# THE TIDINGS

further extracts from:
## THE BOOK OF TIDINGS OF
## THE ALMIGHTY AND HIS SPIRITS TO HUMANITY

VOLUME SIX
APRIL 1964 TO JANUARY 1971

translated by
# Nick Mezins

Order this book online at www.trafford.com
or email orders@trafford.com

Most Trafford titles are also available at major online book retailers.

Print information available on the last page.

ISBN: 978-1-4907-7463-3 (sc)
ISBN: 978-1-4907-7462-6 (e)

*Trafford rev.    08/11/2016*

 www.trafford.com

**North America & international**
toll-free: 1 888 232 4444 (USA & Canada)
fax: 812 355 4082

Dedicated to the memory of Alexander Upenieks, Alexander Homics, and Mary and Janoss Mezins, all of whom contributed through time and effort to the receiving and preservation of the material in The Tidings/Messages to Mankind series and enabled Nick Mezins to bring all the pertinent material together in six volumes.

# CONTENTS

# Foreword

The material in this book came through human vehicles, but is not of human origin. It started in mid-1943 in Latvia, one of the three Baltic countries that regained their independence from the Soviet Union when it broke up in 1991 after its long stranglehold on those countries since World War II. Two women had gotten together and tried to communicate with the spirits in the days of uncertainty in the midst of World War II. One of them was Mary, the mother of the translator of this book, Nick Mezins.

What eventually started coming through was a series of communications from entities who gave their names and identified themselves as spirits that are behind the workings of the Universe, including the planet Earth, and the development of matter and the spiritual nature of humankind.

As things progressed, Mary invited others to join. Some did, and then left for personal reasons, while others stayed to become the core group: Mary and her husband Janoss (initially referred to as John M.), Alexander Upenieks (who soon became the leader of the group), and my father, Alexander Homics, (Alexo, who initially was referred to as Alexander H.). Mary and Alexo were the two individuals who each could, jointly with Alexander, establish communication with the spirits. (During some of the longer communications, Mary and Alexo alternated back and forth, and short intermissions were given for this purpose.) Alexo came to be the main transcriber for the group, typing up the handwritten material after each session and distributing it to the group members.

In late summer of 1944, when the Russians began to gain the upper hand over the Germans in Latvia, the members of the group at different times fled from Latvia and went to Germany, where they fortunately settled in what was to become the American Zone, and resumed their sessions. Later, several years after World War II was finally over, the members immigrated at different times to the United States, settling in New York. There, starting in 1950, they resumed their sessions. The last session took place in January of 1971.

When my father retired in the late 1970s, he translated virtually all of the material into English. He had organized it into ten volumes, plus two separate volumes that consisted of material in a fictionalized form. Sadly, he succeeded in publishing only the first two volumes before his death in 1982[1].

In 1992 Nick Mezins – the son of Mary and Janoss Mezins – published *REVELATIONS: Extracts from the Book of Tidings of The Almighty and His Spirits to Humanity* (Winston-Derek, 1992), which highlighted excerpts from the message material 1943 - 1970; it was reissued in 2000 by Trafford Publishers with the title *REVELATIONS: Extracts from the Book of Tidings of The Almighty and His Spirits to Humanity 1943 - 1970.*

Since then Nick Mezins has been publishing the messages/tidings in greater fullness, not just highlights. In 2005 *THE TIDINGS, Volume One: Further Extracts from the Book of Tidings of The Almighty and His Spirits to Humanity* came out, covering November 1943 to January 1945. In 2010 came *THE TIDINGS Volume Two: Further Extracts from the Book of Tidings of The Almighty and His Spirits to Humanity* covering January 1945 to January 1946. Then in 2014 was published *THE TIDINGS, Volume Three: Further Extracts from the Book of Tidings of The Almighty and His Spirits to Humanity* covering February 1946 to June 1949. In 2015 was published *THE TIDINGS, Volume Four: Further Extracts from the Book of Tidings of The Almighty and His Spirits to Humanity* covering June 1951 to December 1956. In 2016 was published *THE TIDINGS, Volume Five: Further Extracts from the Book of Tidings of The Almighty and His Spirits to Humanity* covering January 1957 to March 1964. At present Nick is finalizing the final volume in this six-volume series, *THE TIDINGS, Volume Six: Further Extracts from the Book of Tidings of The Almighty and His Spirits to Humanity* covering mid-1964 to 1971.

As can be seen from the titles of the volumes cited, there are the usual problems of translating from one language to another while trying to retain the original meaning. For example, my father chose to use the word *messages* as opposed to Nick Mezins translating the same word as *tidings*, (which could also have been translated as *communications*). Another example: my father used the word *messengers*, and Nick prefers the word *heralds*. I myself like the word *envoys*. But the important thing is to make the material and the concept therein, available to all seekers on the Path to truth, and so it is encouraging to see this voluminous material still being worked on and put out further to the public.

Maya Homics

New York, 2016

---

[1]   *Messages to Mankind From The Almighty and His Spirits* (1976, Vantage Press); *Messages to Mankind - Part II* (1977, Valkyrie Press); and one of the fictional ones, *Ipsis: A fairy Tale by Ali* (1977, Valkyrie Press).

# Introduction to Revelations

The material in this book is not of human origin. It has not been thought of by a human mind. The material in this book originated from The Almighty, from God, from the chief spirits and the spirits. It has been passed on to humanity on the planet Earth by the chief spirits and by the spirits. It has been passed on through The Almighty's heralds to the planet Earth, who, outwardly, were ordinary human beings.

Initially, the heralds wrote down this material in longhand. Afterwards it was typed, and several copies were made. Care was taken to see that no accidental alterations were made. The original and the typed version were compared carefully. Some errors in grammar were found and corrected, and it was agreed that the corrections did not alter the meanings of the phrases or the sentences. In each case, the heralds concurred that the correction did not alter the meaning of the material.

The chief spirits and the spirits passed the material down, through the heralds, in a language other than English. My involvement is limited to translating it into English. I have taken great pains to translate the material so as not to alter its original meaning. At times, I have sacrificed the quality of English, or its proper usage, in order to avoid possibly altering its original meaning.

Some explanations are in order to assure a full understanding of the authenticity of the material. Unless otherwise indicated, the contents of this book came from the chief spirits and the spirits. For the sake of clarity, some questions and statements by the heralds have been included. These have been enclosed in double brackets ([[]]). All material enclosed in double brackets is of human origin, such as questions posed by the heralds, reading of material from the Bible, and so on. In addition, at times, I have inserted a word, or words, not in the original. These are enclosed in single brackets ([]) and were inserted due to the peculiarities of the two languages. Sometimes, English requires a word or phrase which is only implied in the original language.

Each tiding begins with a title line. This title line consists of the name of the spirit or chief spirit talking, the date of the conversation, and, generally, the starting time of the conversation. These are not part of the tiding itself and should have been enclosed in the double brackets, except for appearance. The ending time of the conversation, when given, is enclosed.

Since this book is a book of extracts from *The Book of Tidings*, not everything is included in it. To denote whenever something has been omitted, the triple asterisk (- ★ ★ ★ -) symbol has been used. This symbol, when used within a paragraph, indicates that part of the paragraph has been omitted. When used in a line by itself, it indicates that an entire paragraph has been omitted. This symbol is not repeated whenever more than one paragraph may have been omitted.

In reading this book, both the brackets and the triple asterisk symbols should be disregarded. They become important only when questioning the exact meaning of a phrase, sentence, or paragraph. Then they indicate that, if the question is of sufficient importance, one should go back to the original language and satisfy oneself as to the exact meaning of the original.

A few words follow, regarding the use of the word *man*. It has more than one connotation in English. Generally, in this book, the word *man* is intended to mean a human, the singular of the word *people*, rather than the male of the human species. *Man* is used synonymously with *human*, *individual,* and *person*. In those cases where it does indicate gender, the text makes it evident. The plural *men*, however, is used only when gender is indicated, otherwise *people* or similar words are used. The expression "man on Earth" should denote what this is all about.

Thank you very much for putting up with these technical explanations. They are superfluous for most readers, but may be important to a few; therefore they have been included.

Nick Mezins

# Introduction

The volume REVELATIONS: *Extracts From The Book of Tidings of The Almighty and His Spirits to Humanity*, (originally published in 1992 by Winston-Derek Publishers, and now available in the revised edition from Trafford Publishing), contains what I consider to be highlights from the extensive material received by a small group of people during World War II and which continue to 1971. In it are included only those conversations which "reveal" something new or else, in a few cases, conversations which present rather concise and explicit summaries of the material.

It would be helpful, but certainly not essential, to first read *REVELATIONS*. It gives the reader an overall idea about The Almighty's teachings, which were received from 1943 to 1970, and give a general understanding of, and appreciation for what they are all about. In his earlier translation, Alexander Homics included material which I chose not to include – strictly a personal judgment. I have to say that *REVELATIONS* is so concentrated that it is not all that easy to read, but it does include the most important messages/tidings. We also differ in some terminology. For example, he used the word "messages" and I prefer "tidings"; he used the term "messengers" and I prefer "heralds".

I have organized the bulk of the material which comprises *The Book of Tidings of The Almighty and His Spirits to Humanity* as much as possible according to directions given in the Tidings themselves:

On April 13, 1944 Ilgya said in part,
"*...systemize all conversations with the spirits into three books. Everything that refers to the faith has to be collected into the first one. Into the second – advice for life, how to bring up the spirit and the body, how to raise children, and so on; as well as those stories which have an everyday significance. Collect into the third book everything that pertains to you and the accomplishment of your work.*"

In *The Tidings* series are included what I feel are what Ilgya calls Books One and Two. In a few cases, brief passages which probably belong in Book Three have been retained, primarily for the sake of continuity in the case of a particular conversation. Material that appeared in *REVELATIONS* is given here in its fuller context and is marked by arrows at the beginning and end. In order to facilitate locating a particular conversation, the Table of Contents lists, in chronological order, each spirit whose tiding is included in that chapter and shows whether there was more than one tiding.

The fuller context in this volume includes explanations and clarifications, stories which illustrate some of the concepts, and, sometimes, related ideas that are of importance. There are also descriptions of interesting events on the planet Earth as well as on a few other planets, some of which are related to specific heralds.

The present volume – Volume Six – covers most of the period of 1964 through the conclusion of the conversations with the spirits in January of 1971. With the passing of Alexander Upenieks on March 10, 1971 conversations with the spirits ended for ever and ever.

Nick Mezins

# Chapter I

# Spring 1964

Aksanto                            04/03/64 2202

Heralds, you were surprised that the previous time we did not note the festival of Christ's resurrection. In fact, you people are at fault. You cannot set a specific day for celebrating this festival, but you celebrate it twice and at different times. Which one is the right one then? We do not want to side with either, because none of you, in fact, celebrate it on the correct day. Similarly, Mary's name day came at the same time, and we decided to note all three festivities simultaneously today – in-between the two Easters and immediately after Mary's name day.

Without any doubt, festivals have a large significance. They unite people toward a single goal, and elicit contemplation and memories, but it is not necessary to overdo them. Christ rode into Jerusalem on a donkey, He did not ride in a carriage nor was He carried on a litter. His deputy – who found it necessary to imitate Christ in washing the feet of His disciples and kissing them – should also have imitated riding into Rome on a donkey, rather than having people carry him while sitting on a throne, as did the earthly kings of olden times, by having slaves carry them. Christ categorically rejected the display of any kingly honors to Him. No one had the right to change this wish of Christ. However, formerly man could not imagine God in any other way than as the King of kings, and considered himself to be a slave.

Now that man has freed himself from slavery and kings, he should thoroughly familiarize himself with Christ's teachings, and discard everything that does not correspond to them.

With respect to The Almighty, He does not recognize any worship and prayers. He recognizes only work; work that draws man closer to Him, and work that leads toward constructing the universe and achieving His – The Almighty's – ideals. He wants to see man as His assistant in this grand work.

On behalf of the chief spirits and myself – as well as the spirits who are close to you, many of whom have alighted together with me in order to congratulate you – I wish you a true, spiritual festival, which alone is worthy of Christ. We also congratulate herald Mary, and join in Alexander's wish to her. May God's blessing be with her.

Aksanto.                    [[2230]]


Santorino                    05/02/64 2223


→Heralds, I come to you today, two days before your Orthodox begin to celebrate Easter. Yet, it is really only one day if we consider from midnight, which is near, until midnight of the starting day of the festival. Days, though, have little significance here. The fact has significance – the departure of Christ from Earth. People themselves do not know accurately the day, as is demonstrated by the transition of the festival, and the celebration of different days by the various confessions.

Today I come in the name of Christ, in order to tell humanity what was either told it back then and forgotten, or else was not told at all. Back then humanity was still too young to be capable of understanding many things, and of carrying them out. Christ asks humanity to return to His pure teachings – by casting aside the thick moss which has grown over them during these past two thousand years.

[Christ says], "Now that every person knows how to read, each individual must read My book and must live like is said in it. No alibis, that he has been taught otherwise by high priests and has believed them as authorities, will be considered. Man himself has to bear all responsibility.

"Next, man should stop praying to God with words, and instead pray only with deeds. God has never considered words, only deeds. Good deeds were considered to be a prayer, and evil ones to be a sin. After all, it is time to understand that there is no sense in doing anything that does not bring any good. Man's life is not all that long that it can be wasted in doing what is unnecessary and superfluous."

What Christ is saying that is new, is to stop thinking of Him as an earthly king. He has never been, is not now, and will never be an earthly king. He is the world's manager, who organizes His establishment and who needs assistants and workers. He gladly talks things over with every good worker, and offers him His hand.

The crowd is not that which takes everyone toward the future – the future of humanity. Therefore, one should not get particularly concerned if the crowd, which consists of various elements, acts barbaric on occasion. Humanity is led forward by its selected few, spiritually endowed people – the inventors, scientists, philosophers, engineers, and so on, as well as a few leaders. The crowd itself is incapable of doing anything that is lasting. It gathers, accomplishes what seems necessary to it, and then disperses. To rely on the crowd is the same thing as to rely on a wave. It may set you on the shore, but it may also smash you against the rocks.

There are some questions which arise while reading the Gospel. For example, Christ says that man must not sin, but simultaneously with that, He forgives the sinners. How can that be explained? That can be explained easily! Christ asks man to live in such a way that it will be good for everyone. Yet, He also knows that man's spirit and body are not the same thing. Therefore, man's spirit occasionally succumbs to the body's demands, and sins. The spirit, however, can overcome the body eventually and redeem the sin which has been committed. Life is a struggle, and victories in it alternate with defeats. Therefore, Christ did not condemn anyone irrevocably. He gave the latter an opportunity to redeem the sin on Earth, for it is already too late to redeem it in Heaven.

Christ had me pass this on to humanity today, on the eve of the Easter Festival, for its knowledge and execution.← [[2305]]


<u>Santorino</u>                06/05/64 2232

Heralds, as directed by God, I – the divine Chief Spirit Santorino – am talking with you. Twenty years have passed on Earth since God has revealed His face. During this time man has been told what has changed over two thousand years, he has been told what man was still unable to undertake and accomplish back then, as well as that new information which came from The Almighty, who spoke to man for the first time.

Christ's teachings have been accepted both voluntarily and by force – which Christians should not have used – by many millions of people. Yet, only a few people followed the demands of Christ's teachings in the manner in which Christ had intended. Even many crimes were committed in Christ's name. Still, Christ's teachings influenced people's souls, and many people not only followed them but even gave their lives for them.

Humanity's road was difficult. Humanity split up into many states — non-Christian as well as Christian. In addition to religious wars, there also were mutual wars among the Christian states. All kinds of things have happened, but the main thing is that man has gone forward, and that he has achieved such a level of development that he is not only capable of looking at the stars but even of reaching some of them. Being the ruler of Earth, man is now getting ready to become the ruler of the planets of the solar system. He even casts his glance at other solar systems.

Even if his scientific abilities could achieve this goal, the extreme distances make this unattainable in a human lifetime. For the time being such achievements are possible only for the spirits, obviously, also for man's free spirit — free from his body. As you know, however, The Almighty's goal is to combine the spirit and matter in a new type of living being. This can be achieved only with the participation of man, or living beings similar to him.

→As it turned out, not everything was clear to you at the time the Tidings were given. There are some points which have to be clarified. The most important of them is the question regarding the forgiving of sins, and the redemption of sins. There is a tremendous difference between these two definitions. God gave me the task of explaining to you how to understand them correctly. An idea about them has partially been given to you already, but you must comprehend fully the difference between them.

The spirits incarnate in order to live as people, with general and special tasks assigned to them. A large number have been assigned general tasks. Christ has told you about them, and before Him, [they were revealed by] God in the Ten Commandments. The special tasks are varied, and are also given to quite a few people. Yet, in this case it is not important what kind of tasks have been assigned to anyone; only their execution is important.

On encountering matter of an opposing nature, the spirits engage in a constant struggle against it. Some of the spirits lose this struggle, and others lose it partially, and in turn win partially. Still, there are others who win almost completely. Occasionally though, in some cases, even these spirits commit some errors, and are incapable of struggling against them. Therefore, they do not carry out their task, and, as is accustomed to saying on Earth, sin. The spirit is responsible to God for the execution of his task on Earth. He can rectify it, but only while still a human.

After becoming a pure spirit once again, he can no longer rectify anything. He can only hope for forgiveness from God. Redemption and forgiveness of the sin, however, are not the same thing. With forgiving,

God does not condemn the spirit, and gives him the opportunity to continue his activity as a spirit. Sometimes, in conjunction with grave errors, He renews him without great losses to his further course. Redemption of the sin is something entirely different. With that, the spirit corrects the errors which he has made, and faces God as though he had accomplished his task completely. He receives recognition from God, and a new task of a higher nature. Now you can see what a tremendous difference there is between redemption and forgiveness.

You, people, quite often wonder why sometimes you have to suffer as if unnecessarily. You do not always remember what you have failed to do correctly. Perhaps you have treated some individual poorly, and thus sinned. In that case, God tries to give you an opportunity to correct this sin, by doing something good even for an individual and individuals who seemingly do not deserve this.

The crux of it is that each incorrect, or evil, deed can be redeemed by performing another correct, or good, deed. Therefore man, despite his errors, his weaknesses, or his sins, is given the opportunity to accomplish his task, and face God with a clear conscience. So, man should not complain if sometimes he has to suffer as if unnecessarily. Instead, man should thank God for giving him the opportunity to suffer.

Santorino.←          [[2329]]


Santorino          06/12/64          2300

→Santorino speaking. Almighty's heralds to the planet Earth, I found it necessary, due to possible differences of opinion, to explain to man on Earth what has not yet been explained to him fully.

In the tiding about the revelation of God's face, there is a discussion of the scale which is located between God and Satan. Don't imagine the impossible – that the deeds of the soul of every living being, whether it be a human or a similar being, are weighed on this scale. No, the activities of the souls of the living beings are evaluated by special spirits, upon the souls' arrival in Heaven. Only events of extremely important significance – like those that generally effect the fates of entire planets and of entire nations, and the evaluation of the activities of God's special envoys – are weighed on the scale of the Deoss Temple. This is because this scale not only settles the differences of opinion between God and Satan, but also reflects the thoughts of The Almighty.

Here we come to a concept that seems to be completely incomprehensible to the human mind. The Almighty seems to be mystical. No one has seen Him and no one knows where He is. It turns out that The Almighty is so remote that no one can reach Him, and is so great that no one can comprehend Him, and simultaneously with that, He is everywhere. Not even the tiniest blade of grass can develop and grow without Him. A mosquito could not fly without Him, and an elephant could not shake the ground with its heavy steps. Man could not walk on Earth without Him, and man's brain would be mute without Him.

Just as a savage's tiny hut does not erect itself, neither does a king's castle come about on its own. Man's hands erect them. Similarly, The Almighty's hands build, create, and direct everything that is alive, and He is the only one in the entire universe who does that. How He does it, that is another question. That is His secret. So far, no living being or spirit has been able to solve or even understand that. You only have to understand one thing – neither you nor the universe would exist without The Almighty, for without Him, there would be absolutely nothing. Can you imagine that? Yes, without Him there would not even be anyone capable of imagining anything, capable of thinking, of being alive, or of existing in any form whatsoever.

The form of The Almighty's power is not the same in the entire universe. God and Satan are the promulgators of His might in your galaxy. God gives laws to the living beings which exist in the galaxy. He sends His envoys to them, the way He sent Christ to Earth, not to mention the lesser ones. God rules, but He does not create the living beings. The Almighty creates them, and not one cell can become alive without The Almighty's participation. You are created, in a language understandable to you – you are built, by The Almighty. From a child He molds you into a man or a woman, and He takes you to the grave, and then turns your body over to the soil. With that He completes His cares for you, and sends your spirit to God.

I hope that, even if you did not fully understand The Almighty, you nevertheless know The Almighty's role in the universe, know how impossible it is to grasp who He is, and how indispensable He is for everything and everyone who exists.←

[[2335]]

Mortifero                          06/12/64

Chief Spirit Mortifero. Almighty's heralds to the planet Earth, God's and The Almighty's envoy – Santorino – revealed to you today, at Their direction, what has never been revealed yet to anyone. Just imagine this situation, when The Almighty's envoys spoke with you, The Almighty Himself was within you, within each of your cells.

Man has developed spiritually – as you say – very much already. He is already able to understand much of that which he and all other living beings formerly were unable to, and which they are still now unable to comprehend. As you can see, though, in order to completely comprehend The Almighty, a road still lies ahead of you that leads into infinity, and that ends somewhere beyond infinity.    [[2343]]


Mortifero                          06/19/64 2301

The Almighty's envoy – Chief Spirit Mortifero – is speaking. Almighty's heralds, in the previous tiding you were told that The Almighty is everywhere and that without His participation not even a tiny blade of grass can come into being and develop, and that the development of life everywhere requires active participation by The Almighty's spirits. With respect to the development of plants and animals, it is more accurate to say that they are not really The Almighty's spirits; it would be more correct to call them The Almighty's forces. Their function is limited to the development of the plant or the animal. These forces have no other functions, and neither do they have any other powers, or abilities to do anything else.

It is more appropriate to use the term – The Almighty's spirits – for those who direct the construction and functioning of the brain, particularly in such living beings like man. But, please, do not make a mistake by thinking that they also direct man's thoughts. No, The Almighty's spirits only develop the brain and maintain its proper functioning, they maintain and direct only those parts of the brain which deal with the functional activities of the human body.

Man's spirit is unable to direct the functioning of the cells of his body, he cannot influence them to do what he wants. He is unable to either control the functioning of the heart or to fight against the germs of diseases. Man is incapable of making one fingernail longer than another, even if he wanted to. In this case, however, he can still achieve his wish by cutting off with scissors the nails of the other fingers.

The human brain has nowadays found the means of participating in the body's fight against diseases, by doing this from the outside. The thinking parts of the human brain have directed their abilities toward research and finding different means and medications for fighting against the germs of diseases, or else for helping the cells of the body to fight against them. The Almighty's forces of the body do not always turn out to be stronger than the attackers, particularly if man himself still weakens them by introducing harmful substances in his stomach and lungs, as well as in blood. [These include] products that are unsuitable for digestion, products that are too difficult to digest, tobacco smoke, narcotics, alcohol in excessive amounts, and so on. Also, by leading an abnormal life as well as placing his body in harmful situations – extreme cold, extreme heat – failing to keep it clean, and allowing blood suckers – such as fleas, and others – to weaken it or to introduce the germs of diseases into the blood.

Man made many mistakes before he found the right paths. Thus, there was a time when physicians in Spain considered that the dirtier the air the better, because then there was less room for germs in it. Such and similar points of view produced countless victims. Yet, those times have passed, even though not completely with respect to some things, as mentioned above.

You may get the impression that the thinking part of the human brain has no contact with the other parts. That is incorrect, contact exists and it becomes ever stronger. That means that the thinking part of the human brain acquires ever more effect on the part of the brain that controls the entire body. To put it simply – the thinking part of the human brain starts to participate ever more in all functions of the organism. Do you realize where that leads? Obviously, yes, because you know The Almighty's goal!

Now I want to talk about the so-called good deeds which you do or try to do, by helping other people who need this help. These good deeds are not evaluated equally in Heaven, but differently. Every good deed is evaluated, but how is it evaluated? You perform good deeds because of different inducements. Most often you hope that the one whom you help will someday help you. This good deed smacks of commercialism, and it cannot be evaluated particularly high. You help someone because he asks you, and you know that refusing may cost you dearly later on. This good deed has ulterior motives and cannot be evaluated too high either. You help because you were helped previously – that is re-paying a good deed.

If you help someone specifically due to compassion, that is already valued highly. A good deed is valued most highly when you perform it without being asked, but on your own initiative. As an example I will use a good deed of this highest value as performed by Mary and Janoss. For all kinds of reasons Alexander had not asked them to feed his old mother-in-law in the morning. When they found out that he had been delayed in the city, then either one or the other went over to the old woman and fed her. That does not seem like a major good deed, but Mary's and Janoss's self-initiative, rather – their conscience, makes it great. They felt that they had to do this – whether they had been asked by someone or not – for otherwise it might turn out that the old woman will go hungry, or else an accident might happen to her.

A good deed is not evaluated as much according to its magnitude, but rather according to the motive why it was performed.

Chief Spirit Mortifero.        [[2400]]

# Chapter II

# Summer 1964

Mortifero                    07/17/64 2140

Almighty's heralds to the planet Earth, The Almighty's envoy, Chief Spirit Mortifero, is talking to you. Important concerns were mentioned in the previous tiding. It is generally accepted on Earth to think that only outstanding, highly talented people shape humanity's history. Of course, people and even nations of a negative nature also have an effect on it. Thus the Mongol nation suppressed the development of culture in Russia and other countries for several centuries. An individual, negative person who influenced history was an actor who shot President Lincoln.

A particularly important question arises – does every murder leave a negative effect on humanity's history? Obviously no! There are murders that benefit humanity by liberating humanity from tyrants and oppressors. There are few people who regret Nero's death. The main thing in this situation is that the victim of the murder can be a good person, but one who travels a path which while seeming to be good, can eventually turn out to be bad and even fateful for the nation. Sometimes this can be seen later on, or it even may never be understood.

For example, currently there is a very important question which may even seem to be upsetting – did Oswald's murder harm or benefit the American nation, and even the entire world? This question cannot be answered today, but later on it will be possible to answer it rather definitely. The situation is never simple under such circumstances, because the judgement depends not only on the individual who was shot, but also on the one who takes over the leadership, and on how he will succeed.

Now I will turn to another subject. The Commandments simply say in one phrase, "Do not kill." Therefore it would seem that this may not be done under any circumstances of life, even while defending your own life. Yet Christ says that an individual who gives up his own life for his neighbor deserves the highest recognition. How can one give up his own life for his neighbor? Probably by fighting for him, defending him, and, obviously, if there is no other choice, by killing the attacker or attackers. By allowing them to murder your neighbor and by not averting the murder, you are, in fact, participating in it.

Killing is always a sin, no matter whom you kill. You will be punished for that. However, should you save someone else's life by killing someone, that eliminates the punishment. Should you save several lives by that, you will earn gratitude and reward from the High Judge, instead of punishment.

Let's say a soldier stands guard in the door of a house, protecting the soldiers sleeping inside. Suddenly an enemy soldier approaches the door, he is followed by others. The guard gives an alarm, but if he will not kill the enemy soldier he will get into the house, and others will follow him. Those sleeping will be killed before they will be able to get ready for the fight. It seems to me that there cannot be any doubts regarding what the guard has to do, and neither is there any doubt as to what every individual has to do if the lives of his neighbors are threatened.   [[2217]]

<u>Santorino</u>                    07/24/64 2237

Almighty's heralds to the planet Earth, I come to you today as God's envoy, in order to talk about concerns that are intimate to us.

A few nights ago Alexander sat in his place of work and looked at the street through a glass wall. There was a dark building on the other side of the street, which also was a part of the complex where he worked. He looked at the dark windows, because it was rather late – two hours past midnight. He saw only dark walls and dark windows. It seemed like that was all there was, that all people in that house slept. But were all of them really asleep? Perhaps some were dreaming, some devoted themselves to love, and some were contemplating the sorrows and joys of life.

Who can tell that? He did not know any of the tenants of that building. In fact, they did not exist for him at all, because only those people exist whom an individual knows. How many people exist for you? A few dozen, a few hundreds, whom you know or about whom others tell you or the newspapers write. They exist at least in your memory, because everyone has heard their names in some manner: great statesmen, writers, painters, musicians, actors, singers, some scientists, sports stars, prominent murderers, and so on.

Millions of others, though, thousands of millions, in fact, do not exist for you at all, just as you do not exist for many millions. Even if you wanted to know all people, that would not be possible, because there are so many of them. If you do not know them, how can their joys or sorrows effect you? Seas of joy and sorrow billow around you, but only a few drops touch you. These drops can bring you much joy and happiness, or else even worse sorrow and calamity, because these drops come from those with whom you are acquainted and whom you know.

That night when Alexander was looking at the dark, mute building, suddenly the telephone rang. The voice of an excited person came from the distant Boston. This voice asked the proprietor of the building to rush across the street, to the apartment from which his daughter had just called. She had said that she intended to commit suicide, and had hung up. Thus the mute, dark building suddenly came to life. People rushed around, telephones rang, police and an ambulance arrived. A young woman was picked up from the floor. She lay there unconscious and did not say and could not say a word. A physician took her to the hospital saying that there was still a chance to save her, but not a particularly good one. Still, she was saved.

Thus this dark building suddenly opened up its walls, and a desperate individual's tragedy of life became visible. This young woman has been saved now, and it seems that she no longer has to seek death. Others learned of her fate, and it turned out that these others were able to make her life worth living. What does this event teach us? What does it ask from you – people? It teaches us much and asks us even more!

You have churches, you have priests and congregations, but what do all of them do, if one of their members is no longer able to live, and she does not feel that anyone is interested in her. The church, priests, and congregation are not intended only for praying to God about things that He knows well on His own. They are not for singing songs of praise to Him, which cannot make Him more glorious. They are not for collecting money for superfluous decorating of the church and for a particularly good life for the priests and other servants of the church, while many members of the congregation have to live in poor apartments; while they are beset by want, various calamities, and sickness; and while many are despairing, and no one sees and wants to see that.

The duty of the church, priests, and congregation is not what they currently do, that is not their main duty. Their duty is not to wait for someone to come to them for help, but rather to find out for themselves who needs it, and to provide that which is possible for people. Not every individual is capable of asking for help, or of expressing what preys on his mind, what makes his life undesirable, and what makes the dreadful Death a welcome visitor.

Christ went, without being asked, wherever there might have been sorrow and suffering, He went to those who did not dare to receive Him, and did not go to those who needed Him only in order to gain more respect. The same thing has to be done by everyone who calls himself Christ's priest, who calls himself Christ's disciple, and who calls himself a Christian. Humanity will become happy only when everyone will look out for his neighbor, just as he does for himself. Very many calamities occur simply because no one takes an interest in his neighbor, in another person. Sometimes – as in the case of the young woman from Alexander's neighboring building – no tragedy of life should, in fact, have happened, had someone come to her and tried to comprehend her, learn her sorrows, and clarify the situation.

During youth, something that is transitory often seems to be unbearable, if everyone around is silent and indifferent. However, the worst calamity can become unimportant if there are people who help.

The old American farmers came together if a neighbor's house burned down, and built a new one to replace the one that had burned down. They brought over furniture for it, so that the house did not lack anything. It did not cost the neighbors so much that they felt that they had done something for nothing. Their good deed also made their hearts better, and if people have good hearts, then it becomes easy for everyone to live.

There is a sect that takes a rather substantial percentage of their pay or earnings from the members of the congregation. However, should something happen to a member of this congregation, the congregation assumes full responsibility for the member, such as in case of sickness, as well as unemployment and old age. I do not say that everyone has to do exactly that. There are other, even better means of achieving the same goal. I use this example only as something that is worth contemplating, rather than kneeling in church and praying to God for Him to help.

[[2344]]


<u>Astra</u>                              07/31/64 2143


Astra will speak. Yes, Astra will talk with you today. That may seem strange, because you are used to me announcing the spirits to you, and being with you. Announcing is the least important of my duties, because we can get by without announcing. My most important duty is to be with you as with the heralds, to know everything that takes place, and in some cases – if there is no other way out – help you to avert whatever can interfere with delivering the Tidings. I also observe how understandable the Tidings are for people, and what should be supplemented or explained.

Today I will talk with you as a spirit who is constantly with you, and who is constantly with the people on Earth. I see that sometimes it is difficult for these people to understand not only what is now revealed to them in the Tidings, but also what they have been told previously. It is particularly difficult for people to understand why God permits things to take place that should not happen; why He allows the possibility of such murderers as Hitler and Stalin to come and rule the people. After all, God could have averted all that, but why doesn't He do that? Does The Almighty preclude Him from doing that? Here, you see, we come to a superficial approach, to a failure to dwell into the essence of the matter.

Humanity already begins to sense how unimaginably large the universe is and what an enormous amount of heavenly bodies there are in it. All that can be controlled only by working out definite laws for everything and everyone. All living beings who are capable of thinking acknowledge that to create and direct this universe is the greatest miracle that can be imagined. To permit something contrary to the law can result in a catastrophe, the entire logic of the work can be disrupted.

You know The Almighty's goal – not to create wonderful machines, which would do everything as The Almighty would order, but rather living beings. These have been given a brain which not only can carry out The Almighty's will, but can also function independently. These beings would not only be The Almighty's creatures but would also be capable of individuality. Based on their brilliant abilities they would create on their own whatever they want to obtain and achieve.

As you know, no one can please everyone – not even The Almighty. For example, a farmer wants rain, a vacationer asks for sun, and so on. Therefore the people themselves have to strive to achieve what a large majority needs and what it wants. The minority will have to be satisfied with what is possible. Similarly, the people themselves have to fight against what they consider to be evil. Whatever benefits only a few people but harms everyone else is evil.

The Almighty can intervene in adopting His laws in some cases. He can very easily help an individual when it is difficult for him to achieve something, or else to avoid something bad. If The Almighty, though, or shall we say – God, will do that, what will happen? People will start relying on God ever more, and eventually no one will want to do anything on his own, while expecting everything from God. If God will have done something for one person, how will He be able to refuse doing that for everyone?

The Almighty has given man the ability to achieve everything on his own, while following God's advice. If man wants to be free, then he cannot ask The Almighty to use His will to limit man's freedom in any manner and under any circumstances. If the master wants to be a master, he may not become someone else's slave under any circumstances. I see people streaming into churches every day in order to do there what Christ – God's Envoy – has not asked them to do. Why do they do that? Why don't they utilize this superfluously wasted time for that which Christ has asked them to do – go visit a sick neighbor, or help someone with his work who cannot complete it on his own. There is so much with which one can serve God better, rather than with prayers and extolment.

There is yet another thing that people do not understand. They ask The Almighty for miracles, considering that The Almighty is capable of anything. Yes, He is capable of anything, but is it necessary and possible even for Him to make use of these abilities? You know that your mechanics and engineers are able to build wonderful machines, such as cars and airplanes. Should one of these machines run into another and turn into a heap of broken machine parts, will those who built these machines be able to make them again like they were? No, they will no longer be able to restore them from the remnants of the machines, and even if they could, it would never be cost effective. Therefore they build entirely new machines, and have the old ones discarded. Each machine has its own process of construction, for which the old, broken parts can no longer be used.

You see, dear rulers of the Earth – people – you have achieved much and understand much, but you have not yet achieved everything that is necessary for perfection, and have not considered everything that you do. Simultaneously with the necessary and the correct you also do much that is unnecessary and incorrect.

Good night, heralds. Astra. [[2250]]


<u>Astra</u>                              08/07/64 2237


Astra. Let us continue our discussion regarding you and the outside world. You – the people on Earth – constantly complain about God, that He has given you a hard life, full of all kinds of mishaps, misfortunes, pain, diseases, sorrow, and so on. You blame God, but who is eventually the real culprit? Of course you do not want to admit this, but the culprit is man, who has chosen this cursed world for himself.

Open the Bible and read its very beginning, where did God place man after creating him? Wasn't that place called the Garden of Eden? As the words indicate, man should have had the very best life there. Why didn't he stay in it, though? Because he wanted to know and experience not just only the good, but the bad as well. He wanted to know and comprehend everything, rather than play with tigers and lions in the shade of the palm trees, like your children play with cats.

Man knew and understood everything that was in the Garden of Eden. He was permitted everything except for one tree, whose fruit were the only ones able to reveal everything to him – the very best as well as the very worst. What did man do? He rejected the small and good Garden of Eden and chose the large, evil world. Why did he do that? Because within him dwelt The Almighty's spirit, who had created and formed the universe over innumerable years, who sought new opportunities, and who gained wonderful successes and made horrible mistakes. He learned from these how to avoid them and how to create something that was better than the previous, because being alone He was simultaneously a student and a teacher for Himself.

He did not have anyone whom to ask for advice or from whom to get help. He did not have anything to look at, He did not have any models of anything. All that guided His work were His fantasy and His will.

You will claim that what is written in the Bible about the Garden of Eden is a fairy tale. No, it is not a fairy tale. It is the truth, even though it did not take place on Earth, but somewhere else countless years ago. The Almighty created ideal conditions for the life of His chosen living being. It turned out, however, that man – or a living being similar to him – did not want paradise, did not want idleness, and did not want everything ready made. He wanted to obtain everything, know everything, and achieve everything on his own. Just as The Almighty, man wanted freedom and wanted it just as much as The Almighty. Man chose his own pathway and chose his own fate.

The proverbs of some nations prove that simple people comprehend God more correctly than is accepted in the wise writings. Today I will use only a few proverbs from the Russian people, who are among the more talented people.

"Na Boga nadejsja, a sam ne ploshai." [[Rely on God, but do not idle yourself.]] What does this proverb express? It says that first you have to try to do it on your own, and you can turn to God only if you cannot accomplish it by yourself. What do you do, though? Initially, you turn to God, and only when nothing happens you start doing it on your own.

To continue, "Bog vse vidit, da ne skoro skazhet." [[God sees everything, but does not speak that soon.]] This proverb is understandable without any explanations.

"S miru po nitke – golomu rubashka." [[A thread from everyone in the world – means a shirt for someone who is naked.]] This means that an individual has to help another even with something very small, but if there are many who do this, then it is possible to help everyone without waiting for major help from someone else.

"Vera silna ne slovami, a delami." [[Faith is strong not by words but by deeds.]]

After everything that we hear from the mouth of the people, it is clear that people understand their responsibilities with respect to their neighbors and everyone else, as well as what they can ask from God, and when.

Then comes the proverb, "Bez Boga ne do poroga." [[Without God, not even to the threshold.]] It seems that this proverb contradicts the previous ones, but quite the contrary – it expresses the genius of the people. Man can do anything, but everything that he will have done will be in vain if it contradicts God's laws. One can expect help from God in all good endeavors, but there is no sense in doing anything that is contrary to God's laws, because sooner or later the consequences will be sad.

As you can see, one cannot say that people do not comprehend God, and that they do not understand what the relationship between the people and God has to be.

Good night, heralds. Astra. [[2327]]


<u>Astra</u>                        08/21/64 2200


Astra. Astra will speak. Heralds, today I will try to continue my conversations with you. First, I will tell you a little story from ancient times.

An old king lived in ancient times. As usually happens in life, he had a son – a dashing fellow who was supposed to take over the throne after the death of the old king. The old man, while being wise, decided to have the heir to the throne get married before his own death, in order to be sure that the prince will get married and will select a wife who will be worthy of being the queen for his beloved subjects. He had the heir to the throne visit all kingdoms that were accessible by horse, and select from among the daughters of the kings the most beautiful and most royal one, according to her nature.

As you – males – know for yourselves, it is not all that easy to find the most beautiful and best girl, because almost every one has something that you dislike in her. The prince wandered from castle to castle, which really did not take all that long, when considering the means of transportation back then. However, people back then also aged just as fast as now, and even faster. The king become concerned that he might not live to see the prince return. He sent several riders to find the prince and encourage him to hurry up with the selection.

Eventually, the prince returned and announced that in a distant and large kingdom he had found a wonderfully beautiful princess, royal according to her nature from the nails of her toes to the hair on her head.

"Why didn't you bring her back?" the king asked impatiently.

"Because she is too royal even for a king."

"How should I understand that?" the king asked. "The more beautiful the better!"

"Yes," the prince said, "but she sets requirements which even a king cannot fulfill."

"What kind of demands could there be that even a king cannot fulfill?" asked the king.

"She said," the prince replied, "that she will marry me only if I will be able to carry out all her wishes within the borders of my kingdom, excluding only the air above it."

"Yes, excluding the air, but what could you not carry out within your realm?" the king asked contemplatively. "I have been king here for over fifty years and I don't remember not being able to do something here which I wanted to. Of course, you are young and are not yet the king, therefore much may seem impossible to you, but not to me. Therefore ride quickly to her and bring her back while I am still alive. That girl will be yours, there is no doubt about that!"

The son wanted to say something, but the king had already vanished behind the castle door.

After six months, the prince returned with the princess, who rode in an unprecedentedly fancy carriage, was accompanied by many courtiers, and escorted by a dozen of the more famous knights of that time.

"So, this shack is what you call a castle!" the princess said while sitting in her carriage.

The king came out from the castle and held out his hand to the princess, helping her climb out of her carriage. The princess stepped out, and when the people saw her, all of them were left with their mouths open – the men from surprise and the women from envy. Nothing that beautiful had been seen even on icons in the church, and they did not lack beautiful angels. When the princess started walking, no one wanted to move any longer, so as not to appear like a cripple. Yes, she truly was a princess, there could not be any doubts!

On getting close to the castle door the princess stopped and said, "My first wish is to have a new castle built in place of this castle, one even more beautiful and splendid than my father's castle."

Surprised by the princess's demand, the prince stepped back a few steps and told his father, "Well, what did I tell you?"

The old king thought for a little while, and then said, "I had already prepared myself for that, and recently accelerated the enhancement of my army. It is now able to conquer the entire world, and also the castle of the princess's father. from it and from other castles, we will build the most splendid castle in the world."

With his arm, he gave a signal and ranks of extremely well armed soldiers started marching past the castle. They marched and marched, until the princess told the king, "Stop them, I withdraw my first demand. When one looks it over carefully, this castle is not all that bad. One can live in it quite well, and there is no need to touch my father's castle, and those of other kings."

The king smiled and told the prince with his eyes, "Well, wasn't I right?"

"The castle is fine," the princess continued, "but it is located in a low place. I want it relocated to the summit of that high mountain, within a period of one month. That is my second demand."

The king thoughtfully scratched behind his ear. "It seems to me that it will be rather windy there," he said, "but if the princess wants to dry her laundry more quickly, that can be accomplished. Now I ask our dear guest inside the castle and to the table. The hungry dogs underneath it already start to howl for bones."

The princess smiled unwillingly, and everyone headed into the castle.

We will continue the next time. Good night heralds. Astra.

[[2307]]

<u>Ilgya</u>                          08/28/64 2232

Ilgya. - ★ ★ ★ -

Since I interrupted Astra's little story today, I will attempt to redeem my sin at least partially with a brief, little story.

God sat on His throne and observed what was happening on Earth. Generally He allowed people to act as they found it to be best. But something happened that did not depend on man's will. An airplane was getting ready to leave the airfield in order to cross the ocean. God noticed that there was a problem with an engine, that it will fail over the ocean, and that all people aboard will drown in the waves of the ocean. There was a very valuable individual in the airplane, who was intimate to other valuable people.

God told me, "Stop the engine on the ground, not allowing the airplane to take off, and avert what people cannot avert due to their ignorance, even though they would want to."

Thus God helped people without them knowing that and without influencing their free will. Man does not know and will never know how many times God has helped him.

Good night, heralds. Ilgya. [[2301]]

<u>Astra</u>                          09/04/64 2203

Astra. Astra will speak. Let us try to continue our little story about the conceited princess.

On the way to the dining room, the prince softly asked his father, "I don't understand anything. Where did you get such a large army? After all, that is completely impossible!"

The king smiled, "You see, my son, guile is essential in politics. I ordered our existing army to march around the castle twenty times. So that the princess would not realize that the same soldiers marched past her several times, I had the soldiers change places in their ranks, and the officers alter their mustaches and beards."

The son started to laugh, "That sure was cleverly done! It seemed to me at times as if some faces which I had already seen were passing by, but I was not certain. With respect to the princess, she probably did not sense anything."

At the table, the princess herself verified that to be the case. "I was surprised to see such a large army. I had not heard previously anything about that. My father did not tell me either that you have a larger army than even he. That will be a big surprise to him."

She sent a messenger to her father that very same night. The neighboring kings, too, were surprised, and began treating the old deceiver with much more respect.

Among the guests was also the so-called king of the great bridge. It was hard to consider this king as being a king, because he had only a fairly small castle and a few hundred subjects. His castle, however, was next to the only bridge which crossed a swift and wide river, in the region of the huge mountains. This bridge was extremely important to all the kings, and none of them wanted a strong king to control this bridge. Therefore none of his neighbors wanted to feud with the weak king of the bridge.

This king had a daughter, a pretty lass. Her father did not have much wealth, because being wise he charged a low fee for crossing the bridge. Therefore the little princess grew up together with the children of servants and farmers. She tried to help her mother in the household. Her father was pleased with his daughter's good nature, and did not hesitate to hire a good teacher for his daughter, the best teacher in the entire vicinity. The daughter was called Ida. Her teacher was not only renown for his knowledge, but also for much else. He taught the princess how to ride and how to fight against attackers, using special methods from far off lands.

The princess once walked all by herself along a forest road. A traveling knight positioned his horse crosswise to the road, and told her to climb on his horse and sit behind him. He said that he would pierce her with his lance if she will not do this.

"I like you rather well, knight, except I don't like your unknightly conduct. A real knight dismounts from his horse and helps a lady mount the horse."

"Look at that," the knight exclaimed, "an ordinary girl and she talks like a princess!"

"Perhaps I am a princess!"

The knight started to laugh, "A princess? Well, all right, if you think that you are a princess, then I can show you the appropriate respect."

He dismounted heavily from his horse, leaned his lance against a tree, positioned himself in front of the girl, bowed low, and said, "Please, my lady, here are my knee and my hand to help you mount my horse."

The princess responded with a curtsy used at court. The knight did not manage to come to his senses before the girl flew on the back of his horse, grasped the bridle, grabbed the lance, and slapped the horse. She shouted while galloping away, "I will see you in my castle, knight!"

Later on, in the castle, the knight apologized for the misunderstanding. He knelt on one knee and said, "I have never yet been defeated so readily and so swiftly as by you. My knightly acknowledgment to you, and also my admiration! I would be happy if we could turn from short-term enemies into friends for life, and today I could conclude my search for a bride, and bring the new queen back to my castle."

The princess replied, "I am still too young to assume the duties of a queen. I will wait for you to return in a few years."

"Your wish is my command. I will return."

The knight bowed low and left the castle.

That was only one example. I could give you many more of them, but this one will suffice for you to be able to judge what the princess who lived in the small castle by the bridge was like.

The continuation will follow. Good night, heralds. Astra.

[[2300]]


Astra                         09/11/64 2134


Astra. Astra will speak. Heralds, obviously you want to hear about what is happening in the world. Everything is, in fact, currently happening almost as you know from the newspapers. The situation is fluid, therefore no one can say anything definite. Ilgya is very busy, and since presently she does not have anything specific to announce, she asked me to continue my little story. I will do that. I could tell you something else, but at the moment I do not have anything better in my collection. So, let us continue.

Many interesting things happened during the period when the old castle was being relocated to the mountaintop. I will relate only what seemed to me to be most interesting. Of course, everything was confusion. There was no decent living in the untouched part of the castle nor in the already relocated part of the castle. Rubble was all over the place. The roads were rutted and muddy.

Late one afternoon, the king, the prince, his fiancée, Ida and her father, and other nobility were riding from the relocated part of the castle to the not yet relocated part. An old woman wanted to cross the road, but Ida's horse became spooked and jumped sideways. It threw Ida from the saddle and pushed the old woman into a mud puddle. Ida rushed over to her, picked her up out of the mud, and started carrying her toward the castle.

The prince rode up, dismounted, and said, "Allow me to put the old woman in the saddle, for it is difficult for you to carry her. Besides, she is so muddy that she will get you muddy as well."

"The mud can be washed off," Ida answered, "but the old woman does not belong in the saddle of your wild horse. She will not be able to hold on."

"Then let me look after the elderly lady," the prince said.

"Your bright attire of a prince is not meant for mud," Ida replied. "Go ahead and ride on to the castle with your princess, and permit me to do what I like."

"What do you like the most then, perhaps mud?" the princess said with a grin.

"Yes," responded Ida, "as I already said, it is easy to wash off the mud, but the slop which some people like to pour on others cannot be always washed off – it is that dirty."

The princess blushed, "Is that intended for me?"

"No, it is not intended. It has been said, and therefore everyone is able to understand what it means."

The prince became confused for a moment, when the princess spurred her horse and galloped off to the castle.

"After all, you are her escort, follow your lady! Do what you should be doing."

"Yes," the prince said, having suddenly made up his mind, "I will do what I should be doing. Since you do not want to trust the old woman to me, I have no other choice than this."

Having said that, he picked up Ida and the old woman in his arms, and carried them toward the castle.

"What will the people say?" wondered the king and the nobility, as well as the princess, as she dismounted from her horse.

The people remained silent in surprise, but when the prince began walking past them along the muddy road while carrying the two women, the people suddenly woke up. They started waving their hats in the air, and shouting at the prince, "May God bless you, prince!"

The prince got to the castle, lowered his burden on the stairs, and turned toward the people. They started cheering, rushed up to the prince, lifted him and the two women on their shoulders, and carried them into the castle.

"Well, did you hear what the people said?" Ida's father asked the king.

"Yes, I heard and I am glad that my son will be a better king for his people than his father."

"And probably also wiser than both of us, old-timers," remarked Ida's father.

Only the princess was indignant about the prince as well as the people. "How can one do that!" she muttered.

After about an hour, both princesses simultaneously walked, through opposite doors, into the hall where everyone had assembled for dinner. The princesses had changed for dinner. All those who were present were surprised – they could not tell which princess looked more beautiful and more royal.

Ida smiled guiltily, "I had not brought along a second everyday dress, and without wanting to I had to wear my fancy dress."

The prince walked up to her, grasped her hand, and said, "We have to thank the mud that it gave us an opportunity to see together the two most beautiful princesses who can be found in our kingdoms."

Ida said with a sly smile, "Perhaps there is a still more beautiful princess somewhere, but she was not fortunate enough to meet a muddy old woman."

The evening came. The guests walked out into the garden. In a little while, the people scattered in all directions. The prince and the princess walked around for a while, but then the princess said that she was tired and had a headache. She would rather retire. The prince escorted her to the door of her room, and then returned to the garden.

Absorbed in thoughts, he walked along the lakeshore. His foot suddenly tripped on something and he fell. His fall was accompanied by cheerful laughter, and a hand grabbed him by his collar just as he was ready to fall into the lake. The cause of his fall as well as the savior of his life – if not the savior of his life, then his savior from a thorough soaking – turned out to be Ida. She had been sitting at the very edge of the lake, with her back resting against a large oak tree.

Having seated the prince next to her in the grass, she said, "Well, after all, show me how mad you are!"

"I am not mad at all. Is it possible to be mad at such a beautiful girl?"

"Now, now, you may use words like that only with respect to one girl – your fiancée," Ida said while laughing.

"Even though I am not yet the king and cannot enact laws for others, I also do not permit others to enact laws for me. I, myself, enact them for me. You know, princess, what I like about you the most – one can never know what you will do and what can be expected from you. You are always pleasant and unusual. The most horrible thing in the world is ordinary people and ordinary princesses."

"After all, your fiancée is no ordinary princess either."

"Yes, she is no ordinary princess," the prince said contemplatively, "but it would have been better had she been an ordinary princess, because her uniqueness is not pleasant."

"Poor prince," Ida sighed. "Those who have recently fallen in love generally do not find any fault with the one whom they love. All that comes only later on, when the masks are thrown away in the trash, after the ball."

"Yes," the prince said, "she asks too much from me in order for me to prove my love, and the main thing is, she asks for things that are entirely unnecessary."

Both of them remained silent for a while. Then the prince as though suddenly woke up, took Ida's tiny hand in his strong hand – but so gently that its great strength could not be felt – and asked, "And you, princess, what would you ask from me if I wanted to marry you?"

Ida did not move at all, only her lips moved as she said softly, "Only your love, prince."

"How come? Only my love and nothing else?" the prince asked.

"Why should I ask for anything else? If you were to love me, then while loving me you would give me whatever I wanted, whatever I needed. Isn't that the case, prince?"

"Yes, you are right, princess. I would give you whatever you wanted, if you were to become my wife – my queen."

He bent down close to Ida's face, wanting to look into her eyes, but it had become too dark. "What will you say, princess?"

"What can I say? After all, you already have a fiancée!"

"Yes," the prince said as he was getting up, "I already have a fiancée, but do not have a queen yet. I do not know now who she will be."

He helped Ida get up, and they walked in silence toward the castle. Similarly, in silence, except while firmly squeezing each other's hand, they parted in the castle and each went to their rooms – to spend the night in dreams or in thoughts, and await the morning of a new day.

We will conclude with that for today. There will be no conversations next Friday. If the evening will be nice, go the World Fair, otherwise you will miss it. Astra. [[2319]]

<u>Ilgya</u>                          09/15/64 1448

Ilgya. Almighty's heralds to the planet Earth, on behalf of all the high spirits, chief spirits, and the spirits who are intimate to you, I congratulate the leading herald with the day of his coming to Earth. Many years have passed on Earth since the high spirit from Heaven – Alexander – was sent by The Almighty to Earth, to start his human course on Earth. Humanity has achieved more during these years than in the previous millions of years. In addition to the many inventions that have completely altered the opportunities in human life, man has taken his first step into the universe, by unleashing himself from Earth and flying around it higher than any bird. Man is now getting ready for his first trip into the universe – to the companion-planet, the moon.

Not only in the material sense, but also in the spiritual, man begins to set himself free from the millions of years old comprehensions of God, by becoming acquainted with The Almighty. Even such frozen religions like the Catholic start to move. The kings who have disappeared from Earth cannot remain in Heaven either. God turns from a ruling King into a creating and directing King. As you already know now, you are no longer on a planet that is the center of the world. In time, the sun became that. Now you know that you are located somewhere in the infinite universe with billions of suns and planets.

The candles-stars suddenly disappeared from the sky, and in their place infinity opened up, with such different suns and planets – so huge and so massive – that formerly the mind could not have even imagined that. There is so much work in this new, infinite world that neither God nor The Almighty have the time and the desire to notice what is unnecessary or unimportant, and to listen to what is not essential. Thousands of years ago, The Almighty and God had already let the people sense and know that They do not need prayers – do not need words – because They communicate with man spiritually. This communication will assume ever different methods until man will be able to understand God and The Almighty, just as God and The Almighty understand man.

The construction of the universe has not been completed yet, it is merely in a phase of construction. Therefore everything in it is not like it should be, and everything is not beautiful and pleasant, just as is the case with the two buildings which are under construction not far from you. Instead of grumbling, dissatisfaction, and criticism you – people – have to involve yourselves in the work of constructing the world, and have to help God and The Almighty with everything that is possible for you.

- ★ ★ ★ - [[1530]]

<u>Astra</u>         09/24/64 2037

Astra. Astra will speak. I decided that it will be more advantageous for you if we will talk today, because otherwise it is difficult for you – and particularly for Alexander – to get to the exposition in the evening, when there is much that you cannot see during the day. Let us continue our short, little story.

When the relocation of the castle to the mountaintop was nearing completion, the prince asked the princess, "Do you have any other requests?"

"Of course! Here the castle is surrounded by an old oak forest, but the mountaintop is completely bare. The forest has to be relocated to the new site of the castle, placing the trees in exactly the same locations as they are here."

"Wouldn't that be too much?" the prince asked.

"Not at all! That is essential! I will not live in a castle around which all the winds in the world howl freely."

"But imagine the work – to relocate these giant oak trees, and with all their roots so that they do not wilt and wither."

"That, my dear, is your problem. You have to do what you have promised!"

"There will be enough work here for all the people," the king said.

Thus the gigantic effort started.

One day the prince noticed Ida sitting on a bench in the garden and knitting something. The prince walked up to her, "What are you knitting?"

"Winter is approaching," Ida answered. "I have to knit a scarf for my father so that his neck would not freeze."

"Couldn't some of the ladies of the court have knitted it?"

"They could have, but not as soft and warm as my father likes."

"Do you carry out all his wishes?"

"Of course! How many can an old man like he have!"

"Yes, but if your father were as young as I am, what would you do then?"

"I would lie in a cradle and scream like crazy to have my father come and rock me."

"For the first time in my life I feel like a fool while talking to a girl. How can you get so much mind into such a small head?"

"You should not stuff all kinds of trifles in it, but should place only gold in it, then there will never be a shortage of space for what is necessary."

"Perhaps you are right, but since winter is not around the corner yet, perhaps you will find it possible to set aside your work and go for a walk with me. It is boring for me by myself, and if I start to think – it becomes even more boring."

"Poor prince! What can one do with such a sad person? After all, he can't be left alone."

She put her knitting items in a basket, and gave it to a girl to take it to her room. Then she asked, "Well, where will my noble prince take me?"

"Nowhere far. Let's just walk around here and talk. Perhaps a few specks of gold will fall from your head into my empty head."

"Well, that head is not all that empty," Princess Ida said, "except you are too lazy to exercise it."

"Yes," said the prince, "so you have found a new shortcoming in me again. I am beginning to get interested in the question – how many will you find if you will search thoroughly?"

"Why should I search for your shortcomings when I don't know what to do with my own," Ida responded. "Let's rather pour them into the well and forget about them. Look at how beautiful the world is. Let's rather enjoy its beauty and talk about that."

"Fine," the prince said while shaking his head, "I have already poured mine out. You pour out your now."

"Unfortunately I can't do that," answered Ida.

"Why?" asked the prince.

"Because the well is already full."

The prince started laughing like crazy. Then he grabbed the princess, lifted her up feet first, and started shaking her.

"Are they really not falling?" the prince asked.

"Sure is falling, my necklace!"

"What? Your necklace? What have I done? I am really becoming ashamed of myself. Such a wonderful and expensive necklace and it falls to the bottom of the well."

"Don't worry about it, it was only my nurse's necklace. I only have one. I keep it locked up in a little box, so that I would have something to wear in the castle."

"I do not know what kind of and whose the necklace was which fell into the well, but you will now have a second necklace, to wear alternatively. Wait a minute, I will be right back!"

He headed for the castle, and soon returned with a small box in his hands. He removed a wonderful necklace from it.

"I bought it," he said, "to give to my bride on our wedding day. It belongs to you now."

"But prince, do you understand what you are doing? You should not do that and I may not accept it."

"You are right, I do not know what I am doing. Yet neither do I want to know what I am doing. This necklace is yours," and he placed it around Ida's neck.

"Prince, later on you will regret this!"

"Perhaps I will regret much in my life, but certainly not having given this necklace to the dearest girl in the world."

Ida blushed, "Your words, prince, are more precious to me than all the necklaces in the world. May I thank you for it?"

"Why not, if you like it!"

Ida walked up to the prince, placed her arms around his neck, looked deeply into the prince's eyes, and slowly brought her lips closer to the prince's lips. They clung to each other for a long kiss, which seemingly drank from their souls.

The princess slipped slowly from the prince's arms, and said, "That was life's most beautiful dream. But dreams cannot be retained by any force. You should not forget your fiancée – the yearning of all fellows, because she is the most beautiful princess in the world."

"You say that it was only life's dream. But if it was merely a dream that cannot be retained, what is then life itself any longer?"

"Yes life," the girl said contemplatively. "What is life, prince?"

"I don't know that either. That is something that an individual has to do, some duty, something as though existing, but I don't know how real it truly is. After all, life does exist – everyone says that – at least until the moment of death. But what is left over after that, perhaps only a dream?"

They sat down on a bench in-between two small houses. In front of one house sat an old, gray man, on a chair that had been brought out from the house, and read a book. Another old man worked in the garden of the other house, he was digging something. He straightened out his back, looked at how high the sun still was in the sky, leaned his shovel against the side of the house, sat down on the steps, and lit his pipe.

An old hag with an ugly and angry face suddenly came out the door. "You are sitting already and smoking! After all, you have not yet finished your work, and you still have to help me in the kitchen. You don't think about me at all, I can break my neck but he sits there and makes smoke!"

"After all, a person has to rest occasionally, and when his back hurts it has to be straightened out at times."

"Someone who is lazy will always find reasons for not working." Having said that the hag disappeared in the doorway.

An old woman with a pot of potatoes in her hands emerged from the door of the other house. She sat down on the stairs in front of the threshold and started peeling the potatoes.

The old man set aside his book and asked, "Ann, why don't you give me the potatoes to peel? You already have much other work."

"Oh no, Michael, I'll manage all of it somehow. You slept so restlessly last night. Your headache probably tormented you again. You look pale and tired. Just go ahead and rest."

Then suddenly she stood up, "And you have forgotten again to take the pillow."

She went inside and brought out a pillow, "Well, dear husband, lift up your heavy, old rear end. It has probably turned blue by now. I'll have to rub it again tonight. Oh husband, husband, when will you for once start looking out after yourself?"

She placed the pillow underneath the old man's rear end.

"Why does a husband have a wife," Michael asked, "if he has to look out after himself? After all, Ann, I have much work to do. I have to thank God every minute that He has sent me an angel from heaven for a wife."

He took his wife's hand, stroked it gently, and kissed it.

"Now, don't start talking such nonsense. What kind of an angel from heaven am I! Just an ordinary broom of the Earth. Well, if you feel up to it and feel like doing it, you might as well peel some potatoes. In the meantime I'll go over to the shed for some firewood."

"Don't you do that! Isn't there a male in the house? Go back to your stove, I'll get the firewood."

The prince looked at the princess, who was absorbed in thoughts, and said, "You see, Ida, they are people, and those are their lives, but what do they have in common? There is hell in one house, in the other – paradise. All that takes place on the very same Earth."

Having brought in the firewood, Michael walked out into the garden, and while smoking his pipe walked up to our couple. "It's been a long time since I have seen such a beautiful couple. May God give you His blessing for a long and happy life."

The voice of the angry hag suddenly came from the other house, "Well, you lazy mule, how much longer will I have to wait for you?"

The lazy mule sighed, stood up, shook the dirt from his pants, scraped his feet on the threshold, and walked in while saying, "I'm coming, I'm coming, my little angel."

"Poor Peter," Michael sighed, "he has a real dog's life. I can see that you are still young and do not know people and life sufficiently well. What you saw here is life, life as everyone has it.

"In our youth, Peter and I were good friends. Then a new family moved in to live in our neighborhood. Martha – that is what Peter's wife is called – was the pride of the new family. She sure was some gal! Lofty and beautiful, awfully beautiful – if I may say so. On seeing her, every fellow could no longer see anything except Martha's face. Before Martha's arrival I had started thinking about Ann. She also was a pretty gal, but could not begin to compare to Martha.

"I fell in love with Martha, but Peter fell in love with her as well. He was somewhat stronger than I, and after a long fight he knocked me down. Martha looked at me scornfully, took Peter by the hand, and both of them walked off while laughing and snuggling up to each other.

"Then I felt a cold and gentle hand touch my injured cheek. 'Poor Michael, you're probably hurting badly all over. Come, stand up, hold on to me. I will rinse off and dress your injuries.'

"Thus Peter got Martha, and I – Ann. My children, every individual possesses two beauties – exterior and the inner. You saw the exterior beauty – both old women are equally ugly, the one as well as the other. The exterior beauty does not last, it fades slowly and everyone becomes old and ugly. The inner beauty, though – which is expressed in cordiality and love – usually does not change, it lasts until old age, until death. You should know how grateful I am to Peter that he beat me back then and took away the beautiful Martha!"

Turning toward the neighboring house he shouted, "Peter, my friend, come on over to my place! There is still something left in the jug from the last time."

"As soon as I finish chopping the firewood, Michael, I'll be over."

Martha's voice interrupted him, "Drunkard, you are not going anywhere until you sweep out the room!"

Then Peter's voice came unexpectedly stern, "Out of my way, you old rag! Who is the master in this here house?"

"Oh you! He's supposed to be the master of this dilapidated shack! We'll see about that!"

The noise of a fight was heard for a while, the falling of dishes, and eventually everything quieted down.

Michael said, "You see, my children, what life can be like – if it can be called life. I will go and clear away poor Peter."

He went into the house and, after a brief while, led Peter out the door. "Come along, brother, we will drink a cup, and then I will lay you down in the barn, to sleep on the hay. You will be able to lie there until Martha cools down."

The prince and Ida stood up and in silence started walking toward the castle. The prince said while parting, "Princess, we were in school, in the true school of life. Yet, have we learned much from it?"

"We have learned much, prince, but whether we will be able to correctly utilize what we have learned – that is another matter."

"Yes, unfortunately that is another matter. It is another matter, because...." but the prince did not finish and went into his room.

Ida looked after him, "Poor prince! Oh God, only You know how sorry I feel for him."

That will suffice for today. Good night, heralds. Astra.

[[2310]]

# Chapter III

# Fall 1964

<u>Astra</u>                                    10/02/64 2242

Astra. Astra will speak. Heralds, the prince, just like some of you, sensed a strange and unpleasant question in his heart. "How could it be that a king's daughter, even though the daughter of the ruler of a small country, could have only one necklace?"

He had the feeling that in this aspect Ida was different than with regard to other indications. Having met Ida's father, the prince was unable to control himself, and asked the old king, "Please forgive me for asking you concerning what may seem to you to be impolite of me. Your daughter has left such an impression of a noble young lady on me, that I cannot understand something, and cannot believe that a king's daughter would have only one necklace, and it is her mother's necklace at that. Could such an unimaginable possibility truly occur that you − a king − would lack the means of providing your daughter several adornments. After all, she is worth all the very best."

The king started to laugh, "You still don't know my Ida well. I am a king, but even I cannot supply her with as many necklaces as she would like to have."

"The further − the worse!" the surprised prince exclaimed. "I refuse to understand how all that could be. What does she do with the necklaces?"

"What does she do? She gives them to girls who get married but who do not have anything to put around their neck on their wedding day."

"Are you saying," the even more surprised prince exclaimed, "that everything that you give her, she gives to your impoverished subjects?"

"Yes, prince, and you know, I have never reproached her for that. I am proud of my Ida. She is the greatest treasure of my poor kingdom. She does not need any pearls, prince. If you cannot see that − then I cannot help you!"

The king bowed to the prince, and left him standing there, not knowing what to say. Having come to his senses, he hurried after the king. After catching up with him, he said, "Please forgive me. My question was awkwardly expressed, and therefor you misunderstood it. I value your daughter very highly, but as you can see, I am nevertheless unable to value her sufficiently high. I have met a princess and a noble girl like your daughter for the first time in my life."

The king smiled, said, "Let us hope, my young friend, that it will not be the last time," and left the prince.

The prince thought, "I am afraid that it was the first and also the last time that I met a princess like Ida. Oh, why didn't I meet her sooner? It is too late now!"

I hear one of you asking, "Is it really too late, and can nothing be done?"

I will answer, "Who can know that? Everything happens in life."

Absorbed in thoughts, the prince inadvertently came to the bench on which he had sat yesterday with Ida. He sat down on it automatically, having forgotten everything, and not seeing or noticing anything.

Michael's voice interrupted the train of his thoughts, "Pardon me, honorable prince, that I conducted myself toward you yesterday as if I did not know who you were. I did not know whether the beautiful girl who was with you also knew that you were the prince. Princes quite often like to play jokes on our daughters. I did not want to be obtrusive and meddle in other people's affairs. Allow me to be like that today.

"I know that you are the prince, and I am an ordinary individual; however, I am old and know what life is and what man is. I will claim that the girl who was with you yesterday belongs among the rare creatures whom we meet only once in a lifetime. A person does not have just one beauty, he has two beauties – the external and the inner. The external beauty is the beauty of the body, it is temporary, and it can fade with years and even turn into ugliness. The inner beauty, though, is spiritual, God has given it, it has been given to man's soul from His spirit. This beauty lasts the entire lifetime.

"You saw my wife yesterday. Her beauty is gone, but only her external beauty; her inner beauty has only increased. I would not trade my old woman now for the most beautiful girl in the world. Poor Peter, however, would give away his former beauty for nothing, to anyone who would take her. Except there are no takers. Peter and I are good friends again, the only thing he cannot forgive me is that I did not fight sufficiently hard against him, thus allowing him to take away my girl.

As for me, I certainly have nothing for which to blame him. Quite the contrary, I am extremely grateful to him for his noble victory.

"Permit me – an old man – to give you some advice. If you have the occasion to fight for yesterday's girl, then fight to the last draw of your breath. She is worth your life."

(A three minute intermission.) [[2350 – 2353]]

"I thank you, my old friend, for your good advice, but I am afraid that even all the wisdom of your long life is unable to help me."

"How come?" asked Michael.

"As I can see, you are a man of honor. Tell me, what would you do if you had given someone your word of honor to carry out something important?"

"I would obviously carry it out," responded Michael.

"Despite anything?" the prince asked.

"Despite anything!" Michael answered in a firm voice.

"Well, you see, my friend, even you with all your wisdom of a long lifetime are unable to help me."

The old man stopped the prince's steps, "Prince, even the wisest human is sometimes incapable of helping under some circumstances. But there is someone who is capable of that."

"And who would that be," having stopped, the prince asked.

"You know for yourself who He is."

"Yes I know, but I cannot let even God break my word of honor. People themselves have to bear the responsibility for their words and deeds."

"Yes," Michael told himself contemplatively, while looking after the departing prince, "he is a true prince. I hope that he will also be a true king once he will become one. May God bless him, protect him, and help him."

When the prince reached the castle he wanted to see Ida, but he was informed that Princess Ida had suddenly departed in a carriage for her castle.

"Why so suddenly?" the prince asked.

"She received news that her old nurse had fallen off a ladder and probably broken some limbs."

"But, after all, the princess is not a physician, and don't they have a physician in the castle?"

"They probably do, but Ida said that she cannot abandon her old nurse at a moment like that, and that she has to do everything in order to help her."

"How do you like that?" the princess asked, having walked up to the prince. "She leaves all of us because of some old hag there, without bidding farewell and excusing herself, and rushes off. What will you say about that? And she is a princess to boot!"

"Yes, she is a princess at that, and I hope that she will remain a princess until...." the neighboring king told them as he walked up.

"Until?" the princess asked provocatively.

"Until she becomes a queen," the old king said. "As requested by my daughter, I will now apologize for her sudden departure, without taking leave from you. She knows that human emotions are not alien even to kings and princes, and obviously to princesses as well. The King of Heaven Himself left everyone and hastened to help a sick pauper along the roadside."

The princess turned pale from anger, but she did not utter a word, and merely bit her lower lip with her sharp teeth. Then she turned around and went to her room.

"Permit me now to take leave as well," said Ida's father.

"Where are you heading?" the king asked. "After all, you wanted to stay here until the wedding."

"I am afraid that it will take too long, and I have my duties in my kingdom, small as it might be."

The prince walked up to him and asked, "Would you have some room in your carriage? It has been a long time since I have been in your castle. I would like to look it over more closely, besides, I want to take along my fiancée's physician. He is the best physician in all the neighboring kingdoms. Obviously, the princess will be only too glad to allow him to help in the case of the accident involving your daughter's nurse.

"Father, would you inform the princess that I will leave her without her physician far a short while. She looks so healthy that she will obviously get by without him."

"Wouldn't it suffice with our court physician, after all, she is only a nurse," said the king.

"Why settle for second best when the very best is available?" the prince asked. "A nurse hurts just as badly as a king."

"It does hurt the same," said the king, "but...."

The prince interrupted him, "Let the 'but' sit on your throne for a while, we have to hurry!"

The neighboring king, the prince, and the princess's physician rushed out of the castle, leaving the king looking at his throne, on which the "but" sat.

Good night. Astra.          [[10/03/64 0042]]

Astra. Astra will speak. Good evening, dear friends. Shall we continue today our famous story about the famous princesses? I will begin to continue it with your consent – kind or unkind. Obviously, you wanted to say that this has not been expressed quite grammatically, but since you are not completely certain regarding how ungrammatical this was, you found it more sensible to remain silent. Hold on, where did we stop the last time? That was so long ago! Well, all right, let us start then. Period. Start with a capital letter.

One day the commander of the reconnaissance unit rushed up to the king and informed him that a large army, led by a king who had not been seen previously in this area, was approaching the castle.

"Order a mobilization," the king ordered.

That order was not necessary. The soldiers, having heard about the approaching army, had in the meantime rushed into the castle yard. The king ordered the army to prepare for battle, which required very little time back then. The king himself, accompanied by his retinue, rode out to meet the guest, or enemy.

The commander of the army turned out to be the knight who is already familiar to us. He was riding here to fulfill his promise. Since he had heard rumors that the prince was interested in Ida, he had decided to bring along a few dozen soldiers. Might as well play it safe! The situation was quickly clarified, and the enemy rode into the castle yard as a guest.

In the meantime, all the people from the castle had assembled on the stairs of the castle. The king presented his son, his fiancée, Princess Ida – whom the knight already knew from his fateful encounter in the forest – and others, to the guest.

On greeting the prince, the knight said, "Where did you find such a beautiful fiancée? I have been in almost all the closer and even the more distant castles, but have not yet seen one like that. You sure are a lucky bird. Had I seen her first, no prince would ever get to see her."

"You have forgotten something, knight," Princess Isabelle said. That was the conceited princess's name, which I had forgotten to mention to you. Make the correction!

The knight did not get confused, and said calmly, "Everyone understands that a man who is talking about a hoped-for bride restrains from praising her incomparable beauty, but you forced me to retreat from this accepted law."

Both princesses blushed, and how could they help blushing when neither of them knew which of them was the more beautiful one. The knight himself probably could not tell that either. One thing was certain, though, Princess Isabelle's good bearing really impressed the knight.

He walked up to Ida and said, "Will the pretty princess be willing to make me the happiest king in the world by permitting me to delete the word 'hoped-for' from my sentence."

Ida responded, "I did not know that you were a king!"

"Yes," the knight replied, "my father left his kingdom to me and recently headed for the King of Heaven."

Everyone hastened to express their condolences to the knight, and to wish him the best of luck as the king.

Ida answered, "A knight and a king are not the same thing. To accept the duties of the queen of a large kingdom is something very important. That cannot be done without contemplation, and that will require a prolonged period."

"Well, fine," the old king exclaimed, "be my guest in this meager castle until Ida will decide what to do!"

The knight gratefully accepted the invitation.

The days passed in much merriment, because the knight – as we will continue to call the young king – was very talented in organizing different amusements. Isabelle in particular liked that, but Ida cared very little for it. Therefore the knight spent more time with the former, rather than the latter.

The day came when all the work in the castle had been completed. The prince announced that to Isabelle and asked her whether there was some other errand for him to carry out. He said that he hoped that he had satisfied all of the princess's desires.

"No, not yet!"

The princess wanted to know what kind of a castle it was that did not have a well. Therefore she wanted the old well relocated to the castle exactly as it is, with all its walls and bottom.

The prince exclaimed, "That is not possible and that is not necessary! We can dig a new well and build it much nicer and more convenient than this old piece of trash."

"That is my wish, prince! May I take your answer as a refusal, as something that you are incapable of accomplishing?"

The prince discussed this briefly with his father, who also shook his head, and then said, "Yes, princess."

At that moment a young man walked up to the prince. He had just returned from distant lands where he had been sent to study construction and other sciences. He apologized and asked the prince for a brief private discussion. The prince and the young man walked aside.

The young man said, "High prince, for God's sake don't do anything foolish and do not refuse. I will relocate the old well with all its walls and even the bottom to the new castle, and will supply it with cold mountain water by underground pipes. in Rome and elsewhere I learned how to bring water wherever you want to, as well as how to relocate large tracts of ground without destroying them. You can safely say that you accept the challenge, and leave the rest to me."

"I don't know," the prince said contemplatively, "whether to thank you or not, because this thing has already become almost unbearable for me.

"Well, all right," he said after returning to the princess. "But let this then be your last request."

"No," said Isabelle, "after this request there will be one more, but a very minor one. It will take only a few minutes, and you will be able to carry it out all by yourself, without bothering other people."

"If that is the case, then I am willing to carry out these two remaining demands."

The well was moved to the new location much sooner than anyone would have expected.

Seeing that the evaluation of the prince was coming to a close, Ida decided to return home. She boarded her carriage in order to drive away. At that moment the prince and the young king walked up and asked her to come to the well, because everything was ready and now will be turned over to Princess Isabelle, who will have no other choice than to accept it. After that will come the final, short evaluation, and then both of them will escort her to her castle. Unwillingly, Ida gave in to the request of the two young men.

Princess Isabelle acknowledged that the job had been accomplished better than she had expected. Ida decided suddenly to go home, and started for her carriage, without waiting for the last requirement.

The prince caught up with her at the door, grasped her by her shoulders, and turned her around facing him, "Ida, don't you even want to say good-bye to me?"

"Oh prince, I am incapable of that. That is more than I can bear, because I love you."

The prince embraced Ida. Their lips met in an unexpected kiss. Then Ida tore loose from the prince's arms and wanted to board the carriage. Princess Isabelle stood in the door, though.

"As a punishment for having kissed my fiancé, you will have to listen to my last demand for the prince. After that you will be free to leave, if you will want to."

She turned to the prince, "Prepare yourself to hear my last requirement."

"I am ready, princess."

While looking directly into the prince's eyes, Isabelle said, "Prince, I am asking you. Are you capable of rejecting love, are you capable of not loving Princess Ida?"

"No, I am not capable of that. I will be a good husband to you, I will do everything possible to make you happy, but I will never be able to stop loving Ida. That is beyond my human abilities."

"I admire the nobility of your soul, prince. I consider that you have lost and therefore I have to – do you understand, I have to – reject you. That is much more difficult for me than it was for you to relocate the castle and the well. When it comes to honesty, however, I am your equivalent. A promise is a promise if it has been made between two honest people, who are different in other respects. I wish both of you a happy future together."

She walked up to Ida and kissed her. Ida embraced her while weeping. Isabelle caressed her hair and said, "Calm down, darling. We will be good friends and all of us will meet often. Allow me now to kiss my prince good-bye."

She kissed the prince and said, "Fortunate one, you are getting the best wife in the entire world, and I am losing the best husband in all the world."

"Aren't you mistaken, princess? It seems to me that the real best husband in the world is standing right here, and he also hopes to get the best wife in the entire world."

Everyone started laughing, and then headed for the castle to celebrate the conclusion of a great phase in life.

At the banquet table, the prince asked Isabelle, who was sitting next to him, "Dear Isabelle, now that we are friends, permit me to ask you. How come that after all your prior conduct – which was not praiseworthy – you turned out to be such a good and noble girl? Excuse me for using the last word!"

"That is the right word, prince. I am no longer the conceited princess, unapproachable by any human emotions. I am now a good, loving, and simple girl."

"How could that have happened?" the prince asked.

"Very simply. As you know, I was my father's only child. I was to take over his large kingdom and find myself a husband who was, in fact, capable of ruling this kingdom. As an only child and only heiress I was endlessly spoiled. Nothing was refused to me. Everyone whispered in my ears that such a beautiful princess of such a large kingdom will be able to get the noblest and handsomest prince for a husband.

"I immediately liked you. I was ready to marry you on the first day, but my father had different opinions. He said that your kingdom was small, that I can get myself a prince from the largest kingdom, and by uniting both kingdoms I can become the leading queen in Europe. On seeing that he could not keep me from you, he asked me to evaluate you. He asked me to evaluate your abilities and the veracity of your love, by requesting the most difficult requirements.

"I told you that back then I was extremely spoiled and conceited. I was surrounded by nothing but apple polishers and flatterers. I did not see any faces of a true human being. Then I met you, and mainly Ida. I saw how people treated her and me. I saw that they admired me, but did not love me and did not even respect me, even though they tried to conceal that from me by all kinds of means. I saw how they treated Ida. I saw that they truly respected and loved her, and that they were not pretending. I also learned from Ida what a princess should be like, and what a human being should be like. I found out that happiness is not in just taking and obtaining, but that true happiness is in giving.

"I felt that I was losing you. That made me mad and kept me from revealing my new, true nature to you and to others. I was able to do that only once I was certain that I will be unable to regain your love, and without it – what value does even the very best individual have? The knight's arrival and his love made it easier for me to decide and reveal my new face."

The prince took Isabelle's narrow, slender hand and gratefully kissed it. "I can see that I am losing just as much as I am gaining," he said.

The voice of the knight, who sat across from them on the other side of the table, interrupted their conversation. "Listen, you two doves, I feel that I am becoming a lonely sparrow and am losing everything! Dear Isabelle, you promised to give me your final answer still this evening. I want to hear it now, I can no longer wait any more. I feel my heart getting so hot that it will burst into flames at any moment. I do not want these flames to burn down this castle along with me and all the people in it. If you do not want to spare me, spare at least them and yourself."

Isabelle laughed out loud. "In that case I have no choice in order to save myself and all these innocent people, and mainly you – my noble knight and king – than to confess that I love you and am willing to become the calamity of your life, providing you give up your hereditary habit of running after every pretty gal; providing you promise to sit together with me in the castle and be a good king and an even better husband to the world's most beautiful queen, and a good father to your many children."

"I promise, so God be my witness, and in front of everyone present I accept all your requirements and demands, impossible for a human, and may God help me."

"That is fine. I accept your proposal, except try to do everything on your own first, and only if that is truly impossible for a human being, turn to God for help only then."

"I promise you that as well. Let's get ready now for a double wedding."

Thus concludes our short, little story. Good night, heralds. Your Astra.          [[10/31/64 0050]]


<u>Ilgya</u>                            11/13/64 2221


Ilgya. Heralds, time passes on Earth. Why did I say on Earth? Because time does not pass everywhere. There are voids in the universe where there is nothing, not even time, because what is time?

Time came into being on Earth thanks to the sun and the living beings. The living beings had the ability to divide time into four parts – night, day, morning, and evening. When man developed his brain for thinking and for activity, he felt that he needed to divide time more finely and more precisely. The durations of day and night were relative, they became shorter or longer depending on the time of the year. Thus hours, minutes, and seconds came into existence, as well as weeks, months, and years. Time was born on Earth, and it grew up.

Man began to adopt his time on Earth to calculating time in the entire universe. He calculated the distances to the stars – distances that are not even subject to the abilities of his mind – in millions of light years. The universe which you see with your eyes is, in fact, not today's.

It is a universe of the past; it is a universe like it was a few minutes ago close to you, and millions and even more years ago in the distance.

Everything that you see is not the past, it is the present. To tell you the truth, the universe, due to its infinity, makes the situation impossible to comprehend. Your Earth does not yet exist for the stars which are far away from you, because not only it but even the rays from your sun have not reached them yet. Even in your solar system, time would not be the same for the inhabitants of the various planets, if they wanted to measure time the same way as you do. On some planets, your entire human lifetime would be included within just a few days. As you can see, everything is relative, the possible mingles with the impossible, and what is impossible becomes more possible than what is possible.

A small, round coin can be useful as an example. A cab driver threw it at a rider who had tipped him poorly. It flew into the collar opening of Alexander's jacket, and slid into the small watch pocket of his tightly fitting trousers. The greatest skill of any individual could not have achieved that. Judging logically, that was completely impossible, but it nevertheless happened. It happened as a miracle, and what does this event prove? It proves that a miracle – even the most impossible and most unimaginable one – can nevertheless happen.

The consequences are that a miracle is possible; as you can see for yourselves, it can happen and does happen. Therefore a miracle should be considered to be real and possible, and therefore man can always hope for a miracle. One can claim that the coin did not end up in the small pocket on its own, that some unknown forces acted there. That does not diminish the value of the miracle, though, perhaps that even enhances it.

Good night, heralds. Ilgya. [[2256]]


Astra                               11/13/64

Astra. I was present when this miracle happened, and I can verify that it really took place like that. Even I consider that to be a miracle.

Astra.                          [[2258]]

<u>Santorino</u>                        12/25/64 2135

I, Chief Spirit Santorino, am talking with you on behalf of The Almighty.

"Heralds, the nations on Earth are getting ready to receive and understand the Tidings. The world's largest religions, while sensing that they can no longer keep people in the shackles of their old dogmas, start to modernize the books of their services and their approach to people. That proves that the elaborate services and the foreign language no longer satisfy the people, that they insist on drawing closer to the living God, and that they want to look directly at God's face and hear God's words, rather than sermons and songs.

"The church has tried for hundreds of years to keep people far away from God. It did not want people to hear God's words, but rather only their – the priests' – words. They summoned people into churches to pray to God, and punished those who did not come – called them sinners. They said that Christ's words to not pray to God in public pertained only to the Pharisees. Of course, they pertained to the Pharisees as well, just as to everyone else.

"It is dreadful to remember how many people these 'servants of God' have tortured to death and burned at stakes in the name of God, while claiming to be defending God – the God who did not allow even the apostles to defend Him.

"The festival of God's – Christ's, because the Son of God is also God – birth has now transformed into a festival of Santa Claus. God has been pushed aside into second place. A children's festival is a very good thing, but it may not take first priority on this day. Yes, Christ loved children, He went to them, but he also loved all people. He went to everyone who needed Him, He went to young people, to husbands and wives, and He went to old men and old women bent under the burden of years. He even went to corpses and rose them from their graves, when that was necessary for the living.

"Yes, the day when Christ came to Earth has to be celebrated as a day of joy and hope, but it should not be turned into a day of merriment. It is good to give presents to your relatives and friends on this day, but it is bad to forget them during the rest of the days of the year. The day of Christ's birth should not be turned into a source of profit for merchants. Instead of the gifts that many people do not need, it is better to help those for whom these gifts are essential. Christ's name should not be used on greetings to those for whom they are intended only as a formality. Too much that is unnecessary and even disgusting has been introduced in celebrating this day.

"In His Commandments, God prohibited to use His name in vain. Almost everyone has forgotten that, but that should not be forgotten, because it is a sin. People will have to bear responsibility for that in front of God."

I pass on to you, heralds, God's blessing. Do not consider suffering and pain as a punishment, because they may be a blessing for your spirit.
Santorino.                    [[2213]]

Ilgya                         12/25/64

Ilgya. Let us part from God's high envoy with bowed heads.

There is much that does not seem to man like it really is. If someone has lived his entire life in nothing but joy, without knowing either sorrow or pain, what kind of a reward will he be able to expect in Heaven? How can anyone be rich and happy, when others are dying or suffering from starvation, be healthy when others ask for help, and not help them? How can an individual be happy if everyone around him is weeping? What will he tell God when he will face Him? How will he justify his life on Earth?

Think about that, people! You have not thought about that, and that is your biggest mistake.

Good night, heralds. Ilgya. [[2222]]

# Chapter IV

# Winter - Spring 1965

<u>Ali</u>                                   01/15/65 2239

The old Turk – Ali – is speaking. Heralds, I am with you again, just as I promised. My best characteristic and worth on Earth was that I always kept my word. Back in those days it would have been better at times had I not kept my word. However, I kept it.

Therefore, on returning to Heaven, I almost received a spanking from God. "You should not have done that!"

"I know, God, that I should not have, but I had given my word."

"Yes, it turns out that you had to keep it," God agreed, "but you should not have given your word [in the first place]."

"I should not have given it?" I said. "Had I not given my word to the sultan, I would have become, in five minutes, shorter by one, insignificant head."

That is how the conversation ended.

You have retained the points of view of prehistoric times – well, not quite of prehistoric times but rather of the times prior to Christ. Back then people could not imagine God other than as the King of kings. What did a king do back then? He ruled, gave orders, punished, and, obviously, also rewarded at times. It was not possible back then to tell people who God really was. Back then, there was no one on Earth to whom God could be compared, in order to make Him comprehensible and accessible to people.

God, rather – The Almighty, has little similarity to a king. The Almighty is the creator, The Almighty is the one who builds and shapes the universe. He transforms the spirits by making them cooperate with matter in a single living being, as for example in man on Earth. However, there is nothing that is more difficult than transforming matter. It has required millions of years, and I do not know if even The Almighty Himself knows how many more it will require. Returning to what I said earlier, The Almighty could best be considered as being the director of the universe's laboratory. He is incomparably closer to that than to some king, even though with respect to might He is greater than any king.

All these paradise, hell, the saints, and so on are simply a fantasy. Nothing like that exists in Heaven. No one has much time for sitting on a throne there, let alone on a chair. Yet, obviously, it does not look like a laboratory either, because the laboratories are on the planets. The work of creating everything and developing life is directed and evaluated in Heaven. The capable spirits receive ever higher tasks there, the less capable ones continue to strive for successes, and the incapable ones return to where they came from. Those who have transgressed The Almighty's laws and orders pass into nonexistence. Death ends only the existence of the body, death does not touch the spirit. The spirit continues to live eternally, unless nonexistence comes. That is the real death – the death of the spirit.

You understood somewhat incorrectly my being on Broadway. A spirit who has been away from Earth for a prolonged period tries to see, on coming back to it, what is new on it. That does not mean that I was seeking amusements. I wanted to see how people have changed and what they have become like. Of course, I did not spend all of last week in New York. I looked over the entire globe. I also was in Vietnam and spent a brief period of time with your soldier.

A few hours ago I was with the great molder of the past World War – the old Churchill. I passed God's summons on to him. I also escorted to God an actress, who had brought very much joy to Alexander during his youth. I was in the jungles of Africa as well, where people still now continue to disgrace the name – man.

I will now take leave from you, but I hope to visit you once more before leaving Earth. Ali. [[2324]]


<u>Ali</u>                                01/22/65 2300


Ali is speaking. Heralds, I am with you again. As it turned out, I have to talk about something that has not been completely clarified. When I talked with you about Winston the first time, I did not know that none of you had read or heard Winston's words about his relationship with God. He said that he is ready to proceed to God at any moment, but does not know if God is ready to receive him. People obviously took that as a joke, and Winston had also meant it that way.

In essence, though, it was not a joke. Winston had come to Earth with a great task; he is among the high spirits. He tried to carry out the task that had been entrusted to him, and he saved Europe by preserving England's ability to fight, until America came to help. America came to help and saved the world from Nazism, but did not help Winston to limit communism – the other equally serious danger to humanity. That was the fault of America's President – his lack of foresight and his belief in Joseph's promises. Thus Winston did not manage to fully accomplish his task, and he had no longer any hopes of accomplishing anything else either. Therefore he could say that he is prepared to return to God at any moment, but does not know whether God considers that he has accomplished everything that was possible, and can return.

My main reason for coming to Earth was to tell Winston that he may return to God. Winston, though, could not break suddenly all bonds with Earth, and he considered that his sudden departure from Earth would come at a bad time. It would cast a gloomy shadow on some important events on Earth, as for example the inaugural festivities of the new President in America. I agreed with his views, for what is the sense of creating unnecessary problems? I left him under the care of physicians and headed for New York, where I also had some things to do. In addition, I visited Vietnam. I did not like it there at all, but I also had something to do there.

Astra's information about meeting me in a place like Broadway gave you a wrong impression about my stay on Earth. I have to say, though, that extremely much that is valuable can be seen inside New York's art exhibits, as well as inside the UN. The fact that there is also much next to them that is worthless, does not diminish the importance of the former, but rather enhances it.

Permit me to conclude my tiding today with this explanation, because other tasks still await me. Ali. [[2332]]


Mortifero                    02/19/65 2231


→Chief Spirit Mortifero speaking. Almighty's heralds to the planet Earth, after a few million years in the development of living beings, man on Earth has achieved a level of development where, by utilizing science, he could transform Earth into Paradise. Yet, does he do that? No, instead he wants to utilize science's advancements for devastating the Earth and destroying millions of people. This goal does not correspond to the goal which The Almighty has given man, and it can lead to the demise of humanity, even though this is not humanity's own goal either.

The utilization of the dreadful means of destruction is restrained by the fact that both leading antagonist nations of humanity are incapable of crushing the opponent without sustaining extremely heavy losses. In a word, the price of victory would be too costly to make it worth paying for it. However, since there is such a large stock of the horrible weapons of destruction, then it is possible that some misunderstanding or mistake could cause them to be activated. Terrible dangers could occur if these weapons fell into the hands of irresponsible people or of fanatics.

Your astronomers occasionally observe the accidental explosion of stars, or even of a solar system. Not all of them take place on their own. Sometimes the living beings are responsible for the explosions. Currently you have not achieved a level of science high enough to be able to blow up your tiny Earth. That, however, does not mean that you will not achieve it.

Sometimes it is not good if science overtakes the spiritual development of living beings. That, you see, is the universe's tragedy – the living beings who should have become rulers of the planets and in turn achieved Paradise in life, wind up in Hell somewhere along the way. A fate like that does not currently threaten humanity on Earth yet, but The Almighty asked me to warn you of the dangers, because humanity could still destroy itself. Also, The Almighty could lose hope that humanity is capable of achieving the task which is intended for it, and could in turn destroy the Earth Himself. That makes it each person's duty to struggle for the continued existence of humanity, rather than merely for its happiness, or for personal goals which have no value as far as The Almighty is concerned.← [[2300]]

Ksenatu                         03/26/65 2222

→I, The Almighty's spirit, Ksenatu, come to you, His heralds to the planet Earth, in The Almighty's assignment in order to explain to the people what seems incomprehensible to them.

First concerning God. God seems to be different in different religions, but in none of them is He like the God which people imagined in earlier times. Back when kings ruled, it was not possible to even attempt to give people any idea of what the true God is like. Obviously, people imagined that He must be like an earthly king, only still greater.

Many thousands of years had to pass for human brains to develop to an extent that they could understand communications from the realm of the spirits.

Part of humanity continues to think and to believe that God is a king who sits on a throne in the Palace of Heaven and rules humanity just like a king. Therefore temples have to be built for Him on Earth, and He has to be worshiped in them. Christ attempted in vain to explain that God is everywhere, sees everything, and knows everything. Therefore, there is no need to pray to Him. Yet, sometimes in despair man wants to know whether God really sees and knows what a predicament he, man, is in. Obviously, God does not have anything against hearing man's desires, but He wants to hear them directly from the individual and only in solitude.

God welcomes building houses in His name, but not as houses of prayer, rather as places for people to assemble where they can, with combined strength, accomplish God's works and help those who are incapable and sick. Obviously, God does not prohibit priests either, but only as leaders of the congregation in the above-mentioned tasks. Therefore, one should never ridicule or destroy, but should transform as Christ has asked.

The second thing is that there is a part of humanity which, being dissatisfied with the form which the church has assumed, denies God altogether. These people only know how to criticize, but they are incapable of discerning the truth.

The third is the notion about The Almighty. Humanity has to become acquainted with the new idea regarding The Almighty. The Almighty, while supplementing man's present knowledge with new knowledge, does not alter the concept of God. For man on Earth, the path to The Almighty is only through God. Without God, man has no possibility of reaching an understanding with The Almighty, for God represents The Almighty to humanity.

Now the final, unifying point. God, as well as all the other spirits, are The Almighty's creations, created from His spirit. They are not, however, The Almighty Himself, just as a father's children are not the father.

Those people who claim that God does not exist, just because they have not seen God, are simply blind. God is everywhere, and He is with everyone and within everyone.

Should you observe the magnificent blossom of a rose, you will see God, for who has created this magnificent blossom, if not God? Certainly not the rose itself, which is not even capable of thinking, and does not see itself. Should you see a stately young man, or a pretty girl, who then has created them, if not God? Could you have created yourself? When you were born you knew only how to cry, and how to ask for your mother's breast.

Why did a butterfly, with its colorful wings, decide to become a butterfly, and the heavy elephant with a trunk decide to become an elephant? If you were to think about all the uncountable living beings and about the conditions which allowed these beings to form, then only someone who is blind can say that he does not see God.

I, The Almighty's spirit, Ksenatu, alight from Earth now, but I will alight back to you again, Almighty's heralds.←

[[2312]]


<u>John K</u>                          04/01/65 1957


My dear ones, the same old John is talking with you, except without the heavy coating of Earth. I want to use this occasion in order to tell you about what is misunderstood on Earth.

Today is not only Mary's name day, but also the day on which an old acquaintance of yours departed from Earth and from you. She was a good person, but because she did not pay attention to the problems of her body, she allowed a disease, that was difficult to treat, to advance so far that human science could no longer save her. Her suffering became so great that God had Mortifero free her from it, by summoning her to Heaven. There was no longer any significance either for her or for humanity in her still remaining on Earth. Thus she is with us again, and you should be happy about that, because she has been set free from bodily torment, and is among friends.

What is human life? It is complicated, and it is, in fact, not one single life. Almost every human being lives two different lives; one is his personal life at home, and the other is his work – that is, serving humanity. A human lives, in fact, in two different worlds. During the period outside of his working hours he lives among his family, relatives, and friends. He combines two entirely different worlds.

Quite often, members of his family never even meet the people with whom a person associates at work, and his coworkers do not know the members of his family. In fact, the people belonging to these two worlds know hardly anything about the people in the other world. Both these worlds do not exist for each other, they exist only for one individual. He meets with one world at home and with another at work, and both of these worlds are familiar and intimate to him. By going from one world to the other, he dies for one set of people and is born for the other.

The spirit's life in Heaven is similar to this person's life in his two worlds on Earth. On incarnating on a planet he proceeds from certain spirits whom he knows, to other entities which he knows – the living beings. There is no death here, there is merely coming and going from one place to another. There is no place here for despair and tears.

Which world is more important to a human being? Mostly the world of work, because in it he assists more actively in forming humanity's life than in his world at home, where he devotes himself mostly to relaxation and family concerns.

The time has come for our get-together to end. Our special tasks summon us, just as they do you. I will not mention by name all the spirits who are present, because only a few of the spirits of people who were close to you have been unable to come. I will nevertheless pass on to Mary kind regards from her father's and mother's spirits.

The spirit of your "boiling pot" has to take leave from you. May God be with you. John.          [[2043]]


<u>Ilgya</u>                          04/16/65 2206


Ilgya. Heralds, since you, people, have separated Easter – some celebrate it this Sunday, but others on another Sunday – then in order not to insult anyone, we will congratulate you next week – that is in-between both Sundays.

I will talk today about a serious matter that is difficult for people to understand. You have already been told that God has given man a free will, so that he could shape his own life and be responsible for it himself. Yet, that is not everything. After all, if a mishap happens to someone, it would not be difficult for God to help him. That only seems to be so simple, but in reality cannot be carried out at all. Why? Because in that case everyone who was suffering would ask for the same help from God. What would happen? God would have to intervene in each individual's life. Where would there be any bounds to this intervention?

You will claim that God could not reveal to people that He has helped someone. Is that possible for God? Man believes in God, believes that God is righteous and does not deceive anyone. Man might not know about this deception, but not his spirit and the other spirits. Faith in God would be wrecked. Do you understand where that would lead?

Therefore even though God would want to help someone, that is not possible for Him. He can do that only in those cases where this help is essential for the benefit of humanity, and for the benefit of God's work of creating and guiding the world. Thus, He helped Janoss in Wiesbaden, because otherwise it would have been more difficult to pass the Tidings on to humanity. The Almighty is almighty, but it is specifically this almightiness that forces Him to restrict His almightiness on His own.

With respect to natural disasters, they take place based on certain laws of nature. The Almighty creates each living being, but does not direct every action of nature. Therefore nature acts occasionally in a way where the living beings have to suffer. Let us say, a railroad track passes in-between two steep cliffs. A piece of the cliff has come loose under the influence of weather. A train approaches. This time the piece suddenly breaks loose due to the vibration from the train and falls on the railroad track.

A human being drives the train. The Almighty could have a human hand stop the train, but the laws of motion do not permit the train to stop suddenly. Even if that were to occur, then based on the laws of inertia that would not help any – the people would be smashed against the walls of the cars anyway. That is the same thing as with an individual. He can jump from a cliff, but he can no longer stop in his jump even if he wanted to. Obviously, I am not talking about planned jumps where mechanical means can be used, for example parachutes.

The main thing that I wanted to tell humanity in this tiding is that God's desire to help man cannot be always implemented, even though He is God. He may not transgress God's laws which He, Himself, has enacted. Man should not doubt God's righteousness!

Good night, heralds. Ilgya. [[2247]]


<u>Ilgya</u>                              04/25/65 1508

Ilgya. I congratulate you with the bright festival of God's remembrance, for who was Christ if not God Himself – except in the form of Christ. God can be everywhere and in different forms. Of course, it is just as correct to call Christ the Son of God, because He was born on Earth as a human child and underwent all human experiences. If someone were to claim that on returning to Heaven He merged with God and that He no longer exists, he would err bitterly. In case of necessity Christ will again continue His task.

That seems strange to you, because you have a body, and a transformation like that seems impossible to you. That is different, though, with respect to the spirits. They can come into being, vanish, and return again. There are spirits with an eternal task. Even though they are the same God's spirits, they do not merge with God. Spirits with a special, one-time task, however, merge with God on completing their task. Christ came with a special task – to proclaim God's teachings to the people, and to give God the opportunity to comprehend and feel what man comprehends and feels.

About the Easter Festival now. The churches on Earth have not been able to reach a mutual understanding in celebrating the day of Christ's resurrection at the same time. Since so far humanity has not managed to determine the historically correct day, then no one can consider his side to be right and the other side incorrect. In this case the split occurred primarily because some Christians did not want to celebrate this festival together with the Hebrew people. With respect to God, He is quite indifferent regarding when and how everyone celebrates this festival. To tell you the truth, the Christian faith has split into a thousand parts. That happened because people did not simply adhere to Christ's words without alterations, but started to interpret them, and began to institute their own dogmas, which no longer were exactly what Christ had taught.

Once the Christian faith acquired secular power, many people started exploiting this faith for their own benefit, and interpreted it according to their needs. Some priest became Christ's deputies, and simultaneously also earthly kings.

Christ said, "My power does not come from Earth, but from Heaven."

The power of these priests began to come more from Earth than from Heaven. The decline of the Christian faith began.

God says that He does not differentiate between religions, and does not consider one or several to be correct. He says, "Whoever adheres to the teachings of Christ and only to them, and does what Christ has asked, is a true son of God and I – God – will receive him as My son, regardless of the name of the religion which he bears. Yet those who already on Earth – in My name – call themselves My sons, but do not act as Christ asked, are not My sons and they will have to travel a long and protracted road in order to reach Me."

That is what God says. I, a spirit sent by God to oversee the nations on Earth, proclaim these words of God to the people on Earth.

On behalf of the chief spirits and the spirits, I congratulate you – The Almighty's and God's heralds – today with the day of

Christ's resurrection. Christ has arisen! May God's guidance be with you. Ilgya.                    [[1550]]

Mortifero                    05/21/65 2229

→Chief Spirit Mortifero is talking with you, The Almighty's heralds to the planet Earth. I have come with the task of warning people against that which is very important, but is taken lightly. I am here to warn against the greatest mistake which too many people make. This error is the conception that once an individual has died, he does not have to be considered any longer. Some people say, "Well, thank God, he has died. We no longer have to consider the promises which we made to him. After all, no one knows what we have promised. The dead cannot talk."

Someone murders another person in order to obtain his money. No one has seen him [commit the murder], and no one has caught and punished him. Now he can live happily and peacefully.

A wife asks her husband to bequeath all his possessions to her, and she will divide everything as he wishes. She will erect a monument on his grave, and will look after the grave. The husband [takes her word for it and] believes her. Then, after his death, the wife sighs happily, "Now, I'm finally rid of this fool! I should give money to his older brother? No way! Whose fault is it if he was not able to earn money for his old age? A monument? A wooden cross will suffice! And, who will then go and care for the grave? It will suffice if I plant a shrub on it."

People, death does not free you from anything, especially from the responsibility for your deeds. Should an individual kill another person, with that he kills his immortality, and he ruins himself for ever. Promises that have been made to the deceased must be carried out. One may fail to carry out a promise made to someone living, for there is still time to do that later on, but a promise made to the deceased cannot be postponed.

It is ludicrous to say that the deceased no longer knows anything, because the deceased knows much more about those who are still living than the living do. Nothing can be concealed from the deceased, and after death, in Heaven, man will have to settle his accounts for all his deeds.

There is still another important matter which I want to discuss. It is that man can redeem his sins only on Earth, while he is still alive. After death, it is no longer possible to redeem the sins which he has committed on Earth. Therefore, an individual should not complain to God that he has to suffer too much on Earth, for perhaps God is giving him the opportunity if not to pay off his sins, then at least to reduce them.

Some people take too lightly everything that has been said about God and about the life of the soul after death. It is so easy to not believe. Let these people consider though, that their lack of belief in God and His laws does not set them free, whether they like it or not, for they will nevertheless have to face up to their responsibility. Man does not risk anything and does not lose anything by carrying out God's laws. Quite the contrary, he gains. Yet, by not carrying them out, he risks that he will be unable to avoid responsibility after all, for it may turn out that God does exist.

With that, I conclude my tiding, heralds. Chief Spirit Mortifero.←
[[2306]]


Ilgya                           05/28/65 2205

Ilgya. Heralds, the previous time Chief Spirit Mortifero spoke about matters that are particularly important for man to know. Christ often mentioned the name Paradise, but did not say anything definite about Paradise. He even said once that Paradise will be on Earth, if people will observe God's laws. In fact, if people were to live and act as Christ taught, Paradise would truly be on Earth, because man himself turns it into hell. The paradise as people portray it is an imagined paradise. May God protect us from a paradise like that!

There are the Solar Fields, however they are intended more [as a place where] the spirits can spend their time when they are free from any assignments. Paradise for the soul is when it carries out God's tasks. God is merciful, but you should not imagine that He will forgive all your sins.

As you know, The Almighty has created the world and the people for His great goal. He has given power to God as well as to Satan. Satan's duty is to evaluate the abilities of the spirits and decide their future destiny. The Almighty has many spirits, and He can create as many of them as He needs. It is simpler for Him to create a new spirit than to try and make too many corrections to a spirit who is incapable to accomplish his task. On incarnating, the spirit demonstrates his abilities, or else inabilities.

Of course, circumstances arise at times which even the ablest spirit is unable to overcome. Some spirits demonstrate their inability to accomplish their task already during their first incarnation. They pass into nonexistence immediately on return to Heaven. Many spirits have not been able to accomplish their tasks, but have demonstrated attempts to accomplish them. They are given an opportunity to incarnate once more, and even several times. They pass into nonexistence only if there is no hope for success. Man should try to accomplish what he has been assigned. He should not rely on God's mercifulness, but only on God's righteousness.

I have to conclude my tiding. Good night, heralds. [[2232]]

<u>Astra</u>                              05/28/65 2232

Astra. You see, heralds, sometimes we also have to consider what can be postponed and what cannot be postponed, and have to give priority to that which cannot be postponed. That is how it is today. I wish you a good rest, and inform you that the worst thing on Earth is not always the worst for your soul.

Astra.                        [[2235]]

<u>Ilgya</u>                              06/11/65 2249

Ilgya. Heralds, we can observe many different events in the book of time. Some of them make much noise, but their significance is minor. Others again make no particular noise, but they have a huge significance. - ★ ★ ★ -

Among the lesser events, I want to note the parting from Earth of two heads of the Orthodox church. How does the church intend to unite humanity if it cannot unite itself? No method of teaching is as effective as an example. The words that are used for teaching cannot compare even remotely to an example. Parents can tell their children from morning until night not to quarrel, but if the parents themselves quarrel, their children will do that as well. If they will be spanked for quarrelling, then they will get used to injustice, because they will not see the parents being spanked. Christ taught not only with words, but even more by example.

The church in itself should not be scorned, because it was established with good intents – to keep the faithful together, teach them how to help the weaker ones, and attract the nonbelievers with its good deeds. What kind of an example, though, do the priests demonstrate to their congregations by quarrelling among themselves? Can anyone really believe that the innumerable prayers, services, and reading sacred books by the beds of the deceased can help any, if there are no deeds behind all that?

With that, we will conclude for today. Good night, heralds. Ilgya.
[[2322]]

Ilgya                                    06/18/65 2234

Ilgya. Heralds, humanity's genius continues along its way toward shaping the future. Another step forward was taken today – a fantastically heavy rocket rose into the sky. I will not repeat the numbers, but it was, in fact, an entire house that rose into the sky. The poor moon has become quite pale out of fear. It feels that its peaceful life is coming to an end. Different items that have been produced by man on Earth fall even now on its face, but once man himself will arrive, then no peace whatsoever will be possible. Beyond the moon, Mars and Venus also begin to feel insecure.

What humanity only dreamt of for innumerable years starts to become a fact – reality. Man was not even able to imagine in any fairy tale the abilities which The Almighty has given the human brain. He has given it His spirit, and he begins to demonstrate his mightiness. Simultaneously with that, however, matter has not yet lost its power. A large majority of humanity has not yet set itself free from it. The struggle will, in fact, continue eternally, but it will become ever lesser.

The spirit of John – whom you remember so cordially – has come to you today from the world in which he currently functions. The Almighty tries out in it the abilities of new living beings. These beings have been created based on other principles than the people on Earth. Neither The Almighty nor John's spirit presently know how successful this experiment will be, but that does not diminish their interest. John has even more work here than he had on Earth, and he cannot even dream of a short nap after lunch, but he does not complain.

A beloved guest is visiting you for a few brief days. God has destined him to take part in the formation of history, by participating in the fight for humanity's future. This future is currently shaped primarily by the United States of America, and, strange as it might be, by its opponent – the Union of Soviet Republics. In their competition to acquire power they not only suffer, but also drive science forward, unimaginably rapidly and successfully. Thus, not only the positive but also the negative is able to accomplish positive work. Had it not been for this competition, all these achievements of science, costing billions, would have required much more time, and perhaps humanity would not have even dared to start some of these inventions. Let us conclude with that.

I wish your guest success along his way, and I wish our friend Janoss many father's days. Good night, heralds. Ilgya.

[[2307]]

# Chapter V

# Summer - Fall 1965

Aksanto                          08/13/65 2202

Aksanto is speaking. Heralds, I observed how you conducted yourselves while seeing old mother Ann off from the Earth. That was truly done right. You knew for yourselves that there is much that is superfluous and that is contrary to The Almighty's and Christ's true faiths. However, knowing that the old woman had grown up and lived her entire life in the spirit of the current church, and that all her friends and acquaintances also belong to those who adhere to her points of view, you firmly adhered to the correct procedure, and buried her as she had wanted it done.

Christ's and The Almighty's religions require every human being to respect other religions and the existing churches and temples for praying. These religions do not permit forcing new religions on people, even if these new religions are the most correct ones. They do not permit fighting against other religions by means of force, and ridiculing or defaming them. These two religions gain people's souls by convincing people that they are the correct ones. Whoever does not join them – while considering that his religion or personal beliefs in what he believes or does not believe are correct – may retain his beliefs. That does not threaten his life as a human, that does not even threaten his soul, but neither does that benefit his soul. Everyone who is capable of thinking will understand why this is the case.

It is a real misfortune that so many people are incapable of relying on their own mind, because they rely on the minds of others, which may be erroneous. A large majority of people are convinced that what their fathers and the fathers of their fathers believed in is correct, and that whatever the majority of the people do is also correct. That is not the case, however, because life does not stand still, and human development does not stand still either. What seemed ideal to a cave man is completely unacceptable to current man.

Man acquired some lasting values in his later course, but not all of them. Formerly, man was entirely dependent on the external world and on the forces of nature, he was their slave. Thanks to his development and the knowledge which he has acquired, he now starts to become the master, and starts to alter his vicinity according to his own discretion. He stops considering the animal and even the plant kingdoms. He destroys everything that harms him, and wages a fight against nature. He lives not only off of what exists, but he begins to follow the footsteps of his Father – God. He begins to transform what exists, and create what does not exist but what he needs.

While you were away, several days of remembrance passed without being observed. That should not concern you, since you did not forget them, which is the main consideration. You were merely unable to observe them like you usually do. All four spirits thank you that you always retain them in your hearts, and that is the most important and most valuable consideration. I pass on to you their gratitude for that.

[[2237]]

Ilgya                              08/20/65 2117

Ilgya. - ★ ★ ★ -

A high spirit told you a few days ago how to deal with other religions. Some of you may misconstrue his words and think that you should not fight against other religions. That is not the case, one has to fight against everything that is incorrect and not genuine. The difference is only in the manner of the fight – hatred can only elicit more hatred. Ridicule and defamation can elicit the same thing. The truth has to win by proving that it is the truth, and that will prove on its own what is untrue in the other religions.

A large majority of people think the same way as other people think, without considering whether these other people think and act correctly. It is very difficult to change the accepted notions. One has to be composed and tolerant in a fight, as well as enduring. You should attempt to obtain the enemies' respect for you as a human.

There is no sense in trying to get as many followers on your side as possible, because in doing this you may recruit many people who are of little value. Being unable to fully comprehend the new religion, they cannot give anything positive for the fight, because they are with you today and with others tomorrow. In addition, under the present circumstances when the fight against communism has to be waged, everything that supports this fight is valuable. It is not sensible to talk an individual into leaving the church, and then allowing him to join the Communists.

Do you remember the time when you asked when Joseph will die and when his replacement will come? You received the answer that he will die once a suitable replacement will have been found. That was essential, and that was not easy to accomplish. Finally, Nikita came along. He did not seem like the type of replacement that you had expected. Yet it was specifically he who wrecked Joseph's divine myth, and showed the people that he had been an ordinary tyrant. He did that for his own benefit, but he did not realize that it was not possible to wreck Joseph without wrecking the party, because it was not possible to relieve it of its responsibility.

Soon people started asking, "Where was the party, though? Why did it permit all that to take place?"

These questions first arouse in people's hearts, but they began to slowly express themselves in words as well. Criticism was born, the blind faith died, and that was the beginning of the end of communism. Nikita carried out his task; he was incapable of doing the rest, and therefore he departed.

Let us conclude with that for today. Good night, heralds. Ilgya.
[[2200]]


Danteos                          09/03/65 2131

The Almighty's spirit – Danteos – is talking with you, heralds. To some extent I come to you unexpectedly. My task is to periodically visit the planets which have highly developed living beings, to observe their progress, and to inform God and The Almighty concerning everything that requires special attention. Quite often everything does not go as is necessary or anticipated. There are many reasons for that. I am currently spending my time on Earth, and my task obviously was to visit you, as The Almighty's heralds. Of course, I will take advantage of this occasion to help you with your work, and will tell you about that which does not appear to me to be particularly comprehensible.

It seems particularly strange to me that the living beings on Earth, while believing in the eternal life of the soul, rather – its immortality, act, in fact, as though once an individual has died, then simultaneously with that the value of this individual's soul is also lost. To put it more correctly, they act as if the soul did not exist, and as though this soul did not know how you behave with respect to it. A large majority of people bury a relative who seemed to them to be a person of a bad character, and feel quite happy once he has been buried.

"Yes, he sure was a rotten one, but now he is finally dead."

Sometimes they even add, "Thank God!"

In this case the problem is that this "rotten one's" soul hears quite well what its relatives say. Not only does this soul hear what the relatives are saying now, but it even knows what they had done which he did not know while he was a human. The situation does not become simpler after death, but far more complicated – no lies and pretending are possible.

Everyone should consider, "Yes, he was a bad one, but what was I like? Was I truly better than he was? Perhaps I was so bad that he could not be good toward me."

You see, every individual should first consider what he, himself, is like, and should talk only then.

Someone murders another person. He thinks that everything is fine now; no one saw him and he will not have to undergo any punishment. That is the worst self-deception there is. He forgets that after his own death, the first one whom he will meet in the hereafter will be the soul of the one whom he murdered. Can you imagine anything worse? Probably not! What can his short years on Earth give him – even if he can utilize the victim's money and even if there is plenty of it – compared to what awaits him, what awaits his soul. There are many things that an individual does not do as is necessary, but if that was not particularly important, and especially if the individual has done much that was done properly, or else has tried to correct what was done improperly, then much if not everything will be forgotten or forgiven.

It is extremely important that people do not forget the deceased. Considering that parting of the souls occurs only for a brief period, one should try to maintain the bonds of the souls as strong as possible, and should not let them break. There are many ways of keeping these bonds alive.

It is time for people to free themselves from yet another concept. Kings ruled on Earth when the religions were forming. Nobility gathered around them, and the rest of the people were slaves. Thus the belief arouse that God is a king, but almost all the others – slaves. Nothing can be further from the truth than this idea. God is the creator, the one who directs and forms everything that is alive, but the living beings are not slaves, they have been given souls – tiny parts of God's spirit.

As you have been told previously, God – in this case rather, The Almighty – tries to shape a beautiful and ideally happy world. Therefore the spirits and the living beings should not consider Him to be a king, but rather as their Father. One can turn to Him, as to his Father, on all occasions of life, by simply saying, "Father, help me, give me advice, save me," and so on.

If God will find that what you are asking for is beneficial for your soul, He will help. You should not forget, though, that currently you are carrying out a given task, which may be difficult and perhaps may require your life, or suffering. What is the key to everything? It is the knowledge that The Almighty is with you everywhere, and most important, not only during the time of your short life on Earth, but also in eternity. The longer you will be with Him in eternity, the closer to Him you will be.

I will conclude with that. Perhaps I will visit you again before leaving Earth, but I will obviously not forget to say good-bye. The Almighty's envoy to all living beings in the universe – the high spirit Danteos.

[[2227]]

<u>Astra</u>                                09/11/65 2243

Astra. I will be the first one to speak. I am someone who is almost constantly if not with you, then near you. You may not always like that, but that cannot be helped. God said that a spirit has to be constantly with the heralds, and looked at me contemplatively. I did not wait any longer, and started packing my belongings. There were not many of them, but there nevertheless was something.

It was difficult to locate Latvia. It could not boast about its size. I almost ended up in Egypt; only on spotting a large crocodile – which looked at me in wonder – I decided that this river cannot be Daugava. I had to rise into the air once more. The first thing that I saw when I got to you was a flock of ducks. They seemed to feel no worse in the little brook than the crocodile had in the Nile. I finally found you in a small room sitting at a round table. No one had bothered to prepare a room for me. I found for myself a quite corner in the room with the large painting of a winter scene, and that is how my activities started.

The small group of heralds started to grow quickly, but then came Joseph with his red army, and everything changed. You assembled again near the Rhine River. Life was easy there, and you had much time to devote to the Tidings. A few years passed and you started looking for a third river, and you chose Hudson. Thus you ended up in the capital of the world.

Today is a special day. It is Alexander's name day. It is really not yet, but will be in an hour. His birthday will be in four days. Alexander decided not to be wasteful, and to celebrate both days this Sunday. This birthday is important because Alexander reaches the age when, according to the American point of view, an individual no longer has to work, but has to start resting and await death. There are people who have to leave the stage of life even sooner, because they have really become old – either physically, or mentally, or else physically as well as mentally. That does not refer to the heralds, and particularly not to Alexander.

Over the last few years, I have observed his endurance in awe. While performing first rate at work, he also assumed responsibility for his old mother-in-law. While often sleeping only three or four hours a night, he carried a burden that would be considered too heavy even for a young man. He carried it without reproaching God even once and even without asking God why He does not recall the old woman, which is what some other heralds did. He did not ask, because he knew that this was probably necessary, and I can tell you that this was necessary. This was less necessary for the sake of the old woman herself than for all of your sake, and not just only for your sake.

Alexander is The Almighty's herald, and the first one among you. You testify with your life about your spiritual abilities. Without thinking about that, but by doing what his conscience asked of him, Alexander proved that to many people, and with his noble conduct even elicited amazement from them. The Hebrew people understood that best, and started comparing him to a saint. Why? Because they were incapable of that themselves, and according to their opinion only saints were capable of that. Of course, that was merely the point of view of practical people on Earth.

I do not come to praise Alexander, I only want to tell you what the truth is and what should not be overlooked, because by overlooking the good you serve evil. The high spirits gave me – as your most intimate spirit – permission to be the first one to congratulate Alexander on his day of festivity, and to wish him to find the right way of serving The Almighty and humanity in the future as well.

The Divine will talk with you in five minutes. Get ready!

[[2333]]

I – the divine envoy, Santorino – come to you, the heralds to Earth, in order to express gratitude to you for your untiring work, and to note jointly with you the entry of the first of the heralds into a new year of life. Many of the great spirits and almost all the spirits who are intimate to you have come along with me, because humanity on Earth has lived up to many of the expectations which The Almighty had placed on it, and with its abilities approaches the most outstanding living beings in the universe.

We allowed Astra to be the first one to congratulate Alexander. With her cares for you, she truly has saved Janoss's as well as Alexander's lives, and has helped Mary much. We completely agree with her evaluation of Alexander's spirit. He is obviously not a saint, as some people who were surprised by his nobility called him. Of course, he also makes mistakes and does not do everything as would have been best. Unlike Christ, he is not the Son of God, he is the very same human being just like any one of you, and specifically that distinguishes his spiritual worth the most. He is incapable of raising the dead from their graves, but he nevertheless was able to perform miracles by preserving a human life on Earth for longer than was possible.

Heralds, it is not only your work of passing the Tidings on to the people that distinguishes you, but also your spiritual worth. This enhances the value of the Tidings as well.

With respect to Ann, Antonina correctly foresaw that without Alexander caring for her mother, she will be unable to live on Earth even for a short period, and she had understood that correctly. Only properly taking care of her, and the help of good medication, could preserve Ann's life. Alexander understood enough in medicine that he could provide her the best possible of everything, and even saved her from the mistakes of a physician. When it turned out to be impossible for Alexander to give her everything that was necessary, and he was forced to commit her to a nursing home, God recalled her.

The other heralds should not reproach themselves for not having understood everything that Alexander was doing, and giving him different advice. They did this while thinking that this would be best, but not just only in order to free Alexander and themselves from the large and difficult responsibility. Mistakes are not desirable, but one is not punished for them if they have been made while wanting to do good.

I pass on to Alexander God's blessing and all our best wishes for his future course of life. Santorino. [[09/12/65 0008]]

<u>Danteos</u>                           09/17/65 2150

Almighty's heralds, I come to you again in order to spend one more
evening in your company. The conversations of last Saturday and Sunday
gave me the subject for this evening's tiding. These conversations gave
me much that is interesting in evaluating the human being. The word
"saint" was often mentioned that evening, and it gave me an opportunity
to evaluate the human spiritual situation, the current situation. I learned
from the conversations and from the spirits some very interesting things
that benefited my task, as well as gave me the subject for this evening's
tiding.

Alexander's mother-in-law outlived her daughter by seven years and
died on the evening of July the thirteenth of this year. Alexander had
looked after her and had taken care of her for all these long years, initially
with Mary's and Janoss's help on special occasions, and more frequently
toward the end. The state of Ann's health was fairly good, and she
required constant caring only during the last year – when she completely
lost her ability to see and could barely hear. Alexander spent much time
working – which, with travel time, took more than ten hours – as well
as shopping, taking care of other needs, preparing meals, feeding the
old woman, and keeping the place in order. Thus, Alexander frequently
managed to sleep only three or four hours. That truly surpassed the
bounds of endurance for a human being.

Prior to her death, Antonina had asked him to give her his word that
he will not leave her mother by herself. Realizing that it was not possible
to give a promise like that without knowing the future, Alexander
remained silent. Antonina, too, while understanding the situation, no
longer repeated her request. Yet, it was obviously not necessary to ask
Alexander for a promise, because he realized his human obligations better
than any other true human.

There are nursing homes in America to which old people can be
committed. If the relatives lack the money to pay for the stay, then the
city pays. In fact, the sons and daughters who earn pay for their work
are the only ones who should look after the care of old people in their
old age. Realizing what difference there was between home and life in
a nursing home, as well as in particular that Ann did not know English,
Alexander decided to keep her with him for as long as that will be
possible, without taking into account the advice of all other people.

When he started going for walks with the elderly lady in a nearby
park and sitting on a bench there, other people in the park obviously
started talking. This part of the city was popular with Hebrew people.

One day a Hebrew lady who was sitting on the same bench, asked Alexander how old Ann was.

Alexander replied, "Around ninety years."

"Is she your mother?" the lady continued to ask.

"No, mother-in-law."

"What!" the lady said as she got up. "We commit our mothers and fathers to nursing homes, and you keep your mother-in-law at home. After all, you are a saint."

That is how it started. There was no longer any tranquility in the park. The Hebrew ladies took everyone who did not know him to his bench, in order to show them a person who does not commit his mother-in-law to a nursing home, to show them the new saint. It is obvious that such idolization became unbearable for Alexander, and he had to change his place in the park. He heard this word not just only from the Hebrews but from people of other nationalities as well.

Prior to clarifying the meaning of the word "saint," I want to say that the word is less significant with respect to Alexander than with respect to other people. It characterizes what spiritual state the current humanity is in, if it thinks that an individual who carries out his human duties as God has intended, has to be a saint.

(Take a five-minute break.) [[2238 - 2243]]

What does the word "saint" mean? As a complete definition of the word "saint" one can consider God, can consider the angels, and can also consider people who, like Christ, did only good, who proclaimed Christ's faith, and if necessary also died for it. It is difficult, though, to consider as being saints those whom people call that. The church has given Heaven many saints, even though it did not and does not have the right to call anyone a saint. Only God can do that. If someone carries out all of God's laws, then he is a true human, whose soul God will receive with respect. Whoever does good but also some evil, is considered to be an acceptable human. Whoever does more evil than good, should be considered as being hardly worthy of the name – human. Yet, whoever does only evil and lives only for himself, should be considered as being humanity's disgrace, and those who murder and steal should be considered as humanity's trash and enemies. There will be no place for them in Heaven.

With respect to those people whom the church has appointed as saints, there are those among them who have no place in Heaven. Can an individual be among the saints if he bore the name of Christ on his sword, and baptized people with blood? Can a monk be a saint, someone who leaves the people, goes into a forest, and constantly prays to God?

Of what use is he to the people and to God? It is different if someone becomes a monk, but while praying to God also helps the poor and takes care of the sick. If one considers good as being sacred, then all the good that an individual does brings him closer to the saints, but in order to become a saint something incomparably more is needed.

We do not call Alexander a saint, but some of his deeds were worthy of the deeds of a saint, because, truly, hardly any human is capable of doing what he did for the benefit of the old lady during her last days of life. He is a human being, however, and as such he does not try to be a saint in his everyday life, but only an honest and good person, which also signifies much.

There is also much to be said about how parents and children treat each other. There is usually no comparison between what the parents give their children and what the children give their parents. The parents gave their children their love, their day to day care, and, in fact, sacrificed themselves for their children. Nothing seemed hard for them, and nothing seemed impossible for the sake of their children. They gave the best years of their life to their children.

How do the children pay back their parents? They provide them with apartments and food, and occasionally visit them. They do not want to live together with their parents, because that is a hardship for them. They want complete independence. It is true that some parents love to interfere in the affairs and life of even grown-up sons and daughters. All parents – just as all children – do not have a good nature. However, I want to tell those children – sons and daughters – who are good sons and daughters, that they forget how lonely their parents feel without them, and how much they long for the love, smile, a kind word, and a kiss from their children.

I will conclude with that. Perhaps I will visit you again sometime, even though I am not making any promises. Danteos.

[[2324]]

<u>Danteos</u>                     09/24/65 2126

Almighty's heralds, in continuing my observations of how man has recently developed, I have to say that the word man is not anything definite or anything unique. Consider the places where space rockets are manufactured and launched, and meet the people who do all that. Then head for a shack in Africa and see a native – almost naked, as God had created him millions of years ago – pick or knock down a nut from a palm tree. It is hard to say that you see the very same man. Almost the same millions of years separate these people.

Had white man, due to his endless curiosity, not penetrated the jungles of Africa, it is hard to tell how long the native would still sit next to his shack, eat nuts from a palm tree, and not know that the entire world is not the same as his jungle. What made such difference? Why wasn't human development the same everywhere? The fight for existence made the difference. Where nature was not benevolent to man, where man had to fight for bread, where he had to learn to produce it on his own, and where it did not suffice to cover his middle with a piece of rag in order not to freeze, he had to think about clothing there. Where he could not live in a shack of twigs and leaves during the winter, there he had to, whether he wanted to or not, start thinking about building a house.

Just as the first paradise did not turn out to be paradise but a cradle of indolence and inertia, thus in other paradises as well, where man could live off of what nature gave him, man remained a savage. A fight is the stimulus of human development, it forces man to think and to work, and once he has started the fight for a better life, man can no longer stop. He always wants ever more. Man senses that he is extremely capable, that he can achieve almost anything that he wants to. He feels within himself the strength and will of God – The Creator. He does not want to become God, but he wants to help God in the work of shaping the world. The formation of the world has not stopped and will never stop. Of course, not everything takes place ideally and without hindrances; in addition to unavoidable mistakes, people of a negative nature also get in the way.

Matter transforms slowly, it is difficult to overcome its inertia. Therefore the cooperation of the spirit and matter does not proceed smoothly. It is a fight between two different substances, and the spirit has to engage in it in order to come up with new achievements of development along his way to the final victory. Yet, strange as it may sound, the negative matter quite often helps toward this victory. Thus, a negative phenomenon like war makes science indispensable and hastens its achievements. They would be unimaginable otherwise, or else would require still many years. All that requires certain sacrifices, but one has to reconcile himself with them. Formerly, cholera and the plague sometimes eradicated entire countries. Human genius has conquered them. In time, it will conquer wars as well.

Good night, heralds.      [[2204]]

<u>Danteos</u>                    10/01/65 2214

Danteos. Heralds, I was slightly delayed, which obviously is not good, but sometimes even the spirits are not the masters of their time. Today I want to continue my examination of man.

Man can be proud of his science. Science can be considered as something that is definite when it comes to exactness, but nevertheless not all the sciences, for example – history. In some places in history there is more that is incorrect than what is correct. Why has that happened? In ancient times, when man did not yet know how to write, much passed into nonexistence. One individual told another – a father his son, and so on – only about the more important events. Obviously, these verbal accounts could not be preserved unaltered, and one cannot completely believe these accounts. The situation improved once man learned how to write. The art of writing, however, was so complicated that only a few people were able to master this art, and they also could not carve much into a stone. Better means and methods of writing were found later on, but even then there were very few of those who could write, and they were generally part of the court and their duty was to praise their rulers.

Every person perceives an event somewhat differently than another. Therefore no event is depicted exactly as it really occurred. Every king wanted to be praised, and since sometimes a new king came to power by killing the previous one, he tried to make him look bad in the eyes of the people, by having historians write what he dictated. There were very many cases like that. I will give you only one example, which you know, regarding Russia's Czar Boris. He was turned from a good czar and person into a murderer and a bad ruler. Therefore one has to be very careful while examining history. The same thing has to be said about the entire history of the Soviet Union. Everything in it has been altered as was necessary for the benefit of the communist party. You saw for yourselves what power these lies had over the people, particularly during the years of Stalin.

However, cannot the same thing that we are saying about history be said regarding all people? Is what you hear about a certain individual always the truth? Unfortunately no, more often than not it is an untruth. If some person invents something bad about an individual whom he dislikes, then this invented story becomes a fact, for how are people supposed to know that what they are told are lies? In order to verify whether what you have been told are lies or the truth, it has to be checked. Who is going to check it, though?

There are people who lie only in cases of necessity; for example – in the Soviet Union people had to and still have to lie in order to save their lives. Very many people lie in order to appear good to other people, in order to obtain advantages in life, and in family life in order to conceal their misdeeds from each other, their transgression of their vows of marriage. That is particularly easy to do with someone who is in love, because he usually believes everything without verification.

Sometimes an individual tells lies about another person simply in order to estrange him from his friend. The ability of actors is to be able to lie, to lie so that the lies appear to be the very truth itself, because while portraying the characteristics of another individual they have to give up their own traits. Some people are excellent actors when it comes to lying, they truly know how to lie so that one cannot help but to believe them. There are hardly any sure means of fighting against lies. All that you can do is be careful, and when you hear something that cannot be verified, consider it but do not take it as a fact.

My task is coming to an end, and I will be taking leave from you quite soon.                    [[2258]]


Ilgya                           10/08/65 2228


Ilgya. – ★ ★ ★ –

The other event was the visit of Rome's Pope Paul the sixth to New York. This visit proves how strong an influence the new developments have had even on the Catholic faith, so obstinate in its principles. Secondly, this visit distinguishes your city – New York – even more as the capital of the world. Truly, there is no city in the world which currently could compete with New York. Even though on the street, here the so-called Christ's deputy on Earth met the leading herald to Earth of The Almighty's new faith. That happened without being noticed by the people, as has been the case with the start of many historic events.

In conclusion, I want to say a few words about the high spirit Danteos's tidings, so that you would not misconstrue some of them. He said in his tiding that not everything in history is depicted as it really happened. History is depicted like the historians saw the events, or else as the ruler who succeeded the previous ruler wanted them seen. As an example he used Russia's Czar Boris Godunov, who in reality was not as bad as historians wrote about him. The more recent historians maintain the opposite. Obviously, all of them have made some mistakes.

With respect to Boris, while evaluating him, one has to consider the period during which he lived. During that period when czars like John the Terrible ruled, boyars fought for power in the court, and the level of human development in general was still rather low. Therefore Boris had to rule with the help of the sword, and quite often brutally. Only while considering all this, can we evaluate Boris anywhere near correctly as a czar and as a human being.

With that, let us conclude for today. Good night, heralds. Ilgya.
[[2255]]

Danteos                              11/12/65 2153

Heralds, as I already said, so much that is interesting takes place on your small Earth that it is difficult to part from you.

_ ★ ★ ★ _

Let us now turn to spiritual matters. It particularly struck me how a large majority of people behave toward the deceased. That is especially conspicuous in the cemetery. All the time there I hear, "Rest in peace." What do these words mean? Who is supposed to rest in peace then? The soul? What kind of a rest can it have? A brief relaxation – yes, but no permanent resting. When it comes to the body, it certainly can be tired, but it starts to return to the soil. It does not feel, and cannot want or feel anything at all. Therefore this wish – to rest in peace – is deceptive and meaningless, because the Christian as well as many other religions acknowledge the existence of the soul.

Nothing and no one rests in peace in the cemetery. It is a place where the mortal remains of the people who have passed into the hereafter are located. It is a place where the people who have remained on Earth can visibly express their love and respect for the departed ones. That is all there is!

People should forget the idea that death separates the living from the deceased for a long time. No, it separates them only for a brief period, and not even completely at that.

I will not yet say good-bye today, heralds. May peace be in your hearts. Danteos.                  [[2223]]

<u>Danteos</u>                              11/21/65  1314

Heralds, as you saw from the newspapers, man states, with the words of his more distinguished representatives, that man has to draw closer to the goal which God has set for him. That is almost the same thing which the Tidings tell you. This proves two things: first – that The Almighty moves humanity toward the goal set for it, and second – that the Tidings have really been given by Him, because this confirms what has been given in the Tidings through you, who did not know about this yourselves.

The Tidings give humanity a strong foundation underfoot, and give it the courage to overcome seemingly insurmountable obstacles. Currently, humanity has achieved such heights in science and its adoption that man can be considered to be a wizard, compared to what he was like less than a hundred years ago. He has acquired wings not only in order to fly so high in the sky as even an eagle is unable to, but he is already getting ready to travel to the planets. That is one consideration. The other is that man works on transforming his body. He develops his spiritual abilities and also strives to free his body from diseases, as well as find the means which would strengthen his body. For the time being he is still unable to control the centers of its activities, but he is approaching this goal as well.

When comparing the road which humanity has traveled to that which it will travel, the stretch of the road that has been completed is short. Not all people are capable of quickly following their leaders, and people are not at the same level of development everywhere. Some ideas are erroneous and even harmful. All that has to be overcome. Currently man cannot be a man always and everywhere – that is, be such as he has to be, which among other things also means to be fair. He has to lie in order to save his life, as for example in Russia or China. He has to hide his ideas there, for otherwise prison or death threaten him.

In the present society, too, an openly expressed idea can prove to be so unsuitable to the current situation of other people that it can greatly harm the individual. That is sad, but it is difficult to currently help that, until humanity develops more spiritually. It is important to avoid lies where that is possible, and to people who try to be fair. The power of the flesh is quite often still so strong that passion forces people to do things which they, themselves, do not want to do. It seems presently that lies reign in the world, but, as I already said, the still relatively low development of people, and the abnormal conditions of life, can explain that.

Let us conclude with that for today, because, after all, it is Sunday and you have a beloved guest, who should be given more time to spend with you, before the start of his long trip.

[[1354]]

Ilgya                                12/03/65 2113

Ilgya. - ★ ★ ★ - It is and will be most difficult for the people of India, because famine has set in due to the extensive drought. There are so many people there that it is questionable whether even the rich America will be able to save all of them.

As humanity's history demonstrates, wars, the plague, cholera, and starvation came in order to keep the number of people within the bounds of reasonableness. Man himself currently feels capable of looking after himself and of keeping the life of humanity within the necessary bounds, as well as fighting against disasters and diseases. Humanity is taking only the first steps in the new era and therefore success is not yet great, except in the fight against some diseases. The plague has been almost forgotten, but just recently it was able to wipe out almost entire countries. The struggle for bread has also been almost won. The scythe can still be heard in only a few places. The conditions of life have become good in many countries, if one may say so – almost too good in some countries.

With that, let us conclude for today. Ilgya. [[2132]]

Danteos                              12/10/65 2135

Heralds, quite a while has again passed and I am still on Earth. It is truly hard to leave Earth, because currently one can see so much here that is interesting and educational, that there is no sense in rushing off to other planets.

Humanity is presently devoting itself to science, and is in such a state of success that at times I truly stop and say, "What will man eventually achieve? It seems that there are no bounds to his abilities!"

What do thousands of years of humanity's history mean compared to one year currently? The Almighty has acquired a worthy and capable assistant. It is strange to call the small Earth – small. It should be called the great Earth. Of course, there is also much on it that is negative, because the majority of humanity is incapable of following the more capable people. That is how it is, however, and even though that is very undesirable, to some extent one has to reconcile himself with that. If all people were to be geniuses, then there would be no one to bake bread and maintain cleanliness. In time, machines will do all that, but still, machine operators will be needed, even though some machines will operate other machines.

The most important point in humanity's history is now – man unleashes himself from Earth and heads into the universe. If he is able to do that, will the day not come when he will start to direct the Earth and even the sun? You will claim that this is impossible, but was it possible for your grandfathers to fly through the air like birds, and to fly around the globe in a rocket? All that was in the realm of fairy tales back then, but what is a fairy tale now, compared to life?

How much time passed before man learned how to speak, write, and read? That seems to you to be expressed backwards, because you learn to read first and only then to write. Yet man – historical man – had to write first, so that there would be something to read. I often visited humanity during its course of development. The first time when I was on Earth, there was nothing yet that indicated what Earth will look like today. Giant dinosaurs walked on it then. They were large, but their brain was small.

When I visited Earth the second time, there were no longer any dinosaurs on it, instead, strange wooly creatures with long arms swung in the trees. They were not particularly well armed for their fight against other animals, but their brain was much more capable of thinking than the brain of the dinosaurs had been. Their hands gave them a particular advantage. They were able to do much that other animals could not do. They were able to pick up a stone and throw it at another animal, and even kill it. They were able to break off a tree branch and even turn it into a weapon, as well as use it for other purposes. This new animal did not particularly transform Earth.

When I came for the third time, I already met man. He still looked like an animal, but he already used fire and primitive weapons, and frequently covered his body with the skins of other animals. What was particularly surprising was that other animals had already started serving him. The most important aspect was that people spoke – they were able to express their thoughts and were able to accomplish joint works.

That was the beginning of humanity's history. Back then nothing testified that this animal, wrapped in a skin, who sat on a rock in front of a cave by a bonfire and looked at the stars, will reach these stars one day. He starts this effort today. How can I leave Earth at such a historic moment? Not even The Almighty can ask me to do that, and thus I will remain with you for a prolonged period.

Good night, heralds. Danteos. [[2218]]

<u>Astra</u>                                    12/17/65 2213

Astra. Heralds, how are you doing? You were lost to my sight today. I am probably getting old and can no longer keep up with you. You claim that I am joking, but, in fact, with what is going on in stores these days, one really can no longer find himself.

The festival of Christ's birth is a great festival, but is that any reason for turning it into a world market? How many of those gifts which you buy for presents and receive from others are ones that you would have ever bought for yourself? How many of them are truly necessary? [Of what value are] these greeting cards – particularly in America, where cards have to be sent to every acquaintance, and he of course has to send them to you? Both of you are quite indifferent about each other. Both of you couldn't care less how the other one will fare in the New Year. Yet both of you write, while wasting time and money, and send thousands of mail carriers to deliver this sea of paper that no one needs.

There is something good in this custom as well. Many people remember each other only over the Holidays, otherwise they would completely fade from memory. The other good thing is combining both festivals – Christmas and New Year. The work is cut almost in half. Still, couldn't these two festivals be utilized much more sensibly? For instance, consider children's toys. Children get so many of them over the Holidays that they do not know what to do with them, and the children get tired of them in a few days. They are forgotten, broken, and discarded. Yet later on, during the long year, some children get hardly any new toys at all.

Once the Holidays are over, everyone feels as tired as after the most difficult work. Why and who needs such an exaggeration? An army of Santa Clauses can be seen on almost every street and in almost every store. Doesn't that make the real Santa Claus worthless? In this entire crowd, Christ is forgotten. Was that the purpose of this festival when humanity first started to celebrate it? Of course not! Thus this festival has turned into a bacchanalia for the merchants.

No one trumpets this festival as much as the Hebrews do, who do not even believe in Christ, but believe in money. Yes, money brings wealth, but does wealth bring happiness? It brings an imagined happiness, which has in reality [only a] trifling value for an individual.

Good night, heralds. Astra. [[2246]]


Danteos                              12/24/65 2235


Heralds, today is the first time when I spend the day of the anniversary of Christ's birth on the planet Earth. Very much that is beautiful and moving can be seen and heard here. Of course, some things are exaggerated and even unpleasant, but when is everything of equal value? The story about Santa Claus, which is intended for children, loses much by the children seeing these Santa Clauses all over the streets collecting donations. Similarly, they see these Santa Clauses in many stores, and they have children sitting on their knees and give them presents. Children lose faith in the real Santa Clause, as well as in their own parents. In general, they lose faith in everything that their parents and other people tell them, and the fairy tale about Christmas loses its magic. After all, donations for the Holidays can be collected without having those doing the collecting wear Santa Claus suits.

Before the Holidays, people do not think about anything else except about buying presents. This does not empty their pockets as much as deprives them of their time. If there are too many toys they become worthless. With respect to giving presents to adults, this often makes the recipient unhappy, rather than happy. Frequently, it is almost impossible to throw away a present without using it, because the one who gave the present may ask why his present is not being used. Obviously, many presents are rather nice. One really has to learn an individual's taste and nature in order to be able to give a present that will truly bring joy.

It seems to me that there is too much of the materialistic and not enough of the spiritual in the current Christmas. The war has also grown silent over the Holidays. That gives people an opportunity to feel how valuable peace is.

I was in the Soviet Union several times. Christmas is not officially celebrated there. It is a workday there. Very many people there, celebrate it privately though, and much more sincerely than here. This festival is much more genuine there. It is also pleasant to see the people there becoming more daring and asking for ever more freedom for themselves.

I wish you to spend the great festival respectfully and worthily. Danteos.                          [[2306]]

# Chapter VI

# Winter 1966

Danteos                                    01/07/66 2225

Heralds, while examining human nature, I observed some interesting phenomena. All people are not the same, and that is understandable. The people themselves separate themselves into good, bad, and tolerable people. The tolerable people are those who are not particularly good or particularly bad. With respect to the bad ones, these are people who live only for their own benefit. First, they can be called egotists. Not only are they not moved by the misfortunes and suffering of others, but they, themselves, are ready to cause suffering for others.

There should not be any bad people. Every child imitates adults, particularly his parents. However, he also learns from his friends, from the street, or from the neighborhood children. Some parents are too lenient. A child should be loved but should not be pampered. There are children who are easy to raise, but there are also children who need a strong and firm hand. They need discipline and sometimes even a spanking. Some children are abnormal – they require medical treatment.

I do not want to read you a long lecture, but I want to point out some peculiarities. As I said before, it is hard to expect anything good from bad people. That should be expected from good people, and specifically here I have to say that good people, while wanting to do good for another person, quite often do something bad for him, because these people do not consider the other person's individuality.

People have different tastes, not only with respect to foods but also with respect to other things. One individual loves chocolate, the other detests it. One likes soft furniture, the other does not. Therefore good people have to strive to comprehend the other person, and should not force on him what they love but what might be unpleasant for him. There are the so-called peculiarities which may not seem to be particularly good to others, but which are beloved to the first one. While wanting to do good, one can quite often do something bad.

I will give you an example. An elderly individual who lived all alone used an old, ugly, and worn-out wallet. He had relatives – a husband and wife. They had tried several times to give him a new wallet. Yet he refused it, claiming that he was so used to the old wallet that he did not want to exchange it for any other. The relatives nevertheless decided to give him a particularly nice wallet last Christmas. So that the elderly person would be forced to use it, they decided to imperceptibly obtain the old wallet and destroy it. They managed to do that.

When the elderly gentleman dozed off while visiting them, they removed the old wallet from his pocket, transferred the money and everything else that was in it to the new wallet, and tossed the old wallet into the stove. When the elderly gentleman woke up and was ready to go home, he wanted to pay back a small debt. He took out the wallet and started rapidly removing everything from it. Then he paled, and asked, "What did you do with my old wallet?"

"Why do you need your old one, when you have a new one that is much better? We burned it."

"What, you burned it? You must be out of your mind! After all, I kept a thousand dollar bill in a secret compartment in it."

"What are you saying?" the relatives paled. "A thousand dollars in a secret compartment? We did not see any secret compartment!"

"You see, that was the value of my old wallet, no one could readily notice this secret compartment."

You see, that is how it is with the affairs of others. A person can never know everything about someone else. There are many things that one individual likes, but the other does not. Therefore you should never impose with your good heart if you feel that the other person would rather not accept it, and even refuses it. This is true even if you are convinced that it will truly benefit the other individual. Of course, you may express your ideas and your intent to do for the benefit of the other what seems to be best to you. If you see, though, that this does not seem to be good to the other, then do not persist.

Relatives and even marriage partners also have to consider that. Forcing your desire – and even good intentions – creates moroseness and can even threaten love, even the greatest love if it happens too frequently. Sometimes one of the greater needs is to consider the other individual and his peculiarities.

I have nothing to say about people who are neither good nor bad. Let us conclude with that for today. Danteos. [[2314]]

<u>Ilgya</u>                                01/14/66 2154

Ilgya. Heralds, the high visitor from The Almighty – Danteos – spoke with you the previous time. He obviously spoke only regarding the main points of the topic. Every law has its exceptions. He talked about man in general, about the majority of people. He said correctly that you should not, without a particular necessity, force your will on another person, even if you have good intentions. Obviously, that does not pertain to people who are unable to take care of themselves, and who can get themselves into trouble with their actions or behavior.

You should definitely intervene as little as possible in the life of another individual, even if there is much that you dislike. Unless it is essential, it is best not to impose. Of course, everyone can express his ideas, but it is best not to repeat them if they fail to gain any support. Not everything that is good in essence is good for everyone.

Consider a bird in a cage. After all, it has a much better life than a bird outdoors. Its life is not threatened, it does not have to look for food, the rain does not soak it, and it does not have to freeze in the winter. A human looks after it, and not only looks after it but even loves it. What better life could the poor little bird ask for? Still, the bird wants to live according to its inclination, look out for itself, and be free.

Similarly, every human being also wants to be free. Whoever tries to limit an individual's will without a particular necessity and without a particularly essential reason, makes a big mistake. Of course, that requires limiting your own will, because you want very much the person to live like you think he should live, so that it would be better for him.

– ★ ★ ★ – [[2227]]

<u>Ilgya</u>                                01/28/66 2132

Ilgya. Heralds, a visitor from the north is currently visiting you – the cold. It is not an invited guest and neither is it a welcome guest, because it does not act politely – it pinches your cheeks, bites your ears, and crawls along your skin wherever possible. It is fortunate that the ocean does not like this visitor from Canada either. It falls on it and forces it back north. This sudden change of temperature does not have a particularly good effect on the state of people's health. What can be done, though? Of course, it is possible to travel to warm lands during the winter, but that is not possible for everyone. Nick has traveled to a warm land, but he is not particularly happy about that. Warm lands have much that is negative, because places where everything is ideally good hardly exist. The Hawaiian Islands are close to the notion of ideal, but neither are they ideal in all aspects.

Man, who has achieved very much in his victory over nature, still has much to achieve. He still has very much to achieve in his victory over his own nature. Since man consists of the spirit and matter – which have different substances, many even of an entirely contrary nature – it is difficult for man to achieve his envisioned human ideal. It is difficult to limit the power of matter, it tries to retain its position. Man cannot become an angel while living in hell, but a devil can readily become an angel while living in paradise.

It was not possible for man to become a human being in the full meaning of the word when he lived among animals. He could not become kindhearted when a lion attacked him or a snake in the grass bit him. The life which the first people lived could be called hell, and man's current life compared to his former can almost be called paradise. Since it is not a complete paradise yet, then man has not become an angel so far. I am referring to humanity as a whole, because some people are capable of becoming angels despite all difficulties. So far there are not many of them. A large majority of people are only halfway there, and many are even further back.

With the help of science – without which man could never achieve paradise – he has to pay particularly much attention to improving his nature. He has to fight against the negative that still dwells within him, and he has to strive to control his emotions. Often, many things do not seem to man like they are in reality. Other people can easily deceive him by telling him untruths, or by expressing one-sided opinions. Similarly, his own conceit can deceive man, as can an incorrect evaluation of another individual's words or nature.

Man generally understands evil better than good. He quite often imagines evil where there is none in reality. Therefore, man should not, without indubitable facts, feel positive about his decisions. Mainly, though, he should not succumb to anger, because anger always results in exaggerations and insults, which are hard to forget and to forgive. That often makes the best of friends part, even though frequently it is based on something trifling, misunderstood, or even simply imagined. Since The Almighty's heralds, too, are merely people, then what I have said, unfortunately, refers to them as well.

The high spirit Danteos will talk with you the next time. I wish you good night. Ilgya.          [[2223]]

<u>Danteos</u>                    02/04/66 2133

Heralds, the previous time Ilgya announced me. It so happened that I had to head somewhat unexpectedly for a very distant planet. Therefore I had to make you wait a little while. I even thought that I will not be able to make it at all, but eventually I managed to get back to Earth.

A large natural disaster occurred on the aforementioned planet. Several millions of the planet's inhabitants perished. Among them also were several close friends of mine who had incarnated. As you can see, there is not complete safety elsewhere either, because sometimes the forces of matter rebel against the spiritual ones. That word is not quite correct, but it is hard to find a better one. Matter functions according to certain laws. Sometimes, though, these laws cease to function correctly due to various reasons, and then terrible things can happen. Sometimes not only a planet but an entire solar system perishes.

With respect to the planet Earth, it finds itself in particularly favorable and exquisite circumstances for life. Of course, such circumstances did not always exist, but you know the history of Earth. Currently the circumstances are most favorable for the development of life and utilization of human spiritual abilities. Just during your lifetime alone, human spiritual achievements have, in fact, been fantastic – unimaginable to man himself just a hundred years ago. Man has conquered not only the Earth itself, but also the air above it. He has surpassed the winged bird, which is no longer able to come even close to man. He has started getting ready for the trip to the moon.

I can say that after some time he will be able to know all of his solar system. Man no longer doubts this possibility. Then the galaxies of the universe will open up before him. How will man be able to reach them? Will man be able to overcome not only the obstacles of distance but also those of time? That is a question to which humanity has not yet received an answer, but that does not mean that someday it will not receive one.

Humanity has already achieved much that formerly seemed completely impossible even in fairy tales. Why should it then not achieve what seems to be impossible today?

I have to return to the aforementioned planet, therefore permit me to take leave. Danteos. [[2205]]

<u>Sineokia</u>                    02/11/66 2150

Sineokia is speaking. Heralds, quite a while has passed since I have been with you. Some things on Earth have happened in the meantime, but it seems that nothing particularly important and historic, in the true meaning of the word, has occurred. What can be called historic? It is the fact that humanity has suddenly realized that the population is becoming too large for the small Earth, and that quite soon it will not be able to feed everyone.

God told man, "Live and fill the Earth."

The moment approaches when man sees that he has carried out this order, and that he has to start considering what to do now. The moon? Yes, it is almost at hand, but what can be done with it? It does not have air, and it cannot be fully utilized without air. The nearer planets? Mercury is out, it is too close to the sun. It seems that Venus and Mars would be more likely. Yet even on them the conditions for life do not seem to be particularly rosy for man. Even if these planets could be utilized, it would still be difficult to move millions of people to them. Therefore, at least for the immediate future, only one solution remains – to control the birthrate.

Why did the number of people suddenly start to increase so much? First, with the development of medicine, man conquered the worst destroyers of people – the plague and cholera. These diseases were able to devastate entire countries. Almost all people in Latvia died out at one time. Similarly, other diseases have also been greatly limited. Secondly, humanity's cultural development – the elimination or limitation of starvation. Several million people would currently die in India, if the neighbors who are rich with grain – as for example the United States of America – had not come to their aid. Obviously, even the United States will be unable to feed the superfluous millions in the future.

In addition to births, the number of people is also increasing because of their longer lifetime. Because of improvements in living conditions and the help of medicine, the number of old people increases much. A large majority of these old people live on pensions and they themselves no longer produce anything. Whether it wants to or not, humanity will have to utilize the ability of medicine not only for saving people from death but also for limiting the birthrate. Man himself is incapable of restraining from passion. That concludes my lecture.

– ★ ★ ★ – [[2244]]

<u>Danteos</u>                    02/18/66 2216

Danteos. Heralds, while observing the development of man on Earth and his notions about the future, I have to say that he advances faster in his deeds than in his thinking and in his attempts to understand The Almighty and His deeds and goals. In his scientific discoveries, man has achieved wonders which he could not even imagine formerly. He has discovered much that he did not know even existed. He nevertheless cannot comprehend the spirit, because so far he has not discovered him anywhere.

After all, one thing is clear to everyone, man himself – or the ape from which he supposedly has evolved – could not have created himself. Similarly, neither could a frog or an earthworm have done that. In order for a car to become a machine that can move and carry out the tasks intended for it, man had to build it and make it "alive." (Put the word alive in quotation marks.) If we were to look at how the car has evolved, we can say that the car, too, has progressed and has become ever more suitable for its duties.

Now consider the new rockets. They act just like man does – head for a definite target, change directions, photograph the planets, and send the pictures back to Earth. They act as if they were living beings, or else as though a man were inside them, even though man remains on Earth. Former man could not have understood all this, and if someone had tried to explain to him that this is possible, he would not have believed and would have thought the teller to be crazy.

Everything in the world proves that there is some force which creates and directs the universe and everything in it. The fact that this force cannot be seen and ascertained with the instruments which man has in his possession, or by other means, certainly does not preclude the existence of this force. If a rocket of alien construction were to land on Earth now – having come from some planet in the universe – and if man would not find any living beings in this rocket, after all, he would not claim that this rocket had built itself. He would claim that some living beings from an unknown planet had sent it.

To those people who cannot understand all this, to those people who claim that the creator of the world – God – does not exist and that they do not have souls, to these unfortunate people only one thing can be said, "Yes, you do not have a soul and do not have God, your life will end on Earth!"

With that, let us conclude for today. Danteos. [[2244]]

<u>Danteos</u>                          03/25/66 2200

Heralds, the last time I talked about the errors of great people. Let us talk today about the errors of lesser people. I have already talked about them once, but I want to return to them once more.

Everyone knows that a person with a bad nature is hard to endure. He is dissatisfied with everything, and nothing can be done to please him. Even good-natured people, though, and even loving people quite often do much that is bad, without realizing it themselves. You should not forget one thing – every individual loves freedom and almost every individual has different characteristics. I will not talk about anyone personally, but I will talk about what I personally have observed. Therefore, if I will talk about something that some of you may possess, do not consider that as being said specifically to you.

Some women tend to be somewhat lazy and do not keep their house in order. When the husband comes home from work and wants to lie down on the couch, first he has to clear some rags from it. If he wants a drink of water, he has to wash a glass first. If he wants to see his wife looking beautiful, he first has to comb her hair and then put a new gown on her. It is obvious that after a prolonged period his love fades. He stops respecting his wife and does not feel at home in his house.

It also happens that the husband loves to stop at a bar on his way from work. He comes home late and is drunk. He goes to bed without undressing. Obviously, his wife cannot respect a husband like that, and generally whomever she cannot respect she cannot love either.

There are also situations of a completely opposite nature, but the results are the same.

A wife loves order and cleanliness. Every item has to be in its place. Nothing may fall down. As soon as he opens the door, the husband hears his wife's question, "Did you thoroughly wipe your feet? Just a minute ago, I arranged the papers and books on your desk. Darling, if you take something, kindly put it back where you got it from. Look for yourself how nice your desk looks!"

Surprisingly, the husband does not feel happy at all. When he wants to pick up a pencil in order to jot down something, he does not do that, because he knows that he will forget to put the pencil back in the place designated for it. He would gladly stretch out on the bed for a few minutes, but what will the bed look like after that? He rather lies down on an uncomfortable couch. He respects his wife as a housekeeper, and loves her, but does not feel like he is in his home, but rather in her home. The love – it slowly pales.

That is how it goes in family life – one wants to go to a dance, the other wants to stay home and read a book. One wants chocolate ice cream for dessert, the other detests it. One wants to have a dog, the other a cat, but they do not tolerate each other. Which one to get rid of? This goes on and on. All that cannot be avoided in life, but even good people turn into bad ones because of all that. What can be done to avert such situations? They cannot be completely averted, but they can be made tolerable.

That can be done by mutual concessions, by respecting each other's desire for freedom, and by asking for only what is essential. If the husband loves to read the paper at the dinner table and the wife does not have anything interesting to tell her husband, then – wives – let your husband read his nasty papers even while eating dinner. Similarly, do not keep your husband from reading the papers while lying in bed. If they make the sheet dirty, cover the sheet with a white rag, and both of you will be happy. Quite often such unpleasant situations can be readily averted, if an individual is willing to achieve the realization of his/her desires without unnecessarily causing displeasure for the other, or depriving her/him of the ability to realize her/his desires.

Important events seldom occur in life, but something unimportant takes place if not every hour, then every day. These unimportant events in their totality become so important that the happiness of your life depends on them. While doing something, people usually think only about themselves. They fail to consider how it will effect another person and how the other individual might like it.

No one can have complete freedom unless he lives in a desert. While living with people he has to limit his desires so as not to harm another person.

Let us conclude with that for today. Good night, heralds. Danteos.

[[2355]]

# Chapter VII

# Spring 1966

<u>Apostle John</u>                    04/08/66 2138

→Heralds, I, the spirit of Christ's Apostle John, come to you and to humanity in the assignment of Christ, in order to relate what is not sufficiently understandable to you, and what causes doubts and differences of opinion.

First of all, Christ had not come to Earth as a ruler, nor as God. He was born as a human and lived like a human, experiencing all human sorrows, joys, pain, and suffering. Only His spirit was divine. Similarly, your spirits are not material, but come from Heaven, as Christ did, with God's tasks, but your tasks are obviously much smaller and much more varied. As you have been told before, God, being a spirit, saw human life with all its hardships and enjoyments. Yet, it is one thing to see, and something else to feel.

You can see someone stick his finger in a fire and then start screaming in pain, but unless you have burned your finger previously, you will not be able to understand what pain is and how it feels. You will understand that it is unpleasant, and that it is something very bad and almost unbearable for a human. Similarly, should you observe a man toiling hard, or walking for a long time, observe him getting tired and stopping to rest, you will see the results of exhaustion, but will not understand what exhaustion itself is, or what feelings it induces. In order to be able to comprehend everything that a human experiences and in order to be able to evaluate what a human can do, and what is within his strength and what one can ask of him, one has to be a human himself. That is one point.

The other point is that man has to know that God knows him as God, knows his capabilities, and knows his suffering and joys. Man has a right to tell God, "Does anything matter to You, up there in Heaven, while ruling us? What do You know about us? You feel no pain, and You don't have to suffer! How can You ask all that from us, not knowing it Yourself? It is easy to talk, but it is difficult to do something."

God understood all that and decided to come to the people Himself, in the form of Christ, not only in order to comprehend man as God and as a human, but also to prove to man that He, God, has undergone all his suffering, and even has died the most difficult form of death. With that, He told and demonstrated to man, not only in words, but in deeds as well, what he has to be like. Also, by coming to us – His apostles or disciples, after His death on the cross – as a spirit in His appearance, He proved that life on Earth is not the most important thing, for only the body dies, but the spirit lives eternally. Yet, in order to live eternally, man must live like God has bid him in the Ten Commandments and in the teachings of Christ.

When Christ, after His death, came to us and talked with us, I asked Him how He could have forgiven those people who tortured Him, for they were, after all, worse than animals. He replied, "In essence, man is an animal. He comes from lions, sheep, elephants, and donkeys, and obviously, most of all from apes. He did not create himself, just as a snake did not create itself. Yet, having been created from the same material from which all animals were created, he was created in a manner allowing him to be able to develop into a human – into an animal who will become a creature which is capable of receiving God's spirit. He will become capable of transforming the brutal characteristics of an animal, will be capable of thinking, and in time, capable of becoming an assistant to God in the work of creating and forming the world."

"To become an assistant to God," I exclaimed, "but is that possible?"

"It obviously is, but that will require thousands of years. Current man is still very close to the animals. All people do not know what God asks and expects from them. A paradise like people currently imagine, does not exist. Souls do not live in it. They have more important tasks than to do nothing in paradise. Yet, man must create Paradise on Earth. God has explained how to achieve that in various words and instructions, and has talked with the people through Me, and will talk through you. Only when every individual knows God's will, knows what he has to do, and what responsibility he bears in front of God and the people – only then will it be possible to demand responsibility for his actions from man. Those people who killed Me did not know what they were doing. How could I fail to forgive them, without becoming unjust? Would you want to see your God being unjust?"

"Oh no, obviously not! How could I serve an unjust God?" I replied, while falling to my knees.

"Get up John, but keep to yourself what I have told you, for currently people are not capable of comprehending that. When that day comes, I will allow you to tell that to the people."

"But how old will I be then, Teacher?" I asked.

"Approximately two thousand years," Christ replied.

"Two thousand years? But there are not and cannot be any people that old," I said again.

"You will not have to be that old. Your spirit will tell that to the people."

"But how," I asked, "will that be possible?"

Christ smiled, "Don't ask that much, but believe Me that it will be possible. Now I have to go."

With that, Christ departed. After He had left, the disciples gathered around me and asked me what I had discussed with Christ. I answered, "I will tell you that in two thousand years."

The disciples looked at each other, and Peter said, "Leave him alone. He has not yet recovered from what Christ told him."

They left me alone.

Today is the day when, with Christ's permission, I can tell humanity what He told me back then.← [[2252]]


Ilgya                          04/08/66

Ilgya. The spirit of Apostle John has alighted away.

In one day, you will celebrate humanity's greatest festival of remembrance, a festival which tells, which reminds people of the day when some of them tried to kill God. With that, however, people only took Him into their hearts.

I wish you to spend this day brightly. [[2255]]


Astra                          04/08/66

Astra. Heralds, I congratulate you with the visit of Christ's apostle on the eve of the important festival. May his words encourage humanity to pursue achieving its task even more successfully.

Good night. Astra.              [[2257]]

<u>Apostle John</u>                    04/15/66 2204

Heralds, as assigned by God, I come to you once more. Currently humanity is concerned about a question which is particularly important to it, even though a question like that should not have arisen at all.

The question is — has God died? First, God is considered to be immortal, even if one does not use the evidence in the Bible, because the universe, which God has created, has existed for billions of years. Secondly, this question is completely illogical. If God has not created the universe, who then has created it? Can a stone create a stone? Can an oak tree create an acorn from which it grows? Could a sheep — whose ability to think everyone knows — have created itself? If they did not create themselves, who then created them? Perhaps a mosquito created the elephant, it in turn a frog, and so on? If a cell could have come into existence due to accidental joining of some elements, then what chance did this cell have to create this unimaginably complicated world? I want to tell you a little story.

A young man had completed school and was getting ready for work, the work of his lifetime. He stood on a cliff by the seashore. The endless sea lay at his feet. Behind his back, a valley covered with green trees dozed in the rays of the sun. A river, like a shiny snake, meandered through it while seeking the exit to the sea. In the distance, beyond the green forests, the edge of the blue sky touched the ground.

"This place is wonderful. I cannot wish for anything better for my mansion in which to spend my old age, having completed the work of my life. I hope to successfully accomplish this. While I will be shaping my life far from here, I will be able to gradually build my mansion here."

He paced out the dimensions necessary for his plans, and then left. Probably no one saw him, and if someone saw him, he promptly forgot that, for there was nothing special to remember.

Many years passed, and then a man arrived from far away. He went over to the cliff. He stayed there for a while and then headed for the nearest town. He went to the mayor of the town and told him that he had received the assignment from a rich and highly placed gentleman to build a mansion on the cliff, according to his plans and instructions. He will need many workers and much material.

Thus, in a few years, a wonderful mansion arose on the cliff above the sea. Guests visited the mansion, they came from near and distant lands. Large banquets were held in the mansion, but the townspeople did not know who the owner of the mansion was. He did not visit it, and if he did — no one knew which of the guests he was. When asked about the owner of the mansion, some guests said that he was a king in a distant, very distant land. They knew him only by name, because they received his orders from messengers.

The inhabitants of the town, too, could visit the mansion on certain days and look it over. It was built of marble, and the halls were spacious and high. They were full of expensive furniture. Wonderful paintings of great masters adorned the walls. Fabulous statues stood in some halls. It was impossible to appraise the value of the mansion. Yet the owner of the mansion was not in it, no one saw him and no one could say anything definite about him.

The owner of the mansion could arrive any day, and then again he could never come. People admired the mansion and said, "The owner of this mansion has to be unimaginably rich, to have been able to build such a mansion and decorate it with such works of art, on which a price cannot be placed."

Even though no one had seen the owner of the mansion, still, no one claimed that he did not exist. One would have had to be crazy to imagine that a mansion like that would have built itself.

That, you see, is a little story. Everyone understands that neither a mansion nor anything else on Earth can come into being on its own. Yet, you see, the universe with its innumerable suns and planets, and Earth with its wonderful living beings and the plant kingdom, could have come into existence out of nothing, without having been created and formed by anyone. God has supposedly accomplished all that. Where is this God then, why doesn't He come to us? Why is He not visible and why don't we know where He is?

I can tell you that God sees the Earth not only with His own eyes, but with the eyes of millions of people, and only those who are spiritually blind do not see Him.

I will conclude with that. [[2306]]


Apostle John                    04/29/66 2158

→Heralds, people do not understand completely Christ going into the desert, and being tested by Satan. That can become understandable only now – now that it has been proclaimed to humanity, through you, who God is, and who Satan is.

As you know, in addition to the spirit and matter, God decided to create a new living being. The spirit, as such, is not capable of that which matter is capable of, and vice versa. The Almighty decided to utilize the abilities of matter in order to make the spirit capable of that which is not possible for him as a pure spirit. He created man, a combination of matter and of the spirit. Matter possesses negative characteristics as well, and man has to overcome them in a long struggle.

In addition to The Almighty, as the creator of the universe, there are two other Rulers in your galaxy – God and Satan. God considers that matter can be transformed with the aid of tolerance and love. Satan considers that these means alone are insufficient, and that force has to be utilized as well. Satan is not hostile to man. He is hostile to matter, and not quite as hostile to it as may appear. He strives to transform the bad characteristics of matter as soon as possible. He also demands of the spirits, who have incarnated in man, a persistent struggle to improve matter. He is also the one who punishes the spirits with meager abilities and a weak will.

Ancient people were incapable of understanding this explanation. You can see that from their inability to understand who The Almighty is. They understood God, the Father, and God, the Son, but did not understand The Almighty. Therefore they called Him [[the Holy]] Ghost.

As you can see, the apostles, too, were unable to deliver to the people Christ's explanation about The Almighty, as well as to deliver the correct idea about Satan. If you know the essence of God and Satan, then it will be easy for you to understand Satan testing Christ in the desert, which otherwise seems absurd.

The decision to send Christ to Earth in order to make known to people the true God and His laws, based on the power of love and capabilities of the spirits, was a tragic one. God believed that love is almighty and that in the end it can break all the negative characteristics of matter, and make it a partner with the spirit in forming and achieving The Almighty's world goals. When God sent Christ to Earth, He gave Him only one weapon for victory – love.

Satan considered that love, alone, is not enough – that Christ has to be given a sword as well, and has to be given the power to give orders and demand obedience. He said that Christ will be unable to conquer the brutal people, and that they will kill Him. God replied, "It is not important if they kill Christ, for with that they will merely strengthen the power of the spirit."

God bid Christ to be a human on Earth, to accomplish everything on His own, without asking for help from God, as well as to select on His own the manner of His activities, and to decide what would be best for humanity's spiritual development. God did not desire slaves, for a slave is incapable of doing anything independently. A man like that, a slave, cannot have any value as far as The Almighty is concerned. Satan, however, said that force has to be used initially, in order to overcome and transform the power of matter more readily. Might has to be used, because currently man is still too brutal. This brutality has to be broken by force, and once it is broken, then the way will be opened for love as well, and for its victory.

"All right," God said, "We will give Christ the right to choose for Himself the method which He thinks is more correct."

(A three minute intermission.) [[2244 – 2247]]

Once Christ reached manhood and had to begin the task given to Him, He went into the desert in order to consider how to carry out, better and more correctly, the task which God had given Him. During His childhood and youth, He had observed people and had learned to comprehend them, as well as to evaluate their good and bad characteristics, plus their abilities to transform. He understood how terribly difficult His task was, and often had doubts. On seeing the horrible brutality of the people, and the hatred of one nation for the other, He sometimes despaired and did not know which way to decide. Therefore, He decided to go into the desert in order to think everything over without being disturbed, and to reach a final decision about how He should accomplish His task best and most correctly.

God and Satan observed Him – initially with patience, and later on impatiently.

"You see, God, how difficult it is for Him to decide. It seems to Me that He understands that Your task cannot be accomplished, that it is not possible to transform man with love alone."

"I see, and know that My task for Him seems difficult to Him, but I believe that He will nevertheless select it."

"I really don't think so," Satan said. "Will You permit Me to go to Him and find out what He has decided?"

"Go," God said to Satan, in response to His question. "A sufficiently long time to decide has passed. Besides that, His human strength begins to be exhausted."

Satan came down to Earth. Christ was rather weakened and hungry from the prolonged starvation in the desert.

"What do You want of Me, Satan?" Christ asked Him.

"I want to help You decide what to do with the people and with Your task. You are the Son of God and You can ask for help from God in those cases when human strength alone is not sufficient. You can even perform miracles. Why don't You turn these stones into bread, which You need so desperately?"

"I can perform miracles in order to strengthen people's faith in God, but not for My own benefit."

While talking, They climbed a high mountain inadvertently, and Satan, while pointing out the wide world with His arm, said, "Look, there are many countries before You. I can give You soldiers and weapons which You can use to conquer the entire world and become its king. In short order, You will be able to destroy all evil and make people obedient to Yourself and to God. Your task will be easy and accomplished rapidly."

"Don't tempt Me, Satan, with the easy accomplishment of My task and the honor of a king. Your way is easy, but it is not the right one."

They came down from the mountain, and went into a city where They climbed to the high roof of a temple. Christ was tired and sat down to rest, while looking at the long stairway which led down to the street.

"After all, You are the Son of God. Why don't You order the angels to carry You down on their wings?"

"The angels have their tasks, and I have mine. If I wanted to, I, Myself, could fly down without wings and the help of angels, for I truly am the Son of God, and have come to Earth to carry out God's tasks as a human. You understand, Satan, as a human! Now You may go and tell My Father that I have decided to travel His difficult paths, rather than Your easy ones, for they are not the right pathways, the ones needed for victory."

Satan bowed His head and said, "I congratulate You with the noble decision. I will relay it to Your Father – God."

Satan departed from Earth and left Christ on it as its Ruler.

I take leave from you, heralds. I have told you what you did not know, and what even we, the apostles, did not know, or did not understand when we were with Christ. May Christ be with you, heralds, during your difficult moments in life. Yet, you must learn from Christ how to live and what to ask from life, as well as how to suffer, and how to be happy in knowing that after suffering comes liberation and the Kingdom of Heaven, in which all of us are – God, Christ, the apostles, and all the people who have departed from Earth.

    John.←                    [[2333]]

<u>Ilgya</u>                              05/13/66 2157

Ilgya. Heralds, I just talked to the spirit of Apostle John. He asked me to tell you that he fully understands your desire to learn more about Christ, but our – the spirits' – task is not to write a new Gospel. We are allowed to pass on to current humanity only a few particularly important and incomprehensible events.

You know most of what Christ passed on to His disciples and what He directly told the people. That is sufficient for shaping humanity's future in the way which God has chosen for humanity. Christ's teachings have reached humanity's conscience and it begins to understand that the road which He indicated toward happiness and Paradise on Earth is the right one. You can see that not only the churches think about how to free the people – all the people – from hunger and worries about shelter, and provide them humane rights to live. The governments of countries enact such laws, and, similarly, the governments assume responsibility for the sick. As you can see, Christ's ideas enter people's lives ever more and deeper.

The superfluous activities which have been incorporated into Christ's faith – such as praying to God and church services – have nothing to do with Christ's faith, and many of them are even contrary to it. Of course, they have to vanish on their own.

God should not be considered to be a king in a realm of slaves. He should be considered as the Father of all people. As a Father, He loves His children, but simultaneously He understands that love should not be blind, and that the duty of love is to raise the children to be capable, good, and just people. Therefore He frequently has to be strict, and has to use means of punishment for the disobedient ones. Since God knows everything that oppresses man's heart, He does not need any prayers. Obviously, He does not prohibit an individual to turn to Him in necessary cases, that is, on occasions when it seems to man that God does not know his need or desire. Entirely superfluous, though, is praying merely for the sake of praying, and the glorification of God. The best prayer is not with words but by deeds.

Now that humanity's development has advanced so far that man himself is able to create something new that did not exist in the world, he also better understands God – the creator of the world. Along his way, man has erred many times, he has even strayed for some time. In the future, too, he will be unable to avoid some mistakes, but there will be ever fewer of them.

God has also made mistakes in His work of creation, but these mistakes have not always been in vain, because one can learn from mistakes what should not be done, and what is useless or bad.

Some people, while reading the Tidings, will claim that all these spirits who have come to you are too human. What should they be like then, if God has even created man according to His essence? Some people will claim that the spirits have come to you simply to chat. Why not do that if it is possible to associate with you? Many of the spirits are your friends, and have even been your relatives as people. Why shouldn't they meet with you on your festival days? Why not do what is good and what is now possible, until you will return to Heaven?

Nothing is too large or too small for God. He looks after the large elephant just as after the small ladybug. Hasn't He given the dung beetle a wonderful, shiny suit that does not get dirty? He has even looked out after it. Why shouldn't He see then how His heralds are faring, and shouldn't give them an extra moment of happiness, as gratitude for their important work?

With that, we will conclude for today. Good night, heralds. Ilgya.
[[2245]]


<u>Apostle Peter</u>                    05/27/66 2154


→Heralds, you are interested greatly in Christ's life on Earth, and particularly in those places of the Gospel where, due to various reasons, the text is expressed so that it is incomprehensible to you, people, and therefore is quite often interpreted wrong. God, understanding that, allowed me to alight to you and attempt to make our, the apostles', writings somewhat more understandable to you.

First of all, I want to make clear to you the apostles' relationship with Christ. None of us were specially prepared for the high task. All of us came from low classes of people. I, for example, was a fisherman. Christ walked around talking with the people, telling them that He brought love to people, brought it from God, for He had been sent by Him. He said that humanity will be able to become happy, and will be able to achieve Paradise only through love. Whenever He spoke, His words went straight to our hearts. He spoke simply, but so sincerely and with such conviction, that all doubts vanished regarding the truth and correctness of what He had said. He revealed to us that He had been sent directly by His Father – God – to redeem the sins of mankind.

We were ordinary people and we reasoned like humans. It was difficult for us to understand that the Son of God did not try in any way to display His divinity, by demonstrating His power. It was difficult for us to understand why we had to suffer just like any other human, or why we had to travel the long roads on foot, rather than riding. It was difficult to understand why we had to struggle and had to eat rye bread, when He, as the Son of God, could have had the angels provide for us. Yet, He said that if we want to prove to the people that we are better than they, then we have to prove that by utilizing our own abilities and our own deeds.

I recall one evening when, scorched by the sun, we had traveled a long desert road. By evening we were thirsty and extremely tired, when we finally reached a village and drank some water from the well. We ate a few bites of bread and rested in the shade of the trees. Christ settled down in the grass next to me and said, "It is so pleasant to rest after a long, hard journey."

He wiped the sweat from His brow and closed His eyes wearily. Doubts overcame me. My mind was unable to answer my questions. After a while, Christ opened His eyes, and I told Him, "Excuse me, Teacher, but I cannot understand with my foolish mind why You, the Son of God, tire just like we ordinary people do."

Christ took me by the hand and said, "Tell Me, Peter, how does My hand differ from your?"

"It doesn't, Teacher."

"And how does My foot differ from your?"

"It also doesn't."

"Why, then, Peter, do you want My feet to tire less than your? My entire body does not differ from your body. Just like you, I have been born from a woman. Then why do you expect something different from My body than from your? Would a king's son, if he traveled with us, tire less than we do?"

I laughed out loud and said, "Less? He would tire much more."

Everyone began to laugh. "How could a king's son endure what we do? After all, he'd be ready to ride even into a castle on horseback."

Silence set in for a while. The disciples began to doze, but the Teacher looked thoughtfully at the sky. I felt that I had put myself into an embarrassing position with my question, and could not reconcile myself in any way.

"Well, go ahead and ask, Peter," Christ's lips whispered barely audibly.

"Forgive me, a simple fisherman, that I ask You questions which seem foolish to other, more educated people."

"No, Peter, they do not seem foolish even to the wisest people."

I became somewhat bolder. "Oh well, Teacher. With respect to a king's son, even though he is a king's son, he still is only the same human as any one of us. He differs from us only with his high position. But You, You are the Son of God. Everything is possible for You. With a wave of the hand You could turn this rock into bread. You could make dozens of horses available for our use. You could oppose thousands of the king's soldiers with legions of angels bearing flaming swords in their hands. There is nothing that You could not do, if You wanted to."

"Wanted to," said Christ. "Here, you see, is the real expression – wanted to! You have to understand how difficult that is, to want to do something and be unable to."

"Be unable?" I asked in surprise. "After all, You can do anything."

"Yes, anything that benefits mankind as well, but not just only Myself, or just only Myself and you. Do you know, Peter, that people's hearts can be conquered only with love – only with love and nothing else? It makes no difference whether you are a human, the Son of God, or God Himself."

"But is that possible?"

"Yes, that is a good question, but if that is not possible with love, Peter, then that is not possible at all. Now then, what is there left for us to do? Reply to God, Peter! What is there left for us to do?"

I raised my head and said, "What there is left for us to do is what You are doing, Teacher. Forgive me my questions, but, You see, we are only humans, but You are the Son of God. You are much closer to God."

"Why do you think that you are more distant from God than I am?"

I did not know what to say.

Christ waited for about a minute, and then said, "Do you have a soul, Peter?"

"I do, obviously!" I replied, almost indignant at such a question.

"And who gave you this soul?"

"God – obviously God! Who else could have given it to me?"

"Similarly, He also gave Me a part of the same spirit of His, as He gave you. What difference then is there between us?"

I did not know what to reply. It seemed that there was no difference, but at the same time, the difference was tremendous.

"You see, Peter, the difference is only in the task which God has given everyone. My task is to bring God's teachings to humanity, and your task, as well as that of the other disciples, is to spread them throughout the entire world."

"Yet, how will You, while behaving like a human, be able to fight against the legions of evil people, and how will You be able to defend Yourself against their swords? They will kill You."

"You express yourself incorrectly, Peter. They may kill My body, but by doing that, they will set free My divine spirit, and with his help, you will bring God's light to all the nations, and no swords will be able to deter you." ← [[2313]]

Ilgya                              06/03/66 2202

Ilgya. Heralds, Apostle Peter will still talk with you, because he has not completed his tiding. However, I cannot tell you exactly when, since he has very little free time.

I want to talk to you about the present. Thursday was an important, historic day again. People achieved the ability to travel to the moon. That is the first step in the conquest of the universe, obviously, not in a military sense. It is not more difficult, but even easier to land on planets that have an atmosphere, than on the moon. Obviously, they are further away than the moon, but distance is not an insurmountable obstacle.

The Russians landed their machine slightly ahead of the Americans, but they were able to do that only after several failures. They figured that the Americans will be able to catch up with them in only two or three years, but the Americans caught up with them within the same year and with far better results, without suffering a single failure. That truly approximates a miracle. Isn't it really a miracle to build a device like that, which reaches the moon so accurately – while its functioning is directed from a huge distance – photographs the landscape of the moon, sends the photos back to Earth, and does still other things toward exploring the moon? Could people have imagined that formerly?

Man has always wanted to reach the moon, even when he did not know what kind of a bird the moon was. Once he learned what the moon actually was, he started fantasizing about reaching it. All his fantasy turned out to be much paler than the truth. The achievements of science turned out to be much more wonderful than a fairy tale and human fantasy. As you can see, The Almighty has not erred in evaluating the abilities of human genius. Some human achievements are equivalent to The Almighty's achievements, and He has acquired a worthy assistant for Himself in the work of forming the world.

Alexander evaluated correctly the historic significance of the new achievement. He sat by a radio and listened to the device approaching the moon, landing on it, and the first news of the great success. Today, too, the Americans continue the conquest of the air, and the evaluation of the capabilities of the many devices.

I congratulate the humanity on Earth with its splendid achievements, and wish it to continue them successfully. What has been achieved so far is only the first step in the conquest of space. The subsequent steps will bring much that humanity cannot even imagine presently.

Good night, heralds. Ilgya. [[2239]]


<u>Ilgya</u>                        06/10/66 2143


Ilgya. Heralds, today I want to discuss some everyday concerns with you. It rained today. New York had a water shortage last year, because it did not rain as usual, but people continued to waste water. There is almost enough water in the reservoir this year — almost twice what there was last year. Conservation of water nevertheless continues to some extent. People have become more careful, therefore the lesson was not lost on them. That is an aside, though. The main thing is to achieve control of the weather, of the rain, snow, and so on. A nasty hurricane hit America recently; it caused flooding and even killed some people.

Man has become the master of several things. He has to become the master of rain as well. Is that possible? Why not? That is not the sun which cannot be stopped, even though an army commander in the Bible supposedly stopped the sun. He certainly could not have stopped the sun, he might merely have stopped the Earth from rotating around its axis. Thank God, though, that he was unable to do that, because then he, himself, and everything that was alive on Earth would have perished. Your knowledge is sufficiently good now for you to know what would have happened. You better not try to order around the sun or the Earth, but try to learn how to order around the rain.

You will be able to look soon at the Earth from the moon, and not just only from the moon but from other planets as well. Can you currently imagine what this ability can bring humanity? None of you can presently answer that correctly. One only has to say that much can happen that is currently unexpected. Where can't something unexpected happen? Thus, one morning Alexander — being accustomed to seeing gentlemen and ladies taking dogs on a leash for a walk — suddenly noticed a tomcat taken for a walk in the same manner. The tomcat did not lose its dignified appearance at all.

This incident proves only one thing – it is not customary to take a tomcat for a walk as you do a dog. Therefore there will be much on other planets that will surprise you, simply because you are not used to it. With respect to the weather, even though the rainfall is generally normal, still, due to different coincidences it may fail and almost cause a catastrophe. For example, [this would have happened] in India, if other countries had not had more grain than they needed themselves.

Good night, heralds. Ilgya. [[2217]]


Ilgya                          06/24/66 2206


Ilgya. – ★ ★ ★ –
Of course, there are no perfect nations. All of them possess something negative as well. Therefore we have to consider whether there is more positive or negative, and evaluate the nation accordingly. In the faraway land of Latvia, people currently celebrate their beloved festival, and it is also John's festival, hence also your festival. Today, though, the dearest one to your hearts – your son – is not with you. He is fighting for the freedom of humanity in a distant land. This human freedom is the most important thing for man, and man does not tolerate having it restricted, even though that would benefit him at times.

Man wants to be free and wants to make his own decisions. Because of this desire, it is not possible for The Almighty to help man during his dreadful days, even if he asks for His help. It is not possible to draw a line between the desirable and the undesirable. The countries fought each other during the last World War, and all of them prayed to God to help them. How could God, though, help anyone who went to slay another human being?

God promised happiness to people, if they will not slay each other but will rather love each other. While knowing this desire of God, people paid no heed to it and caused calamity for each other. God gave man paradise, but man lost it by failing to abide by God's only requirement – not to eat the apple. After all, there were so many other fruit in paradise that were much tastier than the apple, but, you see, man wanted to be free – despite the possibility of losing everything because of this trifling apple.

Today we – the spirits, your guests – wish Johnny and the entire Latvian nation the desire and the strength to become free, while considering justice, and while considering and respecting the desire for freedom of all other nations as well. Mainly, [we wish them to] comprehend that this desire for freedom can be directed against the desire for freedom of others, and while knowing this to try and achieve what is possible, by mutually giving in to each other and not becoming unjust, as perceived by others.

We take leave from you and wish you a pleasant evening tomorrow. Ilgya.          [[2254]]

# Chapter VIII

# Summer 1966

<u>Ilgya</u>                                    07/01/66 2221

Ilgya. The heat of summer is here and you look sort of tired. You see, that is how it is. Science is able to regulate the temperature inside apartments, but is still unable to do that in the open air. Just because it is unable to do that today, though, does not mean that it will be unable to do that in the future.

I remember the times when lamps stood on tables and lanterns illuminated streets. A man would light them every evening, and he would put out the light every morning. How much light did they give? A long path had to be traveled before electricity was understood and put to work. Where are the times when fireplaces assembled freezing people in front of them? Where are the times when ladies would cool down their hot faces on dance nights with fans? Where are the times when the hoofs of horses were heard in the streets? Those times have passed into history.

Was everything bad back in those days? No, there were some good things as well! Life was more intimate. You will claim perhaps that it was also simpler. No, it has become simpler now. Because everything has become simpler and more accessible, people no longer pay any attention to it. Man has acquired much more free time. He does not have to build a fire in a stove any longer, carry firewood, and fill lamps with kerosene. Neither does he have to mess with firewood in the kitchen, go with pails to a well for water, sit in the evenings by a spinning wheel, knit clothing and socks, or darn them any longer. The evenings are no longer empty either. He only has to turn on the television and look up in a program what to look at, see, and hear.

Presidents, the few remaining kings, world famous people, singers, actors, musicians, and so on visit you in your home. You do not even have to travel in order to see other lands. You do not even have to go to war in order to see what happens there. During the period of your short lifetime, man's life has changed so much. Yet do you notice that? No, you return to the old times only infrequently in your thoughts. Your children no longer know your old world, just as their children will not know today's world.

Man tries to make life better, easier, and more beautiful, but not everything that is new has only good aspects. For example, a three-day weekend lies ahead. Will the achievements of science bring everyone happiness and joy over these three days? No, they will bring death to several hundred people, and calamity and despair to several thousand.

The former wars were horrible, but what were they compared to the current ones? Does that, however, mean that one should return to the past? No, that means that more effort should be exerted in order to avert the negative aspects!

I wish you three happy and lucky festival days. Ilgya.

[[2301]]


<u>Mortifero</u>                           07/08/66 2128

Chief Spirit Mortifero is speaking. Almighty's heralds, as a chief spirit who is most intimately involved in the relationships between those who are deceased on Earth but alive in Heaven and the people who are alive on Earth, I want to talk about what people either do not know or else ignore. All Christians and also many adherents of other sects know that the human spirit – or soul – is immortal, and that only the human body is mortal. Many people somehow do not take notice [of the fact] that since the soul does not die, then there is no particularly large difference between the deceased and the living. If people were spiritually intimate on Earth, they also remain like that after one of them departs from Earth.

Since the living people are generally incapable of meeting the souls in a tangible manner, they usually do that in their memories and dreams. All dreams are not preserved in memory. It is particularly those which have an important significance that do not remain in human memory. With respect to the spirits, they are in a much more advantageous position. They can visit people, and can see what they do, hear what they say, and even hear what they think. As you can see, that precludes any possibility of pretending or lying. True friends remain friends even after death, but not those who ended their friendship for various reasons – generally of a materialistic nature. Of course, enemies do not try to meet with each other.

Do not take literary what I have said. There are people who, for different reasons, have been wrong about each other, and by some means have understood their errors later on, and therefore have also changed their attitudes. For example, some enemies told lies to a man's wife. The wife lost her love for her husband and even started detesting him. After her death her spirit learned the truth. Obviously, her feelings of love o returned again, and the situation completely changed.

It may also happen that due to his weakness an individual succumbs to the negative, but later on begins to regret that. Of course, later on one spirit can forgive another, if the one who had erred sincerely regrets his delusions, and the negative conduct caused by them.

The main thing is that you should not forget that death parts you only for a while, and that there are only corpses in the cemeteries. The spirits can stand next to you closer than living people do. A person cannot display his true characteristics with words, because they are often lies. How can he display them? With deeds, only with deeds! You can talk your entire lifetime about how good you are, but if your deeds do not testify to that, then nothing will justify you.

_ ★ ★ ★ _

All of you are people, and therefore whether you want to or not you are influenced by events on Earth. You had to experience the dangers of two World Wars and the horrors of communist power. I heard one of you ask, "Why did God permit that?"

Because you – people – permitted that, because you did not do everything that Christ told you to do for your own good. You wanted to be free, and The Almighty wants the same thing. In order to preclude these wars and the revolution, The Almighty would have had to take away your freedom and turn you into the slaves of His will. The significance of humanity would have been lost with that. In order to preserve it, it was necessary to let you err and suffer, to learn from your mistakes, and to learn how to avoid them in the future. It was also necessary to prove that beautiful ideas cannot always be instituted in life, and that they cannot be achieved by force, but only by convincing people that they are truly good for them.

Yes, the bodies experienced terrible pain, they were consumed by fire, but the spirits of those people gained greater strength. They became more capable of further achievements. Others demonstrated their weaknesses and returned to The Almighty. Many spirits demonstrated their worthlessness and passed into nonexistence.

What you experienced during your lifetime was the selection of the spirits and the evaluation of humanity's abilities. Many ascended and many fell.

- ★ ★ ★ - [[2250]]

Apostle Peter                    07/29/66 2140

→Christ's Apostle Peter speaking. Almighty's heralds, I want to discuss with you once more the days when Christ walked the fields of Earth, while teaching people how to establish Paradise on Earth.← Much has changed on Earth to the extent that it is hard to believe that it is the same old Earth. Now there are fields where forests used to be. There are huge cities now where small villages used to be. Countless roads cross the Earth in all directions, and airplanes fill the air. Man rises into the air above the Earth in machines, and walks in space from one of them to another.

He will soon build ports in space and will walk on the moon, and in a few years on other planets as well. Much has changed in human society. Beggars have disappeared in many countries, and the old and the crippled do not have to starve to death. The state looks after the people, but some countries have remained behind, and people in them still live almost as they did at the time of Christ. Brutality also returns at times, as in those places where communism is in power, but all that is no longer able to hold humanity back from its path toward a better and more just life – toward Paradise on Earth.

→Now let us return to Christ. The previous time I talked with you about the difference between Christ and the apostles, between Him and the people, and between the apostles and the people. He said that He, Christ, had a soul – God's spirit given to Him by God. Similarly, it has also been given to the apostles, and to every human. The difference is in the task which each individual receives from God. It was difficult for me to understand that, when I saw the huge difference which existed between Christ and us.

When Christ died on the cross, I felt utterly desperate and insignificant. I could not agree with Christ's ideas. It seemed to me that I will never be able to draw closer to Christ, even the least bit, or to accomplish what He was capable of. Yet, years passed. We had to accomplish the task which we had been given, and to my surprise, this task became ever easier to accomplish.

It seemed to me that my spirit grew. As you know, I and some other apostles traveled Christ's pathway, and even died in the same manner as He. No bodily tortures were able to smother our spirits. Christ awaited me after death, and with a smile He told me, "Well, Peter, wasn't I right?"

"Yes," I replied, "You were right. Yet, still, the task which we had been given could not have been accomplished without Your help."

Christ smiled once again and said, "I am not sure, Peter, about you. Perhaps you would have accomplished it even all by yourself, if you had decided that you have to do it, for within you, after all, is the very same spirit of God, which is capable of everything – if you have the desire."

On every step of the way in life we meet people on Earth who achieve much more than other people. They achieve goals because of their willpower, and their belief in themselves – in their missions. Every day you see many people complaining about their failures, but none of them will tell you how little they have done in order to achieve their dreams. Hope, by itself, will not help anyone, unless one strives to realize it with actions.

One has to utilize those abilities which God has given everyone. If a person has not been given the abilities of a poet, or a singer, he will not achieve success in that particular field, no matter how much he desires and works toward it. Millions of people may try to paint the Madonna as Raphael did, but they will never be capable of that, for they were not given Raphael's talents. By means of a well-rounded education, man has to be given the opportunity to find out what his abilities are, and then he has to utilize them in order to achieve happiness and serve humanity.

The most talented individual can be destroyed by succumbing to drinking, narcotics, or idleness. The same can happen by a choice of work which is unsuitable to his abilities. Similarly, one should not climb aboard any train waiting in the station, but board only that train which heads in the direction appropriate for him.

I will return once more to the part of my story of life which hurt me the most in everyone's eyes. That was my denial of Christ three times on that dreadful night when Christ was arrested. Everyone has understood and explained this denial as my fear of death. Obviously, I was afraid, as any human fears death and torture, but this fear was not the most important consideration at the time. There was another more important factor – something far more significant. No one ever talks about that. This most significant consideration was my task of passing Christ's teachings on to the people.

On that night, overcome by emotions, I could not think of anything else, other than how to safeguard Christ and how to try to save Him from death. Yet, later on, I understood that it was not possible to save Christ, for He did not want to be saved. Also, He did not want us to abandon our tasks in order to die with Him, for we would not have achieved anything by doing that. I understood that when Christ predicted that I would deny Him three times, it was not as a reproach, but rather as a prediction of what had to occur. [[Alexander's correction: "I understood that Christ's words that I would deny Him three times, were not meant as a reproach, but rather as an inescapable decision."]]

With that I take leave from you. It is not my intention to return to you some other time, and therefore, until we meet in Heaven. Peter.←
[[2247]]

Shota Rustaveli                    09/02/66 2241

Almighty's heralds, the spirit of Shota Rustaveli is talking with you. Several years have passed since I have talked with you. Since you started talking about me in conjunction with my anniversary, it would of course not be polite of me not to thank you for your interest in a poet from ancient times. It is truly wonderful that my work has survived for so many years and has reached you. Compared to the world's greatest poets, it cannot be considered to be the very best. It has several weak places, but it nevertheless gives much that is valuable, and it permits current man to look into the life and the souls of the people back then.

Many people are interested in knowing the year when I was born, but as you already know, we are not allowed to give that type of information. If we were to start doing that, there would be no end to such questions. Our task is different − it is not to tell you about the past, but rather to prepare humanity for the future; and most important, to give humanity as much of an idea as possible about The Almighty and God, and the goal intended for man.

The church was established almost two thousand years ago, at a time when science had not yet achieved much and when kings ruled on Earth. Therefore it accepted the view that God, too, rules just like a king, and that people are His slaves. For a short period, when almost all people still lived in ignorance and could neither read nor write, the church became the place where science was preserved and supported. When a large majority of people learned how to read and write and when many people began to devote themselves to examining life and formulating the sciences, and hence discovered things which were contrary to the views of the church, the church became an impediment to science.

Many concepts that were accepted in ancient times turned out to be incorrect, as did the opinions about God, which were established at the time of kings. Unfortunately, the church remained behind the times and did not try to catch up. Something like an awakening began only in the last few years, when the church began to lose many adherents. This stubborn refusal of the church to recognize the new discoveries of science, estranged humanity's most capable sons – the scientists – from it. The long since antiquated tales about the world coming into being and its form became ridiculous to them. Of course, that is very regrettable, because God's priests should have traveled together with the scientists, for the God of Abraham is, in fact, very insignificant compared to The Almighty, and the world of the old God is extremely tiny compared to The Almighty's universe.

As Christ said, man's task was to turn Earth into Paradise. From this Paradise, man could start seeking the roads to other worlds and truly could begin to draw closer to God and draw closer to the universe and its creator – The Almighty.

There is little significance in knowing the year when I was born. That will not change anything in the work that I have left behind, which perhaps everyone should truly know.

Good night, heralds. Your Shota. [[2322]]


Ilgya                              09/09/66 2212


Ilgya. - ★ ★ ★ -

Humanity moves forward – sometimes stopping and sometimes even going backwards. Yet that is the course of humanity, and there are prospects that someday it will nevertheless reach its goal.

With respect to you, the summer is over for you, with all of its joys, and obviously sorrows as well, without which there cannot be any joys. When one looks at how people still live in some lands, then it seems as if you almost have a paradise here. There are people who work from morning until night for trifling compensation. They think only about eating and resting. They do not have any summer vacations, they do not even have decent apartments, but only shacks, somehow nailed together. Yet they grumble less than you do, who have almost everything that you want. Still, as long as hell still exists in some places on Earth, those who live in almost a paradise should not forget this situation, and they have to devote all their efforts to see that the word "unhappy" will disappear from the dictionary of the nations on Earth.

Good night, heralds. Ilgya. [[2245]]


Aksanto                              09/15/66 1759

Heralds, today is a day that should not be forgotten. This day is called birthday, the day when an individual arrives personally on Earth. Therefore, on this day, people gather around the person in order to remember his course on Earth. There are people whose birthday is remembered by the entire nation, by the entire humanity. The birthday of The Almighty's herald is such a day, which has to be observed not only by the people but also by the spirits who are bound with the destiny of Earth. Obviously, there will be critics who will claim that the spirits will not come to Earth merely for an event like that. Only complete ingnorami can talk like that, those who have no idea whatsoever about the spirits and their relationship with people.

When God's prophets, particularly Christ, came to Earth, they maintained spiritual contact with the spirits. There is little written about that, because the prophets themselves did not like to talk about that. Seldom has there been a situation on Earth like there is now, when The Almighty has permitted the spirits – during the time of passing on the Tidings – to maintain direct communications with the heralds, even in their personal life.

If human development will continue according to the envisioned course, the time will come when man will communicate directly with the spirits. The more recent developments in science, particularly the conquest of space, are truly gigantic, and even surpass what was expected of man. Man begins to approach his goal – to become The Almighty's assistant in forming the universe, thus bringing to life with rapid steps even the lifeless matter. This will mean a completely new situation in the universe.

I congratulate Alexander on his birthday, as well as his name day which was three days ago, and wish him – on behalf of the highest spirits, the chief spirits, and myself – the strength to accomplish his difficult but great task. Thanks to his and a few other heralds' unique spiritual abilities, it was possible to establish this contact. It is possible for the spirits to establish communications only with people who have extremely great and rare spiritual abilities.

Aksanto.                    [[1824]]


<u>Santorino</u>                    09/23/66 2120


→Santorino speaking. Heralds, there is a very important subject which has not been clarified completely. The Bible talks about the Garden of Eden – of God creating a wonderful place where everything was beautiful and good, and ideal for human life. Some people call this story a fairy tale, and others call it an allegory. By no means is it a fairy tale, even though everything was not exactly as related in the Bible. Therefore, it can be considered partially an allegory, as well.

God created the Garden of Eden for the purpose of seeing which path man will travel, after he was given a free will. Paradise was created so that man could have everything necessary for a good, peaceful, and happy life. Evil could not enter Paradise. Therefore, man knew nothing of the evil in the essence of the universe, and God protected man from it. Yet, in order for man to feel independent and be able to act in consonance with his will, God had to let him know that things in the world are not like they are in the Garden of Eden, and that Paradise can be preserved for man only if he will obey God's advice, and will act only in harmony with it. He wanted to know whether man would desire, or even would be able to relinquish even a little bit of his complete freedom – even if this was for his own good.

The Garden of Eden was full of various fruit trees which had much tastier fruit than those of the apple tree. God asked man to refrain only from eating the apple, advising man that it would bring much misfortune for him. God would have to allow man to encounter that which was evil for him. By giving man complete freedom, God would have to cease intervening in man's fate. Man himself would have to form his life on Earth with his own strength and capabilities.

Man relinquished complete, unlimited happiness solely in order to be completely independent. He picked the apple and ate it, and thus relinquished God's help. With this decision, he deprived himself of the right of praying for God's help even in those instances where it was essential for him, and also lost the right of reproaching God because He does not help him.

God did not punish man for his disobedience, but man punished himself, for he knew that altogether unimaginable dangers and difficulties could await him. God simply permitted man to try and win with his own strength. God was proud of man for this choice, because there was His spirit within man. This spirit, by himself – without anyone's help – created and guided the universe. God hoped that this spirit will be able to cooperate with the living matter, and that this union will be able to develop. God also hoped that the spirit will succeed in transforming the living matter, and thus man would become capable of not only overcoming his own difficulties, but also of becoming an assistant to God in the development of the world.

Undoubtedly, God helped man in some critical situations, but not because of man praying. Instead, God helped man because He found it essential for man as well as for His own purposes.

As you can see now, man turned out to be capable not only of creating his own Paradise for himself, but now is able to start helping The Almighty as well.

Man should have been more cognizant of the fact that what many people consider to be the most dreadful occurrence – the death of the body – God does not consider to be that. Death merely means the return of the spirit to Heaven. With respect to bodily suffering, which take place in wars and in prisons, man himself inflicts this on himself and on others, while being guided by his free will, and by refusing to have it limited by God. With that, he also deprives God of the right to help him.

The Almighty assigned me to announce this to the people so that it would be quite clear to them what the situation is like, how it came about, and what it should be like. Also, what man may and may not ask from God, and why he may not.

Santorino.←                    [[2215]]


Aksanto                           09/30/66 2137

Aksanto is speaking. Heralds, in his tiding the previous time, the Divine touched only the more important aspects, and did not talk about some important concerns that have been discussed previously. Still, he found it necessary to once more examine some subjects in more detail, and mainly stress that one should not forget that the spirit and matter have nothing in common. The spirit needs matter for accomplishing those functions that cannot be accomplished without the help of matter.

Since matter is inert, it is hostile to the spirit and fights against the spirit. Matter submits to the influence of the spirit and changes its essence only slowly. Even though slowly, it transforms with each generation, and becomes a little bit more intimate to the spirit and less hostile to him. This transformation does not take place evenly. Quite often – as one says – matter rebels against the spirit and gains an upper hand for some time, as we can see from humanity's history.

As you have already been told, The Almighty had to create everything without any models and without any knowledge, being guided only by His will. He created man according to His form, but The Almighty Himself changed along with the universe which He had created. His ideas changed, and His demands changed as well. He had to learn from what He had created, He had to transform what had been achieved, or even give it up and start something new that was better. He had to research and learn from the work, from the achievements, and from the mistakes. That required countless years. His first man bore little resemblance to the current man.

The Almighty had underestimated the strength of matter's resistance. The paradise, which He had created for man, turned out to be a grand mistake. It turned out that man was unable to develop if he was in paradise, if he had everything and did not have to fight for anything. You can see that from some places in the tropics where man lives still now in a cave and walks around naked, just as his ancestors did millions of years ago.

The living matter feels hunger, cold, pain, and joy. If it lacks something that it needs, it starts to seek what is missing and to fight for it. Similarly, it starts to fight against that which causes it pain or other suffering. Under such circumstances it accepts the help of the spirit and begins to cooperate with the spirit. As this cooperation develops, matter starts to submit to other demands of the spirit as well.

Thus it turned out that man should not be given a ready-made paradise, but should be allowed to establish it for himself. Accustomed to cooperating, the spirit and matter begin to strive not only toward obtaining material needs, but also attaining spiritual goals. This means understanding everything and achieving everything that is possible, and even impossible. Man starts to reject the old God – a king – and begins to acknowledge the creator and guide of the world – The Almighty. He does not want any longer to be the slave of a king, but rather an assistant to The Creator in the endless work of creation.

With that, we will conclude for today. Aksanto. [[2222]]

# Chapter IX

# Fall 1966

Ilgya. Fall is here once again and winter is not that far off. Unless it is wet, sometimes fall is the most beautiful time of the year. For example, today I was in the cemetery together with Alexander. The tree leaves in the cemetery have acquired different colors. They were never this beautiful during the entire year. The leaves die, but they die beautifully. Thus they part from the trees, and bid farewell after having completed their work. There will be new leaves next year, but the tree will be the same old one.

The same thing is also true of people. They carry out, over the decades, the tasks which they have been given, but humanity remains. It continues to live on, but just as a tree is not eternal, neither are the nations eternal. They come and go just as trees do, but the forests remain. Humanity remains as well. Will it be eternal? Scientists claim that it cannot be eternal, because neither the sun nor the Earth are eternal.

Yes, humanity itself might not be eternal, but man has been given something that is capable of outliving the Earth as well as the sun. That is his soul, his spirit. It depends only on the spirit whether he will remain eternal, or else will lose his eternity by passing into nonexistence.

Those people who not only fail to carry out their tasks but harm other people by hurting them, or by not allowing them to carry out their task because they murder them, lose their eternity and become animals, because they kill their own soul – they kill themselves. They cannot destroy another individual, because his soul continues to live, but they completely kill themselves. All these murderers, bullies, thieves, tyrants, and others similar to them should not be considered to be humans, but rather humanity's parasites. Their weak spirits have succumbed to the negative power of matter and have turned out to be worthless, therefore they pass into nonexistence.

There are very many spirits who pass into nonexistence, because very few of them find mercy in God's eyes. No prayers on Earth can help them, and they can hope for forgiveness only if they, themselves, come to their senses and try to rectify what they have done. Therefore, be very careful in your deeds, people. None of you want the fate of a pig or a rat, but that awaits everyone who rejects the rights of a human, by becoming hostile or unnecessary to humanity, and hence to The Almighty as well.

I was in the cemetery – a place where people's bodies rest. This place is not a mute place, it speaks, and speaks in a loud voice. It talks about those resting there as well as those who have remained behind on Earth. Through the monuments on graves that have been erected in honor of the deceased, it speaks about the gratitude from those remaining, but it speaks even louder about those who have remained behind. It tells about them, what kind of people they truly are and whether they are grateful, because gratitude is the highest value of the human spirit. It tells whether their love was true, and whether it is worthy and capable of crossing the border of death and entering the realm of eternity.

The words "rest in peace" are empty and erroneous, because the body cannot rest in peace in the wet soil, and there is no rest for the spirit. He can only have a shorter or longer period of relaxation. No settling of accounts has taken place with the departed one, because the settling of accounts – the final settling of accounts – takes place only between spirits. Therefore no one should rejoice that he has gotten rid of an individual who was unpleasant or unnecessary for him. He has not gotten rid of anything, because he will have to settle, in various forms, all injustices and debts with the spirit of the deceased, and in the presence of God's spirits.

People, you have to understand how serious life is and how unavoidable is the responsibility for what you have done during it. Do not deceive yourselves into thinking that everything will somehow work out, and that someone will help you if you will pay him well. Nothing will work out unless you yourselves will work out your affairs. When facing God, no one will help you with the prayers which you have purchased – even if they have cost you millions – unless you, yourselves, will try to redeem your sins with good deeds.

I have often been to the cemetery with Alexander, somehow we became closer there and understood each other without words. I noticed that before Alexander somehow did not find peace in the cemetery. He felt that something was missing and that he had not done everything that he should have for the sake of the departed. When the cross on Antonina's grave broke off last winter, he understood what he still had to do, and had to do as soon as possible, because it could turn out that it will be too late to do anything. He erected a granite monument on the graves of the departed. It was rather expensive. Therefore he still has to continue working, so that he will not retire without the money which is essential in some cases. Now he feels tranquil in the cemetery, because he knows that he has done everything that he was able to do for the sake of the departed. He tried to preserve their names for as long as possible after he will no longer be there to look after their graves.

I have to alight to the Deoss Temple, therefore I will take leave from you, heralds. Ilgya. [[2221]]

Mortifero                                  11/18/66 2124

→Almighty's heralds to the planet Earth, I come to you in the assignment of The Almighty in order to explain The Almighty's relationship with man, and with other living beings. In order for my tiding to be complete, I will have to repeat some things which you have been told previously.

As you already know, The Almighty is the creator of the entire universe which currently exists. Everything that is alive is bound with His spirit, just as it is with air, without which no living being can exist. Just as no building can erect itself, similarly, no living being can form itself without the help and guidance of The Almighty's spirit.

The Almighty's spirit is diverse, though. There are spirits who shape bodies, animals, and even plants. These are the so-called spirits who form life. These spirits live only as long as the animals or plants live. Then they merge again with The Almighty's spirit, as drops of water merge with the ocean. As you can see from this, the sacred cows of India are not anything ridiculous, for after all, they also have The Almighty's spirit within them. Yet, obviously, they do not have to be worshiped just because of that.

After them come the spirits of the so-called higher living beings, such as the spirits of humans on Earth. These spirits have been given the task of establishing cooperation between the spirit and the [living] matter, in order to create a being with the capabilities of the spirit and of matter, and to form eventually living beings which are capable of cooperating with The Almighty in the construction of the ideal universe.

Every human is given his own spirit with a specific task assigned to him. The spirit, who has accomplished his task successfully, receives an even higher task the next time. The one who has not demonstrated great abilities is sent back again a second and a third time with a similar task. After the third unsuccessful time, the spirit merges again with The Almighty's ocean of spirits.

The spirit, who turned out to be incapable to accomplish the task assigned to him, merges with The Almighty's ocean of spirits immediately after the first time. Those spirits who have acted contrary to the tasks assigned to them, pass into nonexistence. You may wonder what is so particular about passing into nonexistence. Should you have to pass into nonexistence, though, you will find out how dreadful that is.

All spirits do not have the same abilities either, for what would happen if everyone was capable of doing only the very same thing? People need leaders, scientists, writers, poets, engineers, and so on, and obviously, also street sweepers and garbage truck drivers. That does not mean that a street sweeper cannot become a poet, or else, by utilizing all his strength and will, cannot become an engineer. Usually, however, people with minor tasks are given new spirits, created for the first time.

The Almighty is not sentimentally merciful. He considers it more desirable to create a new spirit in place of a useless spirit. Since humanity multiplies rapidly, many new spirits are needed. Obviously, the day will come when humanity will have to maintain a balance. With time, the more capable spirits become full-fledged spirits. They become spirits who carry out only the tasks of the spirits, and no longer incarnate, or incarnate only on particularly important occasions, such as in prophets, or in The Almighty's heralds.

With that, I conclude the first phase of my tidings. Later on, others will follow it. Chief Spirit Mortifero.← [[2204]]

<u>Ilgya</u>                                    11/25/66 2135

Ilgya. Heralds, as you can see, spring has almost returned here in New York. You can see, though, what happens when the wind completely dies down. So many poisonous substances can accumulate in a large city that the air becomes almost unusable. That does not happen often, but it would nevertheless be better to consider the possibility that such windless conditions can continue for several days. What can we learn from events like that? We learn that wind is essential, even though the same wind can cause horrible catastrophes if it becomes too strong.

The same thing is true of water, without which life would be impossible on Earth. Rain is not pleasant but it is essential, and the same water that sustains life, can cause flooding and bring a disaster and death for people. The same thing can be said about fire. Fire is being replaced now by electricity in many places, but even this electricity can cause house fires. All of these so-called elements function in conjunction with the laws of nature, but sometimes mistakes happen, and everything that exceeds the norm can bring a disaster.

Currently man does not know how to control these elements, but he has all the abilities to eventually be able to regulate their functioning, if not completely then at least to some extent. For example, the so-called hurricanes are not a permanent phenomenon. They are born when conditions arise which are favorable for them. The arrival of a new force can disrupt the development of a hurricane, and man can provide this new force. Man already begins to surpass the ability of a storm to cause destruction. The name of this new force is atom and hydrogen bombs. As you already know for yourselves, this destructive power can also be used for positive work, for work that can bring happiness to humanity.

It is like that with almost everything. Everything depends on the purpose for which man uses these forces. The world's two largest countries have presently produced weapons with such destructive power that their use can not only destroy the enemy, but can even threaten the existence of the entire humanity. This gives some assurance that these weapons will not be used, because they are too powerful to take a chance. That would, in fact, have been insanity, and whether humanity wants to or not, this insanity leads it to sanity. Thus, gases were used toward the end of World War I, but no one dared any longer to use them during World War II, because no one was sure how all that could end. As you can see, if evil become too powerful it limits itself. Evil stops evil – that seems absurd but that is how it is.

The high Chief Spirit Mortifero will not speak next Friday, but a week later. Therefore you can rest for a week and devote yourselves to other duties.

Good night, heralds. Ilgya. [[2217]]

---

<u>Ilgya</u>                              12/09/66 2120

Ilgya. Heralds, I congratulate Janoss and Mary with their son's safe return from the battlefield for the second time already. War is a crime against humanity – war as such. There are wars, however, which bring humanity salvation from a calamity. In ancient times, the wars against savage nations were like that. These wars tried to save culture – humanity's achievements – from demise and destruction. In recent years, that was true of the war against Hitler's gangs, which wanted to turn people into slaves. That is also the case with the current American war in Vietnam. With it, the Americans want to protect humanity from the calamity of communism. Nick already risking his life a second time in a short period is a noble deed. He can only be praised for that. Only the more distinguished people are generally capable of a deed like that.

We are glad that the mother's and father's concern about their son's fate has ended.

The high Chief Spirit Mortifero will speak in four minutes.

[[2131]]


Mortifero                                    12/09/66 2135


→Chief Spirit Mortifero. I continue my task, given me by The Almighty, of familiarizing humanity with The Almighty's thoughts, goals, and demands, which He sets forth for humanity as one of His chosen people in the universe, that is – living beings similar to man. As I already mentioned the last time, for the sake of clarity I will have to repeat some things that have already been said previously.

No one knows what the universe is, for it is infinite. Therefore we, the spirits created by The Almighty, also cannot tell you that. We cannot even tell you who The Almighty is, in His entirety. We can talk only about one part of the universe. We are only familiar with the worlds closest to us, the closest galaxies, the closest Gods and chief spirits, and that is the extent of it. What we do know, however, is unimaginably grand and difficult to grasp, even with the mind which has been given us, and is not always understandable. Yet, how can one understand and grasp infinity?

Man has achieved very much, particularly recently, in his knowledge of the universe. What has been achieved, however, is still trifling, in truth, compared with what has not been achieved yet, and that which still remains unknown. You already know The Almighty's goal in creating the universe. He did not want to exist alone in the universe. He did not want to be the ruler of a void, but rather the ruler of worlds on which He could create life and living beings. In order to oversee these worlds, He created innumerable spirits from His spirit, and gave them uncountable tasks.

As has been said previously, He had no models from which to learn. In the beginning, He did not even have any idea regarding what to create, what to select for creation, and most important – how to create. He had only unlimited capabilities of turning His will into existence. Most important though, He did not want to be alone. Creating the spirits did not let Him escape loneliness, for the spirits were just like He. He had to create something that would not be entirely like He – that would be capable of forming its own "I" – something that would be unique eventually, and whom it would be interesting to meet and talk to. This creation could give Him new ideas eventually, and could even help Him in forming the perfect essence of the universe.

As you know, matter was hostile to the spirit. It was incapable of transforming by itself, and of acting logically. Living matter had to be molded from it. This living matter had to be given spirits for its guidance. By making the spirit cooperate with the living matter, living beings had to be formed who would be able to think and transform.

Innumerable experiments failed to achieve what was expected of them. Many planets were destroyed. Then, after a long time, hope arose on some planets that the desirable results will be achieved. After many millions of years, living beings who corresponded to The Almighty's demands developed on some planets. However, new difficulties arouse – what should these beings be like?

If they were to act only as The Almighty desired, what would have been achieved by that? Nothing! The Almighty's slaves would have been created. Therefore, the living beings had to be given the freedom to act as they themselves found it to be better and more correct. That meant that the living beings could choose roads and goals that were contrary or even hostile to those of The Almighty. What could be done? Beings like that would have to be destroyed. And, so it occurred that only on some planets the living beings chose the goals of The Almighty as their own goals. Your tiny planet, Earth, turned out to be among these planets as well.

By acquiring a free will, though, the living beings had to consider that they cannot ask for help from The Almighty in all cases. Should man get into tragic situations – like in wars, mutual struggles, and so on – then each side could ask The Almighty for help. Obviously, The Almighty could not please both sides. In the end, The Almighty had to relinquish intervening in people's fates and had to leave them in the hands of humanity itself.

That may be extremely difficult for humanity to achieve. On occasion it may suffer greatly. But by suffering it will also learn how to live so that everyone will be well off. If you think it over carefully, then you will understand that it is best not to rely on anyone but yourself. Man has been blessed with the desire to know everything, and achieve everything that he wants to. Therefore, The Almighty does not want to deprive man of the joy of learning for himself everything that is within his capabilities. He permits us to reveal to people only that which is not, and will never be, possible for them to achieve and learn.

Let us conclude with that for today. Mortifero.← [[2230]]

<u>Ilgya</u>                                    12/16/66 2110

Ilgya. Heralds, this evening will be historic for humanity on Earth, because The Almighty has allowed God to reveal what only the chief spirits know. On seeing man's vast abilities, He finds it possible and necessary to tell man about the spiritual aspects which man himself is unable to learn.

The divine Santorino will alight to you today. Get ready to receive the high spirit. He will alight to the planet Earth after seven minutes according to the time on Earth. [[2114]]

<u>Santorino</u>                               12/16/66 2121

→The Almighty's and God's heralds to the planet Earth, I come to the nations on Earth in order to proclaim to them what they do not know yet, and will never be able to learn on their own. There are matters which are not visible and cannot be discovered with devices, but which are extremely important for the existence of the universe, and therefore for man's existence as well.

When the Tidings first began, we, the spirits, did not know yet The Almighty's designs in their complete entirety, with respect to you and humanity. Therefore the explanations which we gave you were not complete or even correct. We tried to make some matters understandable to you, which, in fact, cannot be explained to man with his current knowledge. For example, a description of the Deoss Temple was given you, so that you could comprehend its grandeur. The Deoss Temple is not constructed of planets, but of a special mass, unknown on Earth.

Therefore, we only used planets so that you could understand just how huge this Temple is.

With respect to the thrones of God and Satan, I have to say that They are not always on them, and yet They are always on them. How can that be understood? That is difficult to understand unless one knows the essences of both God and Satan. They are spirits and They can be in several locations simultaneously.

Only the souls of historically important living beings are weighed on the scale – beings who have carried out important tasks of God, or of The Almighty. Frequently the deeds of great historical persons are so varied – good and evil – that it is extremely difficult to evaluate whether they have brought more good, or more evil, to humanity. With respect to the spirits of ordinary people, since their deeds are already known and have been evaluated by special spirits, they only come to receive new assignments or punishment.

Now, let us talk about The Almighty and the Gods. The Gods are the very same Almighty – only in the form of God – and with the capabilities essential for God. The Almighty's own capabilities are unlimited, and only The Almighty Himself limits them. He decides on His own what He must do, and what He may not do. He adheres very rigidly to the laws which He has given Himself, in order not to give in to weaknesses.

These abilities of the spirit, in a way that you can understand, are expressed in Alexander, as well. In visiting the graves of his relatives every Friday, Alexander knows that reasons can always come up for not going on a particular Friday. Eventually so many reasons will come up that he will not have any time at all for going there. Yet, his desire is to go. Therefore, he forces himself to carry out his desire. That is a small example of how The Almighty acts.

The Gods, being The Almighty's spirits Themselves, communicate with The Almighty directly and instantaneously. They know what They have to do, and how to act, without even using a wireless telephone. However, They do not know what They do not need to know, for what They need to know is so grand in itself that there is no time left over for other things which are not as essential. The Gods of the various galaxies communicate among Themselves in a similar way.

Now let us turn to the lesser spirits. The chief spirits have been created in order to accomplish special tasks. The Gods, as well as the chief spirits, and even many spirits with lesser special tasks, never change and do not incarnate. They are pure spirits of The Almighty. Then come The Almighty's spirits whose task is to incarnate in living beings, and while cooperating with the living matter, form a being consisting of the living matter and of the spirit. The formation of this new being requires millions of years. Yet this formation has already achieved a level where it starts to materialize ever more rapidly. Man's cooperation in the formation of the universe becomes ever more rapid.

Initially, man transformed life only on his planet. He accepted everything that The Almighty gave him. He utilized the animals not only for food, but also as his helpers. He made the horse, the ox, the camel, and the elephant work for him. He made the cow and the goat give him milk, and from the sheep he got wool for clothing. The dog guarded him and his home, and the cat protected his food from mice. Similarly, he started to utilize water and the wind for mills, and fire for warmth, preparation of food, as well as for melting iron.

Then came the age when he started to explore the energy which fills the space of the universe. With the discovery of electricity, he began to stand on his own two feet. He started to invent things which The Almighty had not given him directly. He began to explore everything, initially that which was on Earth, and later on also that which was in the universe.

Man did not have wings, but the bird had them. Man envied it and thought, "Why can't I fly like a bird? Since I don't have wings, can't I invent something similar to wings?" He not only invented something similar to wings, but machines which carry hundreds of people, and rockets in which he can fly around the Earth and much higher than any bird. Man is now getting ready to visit the poor recluse – the pale faced moon. Similarly, man thanked the horse and other animals, and sat down in machines which carry him with maddening speed over endless highways, plow his fields, thresh his grain, and so on.

Man has completely transformed the face of Earth. Instead of the vast forests of trees, we now see gigantic forests of skyscrapers.

Now the final item, concerning the spirits of the living beings, or souls, as they are called. That will be something entirely new for you. The Almighty gave His spirit to Adam and to Eve. They were the first people, as told in the Holy Scriptures. Let's not argue with your Holy Scriptures, for because of their simplicity, they are very useful to us for carrying out our intentions.

Sons and daughters were born to Adam and Eve. Adam's spirit divided himself into their sons, and Eve's spirit into their daughters. After Adam's death, his spirit returned to Heaven, and so did Eve's spirit. Yet, the parts of their spirits which had split off, continued to live on Earth and to divide again. Thus, the spirits of Adam and Eve still live within you, and they live in all the people, but they are no longer fully the spirits of Adam and Eve. They have transformed over the long period, just as the living matter has transformed.

As you can see, by living together with the bodies for hundreds of thousands of years, the current spirits have become entirely different spirits than were the spirits of Adam and Eve. Since the spirit passes from the father's body into the son's body, and the mother's spirit into the daughter's body, the same spirit continues to live together with the bodies, which also transform under the uninterrupted guidance of the same spirit. What takes place? The spirit of Adam's son, after leaving his body, meets in Heaven with the spirit of Adam, the father. Two of Adam's spirits meet each other, but while being the same spirit, they are nevertheless somewhat different already. They receive new tasks, which depend on the abilities which they have demonstrated during the time of their incarnation on Earth.

Occasionally the father's, as well as partially the mother's spirits incarnate into children. On occasion, even though very rarely, the spirit incarnates into the wrong child. Thus the father's spirit could incarnate into a daughter's body, or the mother's spirit into a son's body. Nowadays, an operation sometimes rectifies this error. Similarly, the mixing of spirits in a child – the spirits of the father and mother – creates people with gentler or cruder characteristics.

Many people wonder why they can neither see God, nor ascertain His existence. There is, however, still so much in the universe that has not been explored, that not everything is understandable yet to man. He forgets, though, that a few hundred years ago, man would not have believed those miracles which man now performs. Consider television. I will not explain to you how it works, for you have created it yourselves, and you know how that takes place. I will, however, talk about that which you have forgotten.

In a room, or somewhere out on a field, people do something, and a device records this, and transmits it over the air in all directions. You are sitting in your room and a box with a glass wall, containing many devices inside, is located in front of you. You turn on this box and miracles take place in front of you. The box comes to life, and a singer stands before you and sings. Perhaps he is singing in another town, or even another country. Yet, he stands before you as though alive, and your ear hears his voice.

What connects you? A void! Not even a wire connects you! Then how does this singer get to you? He comes through a void. You cannot receive him within this void, except with a television set. This singer and his voice travel through this void neither in the shape of his appearance, nor in the form of his voice. They do not exist there. They come to life only within your apparatus, and this singer can sing to innumerable viewers and listeners. He fills the entire air invisibly and imperceptibly. Human genius has achieved this miracle. What miracles then hasn't man's creator, The Almighty, achieved?← [[2307]]

<u>Mortifero</u>                    12/23/66 2157

→Chief Spirit Mortifero speaking. Heralds, I will discuss initially what seems to you incomprehensible in our tidings. The previous tiding of the Divine does not in any way change the principle that The Almighty gives every individual a spirit. Overall, it occurs like the Divine said. The spirits of the father and mother give their spirits to their children – that is, a part of their spirits. Yet, that takes place as The Almighty has determined.

He determines whose spirit has to give a spirit, or a soul, to the child. Quite often He has both spirits give a part of their spirit to the child. However, when He finds the child particularly suitable for this spirit, He may give the child an entirely different spirit – one who has to incarnate in man to accomplish exceptional tasks. It may happen that the father's or mother's spirit may incarnate into the child of the child's child, in order to influence the spiritual development of the chosen child even more. Sometimes you say that a child takes after his grandfather, or some earlier predecessor.

Since nothing in the universe can occur without The Almighty's decision, the expression that The Almighty gives each child a spirit, is completely understandable.

Now let us discuss something rather critical. One often hears people on Earth asking, particularly during the atrocious years of Hitler and Stalin, how God – if He exists – could have permitted such atrocities to take place. Doesn't that prove that God does not exist at all, or that God has died?

First of all, the immortal cannot die. Secondly, people talk without comprehending The Almighty. By giving man a completely free will, He cannot limit it under any circumstances, not even if humanity would have to perish because of that. In a case like that The Almighty would cross off His unsuccessful experiment on Earth, and would start a new one on another planet.

Man has been created from the living matter and from the spirit. Matter is passive; it demands only peace. The spirit is active, and he demands activity from matter. Matter has its own characteristics and they are very strong. The struggle within man between the spirit and matter has lasted for millions of years. You know how brutal the man of former times was. You know that one individual destroyed another, and that one nation destroyed another, or else turned it into slaves.

Overall, humanity has advanced greatly – so much that Christ's demands are being incorporated into laws. Beggars are no longer dying of starvation. In the more developed nations, old people no longer die in their old age abandoned in the streets. The state takes care of them, and similarly the state also helps them in case of sickness. One no longer has to depend on the help of merciful people, and wait by the church door with a cup in trembling hands.

As you can see, Christ's teachings have achieved much. In some cases, however, the power of matter breaks the might of the spirit, and man becomes a savage once again. He rages for some time, until humanity comes to its senses once again and continues along its path toward a happy future, and toward the Paradise promised it. Yet, man has to be capable and worthy of entering it. Otherwise, he will lose it, as Adam and Eve lost it.

It is extremely painful for The Almighty, for God, and for us, the spirits, to observe the suffering of people during periods of degradation. Humanity itself, though, is at fault here. It has to resolve that for itself, because under no circumstances may The Almighty transgress His most important law and limit man's free will. Later on, the people themselves would condemn Him for that far more than they would for nonintervention.

Now, let us discuss the relationship between God and man. Through His prophets and Christ, God revealed to humanity how to achieve a happy life and enter Paradise, by carrying out what Christ told the people, which is indispensable for achieving this goal. Christ's teachings were simple, but they were not favorable to those who wanted to rule and who wanted an easy and merry life at the expense of others. Thus began the era which Christ inaugurated.

Hundreds, and even thousands of years passed. They were years of struggle between the spirit and matter. They were years of an enormous, and at times even insane, struggle. Christ gave His laws to His disciples, and commanded that they be proclaimed to the people. Yet, He already saw, while still on Earth, that some apostles did not carry out His teachings exactly as He had intended. Therefore He said, "Do as I have commanded you."

It was not easy to live like Christ asked. Only those people who devoted their lives to saving humanity were capable of doing that. These were the first Christians, and there were not many of them, but they were spiritually strong. These first Christians experienced persecution and died on crosses, in torture chambers, or else in the arena of a circus. Their examples gained new adherents though, and the Christian faith became so strong that it took over entire countries. Consequently, this victory almost became its ruin.

Kings decided to spread the faith of Christ with the help of weapons, and turned the worshipers of idols into the worshipers of Christ almost overnight. Obviously, an individual could not be converted to a Christian by simply baptizing him. Thus, the Christian faith became diluted with other faiths.

Having acquired many adherents, the successors of the apostles established congregations and built churches. Priests deviated from the main demand which Christ had laid down – God knows for Himself what you need, and should He find it to be necessary, or possible, He will help you without your prayer. Should you, however, still want to pray to God, then do it so that no one sees you. Do not do as the Pharisees do – do not pray to God in front of a crowd and in a temple. By doing so, they have already received their reward from the crowd – its admiration.

Later on, some priests even became rulers and kings, and acquired all the bad characteristics of a king. The most unpardonable act was their decision to protect God from Satan. They could not reach Satan. Therefore, they began to accuse people who did not live as they demanded, of being possessed by the devil. They turned them over to atrocious tortures and burned them at stakes. In a word, with the cross in hand they did exactly what Christ had prohibited. They exploited the name of Christ for their own benefit, by committing the gravest of crimes. They scared the people away from Christ, who, in the eyes of the people, turned from the most merciful [redeemer] into a merciless monster. Obviously, all these priests passed into nonexistence.

Some nations printed the books of God in foreign languages, so that people would not know what Christ had said, but would know only what the priests told them. Yet, the human spirit lived through this temporary darkness, as well. The church itself is at fault if people begin to forsake it. And now, supported by science – which the church also attempted to stop – man comes to the aid of the spirit. This aid is so great and versatile that man's struggle for justice and a better life becomes ever easier and more successful. No delusions of Stalin, or Mao, will be able to stop it again. The day will come when man will reach out with his arm toward the stars and will say, "My Creator – The Almighty – Your son, the man on Earth, comes to You. Give me Your hand and we will jointly continue Your great work."

Chief Spirit Mortifero.←     [[2323]]


Santorino                    12/25/66 1406


→Santorino speaking. Heralds, I congratulate you with the most prominent day for humanity on Earth – the coming of God's Son, Christ, to Earth in order to make God's thoughts known to humanity, and to tell it how it can achieve Paradise on Earth, or else – perish.

What weapon did the Son of God bring humanity? He brought it something else with which to vanquish evil and achieve Paradise. What He brought was neither a spear nor a sword. He brought love to people, for only love is capable of conquering without killing. He came in order to show, by personal example, how that should be accomplished. That should be accomplished with love, and if necessary, even by suffering and dying for it, because death not only does not kill love, but gives it a new, unbreakable strength, which slowly but definitely achieves the goal.

The Christian faith did not perish during the times of persecution in Rome. Instead, it became so strong that it took over entire nations. This proves that nothing can conquer the love which Christ brought. You can see the same thing now in the Soviet Union, where Communists have utilized all available means in order to destroy the faith of Christ. They tried to accomplish that with punishments. They tried to achieve that with the help of science. They deprived parents of the right to raise their own children. They also tried to re-educate the children by claiming that God does not exist, and that the Christian faith is the faith of fairy tales – that it wants to keep people in slavery. But nothing worked, even though almost all churches were closed and the faithful were ridiculed and persecuted.

Several decades have passed, but nothing has been accomplished. The old people who believed have been destroyed, or have died, but it still has not been possible to drive Christ out of the hearts of the youth. Quite to the contrary, the Communists have hardened the people in their faith, and they cannot be broken.

What do we see if we examine communism, and teachings similar to it? We see that Communists want to make humanity happy. Therefore, their goal would seem to be the same – like the goal of Christ. They, however, want to reach this goal quickly, in a few years. Since people do not want to follow these appeals voluntarily, they attempt to accomplish that with force, with power, by destroying those who oppose them actively and by forcing the rest to carry out their orders slavishly. That seems to be easy to carry out, by establishing conditions of life under which people will have to do what the government orders because, after all, the government does that for the good of the people. Yet, all these people forget one thing – human nature.

Man wants to be independent, and wants to do what he likes best. A poor peasant would rather remain in his hovel and work from morning until night than abandon his tiny house and go live on an estate as a servant, even though he would earn more money there. Man wants to be his own master, no matter how small, he still wants to be a master where everything belongs to him, and he can work as he pleases.

A government similar to the communist government existed once in Sparta, in ancient Greece. However, it did not achieve anything. The great French revolution tried to achieve it, but ended up with the world's great conqueror, Emperor Napoleon. Similarly, communism has begun to change in the countries of Europe. The government of the Soviet Republic, having reached a desperate dead end, has started to seek salvation in capitalistic methods.

As you can see, the best ideas cannot achieve anything if they are not suitable for human nature. They only bring horrible suffering. Yet, a free man emerges from that still stronger and more beautiful, as the phoenix emerges from the flames.

Briefly, that was what I wanted to tell you today. No matter how much humanity has to suffer at times, due to its errors and delusions, it only emerges from them stronger and more capable of avoiding new mistakes. Ignorance helped different leaders to deceive the people. The Communists, though, committed a fatal mistake by teaching people how to read and write, and by sending them to schools. With that, each person was given the opportunity to comprehend life, and to strive to find the right pathways toward a better life, and most important, toward a freer life.

Some time will still pass, and then every human will begin to understand what the most capable scientists are starting to understand. This is that the universe could not have come into being and formed by itself. There was and is a Creator and a Guide of life. It is immaterial what He is called, for the essence remains the same.

Children think occasionally that parents are not necessary, and that they would be better off without parents, for then they could always do whatever they please. Yet, when the children grow up and begin to understand the world and the struggle for a better future in it, they start to acknowledge that the parents were indispensable, because without their guidance they would have turned into worthless tramps.

In concluding my tiding, I wish you, heralds, in all sincerity, to spend this day well – the Great Prophet's anniversary day. It is nice to see the very many, magnificent Christmas trees, and the joy that overcomes people near them. It is also pleasant to see the overcrowded churches, for even though they do much that is wrong, they nevertheless do proclaim the words of Christ. It is up to each individual how to adhere best to these words.

In ancient and middle ages, priests took advantage of the ignorance of people and introduced much that is superfluous, and even harmful, in order to obtain more benefits from the congregation for their own personal use. However, they still had to preach Christ's faith as well, and thus this faith remained in the hearts of the people. Now that each person has acquired the ability to criticize, and to differentiate between the correct and the incorrect, the church, too, is forced to start conceding. Under no circumstances should the church be destroyed. It has to be transformed slowly into a true house of Christ.

I pass on to you, heralds, and to all the people on Earth, no matter of what faith they might be, the blessing of God.←

[[1515]]

# Chapter X

# January 1967

Santorino                    01/06/67 2140

→Santorino, speaking on behalf of The Almighty and of God.

Heralds to humanity on Earth, I come to you in the assignment of The Creator and Guide of the universe, and of the God of your galaxy, in order to convey to you the decisions of the High Rulers.

The twentieth century draws to a close. Almost two thousand years have passed since Christ brought God's faith to Earth. Millions of years had to pass before humanity became capable of accepting the new true faith.

Having originated along with the other animals, man did not differ from them for a long time. Yet, once he began to differ, the habits of the animals still controlled him. He had fought furiously the other animals for his place on Earth. Many of them, much stronger than he, attempted to destroy man, but man won. Thanks to his mind, he became the strongest animal on Earth.

Initially, he invented gods for himself, because he needed a master and a guide. Obviously, he considered God to be someone still higher than his ruler. He called God his master and king. One God, however, was not enough for him. Not only did he fill Heaven with gods, but also the Earth and even the seas. They were called gods, but their spiritual qualities were the same as those of people. They were merely mightier than people.

Humanity developed slowly. The time came to proclaim the true God to it – who He was, what He wanted from man, and what man must be like. Prophets – people with highly talented spirits – came to the people. The Ten Commandments came into existence – ten laws which expressed the will of God. These laws commanded what man must and must not do. These laws had been given to a man who had barely stood up firmly on his own two feet, but one who still had a lot to learn and understand, as well as learn how to form his life better. Thus, humanity received God's highest Envoy, in order to proclaim to humanity that its highest law is LOVE. It is not force, the sword, or heroism, that can take man to a true, happy life on Earth. [It is LOVE!]

The words of Christ were simple and understandable to everyone. He brought love to man, and a happy future dependent on it. Man crucified Him, though, and continued to crucify for over a thousand years. The road of the Christian faith was a difficult one, because it was difficult for man to change his nature, which had been molded over hundreds of thousands of years through constant battles and wars.

The apostles were replaced by their successors – their disciples, and the latter again by their successors. The trade of priesthood developed. Yes, it was a trade! The priests wanted to live better than the rest of the people. They wanted to guide and rule humanity as it would be better for them personally. They enacted their own laws. Next to God and His angels, they placed the King of Hell – Satan – with His uncountable legions of devils. They made the devil mightier than God. Since the words of Christ did not allow them to act like they were, they used a foreign language, which the people did not understand, in order to keep the words of Christ from the people.

The English burned at the stake the first man who dared to translate the Bible into a language which everyone could understand.

In order to save the people from the power of the devil, [the priests themselves] became more dreadful than the imagined devils. In order to protect God, they tortured people mercilessly, and burned them at stakes. That sounds unbelievable, but that is the way it was.

In lieu of Christ's teachings, they introduced innumerable prayers in the church, even though Christ had prohibited to do this. They implemented the confession of sins, and the absolution of sins, and took money for that. They built palaces for themselves, while people lived in hovels. They held lavish banquets, while other people were dying of starvation. They also tried to halt the development of the sciences.

You will claim that those were delusions. I, however, will say that it was a crime and the betrayal of Christ.

The progress of humanity is unstoppable, though. Printing the Book of Holy Scriptures in a language understandable to the people and its reading in churches had to be permitted. The church lost its secular power, and began to draw closer to the demands of Christ's teachings.

Whenever an unjust power collapses, the people who have been liberated, having lost faith in the old, go too far and begin to deny the very existence of God. Thus came the time for The Almighty to give humanity a broader concept of Himself, the Gods, and His goals and demands.←

(I will continue in ten minutes. Relax.) [[2235 – 2245]]

→There were times when it seemed that nothing good would come of humanity, and that The Almighty would give up on it. However, that did not occur and humanity, if not in its full entirety, at least to a great extent, began to travel the right road.

By giving up the normal form of faiths, many people fell into extremism, and being unable to discern God, claimed that He did not exist at all, or else that God had died. Yet, who had created this ungraspable world, including these animal and plant kingdoms on Earth? Did everything come about on its own? That, after all, is still more difficult to understand and less possible than the existence of God.

Yes, thanks to his scientific abilities, these days man can almost undertake the creation of a man. Yet man, after all, originated from an animal which had absolutely no idea of the construction of its body. How could it have built that, of which it had absolutely no idea?

Do you imagine that a sheep could have been sufficiently smart in order to create a sheep? That, after all, is a complete absurdity. The development of matter? Where, though, is the knowledge of this matter to do all of that?

All right, let God die for those people who cannot understand or acknowledge Him. However, God will continue to live for those who acknowledge Him.

If God does not exist, then obviously neither does The Almighty exist. Some people will deny The Almighty as well. Perhaps they will even try to rebel against The Almighty, should they find out that He is not like they want Him to be. Perhaps they will even get the spirits to join their side, and they, too, will rebel, along with the people, against The Almighty.

Nothing, though, can threaten The Almighty, for no one knows Him personally, and no one knows where He is, while being everywhere. Only a momentary will of The Almighty is needed for all the living beings, and all the spirits, to disappear from the universe in a second. And the next second there will be new spirits of The Almighty in the universe, and new living beings will be born on the planets.

The Almighty does not threaten humanity. He merely tells it like it is, and what may occur. The Almighty has created the universe the way He desires, and He asks all creatures to carry out His will, and to adhere to the laws which He has given.

He has entrusted the guidance of your galaxy to its God, your God. God gave laws to humanity concerning how it must live in order to carry out The Almighty's will, so that He could achieve the goal of His creation – to form an ideal life for man, the life of a happy and spiritually brilliant man. He needs this man. Yet, in order that this man would be responsible for himself and his deeds, He gave him a free will.

You, and all the people, have to understand that you have no other alternative than to carry out The Almighty's will.

His will was announced to you through Christ. The teachings of Christ remain the main ones, and the only ones for the entire humanity. You, heralds, have not been called forth to alter them, but only to supplement them, and to point out to humanity the errors which have been committed.

Your other main task is to give humanity the explanation for its existence and the goal of its existence. Some people will ask, "What goal does man have? Why does he exist and what must he achieve?"

You also have to explain to man that he has two goals. One, specifically as a human, and the other as his spirit after the death of the individual.

Your task is extremely difficult, for just as the prophets and Christ, you will have to struggle against hostile people who receive with hostility everything that is new. You will also have to struggle against overly smart people who will demand proof from you that the Tidings have truly been given you by The Almighty, rather than fabricated by yourselves. Similarly, critics will strive to grasp at everything that appears doubtful to them.

I, however, give you only one reply, "ALL THESE PEOPLE WHO DO NOT BELIEVE, WHO CANNOT BELIEVE, WHO DO NOT WANT TO BELIEVE IN THE TRUTHFULNESS OF THE TIDINGS – THEY ARE FREE TO NOT BELIEVE. I SUMMON ONLY THOSE TO FOLLOW ME WHO ARE CAPABLE OF BELIEVING IN THE TIDINGS. I DO NOT NEED ALL THE PEOPLE, I ONLY NEED THE MORE CAPABLE ONES! THUS SAY I, THE ALMIGHTY!"

Having passed theses words of The Almighty on to you, I suspend my tiding until the next time. Santorino.← [[2334]]

→The divine Santorino speaking, on behalf of God and The Almighty.

Today we will talk about the Ten Commandments which Moses brought down from Mount Sinai. Having spent several days on it, he received directions from God about how people must live in order to become free from doubts, and so that they would do only the best, and what is necessary for a happy and just life.

Back then, conditions of life differed sharply from the current ones, as they are in cultural nations. People were brutal back then. One of their gods demanded, "A tooth for a tooth, an eye for an eye." That god, obviously, was a god which had been invented by the people themselves. Yet the true God, too, had to demonstrate a certain amount of harshness, and had to utilize threats against those people who did not obey His laws. If we wish to compare, people back then were like children, and many children occasionally require a spanking by their father.

God did not give the Commandments to Moses in writing. He told them to him, and Moses wrote them down on his own. Besides that, he supplemented them with the laws of other nations, which seemed to him to be good and useful for the Hebrew nation as well. I will not criticize the Commandments of Moses, for that is no longer necessary. I merely want to tell you what is still important in them nowadays. I will also supplement them with new ideas, where that is necessary.

Janoss, read the First Commandment.

[[Janoss reads, "I am the Lord, thy God. Thou shalt not have other gods before Me."]]

This commandment talks about God. Now it can be expressed in this way: "I am your God, and there are no other gods in the world. All those who seek other gods and worship them will lose Me, and after their deaths, they will not have a pathway to Me. You must not worship Me with words, but only with deeds. Those who sin, but confess their sins, will be heard, and it will be possible to forgive them their sins. I am not revengeful, and no one will be punished for somebody else's sins, unless he has participated in them."

Janoss, read the Second Commandment.

[[Janoss reads, "Thou shalt not make to thyself an image or the likeness of anything that is in heaven above, or that is in the earth beneath, or that abides in the waters under the earth. Thou shalt not worship them or serve them."]]

[[No remarks from Santorino.]]

[[Janoss reads, "Thou shalt not take the name of the Lord, thy God in vain."]]

[[No remarks from Santorino.]]

[[Janoss reads, "Observe the day of Sabbath, to sanctify it. Six days shalt thou labor, and shalt do all thy works. The seventh day is the Sabbath of the Lord, thy God."]]

Man requires rest. The Hebrews had chosen this in ancient times. Times have changed now and man may give himself rest after a shorter period of work – after four or five days, or whenever he finds it to be best. My only demand is that rest be given to everyone. Sundays, as we call the current day of rest, have to be devoted to rest and to labors dedicated to love. This means to labors devoted to the benefit of the people, particularly those who are sick, old, and all those who suffer misfortunes and who have been struck by poverty. Similarly, this day should be devoted to worthwhile amusements, worthwhile performances, worthwhile games, and worthy instructions.

Janoss, read on.

[[Janoss reads, "Honor thy father and mother, that thou mayest live a long time, and it may be well with thee on Earth."]]

This commandment remains as it is.

Janoss, read on.

[[Janoss reads, "Thou shalt not kill."]]

Do not kill. What does the expression, "Do not kill," mean? It means that you may not deprive anyone else of his or her life. It also means, however, that you may not permit someone else to take some other individual's life, if you can preclude this murder. It also means that the state has to provide laws which do not permit anyone to kill someone else. The state has to assure the safety and life of every person.

That should be achieved initially by the correct upbringing of children in their families. Besides that, it should be assured that all parents do that correctly. Furthermore, not only should knowledge be taught in schools, but the youth must be brought up as well. Its free time must not be left without notice. The youth should be taught how to utilize it. For its own good and that of everyone else, games have to be organized, competitions, field trips, dances, and everything that is interesting and worthwhile. Left without attention, children quite often engage in mischief, come under the influence of delinquent people and in turn are ruined, and thus become unfit for society.

Often compassion for someone becomes a lack of compassion for others. For instance, a murderer who has been sentenced to, let's say, twenty years is paroled in ten years. This murderer, once free again, sometimes murders several more people. Whenever anyone who had committed a serious crime is released from prison, he must be placed under strict surveillance, and must be prevented from resuming any criminal activity. Particularly great attention has to be paid to those who are spiritually weak. They have to be treated, and should that not be possible, and they cannot be cured, they should be placed under conditions where they cannot harm others.

The entire society becomes an accomplice to murders, if it has not done everything to prevent them.

[[Janoss continues to read, "Thou shalt not commit adultery."]]

There were times when the guilty ones were stoned for transgressing marriage, or for the so-called easy life. Those times have passed. Man considers himself to be the master of his body. He no longer considers lust to be a sin. Obviously, love and lust are not the same thing. Love is of a spiritual nature, and lust is of a bodily, materialistic nature. True love and true happiness is when love combines with passion. A happy family life is then established, in which the children may feel happy as well.

People have to strive to select suitable companions in life for themselves, and must try to be faithful to each other. That is a blessing. Should you choose to, you can call its opposite a sin, but it cannot be called a crime.

[[Janoss reads, "Thou shalt not steal."]]

This commandment remains as it is.

[[Janoss continues to read, "Thou shalt not bear false witness against thy neighbor."]]

[[Janoss continues to read, "Thou shalt not covet thy neighbor's wife, nor his house, his field, his man servant, his maid servant, his ox, his ass, or anything that is his."]]

Let's conclude for today. Obtain a separate text of the Ten Commandments for the next time. Good night, heralds.← [[2235]]


Santorino                    01/20/67 2129


→Santorino speaking. Heralds, let us conclude the evaluation of the Ten Commandments.

Janoss, read the next one.

[[Janoss reads, "Thou shalt not bear false witness against thy neighbor."]]

Do not bear false witness against anyone, not a friend, or an enemy, for by testifying unjustly against anyone, you testify that you are a base liar.

Read the next one.

[[Janoss reads, "Thou shalt not covet thy neighbor's wife, nor his house, his field, his man servant, his maid servant, his ox, his ass, or anything that is his."]]

Do not covet that which does not belong to you.

With that, the examination of the Commandments according to number is completed. The last commandment seems to be ludicrous these days. In enumerating all that which not to covet, it seems that everything that exists in the world should have been enumerated. Moses found it essential to enumerate that which he considered to be most important. It seems to me that in our current times hardly anyone would covet a donkey.

With respect to someone else's wife, it seems that the situation has not improved at all. There is little hope that it will ever improve, for every male covets a beautiful woman, no matter to whom she belongs. Yet, it is one thing to covet, but another thing to try to possess her at all cost.

It may seem to you that the commandment about not using God's name in vain would not be necessary. In truth, though, it is necessary – not so much for God, but for man. Man does not love to talk a lot and superfluously about someone whom he respects, and especially out of place. Therefore, it turns out that whoever uses God's name in vain, does not respect God.

The Commandments ask children to respect their parents. The parents, however, also have to be worthy of being respected. The parents have to demonstrate to their children what a human being has to be like. This has to be done by example, and not just by instructions and flogging.

How can a drunk parent ask his children not to drink? How can a mother expect her children to respect their father, when she herself curses him and even beats him? How can the parents demand that their children be polite when they themselves are rude and impolite?

How does a child become an adult? How does he learn how to talk and how to behave? Only by imitating his parents and other adults. You forget that this imitating continues later on, as well.

Obviously, while growing up and meeting other children, children may begin to imitate their bad characteristics. That occurs much easier, though, if they do not have a foundation of proper upbringing from their parents.

Upbringing must continue in schools as well, because this subject is the most important one. In order to retain the foundations of upbringing for the entire life, the state must enact laws concerning what is permitted and what is prohibited. As you have already been told, absolute freedom is not possible, for it may limit the freedom of another person. Therefore people have to work out limits in exercising freedom, by taking into consideration how life can be made as good as possible for as many people as possible.

Once the children grow up, they have to look after their parents. The parents, though, have to take care of their children, so that the children would have to look after their parents in order to repay them for their caring. Obviously, a good child will look after bad parents, as well. However, here is a dilemma. How can bad parents bring up good children?

Marriages. Today priests in churches ask those being married to promise to love each other for life. The words "for life" are only for the chosen ones. Ordinary mortals do not know them. Initially, when passion binds young people, and their natures do not express themselves, love truly does seem to be for life. This "for life," though, is sometimes shorter than a year, and usually lasts only a few years.

Whenever two people no longer love each other, but even detest each other, there is no sense in them continuing to live together, because life should be based on happiness. Obviously, their children suffer the most in these cases when the married ones get divorced.

People must strive to get along in marriage by avoiding sharp corners, and by trying to give in whenever possible. Ceremonies and vows are not important in a marriage; rather, the desire of both young people to establish a family is important. Obviously, there are people who are incapable of living in a marriage. It is better for them not to establish one [in the first place].

What is a sin? The Almighty has given passion to living beings in order to compel them to bear children. Since children require effort in raising them, life could not continue without the force of passion. Love plays no role whatsoever among many animals. Yet, in a human, love, as his spiritual part, plays a large role. The circumstance when passion combines with love should be considered to be ideal, and each individual should strive for that.

I examined the old Commandments because they hold a very important role in the religion of people. They determine what is permitted to man, and what is prohibited, so that human society can exist and not collapse.

It is not possible to repeal these several-thousand-year-old Commandments, which have coalesced with man. However, since man has changed during these thousands of years, these old Commandments have to be renewed, as well.←

There is still much that is important in human life and that has not been examined. I assign this duty to the high spirit Inrak. He will talk with you the next time.

→May God's blessing be with you, heralds! Santorino.←

[[2233]]

Inrak                          01/27/67 2126

The spirit Inrak is speaking. Almighty's heralds to the planet Earth, I come to you as assigned by the Divine in order to examine the mistakes which people make during their lifetime. Perhaps they may seem to be minor and unimportant, but in reality – what is unimportant? Life consists mostly of things that when taken individually are unimportant, but in their totality these unimportant things can eventually have a larger impact than what you consider to be important.

People observe each other, how they conduct themselves, and from their impressions form conclusions about what an individual is like. If a person behaves frivolously, he can often cause harm for himself. People are frequently not hired for a new job simply because they did not leave a sufficiently good impression on the new boss. There are also other similar examples.

The Divine chose me for the purpose of familiarizing humanity with its undesirable mistakes, because I have already been the observer of human nature for many centuries, as directed by him, on the other side of the globe. I have not had any dealings on this side of the globe, and I know you only from those occasions when the Divine visited you.

Since you are people and undoubtedly you have different undesirable ways and habits, then so that you would not think that it is specifically you who are being discussed, a spirit was chosen who does not know you and does not know what you are like in life. Should something correspond with your negative habits, then you can blame only yourselves.

Many people do not pay attention to what kind of an impression they leave on others. If you talk about something or do something in the presence of other people – do not rely on what seems to be correct to you. Rather, observe people's facial expressions, because people may praise you with their words, but may feel the opposite on the inner. Generally, their faces cannot always conceal their true thoughts about you, and about your conduct and deeds.

An individual should learn how to criticize, but most of all he should criticize himself. You should never judge another person about whom you know little, if someone slanders him. If you listen to one side, then this side seems almost like an angel to you, but whoever is being discussed – that is, the other side – is completely worthless in all aspects. Should you now listen to the other side, though, it turns out that the first side is the bad one. Quite often that does not happen because one side wants to tell lies about the other side, but because this side truly believes that to be the case. Therefore, whenever there is talk about people who are intimate or important to you in life, always try to find out the real, rather than the imagined, truth. People generally love to fantasize, and hence – lie. Such lies are usually not harmful, but neither are they desirable.

The other particularly important consideration in human relationships is not to be overly hasty, and not make any decisions without thoroughly considering them. Always try to stay calm, and not flare up. Should you flare up, you will lose self-control and may do things that you will have to gravely regret later on. There are cases where even the very best of friends often became so enraged over a trifle, that they can even start fighting and kill each other.

What should be considered in marriage? Marriage is generally based on love, which is reinforced by passion, but life is not always like a fairy tale, which is what it seems to be at the beginning. Moments of passion become cooler and turn into a habit. Love cools down and becomes monotonous, but people should not become monotonous. You should unexpectedly whisper in your wife's ear, "You know, Olga, I love you!"

These few words which are so easy to pronounce can perform miracles. The next moment Olga, too, will feel that she loves Peter, and obviously will tell him that.

You should not forget to kiss your wife an extra time, to bring a little joy in her life, and to tell her that she is still beautiful. She will not believe you, but pleasant doubts will nevertheless arise, "Perhaps really I still look good?"

The wife should not become particularly slovenly and look unkempt either. She should dress well and take good care of her body. She should not become like a rag – something that is essential in the home but that cannot be respected and loved.

Everyone can occasionally slip up and commit the so called "sin," but quite often this "sin" passes just as quickly and readily as it began, and everything is fine once again.

A married couple also has to take the happiness of their children into consideration, and often has to sacrifice much because of them.

Something else that should be observed in life – if two or more people have made a decision, then it may not be altered without consulting everyone who had participated. Such unilateral action can greatly insult the participant who was not informed of the change. That can even wreck a friendship, because it is insulting.

As I said earlier, you should always firmly control yourself. You should not be too loud. You should control your emotions, and should not display them by a somber appearance or with loud laughter. In general, you should laugh only if there is something truly worth laughing about. Similarly, you should not obtrusively interfere in the conversations of others. You should let the speaker finish his sentence, and intervene only then. I have frequently observed that everyone was talking but no one was listening. What did that accomplish?

Tact – it is a short word, but it has a huge significance in life. You will not achieve respect in society without tact. Tact has to be particularly observed at a party. Many people err merely because they think that they act correctly, but do not notice how the host and hostess react to their conduct. Some people refuse to eat, because they have eaten at home. That leaves a bad impression on most hosts and hostesses, as a rejection of their hospitality. It truly is a strange feeling to see everyone eating, but one or two sitting in front of an empty plate. The best thing would be not to eat anything when going somewhere where eating is definitely anticipated, or else to leave some room for a light meal.

Some people – as one says – love to be late. There is a proverb that arriving on time means displaying the kindness of kings. Obviously, arriving on time is very important, because being late makes others wait. However, the circumstances have to be considered. People who are involved in many activities often cannot always arrive at the set minute, no matter how much they want to. People who have plenty of time cannot understand that.

There also are people who in general are incapable of arriving on time, as for example the famous movie actress Marilyn Monroe. Yet, anything can be forgiven this wonderful girl. Still, beauties, do not attempt to emulate her!

Now I want to talk about fathers. The problem – fathers and sons – has been eternal. Fathers do not understand their sons, and the sons – their fathers. Why is that the case? Simply because fifty years separate them. Life does not stand still. It changes, and quite often it changes in fifty years in many respects. However, fathers and mothers want their sons and daughters to be exactly the same as they were.

In ancient times, when life changed slowly, human nature also changed slowly. These days life changes more in fifty years than during the previous fifty thousand years. Man has acquired wings. Man can converse with someone who is on the other side of the globe. One person can talk to millions of people. Thanks to the radio, instead of performing for a few dozen people, actors can now perform in all homes and for countless people. In recent years, man began to implement in life his designs to fly to the moon and other planets.

What did people formerly do at home in the evenings? They sat by the fireplace, read books, played cards, received visitors, and that was the extent of it. To drive over to a dance or a theater was an entire event. Now they are served by movie theaters which show them the entire world – all of the world's more famous actors, musicians, and singers. Reality has surpassed all of man's abilities to fantasize, and all of his most fabulous fairy tales. During these fifty years man has achieved what he was not even able to dream of during the previous millions of years.

How can man help but to change, if everything has changed so unimaginably? Obviously, some young people exaggerate, but the youth in general does not intend to perish, even if marriage will assume entirely different forms.

I sense that you are tired and that I have become tactless. Therefore I take leave from you, my dear friends, and wish you good night, and particularly ask you not to be mad at me if I have inadvertently rubbed you the wrong way. [[2310]]

# Chapter XI

# February 1967

Inrak                    02/03/67 2106

The spirit Inrak is speaking. Almighty's heralds, with respect to my tidings, you have to consider that they are not intended for the heralds but for all people. If they effect the heralds, then merely because the heralds are also people.'

My tidings are intended for the people in order to point out their mistakes, and thus make their life happier and more successful. Obviously, one expects an example from the heralds, but in general there is no intent to restrict their free will.

As I already said, minor mistakes in life can cause grave consequences. The most important consideration for man is his respect, and it is hard for people to respect an individual whose behavior is ridiculous or impolite. Great people have experienced that, simply because they did not pay any attention to what to them seemed to be too trifling to be noticed.

Normal people generally act similarly, with minute exceptions. That is achieved through proper upbringing by their father and mother, and after that by proper schooling. There are exceptions, though.

This can happen if a person has a lazy nature and he does not want to do anything, or else starts to engage in drinking or perversion. Then come the so-called mistakes – people who lack something that normal people have. People like that should be considered as being abnormal, and their actions have to be measured with a different yardstick.

The final category includes cripples and those who are physically ill. Science, in the form of medicine, has to help them as much as that is possible. If that is not possible, society has to place people of the second and third categories under such conditions that they cannot harm people of the first category.

The last two categories specifically include thieves, swindlers, and murderers. Humanity has to be liberated from them in a timely manner, so that they cannot harm society.

That may perhaps sound excessively merciless, but it would be even more merciless to have decent people suffer because of these trash of society, and in fact – enemies, just the same as rats, crocodiles, and wolves. A murderer is, in fact, worse than a wolf, because a wolf does not kill another wolf, except in exceptional cases, as for example when a wolf becomes incapable of living, or is fatally hurt.

Let us talk now about something else, something that has been discussed before, but not completely. This is what happens to man's soul after the death of his body.

What you have been told about God and Satan weighing the good and evil deeds of a soul in the Deoss Temple, pertains only to very high people with especially important tasks, because it is not easy to tell which predominates – the good or the evil. That pertains to the high spirits, and to God's or The Almighty's envoys or heralds, regardless of how long the herald has been incarnated or what his achievements might have been. Thus the heralds who have departed from Earth, as for example John, have already faced the High Judges, and all of you will.

Next come the lower categories. These come to the Temple, but do not face the High Judges, rather – lower ones. These are the people who have carried out particularly successfully the tasks which had been given their spirits. These spirits are given a choice. They are offered new tasks, and they have the right to choose the task that they like best.

Then comes the third category – the spirits who have carried out their tasks. They receive their new tasks immediately right here on Earth, and then spend a set amount of time resting in the Solar Fields. With respect to the category of spirits who have not carried out their tasks, they merge with The Almighty's ocean of spirits immediately after the death of their bodies, without even realizing that they are lost.

The spirits in the last category – the spirits who have committed crimes on Earth – face Satan's judges in order to undergo their punishment.

In the category of spirits who have carried out their tasks well, are included also those spirits who have been unable to accomplish their tasks due to circumstances over which they had no control.

_ ★ ★ ★ _

Many people complain to God that they are faring poorly on Earth, but it is mostly their own fault, because they do not try to make a better life for themselves. If a father has given his son the highest education, then he – the son – has many doors open for a good life. If he, however, does not try to perform his duties well, starts drinking, or else becomes dishonest, then obviously his life can no longer be happy.

An individual with a High School education – which is free in many countries – can also live quite decently, if he tries hard. People without an education are worse off, but these days the pay even for ordinary work is fairly good, and with diligence even a person like that can feel tolerably, and even well. Therefore, people should spend less time complaining and superfluously praying to God, but rather should grab a broom or a shovel. That will help much more.

Many people, of course, make a mistake by choosing positions which are unsuitable for their abilities. Every individual is more capable of something than the next one. For example, some people are so capable of kicking a rubber ball that – even without an education – they surpass the best educated people when it comes to earnings.

Now, with respect to Christ's faith. Many people think that it has lost its might. The reality, though, is quite the opposite – Christ's faith begins to completely take over humanity, with humanity itself hardly perceiving this. What are all these new laws about treating the sick, taking care of the elderly, and so on? Nothing else than the fulfillment of Christ's demands!

Humanity has quite imperceptibly reached the conclusion that it has to help everyone who cannot help himself, and has to take care of the elderly and the sick without them even begging for help. Formerly, each individual helped the unfortunate ones separately, and there were not enough such people. The state now has to help them, which means that every person has to help.

People have not developed equally in all lands. In some they have progressed with fabulous steps. In others again – as in tropical lands, where nature gave people almost everything ready-made, and there was no particular need to be concerned about an education – the people have remained almost in place.

As the Europeans came into these lands, they started forcing the savages to work for them, thus teaching them to work and to take care of themselves. The whites brought along culture, too, but utilized it differently – sometimes only for their own benefit, and at times for the benefit of the savages as well.

Culture bearing nations such as the North Americans – who achieved all the benefits of freedom after the First World War – started to insist that the colonial nations give freedom to the people belonging to them. However, an individual who has been able to achieve freedom, can utilize it, but not someone to whom it has been handed. He has to acquire an education first, without which it is not possible to govern a country; and education takes time.

You can see for yourselves what is happening in Africa. That proves that sometimes even good things have to be done carefully, so that they would not turn into bad ones.

With that, we will conclude for today. I thank you for your patience. Your friend and guest. Good night, heralds. [[2249]]

Inrak                                        02/10/67 2124

The spirit Inrak is speaking. Every individual has to understand that the freedom which he has been given has a positive meaning only if he uses it to achieve the very best results. If he uses it worthlessly or even harms humanity, then this freedom can only hurt him. That is not the only thing either. Whenever he does something, man has to always consider whether that might harm others, or else is unnecessary.

New ideas appear to be strange and do not always gain success. Besides, ideas have to originate at a time appropriate for them. Thus, Leonardo da Vinci's brilliant ideas lay around unused for centuries. There is a problem, however, if the necessary new ideas come too late. That hinders humanity's progress.

It is unfortunate that a large majority of people is destined to perform work that is necessary for humanity, but is very simple. It turns out as if two classes of people are again created. In fact, that is how it is, but it should be noted that this class includes people who either incarnate for the first time, or else have not demonstrated particular abilities in their prior or previous incarnations.

That does not mean, though, that none of them have any prospects for advancing. Everyone has been given [a chance to advance] – anyone who wants to advance, and strives to do this. Some spirits turn out to be so diligent and capable that even during the first incarnation they already advance to a higher category, and some even to the very highest. Of course, that happens seldom, but everyone has been given a genuine opportunity to gradually advance – it depends only on a person's own desire to advance.

God has come to the people several times. In the beginning, He visited the people often, spoke to them, taught them, and even helped them when that was essential. Later on He sent prophets in His stead, and then again came to the people in the form of His Son. Now He talks to the people through you – the heralds – because progress is necessary everywhere.

An individual's worth and his success in life are three-quarters dependent on his upbringing, while he was a child and a youth. The most attention has to be paid to that. A new subject – the upbringing of an individual – which is intended for new teachers and the heads of families, fathers and mothers, has to be instituted in schools, and particularly in colleges.

As I already said, a child's upbringing has to begin from the moment when he starts to cry the first time.

Since you are very much interested in how things went for John when he faced God and Satan in the Deoss Temple, he himself will immediately tell you how that occurred. A five minute intermission.
[[2158]]

John K                              02/10/67 2203

→The spirit of John, herald to Earth, speaking.

Dear friends, heralds, with the permission of God, I want to relate to you how I departed from Earth, and what happened to me in Heaven.

I recall that, while riding my bicycle, I received a blow. That was followed by severe pain, and then it stopped suddenly. When I looked around, everything seemed to me to be unusually bright and peculiar. Ilgya stood before me, with a smile on her lips.

"Your death came so unexpectedly that Mortifero did not manage to arrive. I was destined to be the first one to welcome you on your return to the realm of the spirits. Now let's proceed to the Solar Fields. You will be able to rest there for a while until God summons you to the Deoss Temple. There He will give you a new task, or else will allow you to continue your rest in the Solar Fields. Then, from the Solar Fields, if you will want to, you will be able to visit your friends on Earth, but no sooner."

In the Solar Fields she turned me over to the jurisdiction of the chief spirit of the Solar Fields, and returned to Earth. Thus I did not even meet Chief Spirit Mortifero. Not everyone is as fortunate as Antonina's spirit, whom the chief spirit of Death, himself, carried in his arms to the Deoss Temple. After all, though, they were old friends.

I will not tell you anything about the Solar Fields. That would require too much time, and I have not been given much time. I will turn to the most important topic.

After some time, which was approximately seven days on Earth, Chief Spirit Mortifero arrived in the Solar Fields and summoned me to proceed to the Deoss Temple, and face the High Judges.

My appearance must not have left the impression of a hero, for Mortifero smiled and said, "Now, now, old one, don't let your courage collapse. Somehow we'll manage to avoid Hell."

I cannot say that his joke improved my disposition much, but I did feel somewhat bolder.

It is not possible to describe the Castle of Light – the Deoss Temple. It appeared unimaginably grand, and nothing on Earth could compare to its beauty. There were innumerable chief spirits, higher spirits, and spirits there. They nevertheless did not leave the impression of a crowd, as on Earth, and there was no congestion. It even seemed that there was plenty of room for many more spirits.

With quick steps – which in fact were not steps at all, but more like gliding along the floor, or floating through the air – we arrived before the High Judges, and Mortifero said, "God and Satan, before You stands the spirit of the former herald to Earth, John, whose life was interrupted by an unexpected, tragic death." Then he repeated, "Herald John," and departed from the Deoss Temple.

"On your return to Heaven, herald John," came the voice of God. I dared to raise my eyes.

God seemed to me to be very large, compared to myself. He did not sit on a throne, but on a chair that had a peculiar form. Still, it was much more impressive than the thrones of earthly kings. God did not remind me of any of His paintings which I had seen on Earth. He appeared like a middle-aged man, without a beard or mustache. His hair was rather long, but it hung barely over the collar of His garment. The garment was simple, made of some sort of glittering white material. His appearance was unprecedentedly noble. His face was handsome, and everything in it was so harmonious that it was difficult to take your eyes away from it. Yet, His eyes were most surprising. When I looked into them, I was absorbed in them, for I saw my figure, but completely naked. I understood that God saw me as I am – that nothing can be concealed from Him. Then my figure faded from His eyes, and a deep, restless ocean lay in them.

"I, too, welcome you," came a voice firm in its expression, but certainly not harsh.

I looked at Satan. His face appeared as if carved from a rock, but it was peculiarly attractive. His hair was short and shiny black, unlike that of God, whose hair was bright white and wavy. Satan's eyes, too, were dark as the night, and nothing could be discerned in them – neither compassion nor hatred.

"John, you know that We cannot devote much time even to a herald to Earth. We know everything about you, but Our duty is to hear you out, as well. What can you tell Us about the accomplishment of your task?"

For a brief second, I felt the floor give away beneath me, but then I took hold of myself and began with a trembling voice, "What can I tell You that is new, for You already know everything about me? Your time is so valuable that I do not wish to waste it needlessly. I will merely say that, being an ordinary human, I sinned much, but I tried to be just, and tried to help people however and as much as I could.

"The duties of a herald came unexpectedly for me, and without being prepared for them. I tried to help the other heralds with that which was less possible for them. I should not have abandoned the duties of a herald, but neither could I abandon my wife, with whom I was bound for almost my entire life, as well as our children. After a difficult struggle I decided to accompany them. It seems to me that I deserve punishment, but ask only to mitigate it, if that is possible."

God and Satan observed me with thoughtful eyes, and I tried in vain to read my fate in them.

Then God turned His head toward Satan and said, "Do You think the same way as I do?"

"Yes," Satan said. "He has sinned, but those sins do not require a punishment. He has done much good, and, within what was possible for him, has tried to do a great deal in the work of the Tidings, considering his age and habits of life. The good, which he has done, deserves a just reward. As to what he has earned, You have to determine that, God."

God looked at me, smiled – more of a spiritual smile than a visible one – and said, "I thank you, herald to Earth, for what you have accomplished on My behalf on Earth. I upgrade you to a higher degree, and, after resting in the Solar Fields, I will assign you a new task. This cannot be higher than the task of a herald, but it is one which is considered very high in Heaven. Do you have some other desire?"

I wanted to reply, "No, God." But then suddenly, almost without realizing it myself, I asked God, "On Earth, we are used to seeing in paintings Your Son, Christ, sitting next to You on the throne."

God did not reply, but then came an unusually gentle voice, full of love, "John, after all, I am here! Don't you see Me?"

In surprise, I turned my head in the direction of the voice. I noticed Christ sitting on the throne next to God. He appeared exactly as He looks in our paintings, with a beard and a mustache. He looked exactly like a living human, and not a spirit. Inadvertently, I asked, "But after all, You do not look like all the others here. You do not look like a spirit, but rather, You look like a real human!"

"I am one," Christ replied with a smile. "Have you forgotten that I ascended to Heaven as a living human?"

"No," I said, "I have not forgotten that, but I thought that You would be a spirit here."

"Yes, I can also be as a spirit here. I want to thank you for the good which, in the name of God and My own, you have done for people. Since you are a spirit, though, then in order to do that I, too, have to be a spirit."

He stood up and came toward me. Along the way his body faded and Christ's spirit shook the hand of my spirit, and said, "Now you may go and prepare yourself for your new task. You will have to help Me greatly in our forthcoming, new work."

I bowed my head low and wanted to thank Him for the honor bestowed upon me. Yet, Christ took my arm, turned me toward the exit, and we departed from the Deoss Temple.

I have to conclude with that. Pass my greetings along to all of my relatives.

May God also be with you, as He is with me! John.← [[2331]]


<u>Alpha</u>                                    02/17/67 2128


→Almighty's heralds to Earth, I come to you in the assignment of The Almighty in order to announce to you what you do not know yet, and to stress the most important aspects of that which you already know.

The high spirit Inrak, who is currently spending his time on Earth, and who has supervised living beings on many other planets in the universe, turned to The Almighty with an allusion. In order for humanity to be completely capable of achieving the goal which is intended for it, humanity must know everything that is possible about its task on Earth and, after that, in Heaven. Humanity has to know how they, the people, will be received in Heaven, and how their deeds will be evaluated there.

The first step in this direction was herald John's story about how God and Satan evaluated him, and assigned new tasks to him. John was very agitated and therefore did not notice everything. Thus, he failed to note the most significant phenomenon of the Deoss Temple – the sizes of God and Satan. He noticed God only when God addressed him. He raised his lowered eyes then, and noticed that God was very large.

The most unusual phenomenon is that once you enter the Deoss Temple, which is extremely large, you can see clearly the figures of God and of Satan. They rise high above the heads of the spirits. You can see clearly the faces of God and Satan, as though they were just in front of you. The most unusual thing is that no change takes place in Their sizes as you approach Them. Thus you arrive in front of Them and see Them exactly the same, as if you had remained in place before Them.

As to how this is achieved, that cannot be explained to you currently. However, that is the way it is. At no moment is God further than a few steps away from you. To express it more correctly, He is always with you, just as in your life, except now He is visible to you.

At the beginning of the Tidings, when we did not yet know fully The Almighty's task, we tried to pass on to you that which would seem incomprehensible to you, in a way that was understandable to man. We gave you the size of God, which was correct in only one instance. The spirit of God encompasses the entire Milky Way galaxy, and can become visible individually to the spirits in different forms and sizes.

John's story demonstrated to you how simply everything is done in the Deoss Temple. God addresses you. You do not have to fall to your knees, as was done in front of rulers on Earth. You address God by simply saying, "God." You feel at ease after God's words, "We know everything about you. If you have anything to tell Us, tell it."

Since you have nothing to hide, and now you know fully what good and evil you have done, it is easy for you to evaluate your own good and evil deeds. Therefore, no unpleasant surprise awaits you, for the High Judges always punish you lighter than you had punished yourself.

The High Judges know how difficult life on Earth sometimes is, and how hard, and occasionally even impossible, it is for a human to decide what to do. For example, consider the best and most honest individual in the Soviet Union, which is under the rule of the Communists. Of what use are your good intentions there, when they cannot be carried out in life, if you wish to remain alive, or else do not want to rot in dreadful jails?

It is an entirely different matter if a human has been given the opportunity to do the very best that God asks of him. In such cases, the verdict sounds different – sometimes very harsh.

The Christian faith was born at a time when kings ruled on Earth, and the majority of people were slaves. Back then, man could not imagine God other than as a king, and himself as a slave. In those times man, like a child, had not yet become an adult. Therefore, in order to keep him from mischief, one had to threaten him with punishment – like a spanking. These days, times have changed on most of Earth. People have become adults, capable of understanding their duties, and capable of controlling themselves and bearing responsibility.

Should you think it over well, you will understand why such great equality is felt in Heaven – and why the highest spirits, and even God, feel equal there to some extent. Which one of you will undertake to tell me, or rather explain, why?

Let us begin with our lady.

[[Mary replies that the reason why all the spirits and God feel equal in Heaven is that all the spirits, and also God, have been created from the very same spirit of The Almighty.]]

Very well put, Mary.

Yes, all the spirits, the lowest, as well as the highest, all are The Almighty's spirits. The Almighty does not segregate them, but merely asks them to carry out the duties which have been assigned to them. If a low spirit has accomplished his task extremely well, he receives the same recognition from The Almighty as a chief spirit who also has accomplished his task extremely well.

Here on Earth, where currently I am with you humans, it is difficult to understand that freedom and sense of equality which the spirits feel in Heaven. In the Deoss Temple, a spirit who has something really important to say, or ask from God, may turn to God from anywhere in the Deoss Temple, wherever he is currently located. He will receive an answer from God, even though God continues to talk with someone else at His throne.

You have been told that the universe and time are infinite, and that The Almighty's spirit is everywhere. Here it is my duty to give you an explanation.

Yes, The Almighty's spirit, in the form of many spirits, is on those planets on which life exists or is being created. The Almighty's spirit is also in the space of the universe, between the stars and the planets. Yet The Almighty's spirit is not on those planets which do not contain life, and on which life is not envisioned, as well as on dead planets. Similarly, He is not in the empty space of the universe.

With respect to the infinity of the universe and time, and their possibility, it is not possible yet to explain that to you, as well as their impossibility.←

(A ten minute intermission.) [[2229 - 2239]]

I, Chief Spirit Alpha, continue my tiding to the people on Earth.

→You have heard and read about the horrible day of punishment, that the day will come, and some await it every day, when the end of the Earth will come. Then the living will die, and the dead will rise from the graves in order to face the High Judges – the Holy Spirit, God, and His Son, Christ. People call this day – Doomsday.

Almost two thousand years have already passed from the time when these threats were first heard. Nothing has happened though, and it seems it is not going to happen either. How can all of this be explained? Will Doomsday really take place, or is it simply imagined?

Neither theory is quite correct. Doomsday was envisaged in the event that humanity would turn out to be incapable of carrying out The Almighty's task, and in case there was no hope for humanity. Obviously, the dead would not rise from their graves, for they would already have faced the Judges. In destroying the Earth, however, The Almighty could not punish everyone for the sins of Earth. He would have to evaluate justly each individual. Those who nevertheless had tried to carry out their tasks, but were unable to achieve anything, would have to receive recognition and new tasks.

During the period of humanity's history, The Almighty began to lose hope three different times. The most frightful situation arose during the Middle Ages when the Inquisition instituted the devil – not to be confused with Satan – as God. Priests began to act contrary to that which Christ had taught, and did so in the name of Christ. Following that, humanity began once again to move forward slowly.

The great wars came, which threatened to set back the development of humanity – particularly the appearance on Earth of inhumans like Hitler and Stalin caused unbearable suffering for the people. The Almighty could no longer bear this, and began to contemplate recalling humanity, and creating new living beings on Earth. After the departure of Hitler and Stalin though, humanity's genius began to emerge. In many countries – as for example, your – the government, which was elected by the people, began to implement Christ's laws in life. Even though without mentioning the name of Christ, the government assumed responsibility for caring for the sick, the old, and the insane. Scientists, having escaped from the shackles of prejudice, began to display their capabilities, and through their achievements surpassed the boldest of people's fairy tales.

The telegraph, telephone, ships, and railroads were created. Cars, movies, radio, and television were created. They were true miracles of science. Formerly, humanity could not even dream of anything similar to them. Then came the breaking point. Man acquired the ability to fly, and even left the kings of Earth – the eagles – below him.

And then man cast his glance on the universe and told The Almighty, "Almighty, I, man, Your son, assume my task to help You form the most wonderful world."

And The Almighty replies through you, "I await you, My children. May your difficult, but successful, roads be blessed!"

Let us conclude with that for today. Chief Spirit Alpha.←

[[2312]]

Alpha                          02/24/67 2057

→Chief Spirit Alpha, speaking on behalf of The Almighty. Heralds, the previous time I had to interrupt my tiding due to your exhaustion, but that was my fault. I had overestimated your strength, as well as my own.

In the meantime I have received new tasks from The Almighty, and that will prolong my tiding.←

_ ★ ★ ★ _

The Almighty also assigned me to explain to you the tasks and the duties of the heralds.

The heralds have been given an exceptional privilege, which even the spirits do not have – they can ask The Almighty about anything that seems to be incomprehensible or unjust to them. They can, so as to say, even argue with The Almighty, which is unimaginable in Heaven. All The Almighty's orders here are carried out by the spirits without any delay, no matter how high or low the spirits might be. The spirits may ask for additional explanations only in particularly important cases, or else raise justified objections.

With respect to you, you are The Almighty's heralds with the previously mentioned privileges, but also with some strict limitations. Only the first one of you – Alexander – and only three other heralds have been selected by The Almighty. The other heralds were selected by chance, and their importance as heralds – as irreplaceable heralds – is not fateful to the work of the Tidings.

Let us talk first about the first of the heralds. He is completely irreplaceable and the Tidings are not possible without him, because the Tidings can be passed on only through him. The first of the heralds has to be particularly talented as a human and also as a herald. The structure of his brain is such that it is capable of receiving the Tidings of the spirits, and passing them on to people. We do not direct his hand, as some people think. His brain directs it, but almost without its intervention.

The duty of the herald who participates in the conversation is to allow his/her hand to follow Alexander's hand entirely freely. The least restraint causes us great difficulties, because it interrupts our contact with Alexander. Alexander has to completely devote himself to receiving and passing on the Tidings. He does not have time to think, and he cannot follow each word, therefore it is not always possible for him to correct mistakes, since that requires stopping the tiding for a moment. Each moment is more precious for us than a century.

_ ★ ★ ★ _

→I, Alpha, am the Chief Spirit of the Past and the Present, and proclaim to you only concerning the past and the present. Chief Spirit Omega will proclaim to you about the future. He will tell you how to handle the Tidings, and about prospects for the future. Obviously, in some necessary circumstances we will look into the time frame of each other's assignment.

The universe is infinite, and the human mind cannot grasp this infinity, for it may encompass within itself completely unimaginable worlds, and may also encompass nothing – absolutely nothing – without an end, and without any sense.

I will talk about the space of the universe which I know. You have already been told how The Almighty created the worlds, with suns and planets. You have also been told that The Almighty had absolutely no notion concerning what to do with this empty universe. He merely sensed that He also had no sense in existing in this dreadful emptiness. He began to think about how to set Himself free from this unbearable and unnecessary void. He felt that He had to do something, and yet, what? Whom could He ask for advice? With whom could He communicate? There was no answer! He began trying to create, and to find an answer to what was necessary, through the act of creation.

The work taught Him what to do with matter and how to shape it. All these suns, planets, and comets, though, while being beautiful and eliminating the unbearable emptiness, were only like toys to a child. One soon gets tired of playing with them. The Almighty began to create the living matter, and various beings from it.

Yes, the universe came to life. But, what goal did all that have eventually?

While looking at the living beings which had been created, and which, led by instinct, roamed the planets, a brilliant thought came to His mind – to give these beings the ability to think.

The universe assumed a much more logical form, but that was all there was to it. The Almighty, however, sensed that something worthwhile had to be achieved, something worthy enough so that it would be meaningful to be the ruler of this universe.

His spirits had much work to do, but everything that had been created lived its own life, paying no attention to The Almighty, and without giving Him any help. This did not lessen The Almighty's spiritual loneliness. Then suddenly the mental lightning flashed and split the universe, while dazzling it with unprecedented light. The Almighty found the goal for everything that existed. He decided to create a living being from matter, and also gave it His spirit, with His unlimited capabilities. Thus living beings came into being. On Earth they are called man. On other planets they are called by different names, but overall they are people, and beings with abilities similar to those of man.

With that, we will conclude for today.← [[2248]]

# Chapter XII

# March 1967

Astra. Heralds, the high spirits and chief spirits will alight later on today, and I was assigned to while away your time. That's fine, I know a few little stories about your brothers in sorrow – people – and I will tell you one of them. Therefore, kindly pay attention.

I like to observe people, and I have to confess that it is not a particularly boring utilization of my free time.

One day a large car had been sent from the capital of the country to one of the world's cities, in order to take a few outstanding citizens to an important meeting. Since there was an empty seat in the car, I decided to travel together with them. They were no ordinary citizens. They were people with exceptional positions. Not having any particularly great knowledge, I decided to become smarter and learn something from these people.

Initially everything went fine and calmly. Then a gentleman of a particularly distinguished appearance suddenly started talking about the driver of the car, who had been directed to take these people to the meeting. "The driver of our car sure is slow. He moves like a crab. We will probably get there only for the conclusion of the meeting."

Another gentleman said, "We will get there too soon, because we have plenty of time. I cannot stand drivers who go fast. When riding with them, there is always the danger of winding up in the hereafter. I think that he could drive still slower."

A third one said, "It seems that our driver does not have much experience. He jerks the car when changing gears."

The only representative of the fair sex – a lady – said, "It seems to me that he drives the car rather well, and he also looks kind of nice."

A gentleman who had already crossed the doorstep of the eightieth year, muttered, "Everything seems fine to you women if a young man is handsome. According to my ideas, our driver is still wet behind the ears, and he has already been entrusted to transport us."

The driver paid no attention to the conversations, except he turned his head slightly toward the lady when she spoke, and smiled. Who does not like flattery?

The intersection of several roads approached. The passengers started to discuss the roads.

One of them said, "We should take road 'A.' It is wide and you can drive fast on it."

Another said, "No, we will be better off taking the narrow road 'B.' It has little traffic and we will be able to move faster."

A third one said, "Neither of the roads suggested by you are acceptable to me. There are frequent accidents on the first one, and the second road goes up and down. It shakes all your guts out of you."

The lady said, "No one can shake my guts out of me. My stomach is young and can endure anything. In general, it is not advisable for people to travel if they have old stomachs, and particularly mended stomachs. They are better off sitting at home."

The old gentleman said, "My stomach is not particularly young, but when it comes to endurance it can compete with the most beautiful lady's stomach. However, I love to doze in the car, therefore I recommend to take road 'C.' It goes through fields and villages, and no city noises can be heard."

He tapped the driver on his shoulder, "Please, take road 'C.'"

The other passengers objected loudly. The driver stopped the car and said, "Honorable ladies and gentlemen, I cannot comply with all your suggestions. Therefore, please make a single decision and I will try to abide by it."

The passengers could not agree which road to take.

"I cannot wait any longer," the driver said, "I refuse to drive on. Choose another driver."

One of the gentlemen said, "I'm game. I have spent all my life behind the wheel."

He started moving toward the driver's seat.

Another gentleman exclaimed, "Oh, no! Anyone but you! I rode once in a car which you drove, and still to this day I am grateful to God that I got out of it alive. Let me do the driving."

"No," exclaimed the first one, "we'd be better off with a crab behind the wheel! We will never make it to the beginning of the meeting with you driving."

The first one said again, "Well, perhaps our oldest passenger will undertake driving the car?"

A few started laughing, "We'd be better off having the car drive by itself. We will wind up in the nearest ditch in any case."

"Well, how about you?" the first one turned to the remaining gentleman. "Have you ever driven a car?"

"Yes," he replied. "A few years ago I drove a car over a forest road when my driver suddenly became sick."

"And you probably hit the first tree?" the first passenger asked.

"No," the last passenger answered proudly, "I hit the last tree."

"Well, then only our representative of the fair sex remains."

"I'll gladly do it. I have won several prizes in car racing."

"Oh no!" the youngest gentleman said. "We cannot permit such a disgrace. Several strong men sitting relaxed in the car and a lady drives the car. We will stop all traffic on the road, because all passers-by will stop and look after us."

"Well, what are we going to do then?" asked the first one.

"What are we going to do?" the oldest one said. "We will ask the driver to continue driving."

"Those are wise words for once," everyone agreed.

"Which road shall we take?"

"Well, let's take the first one," said the lady.

Everyone agreed, and got back happily into the car.

"Driver, we request that you resume driving the car, and please take the first road."

"I will not do that," the driver answered.

"Why not? We chose it unanimously."

"Yes, you chose it unanimously, but nevertheless I cannot comply with your request."

"That is something unheard of!" everyone exclaimed in one voice. "What does that mean?"

"You see, my friends, on leaving your city I obtained information about the road conditions. There are bridge repairs on the first road, and it is closed to traffic until tomorrow morning at ten."

"I drove on it just yesterday, and everything was in good shape."

"That was yesterday, my friend," the driver said, "but not today. Not everything that was in good shape yesterday is also in good shape today."

"Why had none of us heard anything about this bridge?"

"Because," the driver replied, "you had no need to hear and know about it. Only I – the driver – had a need to know, because it is my duty to know so that I could get you to your destination successfully and on time."

He started the engine.

Soon the passengers became absorbed in interesting conversations and completely forgot about the driver and the roads.

I conclude. – ★ ★ ★ –          [[2233]]

Alpha                              03/03/67 2308

Chief Spirit Alpha is speaking. Almighty's heralds, let us continue our tiding.

While looking at you, people, one has to be pleased how soft and round your bodies look. On bumping into each other in a crowd, or while passing someone, there are no unpleasant feelings or pain. It almost seems that this causes you pleasant feelings, but it seems like that only while looking at you with human eyes. In reality, you are not all that soft and round.

When looking at you with the eyes of a spirit, you are awkward. One more so, the other one less, but all of you are awkward. Bumping into each other or even being close to another person makes you uncomfortable, and even causes pain of a spiritual nature. That can be particularly felt in a throng or a crowd, but also [holds true in your] personal life.

This awkwardness can be particularly noticed with respect to your neighbors and acquaintances. One individual causes all kinds of problems for another. People slander each other, and notice all the negative phenomena in another person, frequently even imagined ones.

People are different, so different that one can say that there is no human being exactly like another. Similarly, there are no similar faces. Each person has his own unique face. It is surprising that millions of faces have been created, but every one is different. Man has the same face – with one mouth, one nose, two ears, and two eyes – but nevertheless it is still somewhat different for each one.

Unlike a machine, The Almighty does not create everything according to one model. He wants each human to be different. That demonstrates The Almighty's spiritual wealth.

With respect to man's awkwardness, every person should strive to minimize it, if he wants life to be good and pleasant for himself and for all people.

Let us now discuss yet another phenomenon. Let us discuss giving presents, particularly at Christmas. This essentially good habit can also cause many bitter moments. People often give presents which seem to them to be good and desirable, but do not seem like that to the recipient, or else he already has too many of them. Everything that seems unpleasant or of which there is too much already does not bring any joy to the recipient of the present. It even causes surliness, because one has to respond with a gift even to an unusable gift.

How can one minimize unnecessarily wasting money on undesirable gifts, or else completely avoid them?

Selecting presents is one of the more difficult tests [of man's abilities]. If it is possible, try to find out what the recipient would like before buying the presents, or else what he could need. If that is not possible, then try to purchase and give him something that everyone can use or would like. For example, almost everyone likes works of art, but they are expensive and everyone cannot afford them.

When it comes to the recipient of the present, he should never tell the one who gave him the present that he does not need the present, or that he does not like it. You should never say, "I already have it," or, "What am I going to do with it?"

You could say, "Why did you spend so much buying presents? I already respect or love you without any presents."

Neither should you say that you already have so many similar presents that you do not know what to do with them. Still, it is wisest to give items that can be used on a daily basis, because they will nevertheless be used, even if it will take several years for them to be used.

Thus, Alexander is not the least bit concerned that almost everyone gives him shirts. He calmly tells himself, "If I ever become poor, at least I will not have to walk around naked. I will be able to wear at least a shirt."

You should also note that you indicate your displeasure not only in words but also with your conduct and facial expression. Pass completely unusable gifts on to someone else, just as unhappy as you, or simply throw them out in the garbage.

_ ★ ★ ★ _

Let us conclude with that for today. Good morning, heralds. Chief Spirit Alpha.                    [[03/04/67 0021]]

<u>Alpha</u>                                    03/10/67 2030

→Chief Spirit Alpha. Heralds, The Almighty permitted me to reveal to the people still more of that which has not been revealed so far.

It has been said that if a human kills another human, the killer will have to answer before the Judges in Heaven, and that his punishment will be just as severe as his crime. He will be condemned to Hell, and no one will be able to save him.

However, it is now permitted to reveal to the people that an exception has been made. This exception is this. The soul of the person who was killed forgives the killer. In this case the punishment is set aside. The spirit of the guilty one is given the opportunity to remain among the spirits, and to start the work of his redemption with a most difficult task in a new incarnation.

As you have been told, an individual is permitted to defend his life. In the event that it is not possible to accomplish this by any other means, it is permissible to kill the attacker without receiving punishment for yourself. The same can be done while defending another, or other people, against attackers, or else while defending your country against invaders.

Now I will turn to continuing my tiding.

I have noticed that somehow you still cannot get used to the idea that you are heralds and not ordinary people. You think too high of us, the spirits, and too low of yourselves, the heralds. That is particularly conspicuous whenever a chief spirit talks with you. It seems to you that a chief spirit has to talk with you only about particularly important matters. He may not talk with you in a friendly manner about your personal affairs, or else about matters which seem minor to you, and therefore insignificant. However, what is minor and what is significant? It is difficult to tell that, for, in some instances, what seems to be minor may become significant. Similarly, what is considered to be great, can be smaller than the tiniest.←

I will give you two examples, one of them taken from very recent events.

What significance does a temperature difference of one or two degrees have? Generally people consider that as being insignificant. "Well, big deal if it is two degrees warmer today than it was yesterday! After all, that has no significance!" Yes, generally that is the case, but occasionally these two degrees can be tremendously important.

A few days back [[during the night between March 6 and 7]] herald Alexander sat by a radio the whole night long and listened to whether the thermometer will remain two degrees above freezing. Rain was pouring down outside, and the weather forecasters predicted that some three inches of rain could fall. That would mean a disaster for New York, because that would mean ten times the amount as snow. What would happen then to the huge city of millions – New York? So much snow had never yet fallen in this city. What could be done with so much snow? How could it be disposed of, not even considering the millions that this would cost? Altogether, what would happen to the New Yorkers?

By chance, a very large mass of water vapor had accumulated and it threatened to disrupt the New Yorkers' life for a prolonged period. What could be done? The only recourse was to not allow the temperature to drop these two degrees. That was an extremely difficult requirement, and I stood next to Alexander and experienced the same thing that he was. Will the thermometer hold on for these fateful two degrees, or even one?

Hours passed, and the radio kept on announcing the same thing – thirty-four and thirty-three. The night passed. Day came and the thermometer started to fall. By then, however, the rain clouds had already been depleted, and New York was saved.

Can you evaluate how important these two degrees were?

(A five minute intermission.) [[2112 - 2116]]

I am continuing. The other event took place last month, when you had the huge snowfall this year. It was not as deep as is expected this month, but deep enough.

It was Thursday night [[February 9]]. Santorino and I – together with the ruler of Earth, Ilgya – were returning from observing events on the other side of the globe. Then Astra met us and said, "Perhaps the high chief spirits would be willing to visit the heralds to Earth, and the place where they live?"

Santorino replied, "Gladly, but by now it will be after midnight there and they will be asleep."

"Obviously, except for Alexander. Does he need us, though?"

"Not this time. Not directly, but I nevertheless think that he as well as a few others will need you, and even the entire humanity could benefit."

We did not ask any more but continued to fly to New York. On reaching it, we wanted to stop, but Astra said, "Let us fly a little bit further."

We flew over New York, and saw Alexander reading a magazine. New York disappeared. Fields, villages, and forests began. Then suddenly Astra said, "Let's set down now."

We descended somewhat and found ourselves in a clearing of a forest, which was covered with crosses. It was a cemetery. The cemetery was covered by deep snow. A small chapel stood on the edge of the cemetery – a monument to soldiers who had fallen in war. Beyond it on the right and across the road was the church, and still further the monastery buildings. Dark night covered the cemetery. Everything was still, and only the white snow fought against the power of darkness.

We wanted to ask Astra why she had brought us here, but then we suddenly noticed a light in the middle of the cemetery, and approached it. We approached this light, and what did we see? We saw a lantern next to a cross, and a candle inside it. The tiny flame of the candle had bravely fought the snowstorm. With its minute heat it nevertheless had melted the snow around it, even though the snow level reached much higher than it. No tracks led to it. No human footprints lead to the cemetery, and the tiny flame in it had fought for several days all by itself, having been lit six days ago.

We stood there in silence. We did not know what to say. This tiny flame in the dark night – in the snow covered cemetery – left such an impression on us that we could not find the words with which to express it.

Then we heard God's voice, "Almighty's Chief Spirit Alpha and you – My Chief Spirit Santorino and the ruler of the Earth, Ilgya – tell Me, what would you do in My stead on seeing this tiny flame of the candle which prays to Me for those whose bodies lie here, and for the one whose hand lit it? What prayer can compare to the prayer of this tiny flame?

"There are hundreds of graves around it and just as many lanterns, but all of them are empty and dark. In those houses there, the nuns who had been paid to keep the candles burning in the lanterns, sleep soundly, but they found it too difficult to wade through the deep snow. Was that even necessary, for all of those who had paid – who found it too difficult to light the candles on their own – slept soundly in their beds in the distant city and other places, and none of them would come to the cemetery on such a day. As you can see, only this one candle with its quivering light – the tiny flame – prays to Me. I await an answer, high visitors!"

What kind of an answer could we give God? Then came Astra's voice, "Oh, God, how can we, spirits, tell what is difficult even for You to tell, God. Yet, can I answer You with the old words of ancient people, which seem to me appropriate for this occasion, 'And then the gates of Hell collapsed, and the gates to Paradise opened.'"

"Yes," God said, "this tiny little flame is capable of demolishing the gates of Hell and opening the gates to Paradise. Alight to Me in the Deoss Temple. I await you."

We left the tiny flame of the candle to continue its fight for the right to pray to God for the people.

(A ten minute intermission.) [[2207 - 2217]]

We alighted into the Deoss Temple. God was absorbed in a conversation with Satan, and we waited for a little while before He turned to us.

"As you can see for yourselves, sometimes life presents us with situations where it is extremely difficult to find the right solutions. We evaluate the spirits on their arrival here, after their course of life, and make our decisions which at the time seem to us to be correct and just. However, life goes on in Heaven as well as on Earth. The people who remain on Earth continue to live and do not forget the departed ones, and the more intimate and more beloved the departed have been to them, the more they look after the souls of the departed, and knock at the door of the Deoss Temple with their prayers.

"How can we fail to note these prayers, because they testify that the departed are dear to those remaining, and only someone who has done good for those remaining can be dear. Thus, it often turns out that we have to re-evaluate our decision and alter it. That is how it is usually, but it turns out that now only one candle out of many hundreds burned on Earth, and with its tiny flame knocked at the door of the Deoss Temple. In this case, this sole flame spoke to us not only about those for whom it burned, but also about those thousands who did not have burning flames of candles. Thus, it turns out that we have to judge many, and have to evaluate the lives of many people.

"Of course, there are the departed for whom no candles burn, because they have not left any friends on Earth, for they have not tried to ease the lives of other people, but rather have made them harder and have even wrecked them. There are also cases when no candle prays even for good people, because those remaining behind are not people of a grateful nature, but gratitude is the biggest worth of the human soul.

"Christ told people that they do not have to pray to Me, for I already know what they – the people – need. He did that so that people would not constantly burden Me with unimportant appeals. He understood, though, that in particularly important cases it is essential for man to talk to God, and to ask for God's help. He told how that should be done. That should be done so that the individual would be in solitude with God.

"One should not pray to God as much with words as with deeds. To light a candle is a deed, if the one who prays does it. This work can be extremely great, as you saw today.

"The flame of the little candle knocked so loud today at the door of the Deoss Temple that I had to open the door and go to meet it.

"Tell the people that there is nothing that is absolutely great or absolutely small in all cases in life. Similarly, tell the people that there is nothing that is absolutely good or absolutely evil, for it can happen that good can become evil, and evil can become good – depending on the circumstances of life. Thus fire is people's friend under ordinary circumstances, but it can become an enemy in case of a building fire. Thus water sustains people's lives, but the same water can kill people in case of floods or on the sea. Similarly, a knife faithfully serves man, but one day in the hands of a murderer it can kill a person, and so on."

God concluded with that and dismissed us, but along the way from the Deoss Temple we returned once more to the lonely candle, in order to bid it farewell.

Good night, heralds. Alpha. [[2256]]

<br>

Ilgya                    03/17/67 2035

Ilgya. Heralds, I was slightly delayed, please forgive me.

The previous time, the tidings brought up questions which were not anticipated, but events cannot always be anticipated. The event with the lonely candle, burning on the grave, unexpectedly brought up very complicated questions, which are extremely difficult for us – the spirits – to answer on our own. Therefore we decided to seek your help. The questions are:

1. What impression did the light – the prayer – of the lonesome candle leave on those for whom it had been lit?
2. On the one who had lit it?
3. On the nuns, who had not lit the candles, but who had undertaken to do this, and for remuneration at that?
4. And finally, on those who had paid to have the candles lit?

Carefully read over what has been written, and remember the questions. After that, everyone should contemplate his answer for five minutes. The answer of each herald has to be written down. I will give you the necessary time. [[2045]]

I will ask Mary first. [[2050]]

[[Mary replies, "I think that the spirits of the deceased comprehend this and are moved by such attention. b. The one who lit it proves with that, that there has been very much understanding in their life together, and he expresses that with this deed. c. That does not testify of high spirits, because they do not carry out the task which they have undertaken. d. They do not turn out to be high spirits either, because a candle lit for payment does not have as much significance as one that has been lit by the individual himself."]]

I will ask Mary for a specific answer whether the nuns deserve punishment or recognition for their actions – or rather, neglect – and in what manner.

[[Mary answers, "The nuns deserve punishment for their actions. In what manner? I will not say that it should be particularly harsh, because their actions are understandable from the human point of view, but are not justifiable."]]

Thank you. I will ask Janoss now.

[[Janoss replies, "The first one – it should be very pleasant and welcome to those for whom it had been lit, because this proves that they have deserved this. b. The one who lit it demonstrates with this action that they have been intimate in life and have helped each other, as well as expresses his gratitude for their life together. c. Concerning the nuns – everyone who undertakes to do something has to do it. If they fail to do it, they deserve punishment. One can punish only if he knows all the circumstances. d. The ones who paid – if they have not bothered to find out if this has been done, proves that they have not had such deep feelings as the one who lit it himself."]]

Thank you. I will now ask Alexo.

[[Alexo answers, "It testifies something good regarding them, for those for whom the candle was lit, and tries to make up for the differences of opinion that have existed during life. b. The one who lit the candle himself did a very great deed, because despite any weather conditions he always demonstrates his desire to do something good for the departed. c. The nuns should be punished. If they undertake to do something, they have to do it. I will not decide the punishment, because this neglect may have occurred due to circumstances beyond their control. d. The ones who paid also deserve recognition, because many people do not do anything, but those who paid show that they believe in immortality. They had good desires and good intentions, therefore they should not be punished."]]

Thank you. I will now ask Alexander.

[[Alexander replies, "It is difficult for me to answer, because it is my fault that the candle burned. There were two reasons for lighting the candle. First – the departed are not forgotten, and the other – communications are maintained with the departed and with God, so that their sins would be forgiven. I would never have lit it had I known that the neighbors of the departed would suffer. On lighting the candle, I intended it as a prayer for all departed. This answer is also my answer to the two remaining questions, and I have nothing more to add."]]

Thank you. I do not have anything to add either.

Now that you have expressed your ideas, I will announce to you God's answer.

"I ask people to pray to Me with deeds, but not with words. In this case a great deed had been performed. The one who prayed did not pray for himself, but as he just said, for all the departed, and obviously most of all for those whose bodies rest below the candle. That was a great deed – to travel many miles, light the candle, and return. It took many hours. A prayer like this cannot remain without an answer.

"Antonina and Ann were ordinary people, but while making many mistakes, neither of them had committed any sin during their lifetime that deserved punishment. Therefore I have nothing to forgive them. The only thing I could do was provide them a deserved reception, give them rest, and see to it that they will receive appropriate tasks, which will raise their spirits ever higher. The flame of the candle always reminds Me whether I have done everything that I could on their behalf.

"The second question. This candle proves that what Alexander considers to be his duty is not of a passing nature, but lasting for ever and ever. What he has started on Earth he will continue eternally as a spirit, which is – to be with Me and The Almighty in our works.

"The third question. Alexander answered it in fact. Obviously, no one may suffer because of this candle, for otherwise it would lose its significance. You cannot pray for one person so that others will suffer because of him. The nuns could have slept soundly that night, because the candle erased their punishment.

"With respect to those who paid the nuns to keep the candles lit on the graves, they suffer themselves because of their neglect to verify whether that was actually done, for they have spent their money in vain."

That is what God said.

A ten minute intermission. The Divine will speak. [[2132]]

<u>Santorino</u>                        03/17/67 2142

Santorino is speaking. Heralds, God asked me to talk today with the heralds to Earth about a subject which so far has not been sufficiently examined. It concerns the relationship between men and women. This relationship is very complicated, and therefore situations often arise where it is not easy to find the right solution.

You know why The Creator has given passion to all living beings. Passion – in consonance with the big pleasure that beings of the opposite sex obtain by mating – is what makes them give birth to offspring. This means continued birth of the living beings, their increase numerically, and most important – them not dying out.

This passion arises in animals only when the mating season comes. For some that is once a year, for others only every several years, and for still others more often.

For animals, love seldom plays any role whatsoever in this act. Some animals mate and part. Others continue to live together while looking after their offspring. Let us not dwell on zoology, though.

With respect to man, God has given him passion that continues almost the entire human lifetime, and which man can utilize whenever he wants to. Yet, obviously, while giving man this freedom, God asks man not to use it excessively, and particularly if the other person does not want to. Moreover, God does not consider intercourse to be a sin, if both people – the man and the woman – want it, but rape is considered to be a grave sin.

Times have changed and laws have changed, but people have remained the same. Just as always, they love or detest each other. Just as always, they are faithful and unfaithful in marriage.

The struggle with passion has been going on since the first days when human life began, and it will probably continue always. In some lands in ancient times infidelity in marriage was punished by death, but passion won anyway, despite anything. The knights when heading for the Crusades kept their wives – if one may say so – locked up, for they had no other means of trusting their wives. Yet, God is not the only one who knows what they themselves did.

A question now arises. Since virginity is no longer considered as being essential for getting married, only one question arises that bothers the conscience, "Is infidelity in marriage a sin?"

The matter is as follows. If an individual promises in God's presence to be faithful, and then it turns out that he breaks this promise, it is definitely a sin. Therefore it is better not to get married using God's name, because that has become an empty formality anyway. On getting married, no one intends to keep his word – to not part until death parts them. Death seldom parts them these days, obviously, unless the husband or wife helps out.

The most important responsibility of marriage is the children, and raising them to be real people – people of whom their parents can be proud and who will support them in their old age.

It is not important where a marriage was performed – in a church, or in a state office. It is only important to observe the above mentioned rules.

Now that the states begin to assume the responsibility of caring for old people and abandoned children, many things change and life begins to be based on different foundations. Formerly, the principal provider for the family was the husband and father. The door to independence has now opened for the woman as well. She can earn the money which she needs on her own. Laws provide for easy divorce. Therefore, on what can family life be based now?

The old has collapsed. The new has not yet formed sufficiently. It is truly hard to currently say what would be best for man. What can I say at this critical moment in the development of humanity's culture?

One thing is clear – love has to be the basis for marriage. Therefore people have to be very careful in selecting suitable partners in life.

First, marriage requires those who are married to love each other, to try to understand each other, to try to help each other, and most important – to know how and be willing to give in whenever that is essential. One should not try to force what one likes on the other, but should always try to find a happy median. Similarly, one should try to forgive transgressions of marriage, if sometimes they happen unexpectedly, elicited by passion.

It seems to some people that the world is coming to an end, but that is not the case. Everything will be overcome with time, and humanity will continue along its bright road toward the starry future.

The sins that you commit among yourselves are unpleasant, but they are your – human – sins. They have to be settled and punished by the people themselves, in conjunction with people's laws. God does not assume any responsibility for these sins, and neither punishes nor praises them, unless they transform into sins of another category.

With that, we will conclude for today. Good night to all those who are tired. Santorino. [[2238]]

→Heralds, today we will discuss some matters which still have remained unexamined, or examined incompletely.

Christ and the apostles spoke about the coming of the Antichrist. Humanity thinks about the Antichrist all the time, but is not sure who that might be. Has he already been here, or is he yet to come? Some people considered Nero, Caligula, and still other Roman rulers to be the Antichrist. Roman Catholics considered Luther as the Antichrist, and Luther considered the Pope in Rome to be the Antichrist.

This matter seems complicated. Yet even though many personalities seemed to correspond to the Antichrist, the Roman Catholic clergy nevertheless corresponded the most. They took on this role completely, particularly during the Middle Ages. Popes called themselves Christ's deputies on Earth, but while exploiting the name of Christ, made a mockery of Christ's teachings. They committed the most vicious crimes in the name of Christ. They tortured people, burned them at stakes, and so on.

Thus, as you can see, this prophecy was realized completely. As you have been told previously, it reached such proportions that God was overcome by despair. Yet people managed to break the power of this Antichrist, and it disappears slowly from the face of Earth.

That was the greatest test for man, and in the end he passed it. The road to a beautiful future opened before humanity.

Humanity gained the experience – not to believe the word, but to believe in deeds. If the deeds do not correspond to the teaching, then those who preach the teaching are impostors, and are Antichrists.

Now I want to talk some more about The Almighty's faith, which has been passed on through you. What does this new faith witness?

It witnesses exactly the same thing that Christ's faith witnessed. However, while based on Christ's teachings, it extends human knowledge about the spiritual world. This is indispensable for the new humanity, armed with new opportunities in science.

Similarly, it supplements Christ's teachings with a more detailed knowledge of the responsibilities of people, as well as with that about which Christ had talked but His disciples either omitted it from their writings, or else expressed it incorrectly. Besides that, these teachings summon humanity to return to the pure teachings of Christ, by casting aside all the superfluous laws which the priests have instituted in their own teachings, in Christ's name.

In particular, this summoning of people to a constant praying to God, from morning until night, must be discontinued. Praying just for the sake of praying [is meaningless], because these prayers are completely useless and there is no need to do that. If you are going to pray, then pray only for that which is essential for you.

As life has demonstrated, it is difficult for man to get used to the idea that [he does not have to] pray to God, for God to hear him and come to his aid – should that benefit man, and particularly his spirit.

As has been repeated several times in the Tidings, man's existence is not the most important consideration. Carrying out the task of man's spirit is. If man's prayer does not benefit the execution of this task of his spirit, then God refuses to help man.

Man had to undergo the most difficult evaluations before he was finally able to prove that he will be able to achieve The Almighty's goal, envisaged for him.

With respect to the horrors in communist countries, they have nothing to do with the Antichrist, because they do not take place in the name of God, but in the name of man.←

(A five minute intermission.) [[2114 – 2119]]

→Just to what extent the Catholic clergy was inclined to keep people from learning the true teachings of Christ, and instead let them know only that which they themselves had invented – in the name of Christ – is proved by them burning William Tyndale at the stake in the year one thousand five hundred and thirty-six. They burned him because he translated the Bible into the English language. What better proof does one need, that this church was the Antichrist?

Once this Antichrist faith had formed, obviously, new priests did not have any choice and opportunity of not following it, for the same punishment – burning at the stake – threatened them. You can see how frightful was the power of this Antichrist. Even now, its influence has not been dissipated completely, but people have already understood its untruths and are returning to the true faith of Christ. Therefore, one should not keep people from attending churches, or ridicule their priests, but should strive to gradually transform the church so that it will become a true house of Christ.

The Almighty's faith, for the time being, is intended only for the chosen people, and its imposition by force is not permissible. It has to convince the people that it is the true teachings of The Almighty, which lead toward a mutual understanding with The Almighty and are intended for the good of humanity.

The promulgators of The Almighty's teachings must not be surprised by any criticism of them, and by other forms of attack by their enemies. Nothing in this faith asks for anything that might be harmful to man.

The revelation of the sins of the old church is necessary for the people, because it is the truth. The truth may not be concealed, and this concealment cannot be justified, regardless of who may [have sinned], even though he might be called Christ's deputy on Earth – the Pope.

With respect to God helping people, the people, themselves, have to try to help themselves first. In cases of illnesses, they have to turn to physicians first, and then have to abide by their instructions, because the physicians know better what the patients need. In case of some sicknesses – as Alexander told Mary today, and quite correctly, too – death may come swiftly, unless all possible remedies are utilized against it.

The situation is particularly difficult with old people, for the tissues of their bodies are worn out, and succumb easily to the consequences of diseases. Thus, at times, it is difficult even for God to do anything.

_ ★ ★ ★ _

With that we will conclude for today. Chief Spirit Santorino wishes you a good night.←                    [[2255]]

William Tyndale                    03/25/67 1346

The high spirit William is speaking. Heralds, since you were wasting your valuable time looking for my family name in all the books in the world, the Divine had me liberate you today from this inhuman torment.

During the conversations yesterday, exactly when my name was mentioned, the high spirit Martin Luther arrived, and while greeting him neither the Divine nor we – the other spirits – noticed that you had perceived and written down my family name incorrectly. It should be written – Tindale. In some foreign languages it should be written with a "y."

Once The Almighty's envoy had alighted away, Martin and I remained for the reading of the Tidings, and discovered the mistake which had been made. Since it was already late, the Divine had me correct it today.

I want to give you some other detailed facts as well. I was born in the year one thousand four hundred ninety, and was burned to death – to the joy of the Catholic Antichrist – in the year one thousand five hundred and thirty-six. I completed translating the Gospel, but not the entire Bible, in the year one thousand five hundred and twenty-five.

It is not particularly easy for me to talk and to correctly give you the dates on Earth, therefore please read back my tiding.

[[It is read back.]]

Thank you. Everything is in order now.

I lived at the same time as Martin Luther. He started translating the Gospel into German a few years after my translation. Luther is extremely interested in your Tidings, and has expressed a desire to talk with you one of these days. God has agreed to that, except the specific day has not been set yet.

With that, I bid you farewell. Martin and William. [[1405]]

Alpha                                   03/31/67 2054

→Chief Spirit Alpha speaking. Almighty's heralds to the planet Earth, I will deviate slightly from my previously planned program. Instead, I will talk about what upset you today and yesterday – the Gospel, and how the apostles, in some places, wrote differently about the same events.

The question about the Gospel is a difficult one. The problem is that the apostles had little education, and some had no education at all. Therefore, not every one of them could write on his own. They had to find someone who knew how to write, and these literate ones were not all that literate either. They made many errors. Obviously, the errors only multiplied with further transcription of their writings.

We attempt to correct the most serious mistakes, but it is not possible to correct all of the Gospel. Neither is it possible to write a new Gospel, for then such confusion would arise that nothing could be understood, as compared with the old text. Besides, the old text is so engraved in the memory of the people, and has grown so much together with man's consciousness, that it is not good to alter it now. No one would benefit from that. Let the old texts remain as they are, for after all, they do reveal what is most important. Besides that, one has to realize that in those ancient times, people's thinking and comprehension of life were different. All that cannot be transferred into a new book.

We examine closely everything that is necessary for current man, and we tell you that man must carry out God's laws. Life has changed tremendously today, and man himself has changed, as well. During

Christ's day people were rude. Their nature was similar, and their laws were merciless. They demanded that people be either rulers or slaves.

There were many small nations, and all of them fought for their place on Earth. In order to make land available for themselves, they quite often killed off its former inhabitants, or else, in the best cases, turned them into slaves. Also, they often – particularly the conquering savage nations – destroyed not only the people, but also the cities which they had built, thus completely destroying some highly developed cultures.

Christ could not change all of that at once, and not even over a prolonged period of time. He had to base His teachings on the old culture, and bring His new spirit of divine love into it. He said several times that He had not come to tear down the old teachings, but only to supplement them.

Considering the subject of Christ's death, and His words, spoken on the cross while dying, which have been passed on to humanity in various ways, the Divine decided to tell you about Christ's last hours on Earth in one of the forthcoming tidings.←

I have to go over to the Deoss Temple, therefore I announce a ten minute intermission. [[2126]]

Four more minutes. [[2137 - 2142]]

Let us continue. I want to tell you about yourselves.

You do not fully understand your own situation, as well as The Almighty's laws. You are chosen people and belong more to the realm of the spirits than to Earth. You are not being judged according to what position you hold in the work of the Tidings, but rather according to your success in this work. This work is considered to be so important that if a herald has functioned as one even for a very brief period, this work will be evaluated much higher, compared to other people's work. Each individual who will personally or otherwise help in disseminating the Tidings, will be particularly rewarded in the realm of the spirits. Everyone has to know and consider this, while looking at the future of his spirit.

Let us talk a little bit now about people. Some people claim that no one loves them. You see, if not more, then at least one or two people love the people who are around them, but no one loves them. Why is that the case? Because people are bad? In that case they would not love anyone! The matter is as follows, and the unfortunate, unloved person does not think about it – it could be his own fault. Perhaps he does not love anyone either, and behaves so that no one has any bases for loving him.

Love does not come unearned, just as people's respect. Sometimes you see the so-called life of the party. Whenever he enters a room, almost everyone welcomes him with visible joy, and gathers around him.

However, when you enter no one seems to notice you. Yes, people are different, and neither is their spiritual wealth the same, but everyone can do much good on his own behalf.

First, you should not wait for an invitation from others but should start conversing with people on your own, and utilize the spiritual talents that you have been given. You should become interesting. That can be accomplished by a good knowledge of literature. You should also read some humor magazines and memorize a few good jokes. Yet, mainly, you should be simple, friendly, and helpful. You should also observe tact and not become obtrusive. Then it will turn out that it is not the case at all that no one loves you.

Some people may ask why the high spirits talk about trifles in life. I will tell you that there is no such thing as a trifle in life – everything in life is important. That is particularly true of trifles, because they occur every day. The important questions, or events, seldom come about, and sometimes, for some people, never in their entire life.

The heralds have to be particularly careful, because each unpleasant trifle becomes significant with respect to a herald, and with respect to great people in general.

→There is still another important consideration. People say that children are not responsible for their parents. Perhaps that is true, but how about the question regarding the parents? Does this also mean that parents are not responsible for their children? No, they are, and very much so!

The parents are responsible for the upbringing of their children and for seeing to it that they become honest, and worthy of their name of man. Should the father and mother not do that, they commit a crime against the future of their children, as well as against the entire society. I have to announce to you that a very harsh punishment threatens the guilty ones, for this failure to carry out the task of parents.←

I wanted to talk some more with you, but my duties urgently call me. Therefore I take leave from you and wish you a good night. Also, on behalf of the spirits who are intimate to you and of myself, I congratulate Mary on her name day tomorrow, and wish her success in the work of the Tidings, as well as in her personal life.

Similarly, I congratulate Janoss on his return to his desk and on shaking off the nasty disease from his shoulders. I also wish him the strength to accomplish the high task, as well as look after his family's happiness and provide it with everything that is necessary, and at times also not necessary.

I pass God's blessing on to both heralds.
Chief Spirit Alpha.           [[2225]]

# Chapter XIII

# April 1967

Inrak is speaking. Heralds, today I have to replace the Divine, who has to be in the Deoss Temple. The same thing is also true of Ilgya.

I want to talk today about the currently popular topic – God has died. Almost all magazines examine this subject. Some are even published with a black cover and the eerie headline, "God has Died."

It would be interesting to ask these wise people exactly when God died and from what disease. Also, why didn't He turn to the famous physicians on Earth? Perhaps He could have been saved. Or else, did He perhaps perish in an accident? If The Creator of the universe has perished, then why doesn't something in the universe testify about that? Billions of stars continue along their way! Life on the planets proceeds as always!

They claim that God has died, but do they know God? Have they ever seen Him or heard His voice?

What kind of a god can be the one whom they call God? Yes, perhaps their god can die, but not the God who created the universe and who directs its fate. He was never born, and He cannot die either.

Idol gods could die. It was so easy to burn them or otherwise destroy them, but no one can destroy the true God. He could not kill Himself on His own, even if He wanted to, for He is everywhere. He encompasses the entire universe and is almighty.

On what do these God's murderers base themselves – for they cannot be called differently – because no one else talks about the possibility of God dying, except for these know-it-alls. They base themselves on the point of view that God does not act the way they want Him to act.

They want God to not allow wars, but allow them to do anything, even call God dead. If they cannot understand God, that does not mean that God has to immediately die.

Who is God? God is the ruler of the universe – of the entire ungraspable universe – but not merely the ruler of the small planet Earth.

These screamers base themselves on the point of view that the ruler is a king, but can only a king be the ruler? The enemies of kings and even their murderers can become rulers, as for example Joseph in Russia.

You will nevertheless claim that he was not a king but the head of the government. Yet, this head of the government was worse than the worst king in all of humanity's history. He claimed that he acted on behalf of the people – people, none of whom were allowed to say what they wanted to, but only what Joseph permitted.

At the beginning of history – when man barely began to realize that he was a human being but not a beast or an animal – no individual considered himself entirely free to do whatever he wanted. He had to obey the elder of the band, for even a small group of people could not exist without a leader. When the number of people increased and the bands had to live next to each other, in order not to fight each other, they had to unite and select a leader, who was called king later on.

The realms of kings existed for a long time, until the development of people advanced sufficiently. Some nations which could not stand the rule of a bad king, overthrew him and established republics. Even the freest people could not get by without a government, and they elected a president and a parliament. The parliament enacted laws, and the president governed the people in consonance with them.

Yes, a president could replace a king, but who can replace The Almighty? Even though He rules the people similarly to a king, in addition, He is the one who decides the people's fate. He possesses characteristics that no human has, and therefore even the most brilliant man cannot replace The Almighty.

While being almighty, though, The Almighty cannot rule the people without laws, but as you know even whoever enacts the laws has to obey the laws which he has enacted. The Almighty did not want to rule a bunch of slaves. He wanted to see man able to develop and become worthy of His almighty spirit. The vast majority of people want to be free in molding their destiny – in forming a life that is just and happy for everyone.

Man's base instincts also exist, and they are still quite powerful and the fight against them is difficult. Sometimes a group of people takes over the leadership of a nation by utilizing beautiful slogans which promise happiness. Having won and being unable to institute their beautifully sounding slogans in life, which are unsuitable for life, they use the help of terror in order to retain people in their power.

Similarly, some wars break out between countries. All that causes people to suffer and to starve.

God could have stopped all that. However, then He would have to deprive man of the free will which he has been given. He would also have to order those who shout that God has died, to close their mouths and shout, "Long live God!" What would those who deny God say then?

The Almighty announced His will to the people through the prophets and through Christ, and now through the Tidings, but He simultaneously leaves man his free will. If this man's free will deviates from The Almighty's or God's laws, humanity ends up in a calamity, starts to wage wars, or else succumbs to erroneous appeals and winds up in the power of villains. Of course, humanity has to pay for that, and at times very dearly, but it learns from these mistakes, and nevertheless, while stumbling and falling, it moves ever closer to its bright goal.

In order to comprehend The Almighty, people also have to see what The Almighty does for the benefit of humanity. Nothing that is alive can exist without the participation of The Almighty's spirit.

Man considers that he has created and directs his body, but is that entirely the case? First of all, man cannot create himself. A father and mother are needed for that. Do the father and mother, though, have complete control over the child to whom they give birth? No, because some mothers and some fathers very much desire a son, but a daughter is born. Therefore, they are not the masters of their own bodies.

Man has a brain. It performs many important functions in the human body, but this brain is not completely independent in its work. A spirit, God's spirit, directs it. Only one part of the brain – the thinking part – is left under man's own control.

What I told you today is only an insignificant part of what I could still tell you, but it suffices in order to respond to the people who claim that God has died. "It is not God who has died, but rather you are the ones who have died!"

To consider God as having died is the worst sin that a human can commit, and a human like that has truly died to eternity.

Good night, heralds.          [[2210]]

<u>Ilgya</u>                                04/14/67 2031

Ilgya. Heralds, in half-an-hour the Divine will talk with you about Christ, but not about His last hours. He will talk about Christ's expressions in the Gospel, which raise questions. Therefore, during this half-an-hour, prepare your questions regarding Christ's expressions which seem incomprehensible to you, or else do not correspond to the spirit of Christ's teachings.

So, kindly start.          [[2035]]

The Divine will speak immediately. [[2100]]

<u>Santorino</u>                    04/14/67 2100

→Santorino speaking. Heralds, almost two thousand years have passed since Christ spoke unto the people, and taught them how to live without sinning and how to avoid Hell, or else achieve Paradise.

Much has changed since that time. Man has become different. From a child, man has grown into a youth. He has learned much, from God as well as from life. The current people know what the people of that time knew. The people of that time, however, did not know what today's people know.

Even though many thousands of years had passed from man's first days on Earth, to the birth of Christ, man was still rude, and his deeds were similar. Christ talked with these people, but not with you. He spoke so that the people of that time could understand Him. He had to base His teachings on the concepts of those times about God, man, and his laws and habits. Therefore, you find much in His speeches that now seems brutal to you. People had gods prior to Him. Yet these gods, like the people themselves, were both good gods and evil gods. The benevolence of the gods had to be bought by sacrifices. Some gods, but not all gods, demanded good deeds from man, but also great sacrifices, for only with them was it possible to obtain the benevolence of the gods.

One talked little of love and in a limited sense. Christ was the first one to call Love, God, and to call God, Love. This means, everything must be based on love, and man must base his life on love. Only when love will completely vanquish evil, Paradise will be able to come to Earth. However, that required an almost complete alteration of man. Such a complete alteration was not possible in a few years, or in a few centuries, but was possible only over thousands of years.

Overall, the more cultural part of humanity has achieved very much along its pathway toward Paradise. Not only the noblest individual people, but even several of the more educated states, have recognized Christ's demands of helping the poor and the old, as well as the sick and the unfortunate ones.

These states do not call these laws of Christ, or rather of God, God's laws, but rather their own state laws. There is no great significance in what these laws are called. The important thing is that these laws are, and that they exist.

Now let us turn to examining the Gospel, and its evaluation. As you know for yourselves, only one of the four books of the new faith was written by the hand of one of Christ's apostles. It is the Book of John. The others have been written by the apostles' disciples, or else based on the words of the apostles. Obviously, because of this method of writing, much that is important was omitted, and much was related incorrectly.

Then came translations into other languages, and errors were made again. Particularly, by translating some words incorrectly the meaning of certain sentences was altered partially or even completely.

Much again has become incomprehensible due to the great changes in times, and has been interpreted incorrectly. For example, as you already know for yourselves, Christ's expression that, "It is easier for a camel to pass through the eye of a needle, than for a rich man to enter Heaven."

This expression seemed completely absurd, for people did not know that, at the time of Christ, an extremely narrow gate of Jerusalem was called the eye of a needle.←

(A ten minute intermission.) [[2142 - 2152]]

Let us continue now.

Try to let your hands move completely freely.

→Approximately one third of Christ's deeds and speeches are missing from the Gospel. Much has been translated incorrectly, or else has been altered. Since it is not possible to write a new Gospel, and since it would no longer have a major significance, we will correct only a little bit of it, and only what is most important. We will leave the remainder as it is.

First of all, I would like to hear from you about what in the Gospel is incomprehensible to you, or what seems to be incorrect. Please begin.

[[Mary asks whether the Holy Spirit truly appeared in the form of a dove, at the time when John baptized Jesus in the Jordan River.]]

That truly was the case, and I fail to see anything in this event that could be incomprehensible to you.

[[Mary reads the first verse from Christ's Sermon on the Mount, "Blessed are they who know their spiritual poverty, for theirs is the Kingdom of Heaven."]]

Read the entire Sermon.

[[Mary continues to read:

Blessed are they who mourn, for they shall be comforted.

Blessed are the gentle, for they shall inherit the Earth.

Blessed are those who are hungry and thirsty for righteousness, for they shall be satisfied.

Blessed are the merciful, for they shall obtain mercy.

Blessed are the pure in heart, for they shall see God.

Blessed are the peacemakers, for they shall be called God's sons.

Blessed are those persecuted on account of righteousness, for theirs is the Kingdom of Heaven.

Blessed are you when they slander and persecute you, and falsely accuse you of every wrong because of Me.

Be glad and supremely joyful because in Heaven your reward is rich!]]

This Sermon was told to the people of that time. It is correct overall, except for certain expressions, as in the first point. One has to say that it has been passed on to the people awkwardly by the writer of the Gospel. All these many divisions into many verses have become antiquated, and they are not worth repeating, for as you know, neither the paradise of those times, nor the hell of those times, exist any more. Christ has expressed the foundation of His teachings more correctly and more concisely in other places.

Mainly though, He stressed that God does not need those people who act arrogant and consider themselves to be better than others. Rather, God needs those people who have pure souls and who are humble. He always stressed that those who want to achieve the Kingdom of Heaven may not be conceited, but rather have to be obedient to God. Similarly, those who want to follow Christ must set themselves free from all earthly bonds. God, as the Father of all people, must be held in higher esteem than all people, even your father and mother, brothers, sisters, and so on.

The words "hate them" are incorrect. Christ said, "Do not honor them higher than Me, and do not love them more than Me."

What else would there be?

[[Mary reads Mathew 15:26, in which a woman asks Christ to save her sick daughter. Christ replies that one has to consider higher people first, and only then dogs.]]

I have already said that what sounds unpleasant to your ears now, sounded different back then, for back then one nation quite often considered another as a nation of dogs.

Obviously, Christ spoke in this manner so that people would understand that even those people whom they considered to be like dogs could hope for God's help if they believed in Him strongly.

[[Alexo says that his questions have already been answered in the previous explanations.]]

[[Janoss asks about the authority given to the apostles to absolve sins, as well as about leading into temptation. The heralds themselves answer these questions in their discussions.]]

Obviously, there are some differences of opinion among the four books. I have already told you, though, that there is no longer any sense in correcting all of them, for that will no longer give anything to today's humanity. The greatest difference of opinion among the evangelists is in the end, with respect to Christ's last words, but I will talk about them in the tiding about Christ's last hours on Earth.

Should you still come up with some truly important questions, I will answer them in my next tiding, or in one shortly after that.← I will also ask you to collect by next Friday, from appropriate books, all possible information about pronouncing a curse, and how it has turned out to be right with respect to some historic persons. Also, contemplate why the curse has worked.

I want to make it a little bit easier for you to give your answer.

As you have been told before, a part of the father's and mother's spirit enters a child's spirit, but can a child's spirit also enter his mother and father?

Let us now discuss a particularly important matter.

What is love? Everyone talks about it, but who, in fact, knows what love really is?

One individual says, "I love my father and mother."

Another says, "I love my wife."

A third one says, "I love my children."

Then someone says, "I love our president."

Millions of people said, "I love Stalin."

Other millions said, "I love Hitler."

Several millions say, "I love the Virgin."

Someone says, "I love my friend Andy."

Someone else whispers in his maid's ear, "I love you, Kate."

A bearded man takes the pipe from his mouth and while looking at it lovingly, says, "I love my pipe more than anything else in the world."

Many people say the same thing about their houses.

A child babbles, "I love ice cream more than anything else in the world."

When you ask him, "Even more than your mother?" the child will answer without thinking, "Yes."

Well, what is love after all? We have to say first that the word "love" is used in the right and the wrong places. By loving everything we do not love anything and anyone, because it is not possible to love everything.

You may like chocolate, but you cannot love it. Love is of a spiritual nature, but quite often it is bound to matter. Parents are bound to their children doubly – spiritually, and also through the matter from which their bodies have been formed.

The purest love of course is a mother's love with respect to her children. A father's love should also be the same, but this poor thing is not sure whether all of his children are really his. You see, this question becomes extremely important, if it is taken seriously. Why? Because as you already know, parts of the parents' spirits incarnate in the child. If this child, however, is born from a lover, then the father – the father by marriage – has nothing in common with him.

That explains why a child, or several children, are often very different and have none of their father's characteristics, neither spiritual nor physical.

Yes, heralds, you are people and modern people at that, so tell me what to do with this love which has never, or rather – very seldom, acknowledged God's as well as human laws?

If love, after all, does not acknowledge any laws, and people could not force it to do so with death or with other most horrible punishments, and now it becomes almighty, what are we going to do with it, heralds?

Perhaps you will find a sensible answer by next Friday.

Good night, heralds. Santorino. [[2300]]

<br>

<u>Nakcia</u>                    04/21/67 2101

Nakcia is speaking. The Divine will not speak today, because all of you have not been able to assemble your answers. He will talk on Orthodox Easter Sunday about Christ's last hours on Earth. The tiding is planned to start at twelve o'clock in the day. It has not been announced yet whether he will speak next Friday.

Today I will tell you a story which we will call – A Different Person.

One night a young man wandered along the semi-dark streets of a small town. He had arrived in town from a large city just that evening. He walked along the street and looked into the dark windows. Everyone was already asleep.

Why had he come here? Let us try to find that out.

He had been born in a large city, in the family of wealthy parents. His parents devoted much effort to bring him up to be a decent and educated individual.

Everything went fine. Then one day he met a very imposing young man. He was the leader of a gang of robbers. In a short while, he talked our young man into joining his gang. He claimed that by doing that he would quickly become rich and could live as he pleased.

Initially the gang engaged in theft and in robbery on the streets. It turned out, though, that the loot did not suffice for their extensive carousing, and they decided to start breaking into homes.

Things went well for a while, but then someone who had been robbed spotted one of the gang members sitting in a restaurant. He rushed off to the police station, and the police headed for the restaurant. In the meantime, all members of the gang had gathered there, except for our young man and the leader of the gang.

The robbers who had been caught were sentenced to several years in jail. The two who had not been in the restaurant headed for another large city, in order to evade the police.

After their escape, the police went to the homes of their parents. The parents of the gang leader were also arrested, and were convicted of possession of stolen goods in their apartment. The parents of our young man were so crushed that his mother died in a few days. His father sold everything that he had and went abroad. He said that he does not have a son, but that he curses the one who calls himself his son, and no longer wants to hear anything about him.

After this treachery, the two remaining robbers decided to play it safe, and kill those whom they had robbed, in order not to leave any witnesses. That was obviously an atrocious decision, and our young man refused to kill, leaving this work to the leader.

Everything went fine for a while, but then one night they wound up in an apartment with several members of a family. The leader said that he could not kill that many people by himself, and that he needed help. When our young man refused, the leader responded that in such case he had no other choice than to also kill Peter – that is what our young man was called. Peter had to give in.

Everything went well for the time being, but then they happened to break into the apartment of a merchant. When they were getting ready to leave and wanted to kill the people whom they had robbed, the merchant fell down at the leader's feet, kissed them, and said, "What will you gain by killing us?"

"What will I gain?" the leader asked. "You will not turn us in."

"I swear by all the saints and by my father's remembrance that we will not tell anyone."

When the leader nevertheless wanted to start killing, the old man said, "If I were to provide you another hundred thousand tomorrow, would you spare us then?"

"Where will you get this hundred thousand?"

"I will withdraw it from the bank, and will deliver it to wherever you tell me, at one o'clock tomorrow."

"How can I believe you?"

"I give you my word of honor, and you will not risk anything, but you will lose these thousands by killing me."

The leader thought for a while. "Well, all right, I will believe you, but if you will fail to provide me this money, I will kill you and your old lady. Thus you will not escape death in any case."

Truly, the old man brought the money at the appointed time and place.

However, when his fear had subsided in a few days, he nevertheless turned in the robbers, wanting to get his money back.

After the police had watched the leader for a while, they learned were he lived, and broke into his apartment.

Peter had gone out to buy some drinks. When he saw a crowd of people on the street in front of his building, he understood that something bad had happened. He asked a man standing next to him what had happened. Yes, the police had broken into the robbers' apartment. There had been shooting and one of the bandits was killed, but the police is looking for the other.

At that moment Peter saw the bloody corpse of his companion carried from the apartment and placed in an ambulance wagon. He waited no longer, and vanished in a side street.

He acknowledged that the leader's tactics had been right, and that under no circumstances should he leave anyone alive, no matter how he pleads and what millions he promises. He continued robbing, and did not leave any witnesses alive.

Everything went perfect, but then on coming out the door after a robbery, he noticed a man with a black beard standing on a street corner. While Peter considered what to do now, the bearded man had vanished. Peter ran to the corner, but saw that there was no longer anyone on the street.

He had no choice but to leave the city. He was sure that the next morning, on reading in the papers about the murder in such and such a building, the bearded man will tell the police that he had seen the murderer leaving the murder scene with bundles in his hands. Therefore he had to leave the city as soon as possible.

Thus he had wound up in this small town. While running in fright, he had abandoned on the street the bundles with the loot, but there had been very little cash. Peter thus wandered along the streets of the small town while thinking about how to obtain money.

He suddenly noticed a light in the window of a small two-story house. Having walked up to the window, he saw through the thin curtains and old woman sitting on the edge of her bed and arranging her gray hair.

"Nothing much can be hoped for here," he thought, "but sometimes these old women sew a bundle of money into their mattress."

He looked around. The streets were empty and the house windows dark. He walked up to the door while thinking about how to get in through it. He pushed down the door handle and as a wonder the door opened. It had not been locked. He slowly entered the hallway, and heard the old woman's voice, "Is that you, son?"

(A ten minute intermission.) [[2214 - 2224]]

Peter did not answer and walked into the room.

The old woman stood up, looked in the direction of the door, and said, "My eyes have become rather weak. I cannot see you that well."

"No, I am not your son. I am a stranger, and came in because your door was not locked and I am very hungry. Is there anything left over from dinner?"

"Why, of course! My son's dinner is in the oven and I can find a few other things as well. Just come, sit down at the table."

She started to fumble with the stove while saying, "I do not lock the door thinking that my son will come soon, but he probably has remained...."

She grew silent.

"Where has he remained?" Peter asked.

The old women wiped off her tears, "Well, wherever he went five years ago by now. I nevertheless wait for him every evening. After all, he was my only son."

"Don't you know where he went?"

"No, he went to the big city and disappeared. All these five years he has not written one word about himself."

"And you make dinner for him every evening?"

"Why, of course, how can I know that he will not show up, and just like you perhaps he will be hungry. Well, please son, sit down at the table."

She raised her head and looked into Peter's face. "You look very much like he, but you nevertheless are not Andy. I am used to calling all young men 'son,' therefore don't get mad if I also call you 'son'."

"Why should I get mad? It sounds so kind of you, for, you see, my mother no longer calls me – son."

"Why not?"

"Because she has died."

"Oh, poor little orphan! Such a good boy and without his mother."

"How do you know that I am good?"

"With my old heart I can feel who is good and who is bad."

"And your heart," Peter asked while eating, "tells you that I am good? Perhaps I am bad, very bad?"

"No, son, my heart tells me that you are good."

She walked up to his back and started stroking his hair. "You have such soft hair, just as my son's, except it has not been combed for a long time. Go ahead and eat son, I will comb it for you."

She came back with a comb and started combing Peter's hair.

"You really treat me like my mother. May I call you – mother?"

"Of course, son, who would refuse an orphan to have him call her – mother?"

The old woman returned to her bed. "My son was called Andy. What is your name?"

"Pe...," Peter wanted to say, but then stopped abruptly.

"What did you say?" the old woman asked. "I did not hear you."

"Yes, I'm called Francis."

"Francis? What an unusual name!"

"What can you do if your parents give it to you?"

"Yes, that's how it is," sighed the old woman.

Peter felt that he had eaten enough, and walked into the kitchen to get a drink of water. He stopped there and thought, "What should I do now? Such a kind old woman, and I will have to strangle her! First I have to find out if she has any money."

He came out of the kitchen, sat down next to the old woman on her bed, and said, "You see, mother, I am all out of money. Could you lend me some for a few days?"

"Oh son, I'm doing rather poorly when it comes to money. Take a look in my purse on the dresser, how much is there?"

Peter walked over and opened her purse, but there was hardly any money in it. "Is that all the money you have?"

"Yes, son, where am I, a poor old woman, to get it? I can no longer work. I get something now and then for baby sitting."

"How much do you have sewn into your mattress?"

"In my mattress? How could you have imagined that? Even the straw in it is getting rather thin, let alone money. If you don't believe me, go look for yourself!"

"No mother, I was only joking."

He stood up and walked out to see if there was anyone on the street, but the street was deserted. He came back, and sat down again next to the old woman.

He reached out with his hands and approached the old woman's neck, but the old woman grabbed them and started kissing them. "Oh son, you wanted to caress me!"

She placed her head against his chest. "You are so dear. Could you come and be my son? I will love you very much. My son's room is empty. You could live in it. I could arrange for a good job for you, and we would live happily!"

"Yes, that would be nice – too nice," Peter said, "but that is not possible."

"Why, son, is that not possible?"

"That is not possible," Peter mumbled. "I have to go now, but I will ask you not to tell anyone that you have seen me."

"Why not, son? After all, you are so kind to me, as to your own mother."

"Oh yes, my mother, my mother," Peter mumbled again, and tears appeared in his eyes.

"Well, all right, if you don't want me to, I will not tell anyone."

"Yes, don't tell anyone. Perhaps I will return some day, and then I will tell you why I did not want you to tell anyone."

"You know best, son, I will not tell anyone."

"Can I believe you?"

"Oh, son, and you still doubt me?"

"No, I no longer doubt you. But it really is time now for me to go."

He stood up and wanted to leave.

"Wait son, I completely forgot! I have some money saved up. You see, my eyesight gets weak and I need an eye operation. The physician said that he will come tomorrow and take me to the hospital. But you, son, probably need this money more. I can still see a little bit."

She reached under her pillow and pulled out some money wrapped in a small rag.

Yes, that was money! He could live on it for a little while. He took the money, kissed the old woman, and started to leave.

When he was already by the door, the old woman exclaimed, "Son, you left the money on the table! Here, take it! I will hand it to you."

She stood up, picked up the money which Peter had left on the table, and rushed toward the door. Her strength gave out, she fell down, and the money, while clanging, started rolling along the floor.

Peter returned, lifted the old woman from the floor, and laid her on her bed. He picked up the scattered money, wrapped it in the small rag, and put it under her pillow. Then he sat down on the edge of her bed, started to stroke the old woman's hair, and thought, "Oh mother, mother, where are you?"

He recalled his childhood, his mother's loving arms – the soft, caressing arms – and the kisses, the many wet but pleasant kisses. He remembered that he had been sick, and the physician had said that he would probably not recover. It was a difficult struggle with death. His mother hardly left him for a moment. She sat on a chair by his bed, changed his compresses, and gave him medicine. She would not let anyone else look after him, and she was so tired that sometimes at night she fell out of her chair – but she conquered death.

The physician said, "You have performed a miracle!"

Yes, that was his mother, and how did he pay her back? He pressed his hands against his temple, as though wanting to squeeze these unbearable memories from his head.

Then came the old woman's voice, "Son, go lie down in the bed and rest. I feel well enough by now."

"No mother, allow me to stay with you and hold your hand."

"Do as you want to, son."

"Mother, dear, if I were to do something bad, something evil, could you forgive me?"

"Of course I could, son!"

"What do you think, could my mother also do that?"

"Why yes, son! Every mother can do that."

"Are you convinced that my mother has forgiven me all the evil that I have done to her?"

"Of course, son! A mother and God can forgive their sons everything."

Peter asked in surprise, "You said that God, too – and you believe that?"

"There is nothing to believe here. That is how it is!"

"Oh mother, how I thank you for these words! You gave me a new life."

"Will you stay with me? You will not leave me?"

"No mother, I will no longer leave my mother. The physician will come tomorrow, he will operate on your eyes, and you will be able to see what your new son looks like."

(A five minute intermission.) [[2346 – 2351]]

Thus began Peter's new life.

The daughter of the old woman's sister came over in the morning, in order to prepare everything for the physician's arrival. Surprised, she met Peter in the doorway.

The old woman exclaimed, "Don't be surprised, my son has returned!"

She was even more surprised now, and Peter found it necessary to clarify the situation. "You see, I made friends with her son in the big city. While dying, he asked me to visit his mother and do everything possible on her behalf. I promised him, but all kinds of circumstances delayed me, and I could get here only last night."

The old woman heard what Peter was saying, and told herself, "Why did he hide that from me? Oh yes, he probably did not want to agitate me at night. What a good boy!"

The operation was successful. The physician refused payment, saying to use the money for buying medication and for follow-up care, until everything will be in order.

The neighbor ladies started to arrive after lunch, in order to see how the old woman was doing, and everyone brought her something. The local storekeeper came as well. He talked with Peter for a while, asked him about his education, and then suddenly asked, "Would you be willing to come as my helper in my store? The work is getting to be too much for one person."

"Is it that hard to find salespeople in this town?"

"There is no shortage of them, but I need a trustworthy individual as my helper."

"After all, you have seen me only for the first time."

"I can see through a person," the storekeeper replied, "therefore thieves don't come into my store."

Peter smiled, and the old woman said, "Go ahead and hire this young man. I will vouch for him."

"Well, you see, you even have a sponsor. Well, how about it? Everything is in order, let's shake hands and start working. Can you come along with me to the store right now? I will show you around it, and we will settle all the official details."

"Go ahead," the old woman said, "I have a roomful of helpers."

Everything had been arranged in two hours. As Peter was ready to head home, a beautiful girl walked into the store. She was surprised, but looked at Peter with some delight. "Forgive me, but I have never seen you in this town. Are you a newcomer?"

"Yes, I was one yesterday, but today I am a helper to the owner of this store."

"What?" the girl exclaimed. "You are my father's helper!"

"Unfortunately, that is how it is."

"I do not regret that at all, I was simply wondering where you had been until now."

Thus our Peter met the heiress to the store.

At the first dance, there were so many gals around Peter that the heiress had to break through them in order to get to him.

"It seems to me," she said, "that you have caused a real avalanche of gals in our town."

That evening, even an avalanche was unable to any longer separate Peter from Molly.

Life began to get ever better. Peter became indispensable everywhere. No singing, dance, or theater group could get by without him. The minister, too, felt happy whenever Peter came to church, because for some reason many more girls started coming to church. However, even the elderly ladies felt unhappy at congregational meetings if Peter was not present. Neither could Peter recognize himself any longer; he wanted to help everyone. It was easy for him to be good even toward the worst old men in the congregation.

One evening, in a box at a movie, Molly sat next to him. Two people happily in love were kissing each other on the screen. She asked Peter, "Peter, wouldn't you like to kiss me?"

Peter felt so surprised that suddenly he could not find any words. "But..., but, Miss Molly, I did not even dare to think about that."

"Look at what kind of a timid boy you turned out to be! I had not noticed that at all. You see, my dear helper to my father, wouldn't you rather become his daughter's husband and a co-owner of the store?"

"I am surprised, Miss Molly! You talk about love as about business in the store."

"One does not hurt the other. In this case they go together real fine. Well, how about the first kiss?"

"The first?" Peter exclaimed, having recovered his senses. "Why the first but not the first ones?"

As they walked home, Molly asked him, "Well, for when shall we set the wedding?"

Suddenly Peter became sad. "You see, Molly, I fell in love with you the very moment when you walked into the store, but I cannot marry you. Not only can I not marry you, but no other gal."

"Why?" Molly asked in surprise. "Are you sick?"

"No, worse than that. I am not sure about my future, and until I am certain about it, I cannot get married. I don't want to make anyone unhappy."

"Not sure about your future? What nonsense! My father dreams all the time about passing his store on to us."

"Yes, Molly dear, it is merely a dream. I cannot!"

"Why not?"

"I already said that I don't want to make anyone unhappy."

"How could you make someone unhappy?"

"Molly, dear, if you can wait for a while, perhaps I will be able to tell you."

"I will wait," Molly answered, "but how long will I have to wait?"

"I cannot tell you that for the time being, no matter how much I would like to."

Thus they parted, and no longer met alone.

One night a fire broke out in the house where the daughter of the old woman's sister lived. Peter rushed over there. People had already gathered, but the firefighters had not yet arrived. The flames had already engulfed the bottom floor, and it was no longer possible to either enter or leave the house. Some people were trying to put out the fire with pails of water, but to no avail.

Here a woman walked up carrying a bundle of blankets. Having noticed the blankets, Peter ran up to her and said, "Let me have them! I will try to save those in the house!"

He grabbed two blankets, run up to the pails of water, thoroughly soaked the blankets, so that water dripped from them, cut out eye openings in one blanket, grabbed the goggles from a nearby motorcyclist, put them on, wrapped himself in one blanket, took the other one along, and rushed into the house through the flames.

"Crazy man! After all, he will burn to death!"

A few minutes passed. The glass fell from a window on the second floor. Peter appeared in the window with two children in his arms.

"Spread out a blanket," he shouted, "and catch the children!"

The blanket which the woman still had was spread out, and six men stretched it tight. Peter tossed the children into it, one after the other.

Then he shouted, "Hold on!" and rushed back into the room.

He returned in a minute. "The entire building is in flames, I can no longer take it! Hold the blanket!"

He jumped into it, and remained lying there. However, he soon regained consciousness, after having been given artificial respiration.

The firefighters finally arrived, just as the house collapsed.

Having regained consciousness, Peter asked, "Where are the children? Are they alive?"

"They are alive, and it seems that they are not badly hurt," a physician replied.

"Let me have them. I will take them home. My old mother will have something to do."

He left.

They were pleasant children – pretty and lovely – a boy and a girl. The old mother, of course, did everything that was possible in order to replace their mother, but she did not lack helpers either. Old women, wives, and even girls came from almost the entire town to help the old woman. The girls, of course, had ulterior motives, but they did not talk about that.

Peter had become a real father to the children. The children could not love their daddy enough, their good daddy. Molly also started coming. She became their second mother, but Peter did not respond to the silent question in Molly's eyes. That seemed to be the only thing precluding complete happiness, but was that really the case? Wasn't there something else as well? That surfaced a few days later.

Peter had gone to a restaurant to have few beers with his friends. Time passed pleasantly. Suddenly Peter sensed something awkward. He could feel something unbearably threatening coming from the nearest corner of the room. Peter looked in that direction and saw the bearded man, who was looking at him without taking his eyes from him.

Peter felt a wave of hot water splashing him. "That is he, that is he! Oh God, everything is over now!"

He tried to remain calm and continued to talk with his friends. When he raised his eyes again, the bearded man stood next to the counter and was talking with the owner of the restaurant. Peter got up, said good-bye, and left by the nearest door.

On the way home, he looked back frequently, but no one was following him.

(A five minute intermission. Mary may replace Alexo, and give him the rest which he deserves.) [[04/22/67 0126 - 0131]]

Peter walked, but his legs seemed strange and heavy to him. "What should I do now? Should I disappear again and leave all these beloved people? The worst of it – then the bearded man will definitely decide that I am I, and will tell everyone about me. That will be my spiritual death. Perhaps he still has doubts, because I have recently grown a small mustache. I think that I will rather wait, I'll see what the bearded man does."

Over the next few days the bearded man went everywhere, talked with everyone about different things, and then among other items also asked about Peter. He asked when he had arrived, from where he came, what he had related about his past, and what kind of a person Peter was – good or bad.

He heard very little, rather – nothing, with regard to Peter's past, but everyone admired Peter as an individual. He was wondering whether it was possible for a person to transform like that, to turn from a merciless killer into a good individual like that, one who had faced almost a certain death on behalf of other people.

He also came into the store and began a similar conversation with Peter. Peter said that he had come here from a large city in order to tell his friend's mother about his death. He stayed here because he had to look after his friend's mother, and he met very many good people here.

When the bearded man asked in which big city he had lived, Peter responded that he had loved to roam and had been in almost all the big cities.

"Have you also been to Chicago?"

"Of course, even several times."

"Do you remember when?"

"No, that is not possible. I did not keep any diary."

"Did we meet in Chicago?"

"How can I say that? What kind of an encounter are you referring to?"

"Well, let's say on the street. I stood on a street corner, and you came out of a building while carrying two bundles."

"And you stopped me and asked me what I was carrying?"

"No, I minded my own business and was not thinking about you. Only the next morning did I read in the papers that there had been a robbery and even a murder in the building from which you came out that night."

"What are you saying, even a murder? Who could have committed that? I have heard about many murders in all the cities. If one had taken place in a building from which I had supposedly come, of course I could not have forgotten such an event and such an encounter. But, unfortunately, I do not remember this and have not participated in it."

"Are you sure about that?"

"Of course! What a question?"

"Sorry for bothering you," and he left.

After spending a few more days in town, he disappeared. There was only one place which he had not visited – the police station. Peter found out that, and did not know what to think. "He probably thinks that I am the one who came out of that building in Chicago. In that case, though, he should have gone to the police, but he did not do that. What am I supposed to think?"

Peter failed to find an answer.

The bearded man had gone to the nearest town and told everything to the police chief there. He said that he had not wanted to tell the local police about his suspicions, because it was hard to imagine that the murderer in Chicago and the storekeeper's helper in the small town could be the same person. After all, it is not possible to transform like that.

The police chief said that he will come along to the town, and will try to determine the real truth. Even if an individual transforms, he nevertheless has to undergo the punishment which he deserves for a murder that he has committed.

They arrived in the town just as Peter was presented an award in the town square for having saved people in the fire. There were many speakers. Every one of them praised Peter for something.

"Your Peter resembles an angel more than a murderer," the police chief said.

"Why did he say shortly after his arrival that his name was Francis?"

"Yes, he supposedly did that when he intended to leave the town soon, but once he decided to stay he started using his first name again, because Francis is his middle name," the police chief mumbled suspiciously. "I can see that we cannot accomplish anything here today. Let's go to a restaurant for some food and drinks, and then to a hotel for some rest. After all, tomorrow is also a day."

Truly, the next day was also a day, and a very important one at that.

After collecting some more information, which did not give them anything new, the police chief said, "There is so much that is suspicious in this case that I have reached the conclusion that Peter has to be arrested, and a thorough investigation has to be conducted. I hope that you, too, will feel certain the he is the same person."

They went to the old woman's house. The old woman was alone with the children. Peter was at work. The police chief asked the old woman to relate about Peter's arrival at night, and what he did.

The old woman repeated what she had told others.

"Are you saying that Peter came in through the door which had been left unlocked, without knocking?"

"I really can't remember such trifles."

"After all, that would indicate whether he had come with honest or dishonest intentions."

"What dishonest intentions could he have had with respect to me – an old woman – if even our prettiest gals don't tempt him?"

The chief blushed. "That is not what I am talking about, but perhaps he was after money."

"Had he been after money, he would not have come to a poor woman, but would have gone to a merchant."

"Perhaps he did not know that you really had very little money. Many people pretend to be poor, but after their death thousands are discovered sewn into their mattresses. Did he shake your mattress?"

"No. I offered him to do that, but he refused."

"But he asked you for money?"

"Yes, he asked me to lend him some until the next day, for he was hoping to find work here. Besides, had he come after money, why did he leave it on the table, and returned only in order to help me get up from the floor?"

"Why did he stay with you?"

"In order to help a sick and lonely individual."

"Therefore, you think that he is an honest person?"

"Think?" the old woman laughed out. "I know that and all the inhabitants of this town know that!"

"Therefore, you have no suspicions with respect to him?"

"Yes, I have suspicions. It seems to me than an angel from Heaven has come to us in his appearance."

"Well, that is saying too much!" the chief exclaimed surly.

"What do you mean, too much? You should say – not enough! No matter where you will go, you will hear everywhere about the good that he does for everyone."

"Perhaps he does that in order to save his life?"

"To save his life? I haven't heard of anyone saving his life by rushing into a burning house."

The chief started feeling uncomfortable. "We will not get very far with this old woman. Let's wait for others."

The bearded man did not participate in the questioning, and became ever gloomier.

Then Peter came in, carrying all sort of items that he had bought at the store. The children rushed up to him to greet him. "Daddy, dear daddy is coming!"

Peter set down his purchases on a table, picked up the children from the floor, and sat them down in his lap. The children covered him with kisses. Their love was obvious.

The storekeeper came in. He brought presents for the children and for the old woman. His daughter followed him. She also had presents for the old woman, and candy for the children. She sat down, and the children started kissing her, just as they had Peter.

"I think that we have had enough of fun and games. It is time to arrest this clever deceiver!"

"Arrest him? What for?" the bearded man asked.

"What do you mean – what for? After all, you said yourself that you had seen him leaving the building in which people had been murdered. And now you say that he is not that person?"

"Yes, he is a different person! I had been mistaken."

Surprised, the police chief asked once more, "Are you definitely saying that Peter is not a murderer, but is a different man?"

"Yes, he is a different person, and there is no law that permits punishing another individual."

While smiling ironically, the police chief asked, "Perhaps you mean a man who has transformed into a different person?"

"You are the one who said that, chief!"

Then he turned toward Peter, gave him his hand, and said, "I wish you the very best. Continue your noble work!"

After that he walked out.

The police chief followed him and said, "I have no other choice, because you are the only witness, and you claim that he is a different individual."

The bearded man turned toward the chief and said, "Chief, don't you really see that Peter is a different man?"

The chief thought for a moment, then gave the bearded man his hand, and said, "Yes, he is a different person. He is no longer a murderer."

They drove off.

Once the bearded man and the police chief had left, Peter walked up to Molly. "Molly, dear, now I can ask you without any hesitation – are you willing to become my wife, the mother of these children, and the daughter of this old woman?"

"Of course I am willing, and very much so!"

She threw herself into Peter's open arms.

The curtain has dropped. The play of life has ended.

Good night, heralds. I thank you for your superhuman endurance. Nakcia.                                     [[04/22/76 0318]]

Ilgya                                     04/30/67 1248

Ilgya. Heralds, I congratulate you with Earth's greatest festival – the day of Christ's resurrection.

The world celebrates this festival for the second time [this year] already. Of course, everyone is allowed to celebrate a festival as he finds it to be more appropriate, or not celebrate it at all. However, if people of a certain faith to which they belong celebrate a specific festival on a particular day, then it nevertheless would be better for everyone to celebrate this festival at the same time.

The Divine, who will speak with you at one o'clock, according to daylight savings time, celebrates this festival together with you – the Orthodox.

A misunderstanding arouse in conjunction with the change to daylight savings time. It is extremely difficult for us in the Deoss Temple to coordinate time, because our time here is entirely different. If the clocks are changed, we do not always realize this ahead of time.

The mistake was of course discovered the following day, but since the conversation was set to take place later, rather than earlier, than the set time, the Divine decided not to unnecessarily bother you.

The Divine will speak in five minutes. [[1258]]

Santorino                                     04/30/67 1303

→Heralds, I, Chief Spirit Santorino, will tell you today about the last hours of Christ's life on Earth. I will not talk about everything that occurred then, and about that which has been described correctly in the Gospel.

As you have already been told, the first three evangelists did not write as eyewitnesses, but wrote according to the words of the apostles and other witnesses. Obviously, errors are possible in a case like that.

The apostle John was the only one who wrote as an eyewitness, and his work possesses the peculiarity that he wrote almost exclusively about events which the others had not covered. He sometimes described along with the others only particularly important events, either by supplementing them, or else by correcting the errors which they had made, but unfortunately not all of them.

FRIDAY. The clock neared five. High above the crowd, Christ looked on it from the cross, and looked out over the Holy City. His hands and feet, having been nailed through, burned horribly. With each smallest movement, the nails slowly tore the flesh ever more. If He wanted to relieve His hands slightly, His feet began to hurt unbearably, and if He wanted to relieve His feet, then His hands hurt just as unbearably. It was not much better even when He let His body hang loosely. Every muscle ached like an overstrained string.

How can this pain be expressed in words? It can be understood only if one suffers it personally.

His suffering was even greater when He saw the suffering of His mother and other relatives. His mother's suffering in particular was not much less painful than the Son's suffering, because it was even more dreadful.

He saw His most beloved disciple, John, standing next to His mother. He could also see a few other disciples in the crowd. He raised His head slightly and cast His glance over the town of Jerusalem. He had suffered there so much yesterday and today. The past hours of the past days flashed before His eyes.

For a moment, different scenes flashed before His eyes − of Him being greeted by the people and accompanied by their cheers, as He rode into this town of torture. Then His eyes focused on the Hall of Feast, where He sat with all His disciples. Here before Him were reborn the torments which He underwent, by permitting one of His apostles to betray Him − the Son of God.

For a long time He had sought the right man − a man He would feel the least sorry for. Yet, how could a man like that be found, when there was no man for whom He would not feel sorry, no matter how bad this man might be? When He broke His piece of bread with this disciple and told him, "Go and do that which you must do!" then, for the first time in His life, the Son of God felt that He, too, had become a sinner. He knew that there was nothing with which He could repay the apostle for the sin placed upon him, and that the only way out was to let his soul pass into nonexistence at the moment of his death. Will Christ be ever able to forgive Himself, or will He have to suffer torment for that eternally?

I reveal to humanity this – the world's greatest tragedy – for the first time, because it surpasses all the tragedies in the world, but the people had failed to comprehend it.

Then the night in the Garden of Gethsemane flashed before His eyes. He had discussed with His Father all His courses of action on Earth, and also how to give humanity an example, so that it could not complain that God had not suffered the way people have to suffer. Therefore, it was easy for Him to summon people to self-sacrifice for the sake of God and humanity.

Obviously, He and God had considered other possibilities, and probabilities that could have arisen during the time of Christ's life on Earth, but they did not arise. People were still so subordinated to the power of matter that it was possible to help them to set themselves free from it only by utilizing everything that was possible for a human. Knowing what His Father's reply would be when facing the foreseeable, atrocious torture, His spirit sought His Father's help. Obviously, not even His Father was able to help Him, without undoing everything that had been accomplished, and what could be done after that?

Christ hoped that His disciples would be with Him during this difficult moment, but their spirits were weaker than their bodies, and Christ woke them up three times in vain. And then, when they were ready to leave the garden, He saw Judas coming with the soldiers. He understood that the hours of torture were beginning.

"You betray your Teacher with a kiss," He said bitterly. That was His parting from Judas for eternity.

This kiss proved that a kiss can bring not only happiness and love, but that it can also bring torture and death. Thus the kiss, too, lost its value that night.

Then before His eyes flashed scenes of how He had been brought before the high priest, and how, with false witnesses, he tried to make Him guilty of profaning God, by claiming to be the Son of God. However, only two witnesses were found who would testify against Him. The Hebrew high priest, though, found fault with Christ's words, and proclaimed Him to be guilty and to be punished.

He was taken to Pilate, but Pilate did not find Him guilty.←

(A ten minute intermission.) [[1403 - 1413]]

→Then Pilate, the Roman, sent Him to the Hebrew King Herod. The king did not find Christ guilty either, and sent Him back to Pilate.

Once again, Pilate could not find Christ guilty, for Christ said that His Kingdom is not on Earth, and that He has come to Earth to proclaim justice and love to the people.

Pilate's wife, too, begged that this Prophet be spared. Yet, the priests, Pharisees, the learned men, and the entire synod demanded the death of Christ.

In order to avoid possible trouble, Pilate gave in once the Hebrews began to threaten him. They said that Pilate wanted to spare a man who called himself the King of Jews, and by doing this, he was supporting the enemies of Rome. Pilate washed his hands in a vessel of water, and having dried them, said, "I wash my hands of this Prophet's blood!"

Then occurred the most dreadful thing of all that the Hebrews could have ever done to themselves. Through the mouths of the priests, Pharisees, and the mouths of the best-educated people of the nation, they said, "Let His blood fall on us and on our children!"

Christ felt as though He had been struck by stunning lightning, and turned to God in despair, "Did You hear what these people said?"

"Yes, My Son."

"But, after all, they take on with that an almost unbearable curse. With that they bring destruction, torture, and misery on their nation. And, after all, this is My nation as well! What can We do now, Father?"

"What can We do? Man himself chooses his own fate and neither I, nor You, can help them any longer. They will have to bear the consequences of this curse for thousands of years!"

"But, Father, will they have to bear this curse eternally?"

"Yes, as long as they will not admit their sin and acknowledge that You are the Son of God!"

"But, after all, they knew from their own writings that I would come. Why then don't they acknowledge Me?"

"Because they had imagined You to be a supporter of their power. They saw, however, that You have come to destroy them. Therefore You have to be destroyed at all cost!"

God grew silent then.

Then Christ saw once more the torture, mockery, spitting in His face, beatings, and all kinds of degradation.

Christ received yet another blow. Representatives of the Hebrew nation found a murderer to be more deserving of being set free than He – the Son of God.

Thus began the road of the cross. He was so weak, and the cross so heavy, that it was given to someone else to be carried. And so, you see, here He was, crucified, in between two criminals.

The sixth hour approached. The torment became ever more unbearable. He looked at His mother and John, and told John to take His mother as his own mother, and care for her as a son, until her death.

The sky began to turn dark, and enveloped in darkness the Earth as well. The ninth hour approached. The people continued to ridicule Him in various ways, saying, "You claimed that You could tear down the temple and build it anew in three days. If You can do that, then why can't You free Yourself from the cross?"

Another said, "If You are the Son of God, climb down from the cross, and then we will believe You."

This went on.

"These people are so merciless and even detestable!" Christ thought. "They deserve to be destroyed."

The voice of God came, "If You want Me to, I will carry that out!"

Christ thought, "But My mother is in this crowd, as well, and so are My relatives, My apostles, and followers. I do not want them to perish."

"I will spare them," God replied.

Christ was absorbed in thought once again. He saw children grasping at the clothing of their mothers, saw some people with compassion on their faces, and even tears in their eyes. Then He thought, "No, they have to live!"

Then He began to think about the others, "Just how guilty are they really? Many of them do not know Me, and believe in all the evil that the priests tell them. It is not they who are guilty, but rather the priests!"

And He said, "No Father, there are very few here who are really guilty, and because of them You may not destroy all the many deceived ones and all the many unwittingly guilty ones, therefore everyone must be spared."

It turned ever darker. Christ felt that it was no longer possible to bear the pain, and moans came inadvertently from His lips, "Oh, God, why have You abandoned Me?"

"I have not abandoned You. I suffer along with You. If You can bear it no longer, then leave Your body and return to Me!"

Christ said a few words, expressing them in thought and a few in words, "Yes, Father, I deliver My spirit into Your hands, for everything has already come true!"

He lowered His lifeless head to His chest.

In order to prove to those people who were capable of understanding that Christ truly was sent by Him, God shattered the cliffs with lightning, shook the ground, and tore the curtain in the temple. He released many of the dead from their graves, and many people acknowledged their sin and fell to their knees in front of God.

Many, however, did as Christ had already told the synod, "If I were to tell you the truth, you would not believe Me anyway. What sense then is there in My replying to you?"

Thus ends my tiding about Christ's last hours on Earth.

I congratulate you, heralds, with the Festival of Christ's Resurrection, and wish you the best of everything, as well as thank you for the great work which you are doing on behalf of God and humanity. May God's blessing be with you!

Santorino.←                    [[1512]]

# Chapter XIV

# May 1967

Heralds, the spirit Inrak is talking with you. As directed by the Divine, I will listen to your answers to the assignment which the Divine gave you with respect to love, pronouncing a curse, and what you can say on your own that will be important for the Tidings and for humanity. Please begin.

[[Alexo: "I have not prepared much, but I remember from the Tidings that love is friendship based on sympathy, where the lover is able to sacrifice himself for the sake of the loved individual to the extent of even being able to sacrifice his/her life for her/his sake. Others say that love is God, and God is love.

"There is also an explanation about pronouncing a curse in the Tidings. I have been told about an incident involving Russia's Czar Alexander the Third, during whose reign there was persecution of Jews in Russia. The persecuted Jews gathered in a secret location and pronounced a curse on the czar, while reading extracts from their writings. The czar became sick, and the physician – a specialist from overseas – whom the court people had summoned, supposedly poisoned the czar.

"Realizing that he had been poisoned, prior to his death the czar asked the specialist who had been summoned, 'Who are you?'

"He replied in turn, 'I am a Jew!'"]]

[[Mary: "Love is the most wonderful feelings that God has given man, but man started to use the concept of love to designate everything that really has nothing to do with love.

"'The wing of death shall touch everyone who will disturb the Pharaoh,' is written on Tutankhamen's tomb, which was built some three thousand years ago. In fact, Howard Carter, who was the first to enter the tomb, lived another 17 years, while peacefully writing about his experiences. Lord Carnavon died suddenly from the bite of a poisonous insect. That same night there was a power outage in the entire city of Cairo, and Carnavon's son and his nurse died soon afterwards. The next year 17 more people died who had been involved in entering the tomb.

"A second event. The Hebrews forced Seneca from their midst and from their ghetto, and subjected him to anafem (a curse). He did not suffer at all, because now he could feel free as a world citizen. Ben Gurion demanded in 1956 that this curse be removed, since he considered it to be a screaming anachronism in the life of the Hebrews, which was taking shape then.

"Also, Christ cursing the olive tree."]]

[[Janoss: "There are two loves, God's love – a pure love, and human love – feelings that attract and bind. Human love is part of God's love, influenced by the human body.

"A shepherd had transgressed, and had been convicted and jailed. After completing his punishment he returned home and met Mr. John, who had convicted him. He cursed John by saying, 'You will die on yellow sand from a human hand.'

"Mr. John moved to a different location. There were battles there, and Mr. John died on yellow sand. The legend tells that at that very moment the shepherd arrived and said, 'I told you so!'

"Tyvre Castle had been built on land which had been taken from the church and with stones from that church. Two stones, one at each end, had these characteristics – one remained dry during rain, and the other was wet in dry weather.

"The Tichborne Curse. During the reign of Henry the Second, Roger Tichborne's Lady Matell, while feeling that she will soon die and being charitable, asked her husband to give some land to charity, on her behalf. The husband, knowing that his wife was bedridden, promised to give as much land as she could walk around. The wife crawled on her hands and knees, and encircled a piece of land the size of 23 acres, which is called The Crawle. Getting back home, she gathered her household and proclaimed 'The Famous Curse' which will go into effect if her instructions to help the poor will not be observed.

"Each year the land yielded 900 loaves of bread for the poor. After several centuries, one of the heirs changed the giving of bread to financial assistance. However, in 1869 the heir at that time was indicted, and the court severely penalized him and ordered to continue handing out bread. Even now, every March 25th, 900 loaves of bread are given to the poor.

"Pronouncing a curse was already described during the Bronze Age in Babylonia, and it is also noted in the Bible. Thus David pronounced a curse, and this is still practiced in Greece today."]]

[[Alexander: "Janoss spoke correctly about love, that there is God's or spiritual love – which we use little, and bodily love – everything that we like. The strongest manifestation of bodily love is passion, and if it combines with spiritual love, it can perform miracles.

"A mother's love is the strongest one, but these days even a mother is not only capable of abandoning her child, but even of killing him. Thus, love transforms into hatred, and is not real. A father's love is not as strong as a mother's, but it is more noble. Christ commands us to love even an enemy, which is difficult to accept, because it is not possible to love an enemy. One can pretend that he loves an enemy, but that is not real love. We have to try to love as Christ commands, but I don't know whether that will be within our abilities, because you can love only someone who is worthy of that, and someone who loves you in turn. Perhaps some people can love their enemy, but a love like that would be blind and senseless.

"What is love? There is no direct answer. The spirits do not have a definition either. We had not been given this question in order to give a clear answer, but so that we would try to understand on our own, would think about it, and would find an answer. The books which I have read did not give an answer. They only contained philosophy, and nothing was clear. Only God can answer this question. God could have created only good beings, while hoping that matter will start to cooperate with the spirit, and thus end the mutual struggle. Then love will conquer matter, and there will be only one love. There will no longer be the spiritual and material loves.

"To pronounce a curse is not a specific expression. Pronouncing a curse is empty words. One curses his enemy, but nothing happens. A drunk individual also curses, but without any significance. These are not significant pronouncements of a curse. If a father pronounces a curse on his sons and daughters, then the father must have particular reasons, but in such case he pronounces a curse on himself as well. An example is the Hebrew nation, which assumed the curse regarding Christ's blood, 'Let Christ's blood fall on us and our children!' They ruined themselves with that. There is more that I could say, but I could be mistaken, therefore I would ask the Divine to continue my thoughts – whether they are correct or incorrect."]]

Christ pronounced the curse on the tree not as on a tree, but as an example.

I thank the heralds for the work which they have accomplished. The Divine will speak in twelve minutes. [[2122]]

<u>Santorino</u>                    05/05/67 2134

Santorino is speaking. I thank the heralds for trying to answer my questions. Janoss had exerted the most effort, but he has more free time than the others do.

The question regarding love is a difficult question, because it is an extremely broad concept and encompasses extremely much of the spiritual as well as the material essence. Only the spirits possess the true, spiritual love. For a human being it is mixed with love of a material nature, containing the body's feelings. The passion of the body can supplement spiritual love and make it almost perfect. However, this passion of the body can also completely destroy the spiritual love, and wreck both people's lives.

The love of parents and their children is the most stable one, but it is not complete either. It also has several levels, and sometimes this love is even replaced by hatred.

Based on the Holy Scriptures, and his own convictions in life, Alexander claims that he cannot love an enemy. He can ignore him and try not to revenge him, but he cannot love him. If he were to say that he could, he would be lying.

As has been said previously in the Tidings, Christ's words have not been expressed entirely correct in the Holy Scriptures. Man has to strive to love the entire world which God has created, with all its living beings, but love has to be answered by love. If one answers it with hatred, then love cannot exist – it dies. Yet while not loving, in order to transform enemies, you have to try to respond to them with good. If you respond to your enemies with evil, you become like they are, and love loses any opportunity to improve humanity.

With respect to pronouncing a curse, Alexander said correctly that there is a large difference between a curse and a curse. Alexo and particularly Janoss gave several examples. We will not argue over how factual each of them is. Pronouncing a curse can have significance only if it is substantiated and justified.

If an individual is tortured by another individual, then the curse of the tormented is justified, and it will have a decisive significance – if not on Earth, then in Heaven.

The same thing is true if a father or mother take upon themselves or on their children the responsibility for something that they do. For example, for condemning Christ to a death of torture, thus absolving Pilate of his responsibility. Taking on a sin like that is horrible and fateful.

Nothing can any longer absolve the people from it, because with that they killed God Himself, in the form of His Son.

I feel extremely sorry for the Hebrew people, because this curse has brought very much disaster to these chosen people, but it was the free will of these people's leading priests. According to the writings of their own prophets, they knew that Christ would come. Yet, when Christ came with teachings which destroyed their power over the people, they declared Christ to be a false Christ.

Almost two thousand years have passed by now, but no Hebrew Christ has come. A large majority of the world has acknowledged Christ, but not the Hebrew people. They have remained under the power of their priests – their blind priests – and they do not attempt to set themselves free from it.

Some seventy years after Christ, Jerusalem was almost destroyed, following the Hebrews' unsuccessful uprising against the Romans. Then around the one hundred and thirtieth year it was completely destroyed.

The Romans treated the Hebrews extremely tolerantly. Back in those days the kings in Rome were considered to be gods, and their statues were placed in the temples of the conquered nations. The Hebrew people were the only people who acknowledged only one God, and they were not allowed to recognize another god. The Romans obliged the Hebrews and did not place August's statue in the temple in Jerusalem. Similarly, because on entering military service the soldiers had to swear loyalty to the king as to a god, the Hebrews refused to take this oath. They were not allowed to acknowledge August as a god, and to swear loyalty to him as to God. Here, too, the Romans obliged the Hebrews and excused them from military service.

However, all that did not suffice for the Hebrews and, as you already saw, they rebelled against the Romans, thus bringing on calamity for their people. This calamity followed the Hebrews everywhere. They were persecuted in many lands. The Spaniards threw them out of Spain. In Germany, Hitler started to eliminate them. The reason for that was that the Hebrew people – being more capable in certain areas than the German people – took over trade, and professions like law and medicine, as well as diplomacy. People are envious in essence, whether justly or unjustly. The Germans did not consider why the Hebrews held the more lucrative positions. They became angry because these positions where held by people of another nationality, but not by them – Germans – who had more of a right to them in their own country. Therefore it was very easy for Hitler to incite the Germans against the Hebrews, and to start eliminating them.

During the times of the czars, the Hebrews had a difficult life in Russia. Their civil rights were greatly curtailed, and only the Christian Hebrews had the opportunity to live a life suitable for Russians.

After the revolution, the Hebrews acquired the same rights as the Russians had. However, having become free, many Hebrews engaged in revenge, and became prison wardens, leaders in the NKVD, and also entered the government. They extensively participated in eliminating and torturing the formerly wealthy, the former officers, and so on. That again was another fatal step of the Hebrew people. The Russian people began to detest the Hebrews, and even started to gradually persecute them.

Thus the curse, thanks to the Hebrews themselves, continues to haunt them.

With respect to the Russian revolution, the Russian clergy was reborn in it from their long slumber, and stood side by side with the first martyrs of the Christian faith. Their place in Heaven is next to them, and the respect for them – the respect of the entire humanity – will be with them eternally.

(A ten minute intermission.) [[2243 - 2253]]

I am very sorry that I have to say so much that is unpleasant about the Hebrew people, but I cannot help that, because the truth has to remain unaltered. If it were to be altered, then it would become lies, and lies have no place in God's Temple. I also realize that my tiding will cause considerable trouble for The Almighty's new faith from the Hebrews, but this topic could not remain unmentioned.

In the seventieth year the Christians were accused of destroying Jerusalem, because that was easy to do with this small group. That is how the persecution of the Christians began.

In order to extricate himself from the responsibility for having burned Rome, Nero found a way out by accusing the Christians. That continued for almost three hundred years – with interruptions, obviously. Then the Christian faith began to spread.

The Persian Mithras faith helped that to some extent. It had much in it that was similar to the Christian faith. It also believed in paradise and in hell, the eternal life of the soul, and the struggle between good and evil. It similarly observed Sundays and the twenty-fifth of December, used bells and candles, and had other things in common. Since this faith did not recognize the rights of women, and failed to establish unity in forming and maintaining the faith, it soon faded from the stage of history. It nevertheless helped the Christian faith to initially establish this faith, by helping many people to more readily understand and accept it.

→Now I will ask the heralds to ask about what seems incomprehensible to them, or otherwise important. I will ask Mary to start.

[[Mary replies that she cannot recall her questions for the time being.]]

Alexo, please.

[[Alexo asks, "Why didn't Christ leave anything about His teachings in a form written by Himself?"]]

Because everything that belonged to Christ was taken from Him. All the apostles, whom the Hebrews knew, and all Christ's relatives were questioned by the high priest's people, and all possessions and writings belonging to Christ were burned. They committed only one mistake. They did not destroy the apostles, and they were able to pass Christ's teachings on to the nations on Earth.

Janoss, please.

[[Janoss replies, "I have no questions today."]]

Now I will ask Alexander.

[[Alexander answers, "There is a very important question about the Old Testament that should be clarified. God said to Noah and his sons, after the flood when they had disembarked from the ark, 'Multiply and fill this Earth!'

[["Obviously, sensible people understand these words – people have to fill the Earth, then about maintaining the birthrate at a level so as to be able to live without famine and disaster. Yet, many people consider that it is a sin to limit the birthrate, and particularly the priests of the Catholic faith, who consider God's words to be unalterable. I ask you, what does God say concerning this now?"]]

God says the same thing as sensible people do. The Earth has been filled, and because of that, God's command has been carried out and it no longer exists as such.

An estate owner orders his people to sow the fields and to fill the warehouses with grain, with seed stock and with what is necessary for sustenance. The servants, however, having filled the warehouses, continue to produce grain and pile it in a heap out in the open. What would the estate owner say to that? I would think that everyone knows the answer!

Or else, he could have them raise goats and fill the stables with them. It is understandable to everyone that once that has been accomplished, then raising goats in unnecessary amounts should no longer be continued.

[[Alexander asks again, "In reading the Gospel, I unexpectedly caused serious thoughts for myself, and cannot free myself from them. I noticed that everything in Christ's life occurred as the prophets and Christ had predicted. Therefore it turns out that everything had been foreseen, and that's how it had to be. Christ had to suffer, the Pharisees had to betray Him, apostle Judas had to betray Christ, and Christ had to die on the cross.

[["These are serious thoughts. It seems that they are not correct, but as a human I do not know how to find an answer, and God has to help me solve this. 'Who is guilty? Who is to be punished?' I have an answer, but I ask for explanations from God."]]

Yes, God followed your thoughts and waited for this question. No one, not even the wisest person, can receive an answer – a correct answer – from other people and from all the books which exist on Earth. Only God can give it, and He permits to give it to you, Alexander, to all of you heralds, and to all of humanity on Earth.

Prior to sending Christ to Earth, God, Christ, and many chief spirits and spirits who had knowledge of man on Earth, discussed the question about how to save humanity from destruction, how to give it the strength to overcome the power of matter's resistance, and how to gradually transform matter and make it a partner of the spirit in the formation of the entire universe.

The Hebrew nation, as the only one which believed in only one God, and believed correctly, was selected as being most suitable for preaching Christ's teachings. Since it had adopted many of God's teachings, it could be presumed to be best prepared for accepting and continuing Christ's faith. Yet, the clergy of this nation had forced their will and their understanding of the Holy Scriptures on the people. It was clear that the Christ whom they awaited would not be [like they had anticipated], but instead would ask for their abdication from delusions and power.

It was clear that the priests will fight for their power, and will do everything in order to ruin Christ and convince the people that He was not the true Christ, but a false Christ. Therefore, particular means had to be used in order to overcome the power of the priests, and prove to the people that Christ, the Son of God, had come to Earth to bring love. He came to supplement the old laws, the harsh laws of ancient times, with new laws utilizing justice and love. The Son of God did not use any privileges of a divine nature, but lived the life of an ordinary human, experiencing human joys, as well as human sorrows and pain.

Based on what the Hebrews and their leaders – the priests – were like then, it was obvious how these people would react and act, and how God's goal could be achieved. However, it was not precluded that the priests might change their views, once they ascertained the authenticity of Christ. Or else, that people might receive Christ's teachings on a deeper level, might understand them better, and therefore would resist or refuse to follow the decision of the priests.

Unfortunately though, the plan which had been worked out turned out to be correct, and nothing in it had to be changed. All the predictions came true.

[[Alexander continues asking, "In reading the Holy Writings I found that Christ talked often about prayers, even though He said that one does not have to pray to God, because God knows on His own what man desires. Besides that, He gave the people a prayer and told them how to pray to God – by secluding yourself in solitude. He recognized that man could not get by without prayers, particularly during difficult moments of life, and said, 'Knock at the door and it will open to you, pray and it will be given to you, and God will listen to you.'

[["Knocking and repeated asking are, after all, the same thing. Therefore one has to recognize that repeated asking and knocking are the same types of praying and do not correspond to the words of Christ. During some difficult times in life I felt helpless and had no hope of saving myself, for there were no prospects of getting help from people. At such moments, my thoughts turned to God. It seemed that help will not come – only death will come. Yet, once I overcame this despair, life did not turn into death, and those prison gates, which seemed as if they would never open, did open after all; and when I was drowning, I did save myself! Now I understand why that happened, for You helped a future herald to escape death.

[["Can only heralds be helped? What about others? Wasn't it possible to save the many millions who suffered in Russia and France due to Communist tortures? I understand that that's how it is, but still, can't that be changed? We fear death, but can't the crossing over from life to death be made easier? I don't know if You will answer my questions, but I ask You as a human."]]

Not only did you ask, but you also answered. As a true human, you are troubled by the suffering of people. You understand that this happens because man himself causes it for himself, by following his free will. [It has to be permitted] in order not to limit this free will of man, which man does not want to give up in any way, and rightfully does not want to give up.

Yes, God is forced to help His heralds, for otherwise these heralds would be unable to carry out all the opportunities of preserving life. Still, God helps you, heralds, only when that is essential.

I am not saying anything about whether God ever helps other people as well. I do not have the right to talk about that. You, however, have the right to believe that He does help sometimes, if that is essential for others as well, because whoever believes usually receives an answer from God, without realizing that himself. You have to understand, though, that despite some possible exceptions, the law still remains the law. These exceptions do not alter it.

I know that God not helping during some horrible times in life makes people claim in despair that, if God does not help, then He does not exist at all.

The Almighty has carried out millions of experiments in the universe dealing with how to transform matter more readily, but not all of these experiments have succeeded. Still, the successes have become greater recently, and there is hope that the day is not too far off when man will not have to say that God does not exist.

God understands that Alexander and many other people suffer along with the suffering of other people. [God understands] their desire to set free those who are suffering. God and all the spirits desire that, too. The only resolution is for God and the people to cooperate in ending this suffering as soon as possible.

God summons every human to take part in this struggle of freeing humanity from suffering, and establishing justice and love on Earth.

God expresses His gratitude to all heralds for their efforts, and for the work of receiving and organizing the Tidings.

I pass God's blessing on to you, heralds!

Santorino.←          [[05/06/67 0027]]


Santorino          05/12/67 2051

Heralds, the previous time I did not manage to complete my tiding, because it stretched out. We still have to talk about the Hebrew people, because so far we have talked only about these people's negative characteristics and deeds. One might get the impression that God is hostilely inclined toward these people. God is not hostilely inclined toward any nation, and the Hebrew people – just as any people – possess traits of a positive nature as well.

First, the Hebrew nation was the only and the first one to worship the true God. The Christian nations adopted the Hebrew faith in God – in the true and only God. That is a somewhat unusual expression. I meant by that, the nations which consider themselves now to be Christian.

The Hebrew people were nomadic people. They wandered from one place to another. They did not build houses but lived in tents. They came from the Arabian Desert to the Mediterranean, and encountered more cultural people who lived in one place, in villages and towns. Thus the Hebrew people, too, had to stop and settle down in one place. Obviously, they also had to adopt a higher style of life, and had to build houses and towns.

With respect to the Bible, in it true historic events mingle with imagined ones. The Bible is not a book that God gave directly. It includes people's laws, customs, and their own former habits. It is a rare instance when religion guides people's entire lives, even tells them what to eat and how, and so on. It seems that there is much in it that is entirely superfluous, and that even unnecessarily shackles an individual. Of course, cleanliness and knowing what to eat are good things, and people should know them. However, they should not have been combined with religion, thus giving the rabbis the opportunity to interfere in all human affairs, and provide a good income for themselves.

Of course, the nomadic nature did not disappear completely, and it explains why the Hebrew people dispersed throughout the entire world. They also ended up in Europe – in Spain, France, England, and other countries in Europe.

The Hebrews possess initiative and a desire to acquire more money, besides which these people are also very talented. They have given the world many outstanding people – in science, in music, as well as in medicine, but mostly in organization.

They organized corporations that brought profits for them, but simultaneously also for humanity. Of course, these outstanding abilities and the wealth associated with them elicited jealousy in the countries where they had settled down to live. People began to persecute the Hebrews and – as in Spain – even made them leave the country.

Spain was one of the stronger and wealthier countries, but it declined after evicting the Hebrews. I will mention yet another fact, which you also know, because it happened during your lifetime.

After the movies were invented, German films stood out with their superiority throughout the entire world. However, one hears hardly anything about German films after the elimination of the Hebrews during the time of Hitler. In America, though, with their financial abilities and energy, they raised American film production to almost insurmountable heights. The films which they produced gained notice throughout the entire world with their artistic value. Similarly – while obviously thinking little about the people but rather about their own profits – they participated extensively in raising American industry to unprecedented heights.

As you can see, the Hebrews, despite some of their negative characteristics, nevertheless helped extensively in the progress of humanity. They should not be only condemned. Rather, the other nations should also try to do more and be more energetic, and then they will not have to complain about the superiority of the Hebrews.

With respect to Israel – the country which the Hebrews have finally established for themselves – difficulties arise due to the fact that Arabs also consider it to be their land. The Arab people, unfortunately, have not turned out to be as capable as the Hebrew people, and have failed to establish unity and acquire, or rather – retain, Palestine for themselves.

Rest for ten minutes now, and then we will again discuss what interests each of you. You will be able to ask me again, and I will try to answer. [[Intermission 2140 - 2150.]]

→I am listening. This time let us start with Alexo.

[[Alexo asks, "I have read in several places that humanity awaits a new religion. It is most unusual that, when comparing the facts given in the Latvian newspaper, there truly is a noticeable phenomenon which makes one think of changes like that. Some religions – for example, the Mormon – hope for the coming of Christ soon. Way back, while awaiting the coming of Christ, the Hebrews had been told about that through their prophets. Has something been told about the heralds as well?"]]

Since the spirits know about the Tidings, and already knew ahead of time that they would come, then, obviously, while meeting with people spiritually, they had them surmise that new communications with God can be expected.

Is there anything else to ask?

[[Alexo: "Thank you, no, I don't have anything else."]]

Then, let us say, would Janoss have a question?

[[Janoss: "I don't have any questions today."]]

And Mary?

[[Mary asks, "I would like to know very much if the so-called apostle Paul should truly be considered as one of the apostles. It seems to me that he introduced many Hebrew ideas into the faith of Christ. That is my question."]]

Have you read the writings of Paul?

[[Mary: "Very little."]]

Too bad. Obviously, Paul cannot be considered a full-fledged apostle, for he was not summoned by Christ. Still, he did very much toward disseminating Christ's teachings. It is unfortunate that he introduced into his sermons so much that is purely Hebrew. The other problem is that he saw that priests cannot get by without any money, and that it has to be provided. He found the means, of providing for the necessities of life for the apostles, which seemed to him to be good and necessary. Yet, as we have seen, the clergy did not stop with just providing for the necessities of life. Instead, they established a life of wealth for themselves, built needlessly expensive churches, and decorated icons with jewels, while permitting paupers to beg for a crust of bread, or a penny in cash at the doors of these churches. They did not even think about the fact that taking care of these paupers was their main obligation.

What else would there be?

[[Mary: "I would like to understand why the Virgin appears so frequently to the Catholics?"]]

How frequently?

[[Mary: "That has been mentioned several times. She has been seen in Fatima, as well as in Lourdes."]]

And why only to the Catholics?

[[Mary: "Yes, that's exactly what I would like to know. That is not mentioned in other religions."]]

It is.

[[Mary: "Forgive me, but I have not heard of it."]]

The question is not expressed specifically.

[[Mary: "I do not know how to ask this question specifically."]]

Let's set it aside for a while. Is there anything else?

[[Mary: "No, thank you, there is not."]]

Now it is Alexander's turn.

[[Alexander: "I will attempt to ask the same question which Mary asked, except in a more specific manner. Recently the Pope traveled to a village in Portugal where, a few years back, the Virgin had appeared to some children, and had talked with them. Everything that she told the children about the future – for example, about the sister and others – has come true. Similarly, predictions with respect to historical events in the present have come true. It seems to me that since everything that the Virgin had predicted has come true completely, proves without a doubt that the Virgin did truly appear to the children.

[["Many instances of saints occasionally appearing to people are mentioned. It seems to me that such phenomena have occurred and they cannot be doubted. This is obviously not true in all cases, for some phenomena are imagined, and others again are mere hallucinations. Does God confirm my words, or have I erred?"]]

You have not erred, for why can't the spirits, and even the Virgin, appear to people occasionally? An appearance like that only confirms the correctness of the faith, and draws God closer to man. Obviously, this may not occur often, but in some important cases this is requisite.

The time approaches when man will be able to meet with the spirits even more often, and even with the Virgin and Christ. Obviously, the greatest misfortune is that some people imagine occurrences like that, and it is extremely difficult to tell just how true a phenomenon has been.

One should not doubt the appearance to the children, for later on, it was proven to be true with certain facts in life.

[[Alexander: "I want to return briefly to the Bible once more. Immediately after commanding the people to fill the Earth, God told Noah that, with respect to slaying of Cain's brother and spilling of his blood, man may not use blood for his sustenance. An animal being slaughtered has to be drained of blood before its final death. Was Noah truly told that? If he was told that, do we, too, have to abide by it?"]]

He was not told that. It was inserted in the Bible by the clergy, for they considered blood to be harmful to man.

In general, the Bible – consisting of many books with various contents, some of which have nothing to do with religion – contains much that is good and useful, but also much that is superfluous and harmful. According to the writings of the Bible, God seems to be a harsh and merciless king who is preoccupied more with threats than with fatherly advice. Obviously, the man of those times was unable to imagine God any other way. Therefore, all these sacrifices and prohibitions to use blood should be considered as the introduction of the laws and customs of ancient times into books – the books of God.

[[Alexander: "I would like to know whether Stalin's daughter, Svetlana, truly believes in God and understands Him?"]]

I do not want to reveal Svetlana's soul now while she is still alive. She will prove that with her deeds. Not even God, however – not to mention the spirits – wants to reveal the soul of a living human.

There is one thing, though, that I can say. No matter for what purposes or due to what conviction would Svetlana have done everything that she did, it is still difficult to evaluate currently the significance of her deeds and words.

With that, let us conclude for today.

I thank you for the great work that you have accomplished recently, and wish you a pleasant rest. Santorino.← [[2250]]

<u>Santorino</u>                               05/19/67 2100

→Heralds, I return to you once more, for not everything has been clarified yet. Obviously, it is not possible to clarify everything completely. Let us try to clarify at least the most important topics. Occasionally I will have to repeat what has been said previously, but such a repetition is only beneficial.←

While talking about the Hebrews, we failed to examine one more of this nation's more important characteristics; that is the trait of dealing in trade.

When they settled down to live on the shores of the Mediterranean, the Hebrews suddenly found themselves on the trade route from Asia to Europe. Trade was particularly profitable back in those times and in that vicinity and, obviously, the Hebrew people immediately realized that. The nomadic nature of the Hebrews only benefited this new activity of the Hebrews. They had many opportunities in it to utilize their natural abilities.

Along with their good abilities in many occupations in life, the Hebrew people simultaneously turned out to be one of the more obstinate people. They blindly adhered – and still adhere – to their old books of faith, the large majority of which they had written themselves. Even the Ten Commandments are not exactly like Moses received them from God.

Times change, but the Hebrew nation does not want to change. It continues to adhere to laws which were needed in barbaric times. It does not want to give up its old and harsh God, and rather killed God's Envoy – who proclaimed the new God, the God of love – than acknowledged Him.

If an individual commits a crime, then this crime can no longer be washed away by anything. Unless they refute their father's crime, it passes on even to his children, and hence it goes along with them.

There have been many savage nations in Asia that have attacked Europe, in order to plunder it, take people into slavery, and destroy them as much as possible. Almost all these nations have vanished from the face of the Earth, or else have altered their nature.

Let it be as it may with people of other religions, but Christian people may not retain in their hearts evil toward any nation. Christians should not condemn the non-Christians. They should not use evil means to help the non-Christians free themselves from their spiritual ignorance. Human nature cannot be altered by oppression. It can be altered only by love, and if that is not possible, then by utilizing only means of self-defense.

The worst conduct is defamation and ridicule. It only causes new hatred, and most of all harms the defamers themselves.

Yes, the Hebrews believe in their old God, but do not believe in His Son. Let them not believe, because they believe in the Son's Father anyway. Eventually they will have to understand that for themselves.

Let us talk now about people's mistakes. First, once more about how to establish a situation where everyone – obviously, not altogether everyone – could become a good person.

First off, an individual's upbringing has to start from the very first minute of his arrival on this Earth. A child has to get used to what is permissible and what is prohibited. You should treat a child well and should give him everything that he needs, but for God's sake, avoid unnecessary pampering! That is a slow poison, which gradually poisons a child and turns him into someone who wants everything and who recognizes only his own wants. A child has to be made to immediately understand that there are things that he may not take and may not even ask for, because he will not get them anyway. If a child still persists, then he can and has to be spanked, obviously, initially so that it will not even hurt. If that does not help, then so that it will hurt a little bit, but if nothing helps, it should be done so that it will hurt.

Everything depends on the child's nature. Some children understand quickly, and for others it is more difficult to understand, but the main thing – you have to be persistent and should not ignore any of the child's impermissible actions.

Obviously, the parents also may not permit themselves anything negative in their children's presence. If you want to have a fight – go to a barn or some other distant location. Watch your conduct in your children's presence. All that requires much patience, but if you want to be surrounded in your old age by children who will look after you, you have to forget about negligence.

Once your children start going out on the street, observe with whom they associate, and don't let them learn bad things from bad children. It would be best of all to send children to good kindergartens, where they can learn how to properly get along with other children. Yet, I repeat once more, the kindergarten has to be truly good, and the parents should visit it more often.

Schools have to be given the right to not only educate the children but also to bring them up. Streets are where children are most readily tempted toward evil. In general, children have a desire to destroy everything.

Children's free time also has to be used to bring them up. Generally children get into mischief if they have nothing good to do. Therefore children's and youth organizations have to be created, which will fill the children's free time with games that are interesting for them, with sport, and so on.

Of course, all this cannot be accomplished in one day and not even in one year. If you want to live in the company of good children – and later on in the company of good people, once these children grow up and become independent – you have to do that within the scope of the family, as well as that of the town and the state.

(A ten minute intermission.) [[2203 - 2213]]

We can continue now. Let us now talk about adults. If adults have grown up without an upbringing as we discussed tonight, then there is obviously no reason to expect much good from them. Let us not talk about us having to love someone who beats us up, but let us discuss how to conduct ourselves so that we could feel as good as possible in human society.

The wisdom of ancient people already said, "Measure it ten times, and only then cut the thread."

This means that if you are doing something that is completely understandable without any consideration, you should always consider it well.

Control your anger. Never act while angry, because anger makes an individual blind and he goes to extremes, which quite often cannot be rectified. If you feel that you will immediately blow up, then excuse yourself and walk away. Act only when you have calmed down and have thought over what happened. Countless calamities have occurred during moments of anger. Many friendships have been ruined, and frequently because of nothing but a trifle. Similarly, never make a final decision regarding what someone has said about someone else. Always listen to the other side as well, because everyone considers that the truth is on his side. It turns out often that both of them are good, "just stick them in a sack."

(As you can see, I even know the Latvians quite well.)

In general, there is quite often no basis for saying anything bad about someone, but since there is not anything good to say about him either, it is more interesting to say something bad. Here of course people's limited education is also at fault. They cannot say much about world events, about the achievements of science, or about new notions and theories. What then is there left for an individual who is too lazy to read, but is not too lazy to gossip? Just look at those rows of people who sit for hours on end on the sidewalks next to building walls and gossip! The short time of man's days on Earth thus passes in idle gossip.

Of course, man needs rest from everything except rest, but everything has to be proportionate. After all, you can read the same book which you read in a dark room, on a bench in a park.

When you accuse an individual of something, you have to be certain that you are right. Nothing is worse than to falsely accuse someone. If you belong to an organization or if you act jointly on something, then never act on matters that effect others without communicating with these others. Similarly, you should not change a decision that has been made by everyone without the same communication with everyone. An action like that will lead to the demise of the organization, because you cannot play around with other people's trust.

If you collaborate with God, then never try to conceal from God what cannot be concealed. It is difficult for people to get used to the idea that if they say something other than the full truth, the results are far worse than a plain admission. The worst calamity is that people forget that they are on Earth only temporarily, and therefore this life is not the most important thing for man. Almost everyone considers death to be something horrible, and exerts every effort to remain on this Earth. Some people have become so old that they are no longer able to either see or hear. After all, they no longer have any pleasure in withering here, but there in the hereafter the Solar Fields await them with new tasks, and almost all their relatives – father, mother, brothers, sisters, and friends. Yet, you see, they nevertheless ask to be kept on this Earth, which they can no longer see.

Many people are not faring badly here, but God knows that they will do better in some other place. If God, however, recalls one of them to something better, those who remain behind cry and howl as though the devil had hauled him off to hell.

If someone is truly a rotten one, and engages in evil, even he is better off departing from Earth before he accumulates too many sins.

(A five minute intermission.) [[2305 - 2310]]

I will now talk specifically about you, heralds. Do not forget that if you converse with us – the spirits – everything that you say reaches God, and God hears every word that you say, even if you are talking with Astra. - ★ ★ ★ - For example, it was very important for God to hear from man – a herald – about his doubts and suffering, and his request to help those who are suffering even if that is, in fact, not possible for God, because with that the herald expressed the pain of all humanity. God replied just as He had to His Son, Christ, that He cannot ease it, because man's free will is in the way. Still, He said that He will try to help humanity as much as He will be able to.

Then still, if you ask God something, then ask only about something particularly important and to which you cannot get an answer from anyone else. If you ask about something with which you are only vaguely familiar, then rather don't bother God without having first bothered yourself by thoroughly familiarizing yourself with the essence of the concern about which you are asking.

I will answer your questions again in five minutes. [[2318]]

Two of you have declined the honor of talking with me today. I completely understand that they do not have any thoroughly contemplated questions, therefore I will give them the opportunity to do that sometimes later on.

→With respect to Alexander, I feel that he will not decline this time, therefore, please ask.

[[Alexander asks, "In reading over the Bible, I came across a passage where it is told that Abel had been murdered by his brother Cain. Cain, however, and his other brothers, whose names are not mentioned, turned out to be married, and they had children. Nowhere is it explained how these children came about. Certainly not from their sisters?"]]

A similar situation, as was with the children of Adam, also arose with the children of Noah after the flood. The situation is rather simple, and it is clear to me that Alexander knows the answer on his own, but asked it for the benefit of other people.

The very beginning of the Bible is simply the fantasy of people. Therefore such illogical errors have been committed in it. Obviously, these names – Adam, Eve, Cain, Abel, Noah, and so on – did exist. Yet, they did not belong to given people like the Bible tells it. After all, the creation of the world and the creation and life of the first people had to be explained somehow. Similarly, the world flood did in fact take place, but not in the entire world. It took place only in those locations where the Hebrew nation and its neighboring nations lived.

These explanations had been given, but they were originated by the wise people of those times. Even though science barely existed, there was no lack of fantasy even then. Honestly speaking, the task was accomplished rather well, and humanity was satisfied with it for thousands of years. Obviously, later on some things were received from God's prophets, once the history of the Hebrew nation began to take shape.

Think about that for yourselves! What could one tell the people of that time, when they still had no idea whatsoever about what the Earth looked like? Even your grandfathers told you, children, about a place where the sky meets the ground, and the sky is so low there that one can set spoons on it to dry after dinner, that stars are tiny candles in the sky, and the moon – a round lantern. Sometimes, someone took a large bite out of the moon, but it grew back nice and round again – much to the joy of night people. All that is understandable and can be forgiven. It cannot be forgiven, though, that these days, when people know so much, they still continue to adhere to the old fairy tales.

With respect to the Garden of Eden, the story about it is not pure fantasy. In the early phases of creation, God really did try to figure out how to best achieve man's happiness on Earth, while at the same time giving man the desire to develop on his own. Obviously, the Garden of Eden did not have to be created specially, for there were, and are even now, many places in the tropics which are similar to it. If you want to, you can find people on some islands south of Asia who have not advanced one step beyond Adam. They walk around naked, live in huts, shoot with arrows, and to this day they have not even invented the ax. If you want to, you may call it paradise, but not I!

[[Alexander asks, "I have only one question, but it pertains to the New Testament and particularly to Christ. We know about all of Christ's torments, which He suffered as a human, but we know nothing about whether Christ also experienced all of human joys, and all the pleasures of a human body."]]

I understand your question and will reply to it with three words, "No, not all!" You and all the heralds, obviously, understand my answer and you do not need any further explanation.

I thank you, heralds. You have truly earned our gratitude, and I wish you a pleasant night's rest. Let Astra take care of that. Good night, high heralds.

The divine Santorino.←     [[05/20/67 0003]]

<u>Santorino</u>                    05/27/67 1230

→Santorino speaking. Heralds, our conversation takes place under rather strained circumstances. Your planet, small in dimensions, but large in significance, once again experiences a moment which threatens humanity's happiness. Still, let us not succumb to the influence of what is temporary, and let us talk about the eternal.

As you already know, The Almighty is the ruler of the entire universe, which according to human ability of understanding, is considered to be infinite. Your part of the universe, in which your galaxy is located, is subordinate to God – that is, The Almighty's Great Spirit to whom this galaxy is entrusted. Other galaxies are entrusted to other Gods.

Every galaxy is not exactly like your, and their laws are also different. Therefore, let's consider only those laws of God which exist in our galaxy, and particularly the laws given by God to the people on the planet Earth.←

(A three minute intermission.) [[1239 - 1242]]

→Man was not always the very same living being whom you know today. In the beginning, man hardly differed from the other animals.

When creating the living beings, God tried to create initially beings who could develop best under the conditions on Earth, beings who were able to live not only in one location on Earth, but possibly on the entire Earth. After many millions of years, He succeeded in resolving this problem. Living beings were capable of living almost everywhere – on solid ground, as well as in swamps, rivers, lakes, and seas. They were even able to stay above ground, in the air.

Once that had been achieved, and several geological changes had occurred, including a reduction in the heat from the sun, and the Earth itself had cooled down, began the adaptation of the living beings to the new conditions of life. Instead of instinct – rather, not instead but in addition to – the ability to think emerged, for which a brain was obviously needed.

Initially the capabilities of this brain were small. It only helped the living beings to adapt themselves better to the conditions of life, to provide food for themselves more readily, and to defend themselves better against enemies.

After all, this Earth, with its plant and animal kingdoms, did not have a universal meaning. It had just about as much significance as a canary in a cage. God had to tackle the most important part, that of giving a meaning – a sense – to this Earth, with its two kingdoms. That was man, blessed with a body which was ideal for the task, and his spirit of God – the soul.

Obviously, this was a difficult task, and God began to experiment. The construction of the human body changed. The space for the brain became enlarged, and thus emerged the master of Earth, whom you call – man.

Finally the ruler of Earth felt like a real ruler. The fight against animals, which had been so important previously, just about came to an end. The struggle against the invisible enemies – the germs of diseases – also became much easier.

Man recognized God as his creator. Initially he had considered that God was all things that were incomprehensible to him, the threatening forces of nature – such as thunder, the life-giving sun, and so on.

The wanderer nation, the Hebrews, found the first true God within their souls. All the nations on Earth began to embrace this correct faith of God. Some embraced it completely, some partially, and others only slightly.

Many other faiths exist besides the Christian faith. Some of them are contrary to the Christian faith, with evil gods. Some are somewhat similar, while others are very similar.←

(Prior to turning to the main subject of this tiding, I will give you ten minutes to rest.) [[1311 - 1320]]

→Thus, humanity began to recognize one God, but what should we consider to be humanity? This question has to be resolved first. Scientists belong to humanity. With the aid of telescopes and other scientific inventions, they explore the universe, build airplanes, prepare to fly to the moon, and so on. There are people who know much, and who are capable of great things. With the help of the microscope, they have discovered the world of the extremely tiny beings – the tiny enemies and friends who are invisible to the naked eye. Man has managed not only to discover the atom, but even to split it.

Man erects buildings that are hundreds of stories tall. Man converts Earth into a land of gardens and fields of grain. Man descends to the bottoms of the seas, and explores plant and animal kingdoms which are new to him. Man enacts laws to enable everyone to live better, and neither the sick nor the old have to die from starvation, or beg for help. They are provided with everything necessary for life – for a good life. People strive to bring about peace everywhere, to end wars, and set everyone free and [give them the opportunity to] become happy.

Yet, on the other hand, these very same people run around naked in the forests on islands in New Guinea, and some even eat each other. They pray to idol gods to provide them with more meat of their enemies. There are people who inhabit central Australia and the jungles of Africa, and who are only just now beginning to march forward with the steps of the past millions of years. Only now do they begin to open their eyes to the new, real world.

There are people who seem to be just as intelligent as the most intelligent people of the first group of people, but who, while proclaiming happiness to humanity, are just as brutal as the above mentioned savages. The only difference being that they do not eat their enemies, but merely torture and shoot them.

That is what humanity is like today. Can all of it be considered as the humanity of the present? No, only the first part can be considered to be such. The second part, though, whether it wants to or not, will sooner or later have to join the first part, because love and that which is good are the main bearers of humanity's happiness and future.

Just how strong the might of love and justice is, is demonstrated best by the example of the daughter of the world's greatest felon – Stalin. There, where it seemed that God had been completely forgotten, He turned out to be invincible.

Svetlana's example is a sign of fate. It proves the weakness of hatred and its inevitable demise. When you asked me whether Svetlana truly believes in God, you still did not know the contents of the letter with which she, in fact, did not turn to the poet Pasternak, but rather to the entire world, as an envoy of God. Therefore, I told you that she will reveal her soul to you on her own. Such are the ways of God. They are incomprehensible to some, but they lead to the final fulfillment of the decision, man's faith in love and justice, and his faith in the creator of the world – God.

Christ came to Earth because that god which ruled on Earth was not the God who rules in Heaven. The god recognized on Earth was a distant god, a brutal god, and a merciless god even when he was just. He threatened people with revenge for every mistake – even the most insignificant one. He threatened man with eternal tortures in hell for every greater sin. He even called that a sin, which in fact was not a sin, but which the kings and priests on Earth considered to be a sin.

Christ came to proclaim an end to the rule of this old god, who had been formed on Earth. However, two thousand more years had to pass for people to find out who the true God is, proclaimed by Christ.

We will discuss that in the next tiding.

May your work be blessed, heralds, and may you yourselves be blessed!←                    [[1400]]

# Chapter XV

# June 1967

→Heralds, let us continue our tiding which we began the last time.

At the beginning of the creation of the universe, The Almighty was all alone. Only the chief spirits and spirits, who had been created from His spirit, helped Him. However, once The Almighty achieved the ability to create living beings who were capable of developing and of carrying out His decision, He appointed Gods in the galaxies. [His decision was for these living beings] to become His assistants in the continued formation of the universe in a spiritual sense, by also involving matter, which thus far had been entirely hostile to the spirit, in this gigantic task. He gave these Gods virtually unlimited power to rule these galaxies, with the task of forming living beings capable of undertaking His – The Almighty's – task.

From Their spirits, the Gods could create the high spirits and spirits. Considering the aforementioned, you may consider everything that has been accomplished so far as the work of the God of your galaxy. Only now – since man himself understands more about the universe and thus has come in contact with The Almighty – has The Almighty undertaken through His chief spirits direct contact with the planets. In other galaxies – and even in your galaxy – there are planets with equally developed and even further developed representatives of humanity of the universe. With that The Almighty is expanding further the responsibilities of the Gods, rather than limiting them. He permits Them to establish contact with the Gods of other galaxies, for the purpose of achieving the mutual goals better.

The Gods of the galaxies are interested primarily in developing the humanity of the universe, and in achieving Paradise – obviously, Paradise on Earth. Man must achieve those demands which God's personal envoy – Christ – established on Earth. Hatred and want must disappear. Slavery of the body and of the spirit must disappear, and envy must disappear. Rulers which have not been elected by the people must disappear. The people have to govern themselves.

The church is not intended specifically as a house of prayer to God. Rather, it is a house which should direct the spiritual life of the people and should teach Christ's teachings. It also has to inform people of the laws of morality and justice, and has to teach the people how to love and help each other. The church has to teach people how to establish a Paradise on Earth – that Paradise which Christ said will be on Earth. Only then will it be possible to speak of the Paradise in Heaven.

God has not come to rule like a king, but rather, like the Father of a large family, for every human is either His son or daughter. God has not come to punish and has not created a hell with devils and tortures. People themselves created them with their fantasy, by using as models the prisons and torture chambers of the kings of ancient times.

Only two punishments await great sinners after death; you know about these. The people themselves have to establish other punishments for their criminals and violators of laws. The people themselves punish themselves by sinning against the tasks which they have been given, or by carrying them out poorly. A degradation, or a failure to advance, awaits them in Heaven. All others, according to their successes, achieve recognition and advancement.

Satan has nothing in common with the devil. He is merely the judge of people's work. He evaluates man's activities and announces this evaluation to God, who is the only one who makes the final judgment.

Neither God, nor the high spirits, nor the other spirits consider people other than as their children, or as their brothers and sisters, and treat them accordingly. They treat each individual plainly and speak with him in a human language. Therefore it is ridiculous to expect some sort of solemn speeches and proud behavior from them.

None of them need man's worship or prayers. Yet, should man want to turn to them with his sorrows, none of the spirits, and also not God, will leave him unheard, and will try to do everything that is possible and necessary in order to help man.

God sends man to Earth to live on it in human society, and to help humanity in achieving its task. Those who shut themselves off in cloisters, do not help humanity, and spend almost all their time in prayers to God, completely unnecessary to God, act incorrectly. Should the inhabitants of cloisters also – and simultaneously – accomplish some or many deeds, like caring for the sick and helping those who have suffered and the weak ones, then these latter deeds will be considered in their favor.

_ ★ ★ ★ _

Only a very small portion of people are of an evil, criminal nature. This portion can still be reduced considerably by proper upbringing of children and the youth. The mentally ill constitute a part of the remaining portion. Some of them can be cured, and the remainder should be placed in homes for the sick.

Everyone who has committed a crime, or theft, must be kept under observation for a prolonged period of time after completing his punishment. This is an effort to keep him from committing a crime again.

The commandment, "Do not kill," should not be interpreted absolutely. It is permissible to kill, if it is not possible to otherwise defend yourself against an attacker, or to defend another person who is threatened by an attacker. As long as individual countries exist, each country which is attacked has the right to defend itself by any means of defense which it has available, to include weapons.

Those leaders of nations who prepare an attack on another country and carry it out, will receive the harshest of punishments in Heaven.

With respect to the relationships of people's lives, and particularly the relationships of family life, the code, "Whom God has joined, no man may part," is not in effect. God, in fact, does not join anyone. What priests do in the name of God is perceived nowadays as merely an empty formality.

Those harsh expressions of Christ – that it is better to pluck out your eye than to look at your neighbor's wife with a desire – are obviously expressed figuratively. They mean that it is better to strongly resist committing a sin than to suffer the consequences.

Passion has been given to all creatures in order to encourage them to multiply. It has been given to animals only during certain periods. To man, however, it is not limited by time, but only by his will, which, as a sensible being, man himself has to control.

Because of the establishment of family life, bringing up and supporting of children, and other responsibilities, certain laws are needed for marriage. The people themselves have to take care of them, just as they have to decide how long should be the skirts which girls wear. It could well be that man will decide some day to walk around in his Paradise just like Adam. Obviously, no one from Heaven will interfere in his personal affairs, as long as they are justified by the mind.

All extremism is undesirable, for it is harmful, just as perversion is. Certain bounds have to be observed in passion as well, just as in drinking. Everything is for the better in sensible amounts. A glass or two of wine is even advisable with a meal, but its unlimited use becomes harmful to man himself and to his health. Similarly, excessive devotion to passion results in loss of morality, as well as of man's worth.

The Almighty's Chief Spirit Omega will talk with you the next time. Should you come up with some important questions for God, I will answer them gladly at some later time.

Meanwhile, I wish you good success in your great work, and today at night – a pleasant rest. Santorino.← [[2210]]

Omega                              06/09/67 2108

→Omega. Almighty's heralds,... Remove the black paper from the light. The black circle will suffice.

[[The heralds carry out the order and remove the black paper from the light.]]

Heralds, as the Chief Spirit of the Present and the Future, I will take you today into the future, but first let us talk about the present.

Humanity has achieved a very high level of development, but not the entire humanity, and not in all areas. For example, man has conquered the air above Earth. Man sends devices to the moon which photograph this companion of the Earth, investigate its soil, and send the information back to Earth. At the same time, several countries attack one country with the intent of destroying its inhabitants, exactly as was done during the darkest and most distant years of history.

The old notion about God could no longer satisfy today's educated man, but the fairy tales of the Bible were unable to give everything that was demanded by man's desire to know. Many people, while accepting everything superficially, began to say that God does not exist at all, that everything in the universe – and even the universe itself – had come about and formed by itself.

You have already been told how childishly absurd such form of thinking is. Very much of that which was invisible now becomes visible, thanks to science and its inventions for the discovery, development, and fabrication of the necessary means.

The Almighty wants to give man the opportunity to be free, but cannot give him absolute freedom, for that is impossible and belongs only to The Almighty. The matter is quite simple, for after all, it is not man who has created and formed the universe, but rather The Almighty. Man has to live in the universe which The Almighty has created, and has to submit to His laws, whether he wants to or not. Man cannot destroy

The Almighty, but The Almighty can destroy him, and has done that innumerable times with those living beings who have not turned out to be useful to Him.

There is a very great difference between The Almighty and the Gods. Santorino explained that to you recently. Pain does not mean anything to The Almighty, because it was given the living beings as a signal that something in the body is out of order, and that man has to, if that is possible, restore order in the body once again.

Birth, as well as death, is bound with pain. It is not possible to escape it. Mercifulness is extremely important, but it is not always suitable for man either. No matter how dear the tiny calf may seem to the mistress, if it is superfluous she permits it to be slaughtered, for otherwise it would not be possible to operate the farm, and it would not be possible to feed all the tiny calves which would follow. There is much that man likes – animals, plants, and trees – but if they interfere with his plans of life, he eliminates them. That is not mercilessness, but a necessity.

The Almighty, the Gods, as well as the people, have to take this necessity into account. The matter becomes entirely different when we consider man's social life. Here, too, at times, necessity plays its role. However, the main concern here is the law – to create such relationships and forms of social life that all people will be as free and as happy as possible, will love each other, and the main law will be the law of justice.

Man's freedom has to be limited. Man is not permitted to kill another human, to cripple him, to beat him up, to take from him what belongs to him, to curse him, and to slander. He has to behave politely in the home, as well as on the streets; without creating disturbances, making noise, pushing, and has to give the right of way and help each other wherever that is needed.

The streets are not places of amusement for children. Children's parks have to be established for this purpose. Children have to be given free time, but at the same time, one must make sure that while giving joy to the child this would also enhance him, rather than tempt him into mischief and even crimes, as we often see these days.

Correct upbringing of the youth is one of the most important issues now, because we can see the consequences of a bad upbringing. Yet, that cannot be instituted today, and not even in a few years, for one has to initially prepare parents who are capable of that. What kind of parents can those young people become who currently roam the streets, not knowing in what new foolishness or stupidity to engage?

With that, let us conclude for today.← [[2159]]

→Heralds, today we will continue to examine the current situation on the planet Earth, and we will try to find the ways of the future, while noting the good as well as the bad.

Man, having come to Earth for a relatively short period of time, is afraid to leave this Earth even when he fares extremely poorly here. Why is that the case?

It is because he knows what it is like for him on Earth, but he is not sure of what awaits him after death. The church says that if he lives a saintly life he will achieve paradise, where he will have to sing continuously songs of praise to God. Obviously, this causes doubts in some people. What great joy could there be in this endless singing, particularly if one has a poor voice?

The other choice, which the church promises, is hell, if man sins on Earth. Exactly what, though, should be understood by this word, "sin"?

Killing, stealing, and fighting, if you crush another person's skull or ribs, are all sins. Yet, what about the rest − lying, beating up your wife, not going to church, not bothering God with prayers, and so on? Would all that be a sin as well, and would one have to journey to hell for all those things as well?

It seems that a punishment like that would be too harsh, and after all, God is more merciful than man! Therefore, in fact, there would have to be a third place for these lesser sinners, but the priests remain silent about it. Obviously, what desire might man have in parting from Earth and heading into the unknown?

Now let us talk about what really happens to the souls.

As you have already been told several times, hell does not exist. Neither does paradise exist. There are the Solar Fields, nonexistence, and remaining as a spirit for a shorter or longer period of time, or else immediate incarnation into another living being.

You see, heralds, the matter is very complicated. The same yardstick cannot be applied to all spirits, for there are some advantages to being a spirit, or to being incarnated in a living being.

The spirit is free from all pain, and from hunger and thirst, but he is also deprived of all the physical joys which living beings know. First of all, the joys of passion, the enjoyment of food or drinks, and so on.

Some spirits feel good as spirits, but other spirits find it more pleasant to be incarnated and to enjoy all the joys and sorrows of physical life. Therefore, many spirits desire to undertake some task again soon, and to incarnate.

Obviously, not all the desires of every spirit can be fulfilled, and not at all times, but God generally tries to oblige the spirits wherever possible.

Unless an individual has sinned greatly against the laws of God, he has nothing to fear when leaving Earth.

Now, with respect to this unwillingness to die. If man does not want to die, then he should take care of himself so that this would not happen as soon. What do we see, though? Many people cause their own death by drinking, smoking, using narcotics, and failing to take care of their body – not caring about avoiding diseases, and so on.

Humanity must eliminate all this smoking, excessive use of alcohol, and the use of narcotics. Medicine, in a simple form, has to be taught in all schools. Each individual should be prepared for life, should be familiarized with the construction and functioning of his body, and has to be familiarized with what is harmful and what is good for his body. A person has to become familiar with diseases, and how to prevent them, as well as with the effect of apartments and cities on human health. He must become familiar with everything that benefits or harms man. The states have to provide good conditions for life, and good physicians and hospitals. As the old proverb says, "A healthy spirit in a healthy body."

Compared to the total number of people, there are very few murderers, thieves, and other evil people. It is easy to get rid of them, and they must be eliminated. You have already been told previously how to achieve that – by upbringing, education, and use of medicine, especially for the mentally ill.

Everything can be achieved with a strong desire, that is already demonstrated by such facts as maintaining cleanliness. There are countries where the streets are clean and nobody throws anything on them, or on the floors either. Also, there are countries where people are polite, give the right of way to each other, do not create disturbances, do not wander around on the streets drunk and singing, and so on. Almost anywhere we look, we can see that everything can be achieved with a strong desire and perseverance.

In the next conversation we will discuss how to organize the Tidings and what to do with them.← [[2244]]

<u>Omega</u>                              06/23/67 2105

→The Almighty's Chief Spirit Omega speaking. Heralds, before turning to the examination of the future work, let us talk some more about the present.

Currently the nations on Earth are alarmed greatly due to the small but important war between the Israeli and Arab nations. Let us hope that this war will end not only with destruction, but that it will also bring new prospects for humanity to cooperate for the good of everyone.

We will also clarify the question concerning freedom. Absolute freedom is completely impossible, for it results in an absurdity. For example, an individual enters your home, looks it over, and says, "I like your home rather well, therefore I am taking it for myself, because that is how I want it. Now, get out of my home and do not try to take anything with you!"

Obviously, having left your home, you can return and tell the same thing to the new owner, and on and on, until eternity, and this is absurd!

There has to be freedom, but it has to be given in a way that will help all people feel as good as possible. Therefore, let us call freedom – SENSIBLE FREEDOM – and let us struggle against those expressions of freedom which benefit only one, or a few people.

To continue, all people have to be considered as full-fledged citizens, without giving particular privileges to the various ages of the individual. Children and old people, as being unable to defend themselves and their rights, have to be placed under the protection of society. Children have to be loved, and protected from life's mishaps, but there is no basis for admiring or pampering them, because later on, the latter will only harm the children.←

As The Almighty's chief spirit, I can announce The Almighty's thoughts about the little candle in the deep snow, at night in the cemetery.

Subsequent to their answers, some heralds felt as though they had been incorrect. They were not that, except the heralds had not perceived what had happened, to the full breadth and depth of the essence. Alexander – as a participant in the event – reasoned entirely correctly that others, who might be personally guilty, should not suffer because of his good deed.

Alexo and Mary said correctly that the nuns who did not live up to their responsibilities should be punished. They merely forgot that this negligence of the nuns was not their first one, that there had been many such cases, and that they deserve to receive punishment for this continuous negligence, which also includes that night's negligence. The Almighty considers that this little candle has a universal significance.

In six minutes now, we will turn to the further goal of the Tidings.

[[Intermission 2126 - 2132.]]

→Now then, let us continue. With respect to the contents of the Tidings, you will be faced with many and most varied objections. First of all, many people will claim that the Tidings are directed against the church.

They are not directed against the church as such, but rather against that which takes place in the church and is contrary to the demands of Christ. The Tidings do not call for the destruction of churches, but merely for their transformation into true churches of Christ.

Some people will object that the Tidings occasionally speak contrary to the teachings of Christ. They do not speak contrary to them, but simply correct on occasion those errors which were committed in the composition of the New Testament, as well as supplement it with what was completely omitted.

Similarly, it is clear to every sensibly thinking person that, in two thousand years, changes have taken place in man's understanding of the universe so that what had been introduced in the Holy Scriptures allegorically, nowadays assumes an entirely different form of the notion.

Back then man was still like a child. He could understand the universe having been created in six days, but he could not understand it being created over millions of years. The writers of the Bible themselves knew hardly anything about the universe and its creation. There is much in the Bible that is true, but there is also much in it that is untrue or altered. Therefore, the Bible cannot be considered as only a book of history, but it has to be considered as a book of legends, as well.

_ ★ ★ ★ _

Good night, heralds. Chief Spirit Omega.← [[2203]]


Santorino                          06/30/67 2107


→Santorino speaking. Heralds, in his previous tiding The Almighty's Chief Spirit Omega mentioned some subjects whose resolution has been allocated to God. One of these topics was the church.

It has been discussed many times. In addition, some spirits have used very strong language with respect to it, and particularly its activities during certain eras. Even though this language was strong, it cannot be referenced to the church during its entire period of existence.

The church, as a building, called the house of God, is a real house of God only when that which takes place within it, is what God has recognized as being correct and as being His.

The name by itself does not prove anything. Similarly, a priest's robe in itself will not transform a man into a priest, unless he carries out specifically the mission which God has given him. Also, a judge's robe does not assure that the judge will always serve justice. - ★ ★ ★ -

In the Soviet Union there were courts which sentenced innocent people to death, or to a slow death in Siberia. Therefore, the name is quite often not only misleading, but contrary to its designation.

We, the spirits,... By these two words I mean The Almighty, His chief spirits, God and His high spirits, and all the spirits who brought the Tidings to you. Therefore, we, the spirits, may not be unjust and fail to tell the truth, wherever it has to be told.

Thus, we condemned the Hebrews for killing Christ, and for their obstinate adherence to the outdated laws. We recognized though, that in the last war they fought for their lives, that they had the right to do this, and we were on their side.

Thus, we are against the priests and condemn those who act contrary to the teachings of Christ. However, we praise and recognize those priests who strive to do everything that is possible for the good of the people, and who teach them how to live according to the teachings of Christ. We express the greatest respect to those priests who died the death of martyrs during the Soviet Revolution, and to those who continue even now to serve God and the people.

Likewise, we respect the church as a house of God, if the true Christian faith is proclaimed within it, and not only in words, but in deeds as well. Even though it is a slow process, the current church is returning to that church which Christ founded.

The goal of The Almighty's new religion is not to divide, but to unite; and not only to condemn, but to bring out and emphasize the good that can be found in other religions. Also, to support them as long as their objectives are the same, even though they may be expressed in different words.

It is not with hatred, but with love, that the hearts of others can be conquered. Understanding, patience, and most important, the ability and the will to convince people of your truth are needed.←

(A two minute intermission.) [[2138 - 2140]]

→One should not forget that The Almighty's faith is based on the teachings of Christ, and only supplements them with new concepts which were absent at the time of Christ.

Man leaves behind him not only his Earth, but even his solar system. Man enters the galaxies of other Gods and seeks the creator and guide of the universe – The Almighty! No scientific devises can locate Him, and no one can tell man anything about Him without the will of The Almighty.

Besides that, man started to lose the goal of his life, for he did not know his real task in the new, wide world. Man had to know what his goal was. He had to know that The Almighty summons him to help Him in the formation of a better universe.

All people will not be able to understand this new religion readily. It is intended for the more capable spirits and for the more capable people. It is intended for those who are able to understand it, and are able to undertake The Almighty's great task, for the benefit of the many humanities on Earth as well as in the universe.

In fact, The Almighty's faith consists of two parts. The first part supplements and explains the old faith of Christ. The second part talks about the new faith of the universe. The first part is intended for all people, and the second only for the more capable ones.←

(A five minute intermission.) [[2154 - 2159]]

→We will talk a little bit about man on Earth, but first, we will discuss the living beings and everything else.

As has been mentioned several times, The Almighty created the universe without any model, or without any idea whatsoever about what to do in this universe. Initially, He felt that unless His existence had some logical goal, then it also had no purpose in being. He decided to create something definite, something hard and solid, and to create life on it – to create the living beings. This would give work to His spirit, which had been divided into many spirits.

Creating the suns and planets was a difficult chore, and their cooling down required millions of years. Just imagine how many different laws had to be invented in order to create these heavenly bodies, and in order to hold them together. All these gravities and other forces had to be invented.

Then [He had to modify] matter. Everything from the tiniest – even invisible in your microscope – and the largest thing, even imperceptible in a telescope, had to be created and made to function according to specific laws.

The period of experimentation began once some planets cooled down, and the opportunity arose for the plant and animal kingdoms to develop there. It was not possible to create the animals first, because there was no food. Grass and trees had to be created initially, and only then could He think about animals living in water as well as on land.

What should the grass, the trees, and the animals be like? No one could explain that to The Almighty, so He began to think and then to experiment. Many attempts failed, but some succeeded, and as His work proceeded, there was more and better success.

With further cooling down of the planets, new forms of plants and animals had to be created. The Almighty based His work on the theory of the survival of the fittest. Thus the animal and plant kingdoms took shape. The less capable ones vanished, the more capable ones took their place, and so on.

It was now possible to start thinking about man, about a being in whom His spirit could incarnate. And man, with his different abilities, was created in several locations on Earth. Then he had to fight for the first place on Earth.

Now we have turned specifically to your planet.

As you know, a struggle is merciless. One plant squeezes out another, and one animal replaces another. Besides that, plants have to provide food for the animals, and the animals, too, have to provide food for other stronger animals. Therefore, in truth, the task of the animals was to provide nutrition for the stronger animals. The task of the stronger ones was to develop even more. Therefore, there was only a struggle for existence. The only concern in life was how to preserve one's life. Mercifulness, suffering, and pain were not issues of importance, for everything came and went. Everything was bound with one another, and as a whole, this prepared a place for man.

It turned out that both kingdoms had only one task, and that was to give man everything that he needed. Obviously, whatever turned out to be unnecessary or hostile to man had to disappear. Some plants knew how to become useful to man with their nuts and fruit. Some grasses, too, such as rice, wheat, and rye, and some vegetables such as beets and carrots, became necessary for man, and he began to cultivate them.

Some animals, such as cows, sheep, horses, camels, and elephants, were intelligent enough to recognize man as their master, and began to serve him. The dog and cat turned out to be particularly smart, and they became man's best friends. Others, however, had to retreat further into the forests, and even become completely extinct.

Once man understood that now he was the master of Earth, he started to think about forming his society, about improving his life, and inventing tools for all of his needs. He began to try to understand everything that was unknown, and tried to comprehend the entire world.

Man also began to think about developing the sciences and writing down his thoughts, so that he would not lose everything that he had acquired for his benefit and knowledge. Instead, it would be preserved for future generations.

The decisive step along man's road to eternity was made with the invention of writing. Knowledge was no longer being lost, it multiplied and became more exhaustive. Millions of ordinary people could join the wise people and share in their knowledge.

Humanity has now become aware that the time for wars has passed, just as the time of kings has passed. Humanity now has to cooperate to improve life, and to further develop science and its achievements. The Earth has been given to everyone and one does not have to fight over it. Hatred will not bring happiness to humanity – only love will. The unification of all of man's positive powers will create Paradise on Earth.

Yet Paradise, man's final goal on Earth, is not man's final goal in the universe, because the universe awaits man both as a spirit, and later on as a living being.

We will conclude with that. I wish all of you a good rest over the summer, so that in the fall you will have renewed strength, with which to continue your great task.← [[2254]]

# Chapter XVI

# Summer - Fall 1967

Aksanto                                    09/01/67 2035

Aksanto is speaking. Heralds, since your summer vacations are not yet over for everyone, today we will talk in a friendly manner about whatever comes to mind. First, I want to return to the painful subject regarding human relationships.

No matter how insignificant he might seem to himself, man has to understand that every person is responsible for humanity's activities and shaping its destiny. Every individual has to fight for those ideals which can benefit humanity the most. It is unfortunate that so many people allow other people to mold their life and future.

"What can I do? Let those act who have abilities and power!"

They obviously act, but not always like they should. Quite often they act as is better for them, but not for the little man. This is particularly true in such free countries as the United States of America.

Everyone has been given an opportunity to influence life, and everyone should utilize it. [That can be done] by talking to other people, by asking them to help you or him, by writing to newspapers, and by turning in petitions to superiors, party leaders, and everyone who is able to do anything for the good of the cause. Energy often performs miracles. You can see for yourselves that a certain Negro can arouse thousands, even for an incorrect action.

If you will read history, you will find much in it that tells about an individual having been able to alter the destinies of nations.

It is necessary to criticize others, but everyone should also do as much on his own as he is able to. What do we see, though? Many people scream that they have been robbed or beaten up. If these same people, however, see someone else being robbed, beaten up, or even killed, they do not lift a finger to help the victims. Some people even refuse to cooperate with the police, not wanting to become involved in the event. If everyone would, in such cases, rush to help – all this violence would quickly disappear. The same thing also holds true of other injustices, which many people often observe, but fail to do anything to avert them.

Yes, everyone knows how to gather in a small crowd and slander those neighbors who are not present, but to improve life, to improve what is bad – let others do that!

Life is so diverse that everyone cannot like everything in it. Similarly, everyone does not like the same foods, because tastes are different. This diversity often expresses itself in an undesirable manner, which makes life unpleasant for many people. If man himself does not always do everything to his own liking, then what can be expected from others?

People who become so wealthy that they can afford to buy almost everything that they want to, generally develop exaggerated demands. The least trifle, which is almost unnoticeable and imperceptible to others, makes the food, drink, or something else unusable for them or for him. Yet that is not the main concern. Everyone can eat what he likes. The main problem is that the individual tells others about these hardly perceptible trifles, and eventually ruins the so-called reputation, and everyone is afraid to invite him to a party or give him a present.

It is advisable to keep your thoughts about foods and the appropriateness of gifts to yourself. People do not realize how much they hurt themselves by such unnecessary display of their taste.

It is a different matter to act like that in a store, because the salespeople are used to such unpleasant situations.

Much has been said about patriotism, but patriotism should not be exaggerated. A person should love his nation, but he should not be blind. He also has to see his nation's bad characteristics, as well as the good traits of other nations.

You have to know how to correctly evaluate everything. An individual often becomes his own worst enemy, or else becomes ridiculous as viewed by others, particularly at times of uncontrollable anger. You should fear anger as you fear fire. Learn how to control yourselves, and control yourselves no matter how difficult this might seem.

_ ★ ★ ★ _

Together with you, I regret the summer that has passed, along with its pleasant vacations. Good night, heralds. [[2133]]

<u>Santorino</u>                          09/15/67 2051

Santorino is speaking. Heralds, we – the spirits – accepted Alexander's invitation today to gather with you in order to observe the leading herald's name day and birthday. We gladly utilize this invitation in order to be together with you on a planet which even though it is one of the smaller ones in the universe, nevertheless is one of the more important ones. It is not even possible for you to evaluate the importance of your work, because currently you cannot grasp its huge significance to humanity. It has outgrown the knowledge and instructions which God's prophets and Christ gave it. Man has entered the infinite universe with billions of stars and innumerable planets, and feels that he has wandered into an unknown world. God remained, but He seemed to be lost in this unimaginably grand world.

Children's fairy tales and stories no longer satisfied man. A new world had to be revealed to him, and he had to be given new goals in life. The Almighty chose you for this work, and also accepted a few others who joined, in order to make the work easier. They have gone in different directions. Some have come to God, and others have returned to everyday life. However, you have lived up to The Almighty's expectations, and you are envisaged to achieve a particularly outstanding position in the realm of the spirits. I will not evaluate the deeds of all of you today, but will talk only about Alexander, because today is his day.

Alexander was blessed with a mind that was clear and capable of correctly evaluating the values which have been given to people, and have been expressed by their more outstanding representatives. He [did not accept] even the teachings of unquestionable authorities. He enthusiastically accepted Christ's teachings, but rejected with surliness what the church and all people had altered. He accepted science and philosophy the same way. He predicted unlimited possibilities for science, but after a brief familiarization with the huge works of the philosophers, he rejected further study of philosophy, because it turned out that this could give him little that was new. He had already achieved on his own what the books of the philosophers told him. He had been given the abilities of a poet and writer, as well. The work of the Tidings kept him from fully developing and utilizing these. I have to say that sometimes we robbed him, and made use of the material of his thoughts.

His parents left him the largest of human values – honesty, the love of man, and a heart that was not indifferent to people's sorrows and suffering. He possessed a rare characteristic – the initiative to not wait for others to do something, but to do it on his own. He also had the trait of understanding people and evaluating them, while trying to elicit their good traits in them. And, oh wonder, some intolerant and hard to bear people lost their negative characteristics with respect to him. Therefore he had very few enemies, because he knew the art of getting along with people. I will give you a few examples from his life, which will clarify what I have said about him.

I will remind you of an event in the cemetery, in which his wife and her mother are buried. His habit – which has several explanations, some of which you know – is to visit the cemetery every week and light a candle. The event with this candle, which burned for an entire week alone in the snow-covered cemetery, elicited the highest notice in the realm of the spirits. It stopped along his way every spirit who happened to be flying over the cemetery. Obviously, many spirits learned about this, and tried to see this candle for themselves. Of course, the first one to express this knowledge was God, who sees and knows everything. Due to chance circumstances, this lonely flame cast its light over the entire universe – as a certain symbol.

Something else happened in this same cemetery. This characterizes human nature and testifies about the tremendous importance of initiative.

There was a narrow path from the highway to the cemetery, which went through the woods and considerably reduced the distance to the cemetery. Alexander started using this path, but it became almost impassable in the spring and fall. Alexander started putting stones in the wetter places, and gradually made the path usable.

One day, along the path, he started talking with a nun. Among other things, the nun began wondering who was putting stones in the puddles, thus making the path passable. Alexander confessed to this "sin," and the nun exclaimed, "We were wondering, and already started talking about a miracle! I will tell the cemetery supervisor to put down some boards, we have plenty of old boards."

A few boards appeared on the path the following week. Then one day last year they disappeared, and the stones had been covered with soil. A little while later, half the path was covered with gravel, and the week before last the entire path had been covered with fine gravel. This pleased all visitors to the cemetery, and obviously pleased Alexander as well. You see, that is how an enterprising individual's initiative works on people!

The worst problem is that people say, "Why should I do that? Why don't others do it, because they also need it?"

Thus, no initiator comes along, and everyone wades through mud up to their knees, because no one wants to work for others without compensation or their help. As you can see from what I just told you, initiative pays off for everyone and it is well for everyone.

An example or a model is just as important. When Alexander buried Antonina in the cemetery, the cemetery looked sad. The graves had not been taken care of, and only a few had any flowers on them. Alexander fixed up Antonina's grave, planted some flowers, and covered the ground around the grave with little white stones. And, you see, the cemetery started to transform. Caretakers appeared, flowers started to bloom on the grave mounds, and the cemetery itself also started to look better, because people started taking care of it and removing the weeds. Now this cemetery looks like a flower garden, and is considered to be the most beautiful cemetery in the entire vicinity.

In the beginning, on seeing nearby graves neglected, Alexander started removing the wilted flowers and weeds from them. People quickly noticed that, and this spread throughout the entire cemetery. There were two neglected graves not far from Antonina's grave. The tablets with inscriptions had fallen off from the crosses. Alexander went to the cemetery office, asked how much the tablets with inscriptions cost, paid five dollars for them, and asked that they be placed on the crosses by next Friday.

Confusion arouse in the office. "Why do you have to pay to have the inscriptions replaced? That is our duty. We cannot understand how none of us had noticed that the tablets had fallen off. We will replace them!"

"Well, fine," Alexander said, "that is nice to hear, but use my money to take care of the graves."

When Alexander arrived the next Friday, the tablets were not on the crosses yet. He asked in the office why they had not been replaced.

"Yes, you see, they are ready, but the inscriptions have not dried yet."

When Alexander was ready to leave the cemetery, he saw the cemetery artist rush over to the graves and nail on the new tablets. Oh wonder, not only are the graves now adorned with new tablets, but even the grave mounds have been fixed up and flowers have been planted on them. You see, that is how people's conscience has to be awakened, and that is how the desire has to be awakened in people to start on their own what is necessary, without looking to others. Then the others will start looking to you. It is extremely important to awaken this spirit of initiative in people, and then humanity will become entirely different.

In conclusion, I will tell you how easy it is sometimes to make an individual happy. Recently Alexander visited an exhibition of paintings, organized by a painters' organization. It was an outdoor exhibition of paintings. Fences and building walls were covered with thousands of paintings. Alexander stopped at a collection of paintings on a fence. A pretty girl sat on the sidewalk, beneath the paintings. Alexander looked at her and said without thinking, "You are the most beautiful painting here, God's painting."

The girl's eyes sparkled, and she said deeply moved, "Thank you, thank you."

She will forget much that was important and beautiful in her life, but she will tell even her children's children that at the painting exhibition an elderly gentleman of distinguished appearance called her the most beautiful painting at the exhibition. One does not forget such things.

I am surrounded by many spirits who wanted to be with you this evening, and all of them asked me to congratulate Alexander on his high days of remembrance, and wish him all the good that is possible in life on Earth.

I also thank the other heralds for participating in this day of remembrance. Their work is also extremely important, and it could not be accomplished without their help and participation.

I pass on to all of you The Almighty's heartfelt gratitude for the great work, which is too important to be remunerated materially.

May God's blessing be with you – Alexander, Alexo, John, and Mary. God's envoy, Santorino.          [[2234]]


<u>Santorino</u>                    09/22/67 2056

Heralds, the previous time our tiding became rather lengthy, and you felt tired, therefore I decided to postpone the remaining part of my tiding until today. I had planned on talking with you today as well, even though about another subject.

We talked about the effect that one person's undertaking can have on people. We spoke of good undertakings, but bad undertakings can also have a similar effect on people. We can now see that from the foul activities of the Negroes, conducted as if for a noble cause – improving the situation of the Negro people.

Good results have to be achieved by good means. Only evil results can be achieved by evil means. World history tells about many good and also evil deeds of people's initiative. Good initiative does not always bring success. Envy and bad people quite often suppress it. Sometimes people who are not capable of anything prominent, have an extremely large effect on an undertaking. In order to somehow demonstrate their own worth, they start spreading imagined rumors, and variously slandering the initiator of the good undertaking. Since people like to listen to what is said about someone else – without any attempts to find out whether it is the truth or lies – then frequently nothing good comes of a well-intentional undertaking. People have to fight against such a phenomenon, have to try to find out the truth, and the slanderers have to be harshly punished morally. You should never be gullible and quick in believing something that has not been verified.

Let us now talk about today's tiding. Currently people in the entire world read the memories of Stalin's daughter about herself and her father, as well as about a few other people. These memories are extremely important, because they reveal much that was unknown. They tell about a man who had become the ruler of a nation of millions. We know about the rulers of this nation – the czars. Some of them, too, were horrible and merciless, but they did not come anywhere close to Stalin. The difference was that they were lawful rulers, but Stalin became a ruler by means of a merciless fight for power. He managed to get at the head of the people who craved for power, push them aside or eliminate them, and grab unlimited power for himself.

It is not easy to retain such unlawful power. Others crave for it as well. I cannot say that Stalin – especially in the beginning – fought only for power for himself. He also fought for the so-called victory of communism, because he believed in it, just like many people back then believed that communism can make people happy, can make all people happy. All that was necessary was to eliminate the wealthy and the parasites, as well as those people who used to hold power – and then reeducate the people. However, the very best idea is useless if it is alien to human nature.

All characteristics of human nature are not praiseworthy, but if an individual possesses them – one has to take that into account. First, man wants to be as free as possible. He also wants to be independent and make his own decisions. He wants to be well off, too, and wants to consider what belongs to him as being his, but not as someone else's there, no matter who that might be. Thus a long and dreadful fight began between the communist government and the people. Millions of people perished in this fight, and even more millions, because they wound up underfoot of those fighting and were trampled.

The daughter tells about her father. It is easy to tell about a good father, but it is difficult and almost impossible to tell about a father whom people considered to be a monster. She says that she had even loved her father. That is understandable, because, after all, a father is nevertheless a father, and this father had occasionally even loved his daughter.

The situation with such rulers – tyrants – as Stalin is understandable. He holds on to power only with the help of power. Since he knows that his conduct does not elicit love, but only fear and hatred, he cannot trust anyone. In order to retain their position and trust, the people who manage to get close to him try to prove [their loyalty] by betraying his enemies to him – real or imagined, who can know that. It turns out thus that he cannot trust anyone, not even his relatives, and not even his children and wives.

He had considered his latest wife – Svetlana's mother – to be an enemy, because she defended those whom he considered to be his enemies. She also did not agree with his politics with respect to the farmers. It seemed to him that he loved this woman and that she also loved him. Then she committed suicide – thus putting him in a bad light in the eyes of the people. After having read the letter which she left behind, in which she told the truth about his actions, he considered her to be among his enemies. He pushed aside her coffin, did not participate in her funeral, and did not visit her gravesite even once.

He could not trust the physicians either, except for one, but he was also slandered, and was jailed. The unthinkable began – a conspiracy of the physicians. Only his sudden death saved the physicians.

Along came Beria, who knew how to grovel up to him and acquire his trust. This Beria hoped to obtain his position. Therefore he decided to eliminate even Stalin's relatives, who might hinder him. He almost achieved the realization of his intent.

→And so, what did Stalin achieve? Happiness? What happiness? Yes, his name was praised as the name of a genius, and lots and lots of monuments were erected in his honor. The designations of very many cities were changed to his name. With respect to fame, Stalin surpassed the greatest rulers of the entire world. It seemed that his fame will endure eternally, but what happened a few years after his death? All the monuments disappeared, the cities regained their old designations, and instead of praising him, people began to condemn him and blame him for all their problems. However, the monuments of people like Pushkin, Lomonosov, and other men on Earth who have been recognized as spiritual leaders, continue to stand in the squares of various cities.

We have now reached the most important phase in Stalin's life, and not only in his life, but in the life of the entire humanity. The end of Stalin's life on Earth had come. He lay in bed and struggled with death, while his daughter sat next to him and held his hand. The right side of his body had suffered a stroke and was immobile.

The daughter sat there and watched her father's struggle with death. A room full of people observed it as well. The best physicians tried to help him in this struggle, [but could not]. The struggle became ever more difficult. Stalin was short of breath, and his body fought desperately against death. His facial features became almost unrecognizable and his lips turned black. Stalin was semiconscious. Occasionally he opened his blurred eyes, but he saw hardly anything. Suddenly in the room, above the heads of the people, he noticed Mortifero's figure. It was the envoy of the God whom he and millions of his adherents had proclaimed to be nonexistent, to have died, and to be powerless.

The envoy of this God now stood before him, and Stalin understood that Mortifero had come for him. Stalin opened his eyes, which were filled with hatred and inexpressible fear. He looked at the people in the room and at the heads of the physicians, whom he did not know, bent over him. He raised his arm and pointed at Mortifero, while shouting, "Save me!"

However, his tongue did not obey him and Stalin knew that no one – not the physicians, nor his generals, the millions of soldiers, tanks, and artillery pieces – could any longer save him from God. He understood that no one could save him any longer, and that he must face the forgotten Judge – God. His arm dropped feebly to his side, and his spirit departed from his body.

The body ceased its struggle with death and relaxed. The face of Stalin became recognizable and peaceful once again. Thus man's struggle with God had ended.←

Extract the description of her father's death from Svetlana's book, and add it to this tiding.

→It is horrible if man, while feeling secure on Earth, forgets that God does exist. God accepts calmly all these cries that He does not exist, and that He has died. God knows that only animals, plants, and people die, and that even entire worlds die. Yet, the ruler of everything and the judge of everyone – God – does not die. Only The Almighty and His spirits do not die.

Good night, heralds. Santorino.← [[2234]]

[[Extract from **Twenty Letters to a Friend**, by Svetlana Alliluyeva.

My father died a difficult and terrible death. It was the first and so far the only time I have seen somebody die. God grants an easy death only to the just.

The hemorrhaging had gradually spread to the rest of the brain. Since his heart was healthy and strong, it affected the breathing centers bit by bit and caused suffocation. His breathing became shorter and shorter. For the last twelve hours the lack of oxygen was acute. His face altered and became dark. His lips turned black and the features grew unrecognizable. The last hours were nothing but a slow strangulation. The death agony was horrible. He literally choked to death as we watched. At what seemed like the very last moment he suddenly opened his eyes and cast a glance over everyone in the room. It was a terrible glance, insane or perhaps angry and full of fear of death and the unfamiliar faces of the doctors bent over him. The glance swept over everyone in a second. Then something incomprehensible and awesome happened that to this day I can't forget and don't understand. He suddenly lifted his left hand as though he were pointing to something above and bringing down a curse on us all. The gesture was incomprehensible and full of menace, and no one could say to whom or at what it might be directed. The next moment, after a final effort, the spirit wrenched itself free of the flesh.

I thought I was about to suffocate, too, and I clutched the hand of a young woman doctor who was standing next to me. She started moaning from pain, and we held on tightly to one another.

The spirit had flown. The flesh grew still. The face became pale and assumed its usual appearance. In a few seconds it was serene, beautiful, imperturbable. We all stood frozen and silent for a few minutes. I've no idea for how long, but it seemed like ages.

The above has been extracted from pages 10 and 11 of **Twenty Letters to a Friend**, by Svetlana Alliluyeva. Copyright 1967 by Copex Establishment. English translation copyright 1967 by Priscilla Johnson McMillan. Published by Harper & Row, Publishers, Incorporated, New York, NY.]]

<u>Ilgya</u>                          09/29/67 2220

Ilgya. Heralds, the Divine asked me to supplement his tiding about Stalin with a few important remarks. It is particularly important to understand the pathway that human consciousness travels. Why did communism have to go so far, and why did it start to retreat from the position that it had achieved, only after a prolonged period? Every idea that has not been utilized to the very end and in which all possibilities have not been tried out, still seems feasible. If all possibilities, though, have been tried out and the results are bad, only then can the consciousness begin to dawn that the idea itself is wrong, and therefore unsuitable for human needs and requirements. Only then can the road back begin, or else toward something new.

The Communists in the Soviet Union used all means in order to make their idea successful. That is what happened at the end of Stalin's lifetime. The first thing which the communist leaders understood was that a dictatorship – the dictatorship of one man – threatened the lives of everyone, even of those who were very high up, and even of those who were closest to the dictator. Dictatorship causes mistrust, because it is based only on power – without any love and without anything else.

Beria made a big mistake by hoping to assume Stalin's place. The other leaders of communism could no longer allow anyone to assume the power of a dictator, because he would again start with their elimination, in order to get rid of competitors.

Khrushchev understood that best, and did away with revenge by death, but by now that was no longer sufficient for the others. They wanted even more security, and therefore they overthrew Khrushchev and established a cooperative government.

The large failures in almost all of their endeavors testified of communism's unsuitability for life and for human nature. The awakening of the people and return to their sense began slowly, as well as a longing for freedom and for the right to be a human being in the full meaning of the word.

More than one person has wondered about how the communist bigwigs could have made such a big mistake as to allow Svetlana to leave the Soviet Union, and to allow her later on to escape from them in India and end up in the fortress of capitalism – the United States of America. After all, they were no fools, and they were also accustomed to not believe or trust anyone. Still, this incomprehensible error took place. How could that have happened?

Yes, you see, sometimes the wisest people become fools, if God needs that due to important reasons. When Svetlana was born, God assigned one of the more eminent spirits to her as a guardian spirit. Svetlana's spirit, too, is one of similar spirits. Her task was to achieve what Stalin's spirit was no longer able to achieve – to at least partially correct the evil that had been done to the people, by opening their eyes to the horrible crimes of communism, perpetrated under her father's leadership.

Not everything in her book directly corresponds to the truth, because initially she was a child and did not understand anything. Also, being secluded from the people she did not know anything about their lives.

Only on becoming older and experiencing family tragedies – like the death of her mother, and the deaths and suffering of many relatives – she began to comprehend her father, as well as communism. In the later years she had little opportunity to be with her father. She had to find out about life in general and about what her father did only from those who visited the places where she lived, and these were not readily accessible either.

She comprehended extremely well her father's terrible moment of death. She said that God grants an easy death only to good people. She correctly understood almost all the experiences of her dying father, except she could not understand why, at the last moment of his life, he raised his arm while pointing at something.

Obviously, you want to know how Chief Spirit Mortifero received Joseph's soul, and how it met God – God, the ruler of the universe. Perhaps someday the chief spirit will tell you that.

He only allowed me to tell you for now that on alighting into the Deoss Temple, Joseph met his mother's spirit, and told her, "Oh, why didn't I listen to you?"

To which his mother's spirit responded, "Yes, why didn't you do that?"

Your idea to write a letter to Svetlana is nice, but how will you accomplish that? Svetlana receives many letters every day, and seldom do any of them get directly to her. Yet why not try? First of all, much will depend on how you will write the letter, so that she will be interested in it, and mainly – so that Svetlana could believe your letter, for, truly, to everyone who is not prepared for a letter like that it may seem like something fabricated.

I advise each of you to write this letter, and we will decide next Friday what to do.

Good night, heralds. Ilgya. [[2315]]

Santorino                          10/20/67 2257

Santorino is speaking. Heralds, The Almighty's envoy just spoke with you. As you can see, the fate of the Tidings is important to everyone, because high expectations have been placed on humanity. This despite some diversions, the latest being communism – which truly was horrible but which nevertheless was unable to hold humanity back from its correct course – which is now dying. It is struggling fiercely, but it is nevertheless dying. It brought dreadful suffering for a large part of humanity, but it also demonstrated the endurance of the human spirit and its ability to win. The souls of the victims rest in the Solar Fields, and none of them even try to think of refusing a similar task, should that be necessary.

Chief Spirit Mortifero explained so much to you that I have nothing to supplement. I only want to say that despite the mistakes which you sense yourselves, your achievements are large, and eventually will be just like God expected from you. Merely work jointly and help each other in a friendly manner, and then everything will be fine.

I pass God's blessing on to you. Santorino. [[2308]]


<u>Ilgya</u>                          10/27/67 2306


Ilgya. Heralds, we understand your situation extremely well, as well as the doubts that arise to some of you. It cannot be any other way, for you are living beings who think, and whoever thinks also criticizes. What is important? It is important to criticize and doubt until all possibilities have been examined and the right decision has been reached, or else a decision that is as good as possible. Sometimes it is not possible to reach a completely correct decision, because the circumstances are so different and unusual that an unswerving decision cannot be made.

You sometimes know someone so well that you can predict how he will react in every situation, but it may happen that he will – perhaps even to his own surprise – suddenly react differently. There is a strange word called "impulse," whose existence one always has to take into account. There are no laws without exceptions, because there are such complicated and unforeseen circumstances that the law turns out to be unsuitable. That, you see, is what life is like!

There are the so-called laws of life, but no matter how many of them there might be, it will always turn out that there are too few of them. The situation is particularly complicated with respect to people with initiative – people who search for something new. Obviously, these people find something that has not yet existed, or else has been unknown, and that immediately changes the situation. You can see what the so-called scientists have done to the situation in which humanity found itself at the time of Christ. You can idolize the sun and worship it as a god, because it sends you heat and light, without which life cannot be imagined. However, once you have learned everything about the sun, then, while respecting its significance in your life, you will seek the God who has created this sun. Thus you proceed ever further and further into infinity, without even knowing what you will still find there. As long as you do not know infinity in its entirety, how can you hope to know God – now called The Almighty?

That bothers you, for you want to know everything, but you forget that not knowing is what makes your life valuable. If you were to know everything, life would become aimless and uninteresting.

– ★ ★ ★ – [[2347]]

Sineokia                          11/03/67 2211

Sineokia is speaking. – ★ ★ ★ –

I want to talk a little bit about something that seems important to me with respect to man's free will.

As I have said previously about free will, it does not already mean that every individual's free will is advisable, and that it either benefits the person himself or benefits other people. How did the Soviet people benefit from their free will to refuse acknowledging God? If you remove something important from where it was, it has to be replaced by something equally important. With what did the Communists replace God? Which one of them can tell you how the world came into being and who maintains its existence? Similarly, have they explained how they, themselves, have come into being, and why man has always felt that it was not possible to live without God?

Had the Communists found the true Creator of the world and the one who directs its existence, then the matter would have been understandable and acknowledgeable. It is a different and regrettable matter to abrogate God, and leave in His place a hole that has not been filled by anything. What would have happened had you destroyed the horse before it was replaced by the car? You would have simply caused a catastrophe for humanity, because man would have had to put a horse harness on his shoulders and start pulling the plow.

Sense has to direct each individual's free will. Without sense, a human being is no longer a human. Of course, even the most sensible person has to [consider at times whether he] acts correctly, because sometimes free will has doubts about how correctly something has been accepted, whether that concerns the people or God.

No one is punished for having doubts, but everyone has to be responsible for his incorrect actions. Do not forget that there cannot be complete confidence concerning any individual, like two heralds already discussed while considering Christ's situation on Earth. He chose His disciples, but, after all, there was a traitor like Judas among them, and also someone who did not believe like Thomas. During the particularly difficult time when Christ was arrested, none of His apostles dared to defend Him. Life proved, however, that they nevertheless — even if not all, then some of them — were capable of dying on the cross, just like their Teacher.

New heralds may join you, and some of them will perhaps start having doubts, but that should not concern you, and neither should you condemn those who have doubts. Those who are able to overcome their doubts on their own are important. Let those who are incapable of that return to their earthly ways, and may they fare well.

You, Janoss, touched my heart of a spirit with your desire to meet with me more frequently. I will try to do better in the future.

A sincere greeting to you, heralds. Your Sineokia. [[2305]]


Ali                          12/29/67 2128


Your old friend Ali is speaking. I often roam the old Earth, and stick my long Turkish nose in the affairs of all nations. That, you see, is what my awful nature is like. I observe how people give frequently rather good advice to other people, but nothing good comes of it. The recipients of the advice do not fully consider the meaning of the advice or of the order, and act literally, which makes everything either meaningless or even ridiculous.

I remember my sultan having invited to the palace a very wise old man who engaged in examining stars and determining time, as well as in exploring some hundred other sciences. He was so busy that he even forgot to eat, and his wife had to feed him and even had to make him drink. You will laugh about this expression, but she had to, in fact, do that, because otherwise the food which she brought could rot on the plate and the water or milk — evaporate.

The great scientist arrived at the palace dressed rather tolerably, but with bare feet. Since it was raining and back in those days the roads were not paved — as is your Broadway — he left rather dull footprints on the bright palace floor. The sultan noticed that.

When the scientist was getting ready to leave the palace, the sultan had me give him a pair of shoes, and said, "Do not forget to wear them the next time you come to the palace. In general, an outstanding person like you should not be walking around with bare feet."

The old man put on the shoes, and said that his feet felt sort of confined in them, but that he will somehow get used to that.

A rather long period passed before the sultan invited the old man to the palace again. It rained again and the roads were muddy. The old man arrived wearing his shoes, took them off at the entrance, and approached the sultan. Oh wonder, his feet left even worse footprints. The sultan asked in disgust, "How come that your feet have become even dirtier with your shoes on?"

"Yes sultan," the old man replied, "the problem is that even more mud gets in through the holes in my shoes than while walking barefoot."

"After all, you should have had a shoemaker repair your shoes when holes appeared in them."

"Yes ruler," the old crutch said innocently. "But ruler, after all, you did not tell me anything about that."

"Does anyone have to be told that, and particularly a wise individual like you?" the sultan asked.

"Yes ruler, I know much, but, after all, no human in the world can know everything."

The sultan thought for a moment, and then said, "Well, my counselors, tell me how to respond to this man?"

The counselors looked questioningly at each other's faces, but the awaited answer did not come from any mouth.

The sultan then said, "Throw his shoes out the door, and the next time have the guard at the door wash his feet prior to admitting him."

You see, these are the results even these days, if people do not consider the full significance of the order or advice, and try to execute it literally. You saw that this evening, while reading the order of a wise shepherd of the people about how to conduct yourselves in the house of God.

Christ threw the peddlers out of the house of God, but He did not say that every individual should not pray for that for which everyone prays, but rather for that for which he has to pray to God. This one example will suffice.

All people are not capable of thinking independently, and they have to do what other people do. Yet all the others – while doing what all other people do – nevertheless have to consider whether they could come up with something better than other people's ideas. When receiving an order or abiding by a law, they have to contemplate all possibilities which this might conceal.

Even though I was a Turk at one time, I am now a spirit just like all other God's spirits. Therefore I congratulate you with the great festival of many nations on Earth, and also wish you a particularly successful and sensible New Year.

Your Ali.                    [[2209]]


Mortifero                    12/29/67 2220


→In the name of The Ruler of the universe, Chief Spirit Mortifero congratulates the nations on Earth with the New Year, and wishes them to achieve everything that is possible in their goals toward preserving peace and reducing the sorrows and misfortunes of mankind. May they also eradicate hatred, understand love, and follow its call.

The path to eventual comprehension of God and abiding by His laws in all corners of Earth, is not easy and short. Each year, though, draws humanity closer to this goal, even a year which seems to take it away from this goal. The best educated people on Earth have currently achieved such a high level of development, with respect to their intelligence, that the old truths have now became untruths, the old sciences become mere children's toys, and in the light of science the old religious faiths become clearer and more wonderful.

From the ruler of the small paradise on Earth, God becomes the ruler of almost innumerable worlds. Hell, based on physical pain and torture, disappears and turns into torments of the soul for deviating from the laws and tasks which have been given by God. Hordes of devils merge with the darkness of eternity and vanish. They are replaced by Satan's spirits of evaluation, who evaluate the worthiness of man's soul and, according to this evaluation, upgrade or demote the spirit, or even send him into nonexistence.

Considered in a physical sense, the pathway to God has become incomparably longer. Considered spiritually, though, the path has become very short, for it begins on Earth and also may end on Earth. God is on Earth as well, just as on the most distant planets in your galaxy.

The Holy Spirit has assumed His real appearance, the appearance of The Almighty – the creator and ruler of the universe.

On the planet Earth, it appears that currently the old religions are perishing. No, it is not the old religions which are perishing, but those delusions are perishing which were introduced into these religions by false priests, who served mostly themselves instead of God.

It seemed strange to you that you are specifically the ones to bring the new faith of The Almighty to the nations. However, as you can see now, The Almighty does not act only through you, but through all the people, by having them feel a thirst for the true faith.

Your task, heralds, is to serve this wonderful drink to humanity. It is a drink which is capable of freeing man from thirst and of giving him the sense that he, man, is not a slave of God. Man is not just a servant of God either; instead, he is an assistant to The Almighty in forming a better universe. Man may feel proud of himself if he realizes that he has helped The Almighty in achieving His goal.

The Almighty congratulates His assistants in the divine work of transforming the universe, on entering the new, nineteen hundred sixty-eighth year from the birth of Christ on Earth. He wishes them – and particularly you, His heralds – the very best of successes, as well as happiness in your lives.

With that, I take leave from you, heralds. Chief Spirit Mortifero.←
[[2251]]

# Chapter XVII

# Spring 1968

<u>Santorino</u>                    03/29/68 2124

Santorino is speaking. Heralds, I want to spend some time with you again, after a prolonged period, and discuss certain topics. First, concerning what may happen on Earth in the near future.

After the two World Wars, a more peaceful era set in. Even though the minor wars did not entirely cease, they nevertheless had mostly a local significance. Then suddenly the Arab-Israeli war broke out, which already had more than just a local significance. The situation in Palestine – the current Hebrew state – is such that it is almost impossible to resolve it.

For example, the Arabs as well as the Hebrews consider Jerusalem to be their Holy City. At one time Jerusalem belonged to the Hebrews, but then, under pressure from the Arabs, a large majority of the Hebrews scattered throughout the entire world. The Hebrews began to return to Palestine after the First World War, despite the prohibition. Thus the Hebrew state was slowly reborn. Despite its small population, but while supported by Hebrews from throughout the world, it became much stronger than its Arab neighbors.

Being used to their camels, the Arabs did not feel comfortable inside tanks. The Hebrews, who were considered to be poor soldiers, had become first-rate guardians of their homeland. They defeated the Arabs in a very short war, unprecedented in history. A truce was signed – but not a peace accord – and prospects for peace become ever poorer. Neither side is capable of waging a war without the help of other countries, particularly the superpowers. Thus, the United States of America supports the Hebrews, and the Soviet Union supports the Arabs. A war between the Arabs and the Hebrews could eventually involve both superpowers, and even the entire world, in a new war – the Third World War.

A fight against the power of communism has started within the communist states themselves, but it is still at the very beginning.

It is difficult to predict its success in the future, because it depends on extremely many factors. With respect to the Communists themselves, they try to destroy the power of capitalism by all kinds of means and wherever possible. Therefore one has to be very careful while evaluating the world situation.

When it comes to humanity in general, it strives to advance in obtaining and utilizing its knowledge. The latest step – a historic step – is reaching the moon. That is a step that costs extremely much, but man nevertheless does not want to reject it.

Humanity is not as successful in a spiritual sense. Much of the so-called "new" is an erroneous search for something better, or even just merely new. Thus the bearded young people who aimlessly ruin the appearance of the streets do not elicit any joy. Similarly, people prefer to engage in slandering their neighbors, and in empty talk. They exhibit too much of an interest in the family lives of others, and in seeking only the bad and the unpleasant in them. It is immaterial to them whether this is true or false, and occasionally they say something good as well, only when they lack something derogatory to say.

It seems that if an individual sees so much that is bad in others, he should try to free himself from the bad in him, but no one does that. The main task of humanity is to improve the conditions of life, make people wiser and better, and fight against their bad characteristics.

_ ★ ★ ★ _

That should cover the most important aspects of what I wanted to tell you today. In concluding my tiding – on behalf of the high spirits, the spirits who are intimate to you, and myself – I congratulate Mary on her name day. It will be on the first of April – not as a fool's day but as a genuine day of festivities. May God help her in her work and her life.

Good night, on behalf of all the spirits. Santorino, God's envoy to Earth and to all planets in the universe. [[2217]]


Ali                              04/05/68 2209

Old Ali is speaking. Be greeted, my old friends on Earth! Inadvertently I wandered back again onto the Earth a while ago, in order to see how well things were going on this small planet, beloved even to a Turkish heart. There was quite a bit to see, but even more to hear. In my old land, the Arabs and the Hebrews waged a rather thorough but quick war against each other. Initially they wondered that a war can be won – or else lost – that quickly, but after many attempts to conclude a peace treaty, they start thinking again about a new war.

Obviously, the situation is complicated, and probably even the wise Solomon could not decide how to resolve it to the satisfaction of both sides. It seems to me, however, that your situation in America with the black people from Africa is not much better, if not worse. Still, it is not about to start a World War.

With respect to people on Earth in general, they don't seem to have changed much, except it seems that gals have run out of the money – or sense – needed to wear longer skirts. As I notice, though, the fellows don't even think of helping them to obtain longer skirts. Let the young people enjoy themselves, it is not for me, an old man, to try to understand them.

One cannot complain with respect to science. Man continues to achieve ever more and more in order to approach comprehending the universe. Yet, there is one thing which people have not managed to understand so far – there is really no such thing as good and bad. The concept of good and bad is relative. For example, man considers a tiger to be bad, and the tiger considers man to be that. My dear ones, which one then is right? From their point of view, both of them feel justified.

The pig considers man to be a good creature, who takes such good care of it that it could not wish for anything better. Whether this taking care of it is truly something good – the poor pig does not know that until one day the farmer, for whatever reason, approaches it with a large knife, rather than with a bucket of feed.

Man is eliminating or has completely eliminated some animals which were harmful or unnecessary for him. Man, however, protects and feeds others – such as the cow, the dog, the cat, and in some lands still the horse – which became obedient and useful to him.

When it comes to man himself, here there is not a complete distinction regarding what is good and what is bad either. I will say even more – is it always a good thing to do good? I will give you events from the life of herald Alexander, whom you know. All that happened during World War One when Alexander, as a soldier, fought for his homeland against the enemy in Poland. This was in a part of the country which back then belonged to Russia, but that is not very important.

As all good people, Alexander had some friends in his unit. You see, one night when Alexander and his troops had to go on a reconnaissance between the Russian and German trenches, a friend approached him and asked to go as the commander of the reconnaissance patrol instead of Alexander. Alexander would in turn go instead of him the following night. He had a date with a girl and she could not make it tonight.

Alexander also had a date in a village just behind the front lines. Still, he was a very good friend, therefore Alexander sacrificed his own interests because of this friendship, and remained in the trenches.

After a while, a firefight broke out in the area between the trenches, and no one from the Russian reconnaissance patrol returned.

How can you qualify Alexander's actions? Did he do his friend a favor or did he help him to perish? Would their friendship had expressed itself better if Alexander had turned out not to be such a good friend? His friend died in his place, but could he – his friend, that is – be mad at Alexander? Of course not! As you can see, in this case the words good and bad have the same meaning.

Another event now. Should an individual rejoice over another person's death, or should he regret it?

The event which I want to relate to you happened in the same place, a few months later. Alexander's unit was in reserve for rest, a few miles to the rear of the front lines. The Germans had spotted some of the huts of the reserve regiment along the edge of the forest, and placed heavy artillery fire in the camp. They simultaneously used high explosive and poison gas rounds. The soldiers put on their gas masks, and headed through the forest away from the line of fire. While running, Alexander felt a piece of shrapnel shatter his gas mask and make it useless. The forest was saturated with gas; there was no way to save himself.

Then Alexander saw a soldier who was running in front of him suddenly fall. Alexander ran up to him and saw that the soldier had been hit by a piece of shrapnel and that he was dead. Alexander tore the gas mask from the fallen soldier and put it on, thus saving his life.

What do you think, should Alexander have rejoiced over the soldier's death, or regretted it? What does Mary think?

[[Mary gave an indeterminate response.]]

Alexo?

[[Also an indeterminate response.]]

John?

[[Janoss: "One could neither rejoice nor regret in the confusion."]]

Alexander?

[[Silence.]]

Of course, it is difficult for you to answer, but try anyway!

[[Alexander: "To tell you the truth, there was no time to rejoice. I was glad to have remained alive."]]

As you can see, heralds, there are times in life when concepts become completely muddled. Life is very complicated and sometimes man does not know what is good and what is bad. Still, try to be good toward your friend, and help him out even if perhaps you have to sacrifice your own life. Do that even if he ends up dying in your stead.

I don't think that you will be able to stand any more of a chain of events like these. Therefore, I take leave and wish you pleasant dreams, in which you can play the roles of heroes, without risking either your own or your friend's lives.

Your Ali.                    [[2319]]


<u>Aksanto</u>                    04/12/68 2148


Heralds, after a prolonged period, I am again with you, The Almighty's heralds to humanity on the planet Earth. The day approaches when many millions of Christians will again remember the day of Christ parting from Earth. Life – spiritual life – had to be bought through death. Gods ruled on Earth who required sacrifices and who asked for royal respect from their slaves – people. The so-called book of God's wisdom even taught the people – an eye for an eye and a tooth for a tooth! It was time for humanity to emerge from the era of barbarism and become acquainted with the true teachings of God, which ask man to love another man, then he will also love him. Even an animal, like a dog and even a lion, can be subordinated to a human will with the help of love. People – who were very deeply embraced in the power of hatred – had to be shown that even death could not conquer love, that it was reborn in the hearts of millions, following the death of one.

Humanity's road to a real civilization and to the real religion of God was not smooth and uninterrupted. You saw this after the revolution in Russia. This was one of the more horrible returns to barbarism. Even there, however, the rebirth begins, even though it is a difficult and long one. The shackles have become corroded with rust and they are no longer strong. The day will come when Christ will return to His Earth once again – enveloped in the rays of sun.

On behalf of the high spirits and myself, as well as on behalf or your friends and relatives who have departed from Earth, I congratulate you with the Easter Festival, and wish you to spend it in peace and happiness. May God's blessing be with you. Aksanto.        [[2212]]

<u>Nakcia</u>                        04/19/68 2057

Nakcia. Heralds, I congratulate you with the past Easter Festival, as well as with the forthcoming one! That sounds somewhat strange, but that is how it is. The different branches of the Christian faith – if one may say so – cannot decide on a single date. After all, though, why not let people celebrate when and how they prefer? Some Easter songs sound very nice, and even God does not object listening to them twice.

Everything would have been fine if the services could be made less mechanical and livelier. That pertains particularly to prayers. There is no shortage of poets or of musicians. Why not create something new? If not for each festival or Sunday, then it certainly could be done for some. God would also enjoy hearing something new, not to even mention the congregation. Even though there are several festivals, peace nevertheless does not want to come about at all.

_ ★ ★ ★ _

Nakcia and Astra wish you good night, heralds. [[2116]]

<u>Ilgya</u>                        04/26/68 2037

→Ilgya. Heralds, various questions have arisen with respect to the Tidings, for not everything seems to be comprehensible to you. Some questions are justified, but the others you could have resolved on your own, if you were to contemplate them more carefully.

First of all, you have to try to understand better the essence of The Almighty and His spirits. All the spirits who originate from The Almighty acquire – or rather, preserve – the characteristics of The Almighty. While existing individually, or merging with The Almighty again, they do not acquire or lose anything. The situation is different with those spirits who incarnate. After freeing themselves from their bodies, they acquire some new characteristics, which neither The Almighty nor the spirits who have been created directly by Him possess.

With respect to the chief spirits – Gods included – they are the very same Almighty Himself. They are only divided into many parts in order to accomplish their task better. Similarly, Santorino, too, is a single spirit, but capable of dividing himself into many parts in order to accomplish his task in many galaxies. These separate spirits of his can remain separate eternally, or can merge once again with the spirit of Santorino himself.

Regarding the subject concerning your planet. The spirit of God – called the Son of God, Jesus Christ – who came to Earth, acquired a few special characteristics peculiar to man, while He lived as a human. When He returned to God, He merged with Him, and passed these characteristics on to God, thus making The Almighty's spirit richer. God retained Christ's new spirit within Himself separately, and on occasions of need Christ's spirit once again assumes His entirely new form, and thus acts independently as Christ.

Thus, He assumed His form of Christ when He met the spirit of herald John in the Deoss Temple, and instructed him regarding the new tasks being assigned to him.

I am not surprised that it is difficult for you to comprehend The Almighty, because that is not easy for us either, even though we are the spirits of His spirit. Therefore, you should not strive to comprehend everything. Just be satisfied with what you are able to understand.←

_ ★ ★ ★ _ [[2113]]

<u>Aksanto</u>                    05/17/68 2040

→Aksanto speaking. Heralds, let us linger somewhat by the questions concerning humanity.

You know the history of humanity – or rather, that of the diverse nations. Therefore, we will not delve into that, but will discuss something else that also effects humanity's present and future.

In the beginning of humanity's history, once man had already started to differ from the animals, he nevertheless retained many characteristics of the animals. One cannot say that all characteristics of the animals would be undesirable. There are animals who possess such human characteristics as caring for their children, and love – which even makes them fight for their children and sacrifice their own lives. Similarly, some animals travel in herds and follow the leadership of the older animals, who also defend the members of their herd.

Man, while being one of the animals at one time, was not the strongest of them. Nature had given him neither horns, sharp claws, sharp and strong teeth, nor particularly swift feet. He was blessed, however, with a wonderful brain and hands, which enabled him to preserve his life against the much stronger animals. Later on, they took him to the throne of the ruler of Earth.

Regarding numbers, the man of those days cannot be compared to today's man. People belonged to families, tribes, and so on. Fighting continued among the people just as it had during the era of the animals. Man was merciless, and did not even relinquish the desire to eat each other. This was something that even some animals did not do. The people's gods, too, were merciless and even bloodthirsty.

Those ancient times have been preserved only in the form of bones and various artifacts. Sometimes current people find these in old caves or other locations where they have been preserved due to favorable conditions. The more recent ones are also preserved in paintings on cave walls. Those of still more recent times have been recorded in people's edifices, sculptures, and even writings.

Much has changed since then – except for wars. They have persisted even in your present time, when man's capabilities are almost comparable to those of God.

None of humanity's imagined gods had the magical abilities of current man, who is even getting ready to fly to the moon, and to the other stars – planets.

Even if formerly wars were often a necessity, then now they are humanity's shame and calamity. Millions of people die in combat, and why? Did all of them have any personal hatred against those who died on the other side? The majority of them did not even know the people whom they killed.

Without doubt, there were many good people among them, who, under different circumstances, could have become the best of friends. They were the same kind of people who longed for their homes, who longed for their wives and children, and for whom fathers and mothers wept.

Why did they have to slay each other? Because the rulers of these nations demanded that! These rulers could not settle their quarrels by peaceful means. Once the era of rulers – of czars, kings, and other royalty – ended, power was assumed by governments which had been elected by the people. However, the wars still did not end.

It turned out that in some countries the people who had come to power, wanted to force their own ideas, which they had embraced, onto other countries as well. Now that the military weapons have achieved unimaginable power of destruction, a frightful calamity threatens humanity.

The time has come when no nation, or country, no matter how small or large it might be, can remain indifferent and fail to participate in the formation of humanity's future.

"Every human being must start a WAR AGAINST WAR!" says The Almighty.

I am tasked with passing these words of The Almighty to humanity, and to every individual who wants to remain alive, who wants to remain free, and who wants to become happy!

With that, I, The Almighty's envoy, the high spirit Aksanto, conclude this tiding.←        [[2126]]


Mortifero                          05/24/68 2102


→Chief Spirit Mortifero, speaking on behalf of The Almighty.

The Almighty's envoy, the high spirit Aksanto, in his previous tiding, warned the people on Earth about the dangers threatening them, unless they exert all their efforts to averting them. The task of the heralds was to receive this warning and to include it in *The Book of Tidings*, as The Almighty's tiding to all the nations on Earth, and to each person individually.

In order to preclude misunderstandings and doubts, this tiding will explain to you how the true tiding of The Almighty should be understood. The Almighty does not consider the heralds as the only promulgators of His will. As you have already seen, He makes the demands of the Tidings known to people in other forms as well. The task of the Tidings, however, is to concentrate the desires and commands of The Almighty into a book which verifies that which has come directly from The Almighty, but not from other sources, or from the people themselves. Without this book, some people might claim that their own works were inspired by The Almighty.

Many people already sense the dangers which threaten them. The majority of humanity, though, pays no attention to these people. Humanity considers that what these people have expressed are merely their personal ideas, and therefore everyone may doubt them.

How should this tiding of The Almighty be understood? It makes each individual responsible for his actions. With respect to the tiding, it means that every human, even if he is unable to work personally toward averting wars, must treat war with hostility, and must explain its dangers to those who do not understand. More important, he should not participate in a war, unless he is forced to do that.

Anyone who summons others to a war, or anyone who starts a war, is responsible for it. With that, he sides with the opponents of The Almighty, and will be punished after his death.

Those who struggle against war will be considered to be worthy of a higher degree after their death. Those who did not do anything, and who simply lived without thinking about anything, will not receive any recognition in the Kingdom of Heaven after their death.

One can conclude from what I have said that exactly under these circumstances under which the Tidings are being given, the main task of the heralds is to include this tiding in *The Book of Tidings*. Also, if possible, another task is to explain personally this dreadful situation to those people who are accessible to them.←

- ★ ★ ★ - [[2151]]


<u>Nakcia</u>                    05/31/68 2045

Nakcia. Heralds, perhaps we should spend a little bit more time on The Almighty's tiding regarding every individual's responsibilities.

Chief Spirit Mortifero told you how each person's conduct with respect to war will reflect on him. He said that this conduct with respect to war will influence the magnitude of man's sins, or else the recognition granted him in Heaven. In order to preclude misunderstandings, you – people – have to know that conduct with respect to war does not free man from his other sins, but influences the severity of his punishment. If man loses his life in the fight against war, then he is set free from all his sins. In other cases, though, his sins are merely reduced – depending on his achievements in the fight for peace.

- ★ ★ ★ - [[2125]]


<u>Nakcia</u>                    06/14/68 2038

Nakcia. Heralds, let's dwell a little bit on the circumstances of life. Humanity has changed with almost every generation. These changes took place much slower in ancient times, and sometimes these changes could be noticed only after several generations. The changes take place much quicker now. They occur even several times in one generation, and the situation regarding fathers and sons obviously becomes ever more acute.

The parents feel that their children advance too much. They fear that life may reach a circumstance where chaos will set in.

Obviously, the young people fail to do everything correctly. They act rashly and even stray, but they do go forward. They want a freer and better life.

Without any doubt, life should not stand still. There was much in the old life that was superfluous and that hindered progress. There were times when parents made decisions regarding the young people's lives, without considering their feelings. Love had little significance, more correctly – it did not have a decisive significance. Now that almost unlimited freedom has set in, love begins to disappear again, because it is destroyed by unrestricted passion. One can sometimes see something resembling the mating of dogs on the street. Young people kiss openly on the street, as well as in subway trains. They not only kiss, but even display openly their feelings of passion.

Freedom is necessary in love, but a human being has to remain the very same human being with a sense of respect, and should not descend to the level of a dog and start imitating animals.

With respect to political events, the situation has not changed much. The same struggle goes on in the new countries as well as in the Soviet Union. The murder of Robert Kennedy obviously has to be condemned. Yet when it comes to its historic value, or significance, it seems that it will be better that he did not achieve the position of President.

We will conclude with that. Good night, heralds. Nakcia and Astra.

[[2104]]

# Chapter XVIII

# Summer 1968

<u>Indra</u>                              08/17/68 2148

Indra is speaking. Almighty's heralds to the planet Earth, I decided to visit you once more after a rather prolonged period. I cannot say that you have become any younger, but neither do you look much older.

I flew around the old planet and saw much that was new and good, but also rather much that was bad. The major wars have seemingly ended, but the minor ones continue in several places, and some of them are quite nasty. According to its essence, every war is merciless, but some of the minor wars do not differ much from the Mongol Wars. Consider Vietnam and Africa, in these wars, those who do not fight suffer the most – particularly in Africa. Thousands of people starve to death in front of the eyes of the entire world. That is a sight that one cannot bear and endure. It seems that humanity has not yet emerged from the Stone Age.

On the other hand, the paupers have disappeared in some countries. They no longer stand by the doors of churches or on street corners. The state provides them shelter, clothing, food, and even medical treatment.

The two largest countries in the world are getting ready to fly to the moon. Obviously, not all of the millions of their inhabitants simultaneously, but certainly a few. The people of science, while looking into the depths of the sky with instruments of different types, have suddenly encountered phenomena which they cannot explain. They have looked deep into the space of the universe, but compared to its infinity they have touched only a tiny part of it, and there is much facing them that is still unknown and incomprehensible. Obviously, human genius will gradually learn to understand and explain everything. Isn't it wonderful that there is still so much in the universe that is new, incomprehensible, and unexplained?

What would happen if one day nothing new could be found, and people would know everything? What interest would there be to any longer live? Doesn't man become mightier and feel greater with every victory over the unknown?

Man wages an eternal struggle against that in the world which is hostile and unknown to him, and man has many victories in this direction. Yet, man has to struggle most vigorously against himself, against the negative characteristics which are within him. This struggle is the longest and the most difficult one. Every individual feels that he does not act in all respects like his human honor and pride require him to act. Quite often he lies entirely needlessly. He frequently acts mercilessly toward others, is reluctant to help others, and so on.

I am not talking about such trash of humanity as thieves and murderers, as well as tyrants. They are the manure of humanity that simply has to be cleared out of the space of Earth.

It is the duty of the parents and of society to try and preclude this manure from coming into existence. The responsibility for it coming into being and existing rests with them.

Everyone has to examine himself and explore himself to see whether he is sufficiently free from negative traits, and whether he is trying sufficiently hard and successfully to set himself free from them. You can judge others only after you have judged yourselves, and have found yourselves to be worthy of being judges!

With that, I take leave from you, heralds. I will be on Earth for a while yet, and will perhaps visit you once more. I bring you – and particularly, Janoss – God's blessing and help. Good night, heralds.

Indra, Ilgya, and Astra.        [[2224]]


<u>Ilgya</u>                    08/23/68 2122

Ilgya is speaking. - ★ ★ ★ -

Let's talk now a little bit about our affairs. I can see that you do not understand everything about the spirits, as for example about last week's visitor – the high spirit Indra. In India, Indra was initially considered to be the main God – the ruler of Heaven, the God of thunder and rain, and still much else. Later on he was considered as one of the eight gods, while mainly retaining the role of thunder maker, but also losing some roles while gaining some new ones. More recently, he came after the three main gods, already as a lesser god, while still retaining control of thunder and rain to the very end.

Obviously, no god ever existed who was like the people of India had imagined Indra to be. There was, however, the spiritual ruler whom God had sent to the people of India. He had a different name in Heaven, but for the people we will retain the name which people gave him – Indra.

As you know, almost all nations initially had many gods. One of the first nations to acknowledge only one God was the Hebrew nation. Later on, other people also adopted this one God, but even now there are many people who believe in many gods, and many of these gods are not good gods either.

The high spirit Indra is still visiting Earth, and there is hope that he will visit you once more.

Good night, heralds. Ilgya and Astra. [[2203]]


Indra                                    08/30/68 2140


Indra is speaking. Heralds, the spirits also have to keep a promise, therefore I visit you once more prior to leaving the planet Earth.

I flew around the entire planet – starting with India and concluding with Latvia. I saw much that was good, but unfortunately also much that was bad. Things are not going well in my old country either. My people are not among the warrior nations, therefore despite their hundreds of millions they continue to live in their India, which lacks the land to feed these millions. Other people would at least have attacked – as did the Tartars, or rather, in this case, the Mongols – Europe and perhaps even Africa. Similarly, another large country in Asia – China – not only did not want to attack other nations, but did not even know how to defend itself. It slowly digested the invaders only thanks to its massive amount of people, and they disappeared in China's stomach.

Compared to the aforementioned countries, Soviet Russia is now the strongest country. Had it not been for the other superpower in the world – the United States of America – it would probably be the ruler of the world now. The United States should, in fact, have been that, because it was the first to obtain the atom bomb. The Americans, however, did not know how and did not want to take advantage of this event – to their own detriment and that of the entire humanity.

Communism – which rules in the Soviet Union, China, and many other countries – has become old over its fifty years, and begins to lose support among the people. The Communists themselves understand that, and their leaders attempt to retain power by all available means, because losing it would also mean losing their own power and even their lives. All the free nations and also the Communists living in free nations, now condemn the Soviet invasion of Czechoslovakia. To tell you the truth, though, the Soviet Union did not have any other choice. This victory over the small Czechoslovakia is not a victory in the true meaning of the word, because it brought a terrible blow to communism itself. The entire world saw what communism's freedom is like.

What can I tell you about Latvia? It is no longer the same Latvia like it was when you were there, but neither is it a communist Latvia. There is only a handful of real Communists in it, but others merely tolerate communism and pretend to acknowledge it as being good for the people. People do not starve to death there, unlike in some countries in Africa and even in Asia. Periods of drought are at fault there, as well as the people themselves, who prefer to wage war rather than produce bread.

(A five minute intermission.) [[2211 - 2216]]

With respect to executing The Almighty's task, the scene on Earth is just as good and as bad as it is in people's politics. When it comes to development, some nations have advanced with gigantic steps, but simultaneously there are nations which have advanced very little. There are even nations in which some people cannot read, and what kind of a life and value can an individual have if he does not know how to read? It was the book that preserved what people had achieved, and only thanks to the book could all the sciences develop.

Still, in some places there are people who live even now as their ancestors – the savages – lived thousands of years ago. These people, though, who have not advanced at all or have advanced little, should not be considered when evaluating humanity. Humanity should be evaluated according to the people who are getting ready to fly to the moon almost tomorrow, and according to the people who have surpassed all the wonders of fairy tales. There are ever more people who, with their inventions, make human life better and worthier.

Man has to overcome within himself his old habit – to consider his life on Earth as his main task, rather than only as a part of his task. You should not try to keep the spirit in the body if he no longer has anything to do on Earth, or else no longer has the strength for productive work. Man may live for a hundred and even more years if he is able to live as a full-fledged human being. If he is no longer able to live a productive life after fifty years – but only kills time – then it is better to set the spirit free, so that he can incarnate in a new being and continue The Almighty's task.

The new religion calls for man to successfully accomplish The Almighty's task which has been assigned to him, and then hasten back to The Almighty to receive a new task. You should grieve for those who die young, without having accomplished their task on Earth. However, you should rejoice, along with the souls of the deceased, for those who die in old age, that they have returned to their Creator.

In ancient times people imagined that the deceased will continue the same life in the other world as it was on Earth. Therefore people placed food and drink in the graves for the deceased, as well as cattle and even slaves and wives.

Current man does not have to take anything along with him in the grave. He only has to take along with him to Heaven a clear conscience that he has tried to accomplish his task. If he has not accomplished it completely – an explanation why he has been unable to accomplish it, and a request to forgive him, or else not punish him too harshly. Those who remain on Earth have to try not to forget the deceased – or rather, those departed – because they perceive each of your thoughts about them. On meeting them again in Heaven, your meeting will be a cordial one.

My time has run out. I pass on to you greetings from those departed who are intimate to you, and their very best wishes. I also wish you the same thing, and with that take leave from you.

The God, Indra.          [[2250]]


Aksanto                      09/06/68 2115

The high spirit Aksanto is speaking. Heralds, today I want to return once more to clarifying the notion regarding freedom. This is in conjunction with the events in Czechoslovakia, where the Czechs are fighting for freedom, and the Soviet Union fights to preserve its communist freedom.

People use the word freedom in so many different senses that it is difficult to tell the real meaning of this word. Absolute freedom, as you have been told before, is not possible. It would lead to anarchy and would make life completely impossible. Even back in the days when there were few people on Earth and they dwelt in caves, they nevertheless limited their freedom by designating heads of the family and heads of the tribe as persons who had to be obeyed. Later on, kings came about and they enacted laws about what was permitted and what was prohibited.

Then came the era of revolutions, when the crowd assumed power. It grabbed power with the slogan of making everyone free, but this "everyone" included only those who had grabbed power for themselves. Just like the kings, they enacted laws which obviously limited freedom, and sometimes even more than the kings had done. For example, during the time of Joseph one could not even think about freedom. Everything happened as Joseph wanted it to happen.

The citizens of the United States of America established a government which was closest to the real meaning of freedom. That happened because people had come from Europe to America in order to escape a lack of freedom in their homelands. Obviously, even here everything is not ideal, and there is still much to be done so that everyone, and not merely just a few, would enjoy freedom with justice.

As you can see from world events, the word "freedom" often means a lack of freedom for those who do not want to blindly follow the people, supposedly elected by the people, who rule them. The people, however, have been given the right to elect only those individuals whose names appear on a list prepared by the government. Doesn't that sound like a mockery of the word "freedom?"

A group of people who have grabbed power for themselves, has ruled several nations for over fifty years by means of terror that is unprecedented on Earth. These fifty years, however, have demonstrated that the freedom which they gave people was no freedom. It was not even a lack of freedom, because it was slavery. People begin to understand that and try to free themselves from this "freedom."

Why do the Communists fear true freedom so much? Because true freedom would mean the end of communism, and the loss of power and even the death of the Communists. Yet by suppressing true freedom in Prague, the Communists make their situation only worse. They show the entire world what their freedom is really like.

It is difficult to completely define the word "freedom." Therefore God gave people, in His Commandments, instructions regarding what man's freedom has to be like, what it has to be based on, and what bounds have to be maintained – that is, what man may not do even if he wanted to do it.

With that, we will conclude for today. We wish you a good night. Aksanto, Nakcia, and Astra. [[2156]]

<u>Aksanto</u>                    09/13/68 2118

The high spirit Aksanto is speaking. Heralds, I want to dwell somewhat on the so-called human fate. You obviously recall the time when Joseph ruled the Russian people. With the word "freedom" on his lips, he devoted all effort toward eliminating freedom. Words lost their true meaning, and sometimes people died not even knowing why [they were dying].

A similar dictator by the name of Mao now rules in the large country of China. This dictator, too, tries to free people from everything that is worthy, and then wants to give them the opportunity to feel completely free from everything that is valuable to them. This hero and leader of the people decided to institute a new culture, and whom did he entrust to carry that out – schoolchildren, who still had to learn everything, and particularly to recognize culture. They were given the right to punish everyone whom they considered to be enemies of the people, or parasites. They were judges – judges without any concept about whom to judge and how.

They were most successful in destroying the old culture. Treasures, true treasures of culture which had been accumulated over thousands of years, were destroyed. Scientists and the intellectuals were ridiculed and thrown out on the streets, or else jailed.

Months and even years passed, and what do we see now? Mao has reached the conclusion that the implementers of his "new culture" had not implemented or instituted anything. They had merely destroyed very much of what has now turned out to have been necessary and valuable. Now the army has been ordered to take over the leadership of the people, to send the implementers of the "new culture" back to schools or to simply remove them from their positions, and to ask the old, persecuted intellectuals to come back to work.

What else do we see? Those who were persecuted begin to persecute their persecutors, and even kill them. The schoolchildren, having spent a prolonged period in the Red Guard, now see that they have missed out on education and have to settle for ordinary work.

You can see from these two examples where good ideas can sometimes take humanity, if such people assume power as was Stalin and is Mao. Yet people can be found who support these people's crazy ideas and their criminal deeds. The revolutionaries begin to perish in China, just as was the case in the Soviet Union where many Communists perished, even from among those who were in the ruling ranks.

Eventually, who benefits from this freedom? Some for a while, and then others, but eventually hardly anyone!

Humanity already knows revolutions since ancient times. They were almost always intended to benefit the people. However, that could happen only if sensible leaders of the people were found, ones who knew how to look after the people and acknowledged their demands for true freedom, limited by sensible laws. They had to be able to fight against extremism and against people with dictatorial tendencies.

As you can see, some highly cultural nations have achieved true freedom without revolutions, and even while retaining kings on their beautiful but mostly symbolic thrones. Humanity has to learn how to sensibly govern itself and others, but this road is neither simple nor easy. You can see that from the current events and from those that you have personally experienced.

I conclude with that and wish you a good night. Aksanto.

[[2200]]


Santorino                          09/20/68 2038

Santorino is speaking. Almighty's heralds to the planet Earth, history marches forward despite anything. It notes the good as well as the bad, the beautiful as well as the ugly, the noble as well as the base, and the praiseworthy as well as the condemnable and villainous.

There have been noble eras when humanity undertook cultural growth, and there have been bad times when due to merciless wars humanity not only stopped the growth of culture but even pushed humanity backward. Hordes of Tartars, Huns, and others came from Siberia, from the east, and destroyed the culture of the nations in Europe. Legions of Turks also came and ravaged southern Europe. Then finally came armies led by dictators who tried to subordinate the entire world to themselves. They were the armies of Adolf, which, while perishing, gave the so-called communism an opportunity to come to power. Communism had been inspired by Marx and Lenin, but it was taken over by Stalin, who formed a dictatorial government from a government that had been intended as the government of the people. This government eliminated freedom, and killed and tortured to death millions of people.

Fifty years have passed since that time. With a few small exceptions, peace reigned on Earth. These years demonstrated the delusions of communism and its unsuitability for humanity, but the system that had been established continues to keep some nations in shackles. The recent events in Czechoslovakia prove that people recognize communism's worthlessness and its evil.

Why do such times have to come? Why do people have to suffer from wars and dictators? That is not God's punishment, as some people claim. That is the people's own punishment imposed on themselves, because they have not fought sufficiently fiercely against the nature of matter, and have allowed people with a materialistic nature to temporarily assume power over other people.

What do hard times like that give humanity? They teach humanity what is good and what is evil. They point out to humanity the true, correct paths toward freedom and universal happiness. They also indicate the means of fighting against matter.

Currently you see the fight of communism not for a victory, but for its very existence and for the continuation of its power. The question is no longer a question, there is only the answer that death awaits communism. The only question is – how soon? That also depends only on the people themselves.

Did millions of people perish for naught? No, they proved the worthlessness of communism! The souls of the victims of torture gained much in their knowledge of matter, and that will help them greatly in the fight against the power of matter, as well as will give them the opportunity to ascend higher in the realm of the spirits.

(I will continue in six minutes.) [[Intermission 2112 - 2118.]]

Now I will talk about you – The Almighty's heralds to Earth.

On coming to this small planet, none of you knew what role was intended for you on it, and we, in fact, did not know that either. We knew that The Almighty had decided to give a new religion to the people on Earth, but we did not know exactly when this will take place and who will be selected as heralds. Even The Almighty Himself, while observing the conditions on Earth, had not yet decided on the exact time. However, a certain peculiarity could be observed in sending Alexander's spirit to Earth with an unusual task – to study the people, find out their needs and desires, and evaluate the religious situation and its suitability for current man's highest comprehension of life, as well as his abilities to comprehend the true spiritual essence of the universe, its Ruler, and the spirits with their tasks.

In the beginning Alexander's life was peaceful. He helped his father and older brother to struggle with the jungles in the Caucasus, and he also learned the wisdoms of life from books, in school, as well as at home. He became familiar with noble and honest people, who is what his parents and brothers were, as well as with similar people – the neighboring farmers. Then came the First World War. It summoned him to participate in the defense of his homeland against the German attack, which had been intended for the purpose of subordinating the Russian people as slaves to the German people. Death was after him several times, but it was not allowed to touch him. He saw how people died and that they were not afraid to die.

Then came the revolution. The war ended, but an internal war started – the people's war for freedom from the power of the czar. A handful of people grabbed this freedom for themselves. They established a power worse than the power of the czar.

Alexander had returned to his home, where the English ruled at that time. When regiments were organized in southern Russia which started a fight against the Communists, Alexander left home and joined them to help liberate the land from the evil rulers. He was hit by a bullet and returned home.

In the meantime, the White Army had lost the fight, and Alexander decided to head for the newly established Latvia. The Communists captured him along the way, and the muzzle of a rifle stared him in the face again. Yet death had to bypass him again. Alexander spent more than a year in prisons, before he was set free and could return to Latvia. Thus within a year's time, he experienced hundreds of years, suffered from hunger, and looked into the deepest depths of people's souls.

He again entered the army in Latvia as an officer, and met his cousins – Nicholas and John, now called Janoss. He frequently visited Nicholas's estate, which John inherited after Nicholas's death.

Then came the great message from The Almighty, "The day has come to give My new religion to the people on Earth. I appoint My spirit whom I have sent to Earth – Alexander – as the leading herald. I will select other spirits, who will help him, from among those who will want to do this and who will visit Janoss's home. I will repeat what Christ did – I will take people who will be able to accomplish the great task. Obviously, only some of those who want to will be able to accomplish that, but many people are not needed for receiving and preserving the Tidings. Of course, the heralds, while being people, in addition to good characteristics are also blessed with other traits which people have. In addition to a belief in their task, in addition to devoting themselves to the great work with their heart and soul, some of them also possess, to a greater or lesser extent, doubts, envy, a desire to slander others, and so on."

Some heralds demonstrated their small abilities and, while succumbing to the call of a better life, left the work. Some retained it within their hearts, and some were summoned by God. Even though they make some mistakes, the remaining heralds successfully continue the work, which has been almost completed. Now it has to be prepared for dissemination to the people.

The God Indra already spoke about those who are accomplishing the work and the gratitude that awaits them in the realm of Heaven. That was not done in order to distinguish them, but so that they could be sure of how The Almighty has evaluated their work. Without this assurance, doubts about their own worthiness might sometimes arise to them during difficult situations. These may not arise to you, even if it will seem to you at times that you are not doing everything like you should, or else not as well as you should, because the opportunities that have been given you are not unlimited.

I pass on to you The Almighty's appreciation for the many years devoted to the great work – by bringing it through fires and waters.
[[2210]]


Omega                          09/27/68 2122

→Chief Spirit Omega is with you, The Almighty's heralds to the planet Earth. Heralds, as you have been told before, you have been summoned to proclaim The Almighty's faith to humanity. It is a faith which, on Earth, is based on the teachings of God's Envoy, Christ.

I will repeat once more what you have already been told – why the faith of Christ was given in a form where, these days, everything in it does not seem appropriate or correctly portrayed. Christ could not reveal that which the people of those times – due to their development – could not understand. Therefore, quite often He spoke in the language of parables, or based His teachings on some foundations of the old faiths, so that the new faith would be more acceptable to the people.

For many centuries humanity changed very slowly. Yet, once knowledge began to develop, as well as the people's abilities to study life and the Earth, and the Heaven grew larger, humanity began to develop much faster. Even The Almighty was surprised in this century, due to humanity's scientific achievements. Therefore The Almighty reached the conclusion that humanity had become capable of receiving His faith. He decided to entrust this high and unimaginably responsible work to you, to the two Alexanders, to Janoss – John, and to Mary, while summoning John, Nicholas, and a few others as helpers.

You had to function during one of humanity's most difficult eras – the period of the Second World War, when security of life was meager. You accomplished your task – that of receiving the Tidings and preserving them – with honor. The Almighty told you that the work of giving the Tidings has been completed, and that now begins their preparation for announcing them to humanity. He also said that during the course of this work, communications will be maintained with you, and that the necessary supplements and explanations will be given.←

It is obvious that such a great and complicated work will raise questions, because everything cannot be always comprehended correctly. The Almighty assigned me today to give you explanations concerning the most important aspects of what all of you do not understand. You were invited to ask if you do not understand something. This asking was intended to be in the following manner. If a herald does not understand something important or has doubts about the veracity of something, he should raise this question during one of the evenings of conversations. Then the heralds will decide whether there is a need to ask, or whether they can comprehend the point on their own.

There were very few questions in the open, but there were rather many [in the heralds' minds]. Some heralds [did not ask questions] based on the fact that the spirits read their thoughts – that is, already knew the intended questions – and could respond to them on their own, without waiting for questions that were expressed in words. These heralds, though, did not think this through to the end. They did not consider in what a difficult and unpleasant situation they would frequently end up if the spirits were given permission by The Almighty to reply to the questions of the heralds' thoughts. They could answer questions which the heralds would not want to reveal. Sometimes you think rather negatively about each other, and by revealing all that, and other thoughts of this type, your further cooperation would become impossible.

All of you would not be satisfied either if the spirits were to answer only questions of a certain type, because not all heralds would consider each question like that to be truly important. Therefore The Almighty decided not to let the heralds know the thoughts of other heralds, no matter what they might be like. [The spirits will respond] only when all heralds will find a question to be worthwhile and necessary.

→Some heralds are bothered by the situation with Christ, who exists and, then again, does not exist. Christ, as a spirit, does not resemble His human appearance which He had on Earth. He assumes this image only on such occasions as described by herald John. Christ, called the Son of God, is in fact the very same God, who in cases of necessity divides into the Father and the Son.

Concerning the question regarding the many Gods in the numerous galaxies, this question of a minor practical importance was not discussed. Only toward the end of the Tidings did The Almighty decide to explain this latest situation as well, which does effect the essence of the Tidings.

The distance to the galaxies is so vast that man has no prospects of reaching any one of the galaxies. He will be capable of that only as a spirit. Obviously, though, it is nevertheless too complicated to oversee the galaxies from the place where The Almighty is located, or from one or several selected galaxies. Therefore, Gods are appointed in many galaxies. Also, the galaxies are of such diverse nature, and the living beings on their planets are also so different, that the supervision of those planets which are located in these galaxies also has to be entirely different than on your Earth. Besides, the God of your galaxy as well as the Gods of other galaxies are the very same spirits of The Almighty.

You know that the universe is infinite, and that there are also infinitely many worlds within it. You also know that it is not possible to relate everything about infinity, and that one should not particularly strive to find out that which has no practical significance for man on Earth. Should The Almighty order me to place a book in front of Alexo, in which the infinite universe is described – a book which would start in front of him and would continue into infinity – would Alexo attempt to browse through it? Obviously not! Therefore, it is better for us to leave that to the next generations. Let us try to understand and find out what is most important for the people on Earth to know, in order to best create a happy life for humanity.

Do not consider my words as reproaches, or else as an indication that they were unnecessary. Instead, consider your thoughts as incompletely thought out. But then, does the human life span permit man to think everything through to the end?

I wish you even greater success, if that is possible, and also a good night.←                    [[2225]]

# Chapter XIX

# Fall 1968

Ilgya. Heralds, your New York is rather cold today, but the last few days were quite warm and even hot. Who is at fault here? The wind from the north is at fault. You see, that is how it is when one lives in a place which is readily accessible to the cold wind from the north as well as to the warm ocean wind from the south.

Humanity's culture has advanced significantly. Science has also advanced much, but so far it has not advanced enough to be able to control the streams of air. They are not easy to control, and if man will nevertheless manage to do that, this will have to be considered to be a huge achievement.

Just now, man has invented a microscope that enlarges fifty-thousand-fold. It gives man new abilities in research and makes many new inventions possible. All that makes human life easier and better.

Man has not yet gone very far in one direction, that is in improving the standard of living for those people who have remained backward. There is also a strange phenomenon – even some old and cultural nations are incapable of ridding themselves of starvation, or else live half-starved.

Yes, in the United States of America it is difficult to find, even with a light, someone who is starving, because there is no shortage of bread here. The only ones starving are those who try to destroy themselves by using narcotics, excessively drinking alcohol, and so on. The state obliges even them, by providing as much help as is possible in such cases. All other normal people live according to their spiritual and physical abilities. If they utilize them correctly, then well and even very well – and even without the help of the clergy.

This means that the basic principles of Christ's teachings – with respect to what has to be done so that all people could feel happy – have been acknowledged to be correct, and have become the foundations for life. God no longer has to give the daily bread, and people no longer have to pray for it. It is hard to imagine this having happened without the teachings of Christ.

The clergy are the ones who have deviated from the right road. Instead of organizing and directing this work of assistance, they devote themselves mainly to praying to God and to accumulating wealth for the churches and monasteries. They transform the houses of God into palaces, which should be done only after the people will have become wealthy, and hunger and other calamities will have been averted.

The mind came to man's assistance. Man understood that it was his duty to try to render help to everyone who could not support himself on his own. Society can feel happy only when everyone is happy.

If the priests complain that people seldom come to church and pray little to God, then it is their own fault, because they have not traveled the paths that Christ had indicated to them. The time has come for everyone to comprehend correctly the teachings of Christ, and not only read the Holy Scriptures from pulpits but also practice them in life. It is most important to do away with these endless prayers which God does not need – as God Himself has said – and start praying to God with deeds.

Man has to maintain communications with God – spiritual communications – by learning the laws which God has given, discussing how to better adopt them in life, and organizing events during which to uplift morality, rather then wrecking it as is being done now. Girls should be taught to attract boys not with their short skirts, which hardly exist any longer, or by revealing their breasts, but rather with their spiritual abilities.

→Much has changed with regard to man's spiritual development. What previously used to be good, and even indispensable, has become superfluous and even harmful. That is the case regarding the subject of children. Back when Earth was uninhabited, when there were large areas over which only animals ruled, then God's advise was necessary, "Multiply and fill the Earth." Once this advice had been carried out, then man had to find the means to regulate the birthrate on his own.

As you know from the lives of insects and animals, whenever they multiply too extensively, a famine occurs and a sufficient number of them die so that life can go on. Man is not an insect, and neither is he a senseless animal. He has the ability to live so that he will never have to die of starvation.

Similarly, the situation concerning men and women has changed. A woman no longer has to spend all her time raising and caring for children, or doing household chores, because machines and other inventions have come to her aid. These perform the work in her stead, or else make it easier, thus giving the woman an opportunity to take part in the work of men as well.

Because of the same reasons, the work of men has also become easier and of a shorter duration, thus making a place for the woman.

A rather acute topic is the one regarding children, or rather, regarding the youth. Bringing up children is the responsibility of their parents, and depending on how they bring up their children, that is what kind of citizens they become. Yet the street also brings up children, and this upbringing by the street is of a negative nature. It produces trash for humanity – people who ruin the worthiness of life. Humanity must pay the greatest attention to the problem of this upbringing in the streets.

With that, we will conclude for today. Good night, heralds.← Ilgya, Nakcia, and Astra. [[2311]]

Santorino                      10/25/68 2020

→God's high envoy, Santorino, speaking.← Heralds, some changes have been made in our anticipated program. First, it has been divided into two parts. The second part will be next Friday.

→Some circumstances – circumstances of current life – require new explanations, thanks to the complicated situation of the Catholic Church.

The head of the church, the Pope, recently made a decision regarding not using artificial means to limit the birthrate. The laws of the church do not permit introducing birth control, even if this prohibition means disaster for humanity.

Man has been given a mind – one of the better minds in the entire universe – and he must understand that laws are enacted for the benefit of humanity. Even the best of laws can become outdated, and then they have to be changed. If the Pope considers himself to be Christ's deputy on Earth, then he can change even God's laws, if that is essential for the good of humanity.

As history has demonstrated, the Popes have not hesitated to introduce new laws, and have often neglected to abide by the old ones. They have even enacted certain laws which are contrary to the laws given by God. The most significant one was the failure to observe the law about praying to God. First, the prohibition to turn unnecessarily to God with a prayer. The second was the prohibition to pray to God in front of other people.

Obviously, the transgression of this law did not threaten man with punishment, but neither did it give man anything good. It required man to waste time by performing an act which had no value.

It was already a sin, however, and a grave sin at that, for priests and especially the Pope to encourage prayers and even demand that people come to church to pray to God for an hour, and even for four hours. It is an unpardonable sin to call yourself God's servant, or deputy, and then force people to do that which God has prohibited.

The priests disliked much else that is written in the Gospel, and therefore the Popes refused to give [the Bible] to the people written in an understandable language. Instead, it was given to them in Latin, which only the educated people and priests understood. The clergy even went so far as to punish the translators of the Holy Scriptures with the death penalty. This was their way of keeping the people in complete ignorance for several centuries.

The Orthodox priests turned out to be better priests. At least they permitted the people to read the Holy Scriptures in the Old Slavic language of the church. The people could understand this at least somewhat. But, the priests had the same attitude toward prayers.

Besides wasting time, why does this encouragement to pray bring much harm to people? Because it encourages the individual to rely on God to help him, instead of relaying on himself and his own capabilities. Many people would have helped themselves if they had known that God will not help them. The pastor, too, is unable to help the people, even though he often receives a generous monetary reward for his prayers.

It is so strange that people continue to believe in the priests and all their deceptions concerning prayers. People have spent entire lifetimes believing in these delusions, even after they have read God's words. They continue to go to churches to pray, and listen to numerous group prayers, without even considering why the church does and orders them to do this, when God has so clearly and unmistakably prohibited this.

The church could have been a true temple of God. It could have helped people to become acquainted with the laws of God, shown them how to help each other, and taught them to create better lives – a Paradise on Earth. It could also have condemned sin and sinners.

God does not come as a judge. He comes once more in order to remind people about His laws, to wake them from their sleep, and to set them free from deceptions.

The church and the priests must remain, just as Christ permitted His Father's temple to remain. But, just as Christ drove out the merchants from the temple, it is now time to drive out the merchants from the churches. It is now time to bring into them those priests who are capable of bringing the true teachings of Christ into them.

Only a brief period passed since this unfortunate step of the Pope when another unexpected test came for the leadership of the Catholic Church.

Jacqueline, the widow of the assassinated President of the Unites States of America, decided to take a divorced Greek millionaire as her husband. Since the widow had no prospects of obtaining permission for the marriage, she asked an Orthodox pastor to marry them. The Pope's reaction to this was to deny the absolution of sins to her. This truly was a real Christian decision – without a heart and soul!

The worst was yet to come. The cardinal of Boston, who was a family friend of Jacqueline's, decided to defend the poor woman. He said that he did not think that it was a sin for Jacqueline to take a husband, and that she could marry anyone whom she desired. Then the cardinal said that people cannot judge who is a sinner and who is not. Only God can do that.

Obviously, this caused indignation in the Vatican. The cardinal announced recently that he would be retiring this very year. That was the action of a true priest of God. Yet, how many priests are there like him?

This event turned out to be sufficiently great to move people throughout the world, and that is good. People must learn to think for themselves, and to seek individually the true pathway to God.←

(A ten minute intermission.) [[2123 - 2133]]

Let us continue. As you already know, man's course of life on the planet Earth has been a long one. It was a path from an animal to a full-pledged ruler of Earth – a human being. He had to completely transform himself and also had to transform his life. Initially, he differed little from other animals, but even after [he began to differ from them] he had to learn for a long time how to subdue the beasts of pray and how to obtain better results by cultivating the soil, organizing hunts, as well as overcoming the strong animals.

Once he had already become a true human being, he still had to continue the fight against the same animals, and also against a new enemy – the same human, except from another tribe. His religious faith changed along with his life.

The Hebrew people, while they roamed Asia as nomads, had developed a brutal, if one may say so, religion with human sacrifices to God. This religion called for detesting and eliminating enemies, and destroying their land. After their return from the enslavement in Egypt, however, this religion changed extensively. The summons of love could be heard in it – to love your enemies, not to harm another, not to kill, not to steal, to believe in and worship only one God, not to use God's name in vain, not to transgress marriage, and not to covet your neighbor's wife, servants, oxen, and donkeys. There even was a requirement that if you saw your enemy's cattle straying, to return them to your enemy. You were not supposed to testify falsely in court, join evil people, tell falsehoods about others, and lie. As you can see, the same religion transformed completely. Christ supplemented this religion even more, and gave it in a form which conquered more than half the world.

However, as you can see for yourselves, for several centuries it strayed from the true pathway. One cannot deny, though, that despite its negative traits it nevertheless kept humanity from straying completely, and taught man much that was good, like Christ had ordered.

→Humanity has traveled a long and difficult road. It has achieved a high culture, but still has been unable to free itself completely from some negative characteristics, such as envy, slander, duplicity, and some of the old, grave sins like killing. The invention of the new atomic weapons, which have almost unlimited power, may lead humanity to a catastrophe, if not to destruction. Therefore The Almighty summons every human to struggle against war by whatever means he may be capable of using. Of course, one has to fight, with all weapons available to him, against an enemy who is about to attack, and no one may refuse to use them. All those who start a war with the purpose of subjugating other nations to themselves will be punished mercilessly by God. Those who defend themselves, even with weapons in hand, will be singled out especially and rewarded by God.

The current war, too, which is being fought in defense of a non-communist nation against a communist nation, should be viewed as a necessary war.←

In concluding, I want to point out still another undesirable phenomenon, which is particularly conspicuous among older people whose memory has become poor. Since they quickly forget everything, it seems to them that others are specifically the ones who forget. Therefore I suggest to them to be more careful and not be that sure that they are not the ones who forget and who make the mistake.

Specifically with respect to the heralds, whose work is very important, you should not consider the Tidings too casually, and should not be fully convinced that what you are saying truly corresponds to the contents of the Tidings. It is always better to double-check an extra time. There can be particularly unfortunate consequences if you take an extract out of context, without completely correlating it with other places in the Tidings where the same topic has been discussed.

You should never insist that what you say is specifically what is intended in a tiding. Everyone makes mistakes and everyone forgets things. The only difference is that some people try to correct their mistake and admit that a mistake could have been made. Otherwise, particularly in discussions with others, an unpleasant situation can eventually arise. You yourselves understand why.

With that, we will conclude for today. Good night, heralds. I will inform you next Friday about the forthcoming, other part of the tiding. Santorino.                    [[2225]]


Aksanto                    11/01/68 2113

Aksanto is speaking. Heralds, the Divine will speak next Friday. He has not set the exact time, but I think that it will be around ten o'clock and not earlier.

Today we will discuss the technique of giving the Tidings, because even you do not comprehend it quite correctly. Giving the Tidings does not consist of simply pushing the human hand toward specific letters. You know that people speak in many languages. Therefore the first requirement is for the spirit who wants to converse with people to know the required language. The language of the spirits is the same for all spirits, and it has little in common with people's language. Sounds are not used in it, but thoughts are communicated to the other spirit in a manner that is incomprehensible and impossible on Earth.

As you know, all people on Earth are not the same either. Everyone has not been blessed with the same abilities. Even their manner of speaking is not the same. Thus, the dumb talk with the help of signs, and the blind read with the help of their fingers. There are ordinary people who only perform work that is essential for day-to-day life, but there are those who perform unique work, which is intended for transforming humanity. There are the so-called inventors, scientists, and so on. There are poets, writers, musicians, music players, and there are philosophers who examine life and try to explain it. In fact, they try to understand and explain everything.

All these people have not been given ordinary spirits, but rather spirits with great abilities and various talents. These spirits are spirits who have incarnated many times, and also have been incarnated in particularly high beings on other planets.

God is able to establish contact in different ways with these people who have particular abilities. However, the many spirits and even the chief spirits can establish contact only with an individual in whom a special spirit has incarnated, one who has been selected by The Almighty. This spirit has the ability to perceive the language of the spirits and transform it into a language which man knows. This is an extremely complicated process, because this translation takes place instantaneously without the person himself even realizing why he uses these words and why he selects the necessary letters which constitute these words.

That is not everything though. Even though the individual as if merely translates the words of the spirits, he also understands them and may even fail to pass them on if he feels that from his human point of view they are not correct. Therefore mistakes crop up at times. Obviously, this person has to have great abilities of comprehending man and knowing life on Earth. He also has to have great abilities of the spirit, and has to have a spirit who has in his prior incarnations seen and become familiar with the abilities and knowledge of the spirits and of people, rather – of the living beings.

These are special abilities, and compared to other spirits there are very few spirits with these abilities, because they are utilized only in particularly essential cases. They should not be confused with those spirits who have incarnated in prophets and in similar people who have to live on Earth so that they would give an example by their lives. Christ was the only one who had the abilities of a prophet and of interpreting the words of the spirits.

The Almighty selected Alexander to convey His new religion to the people on Earth. Alexander was capable of translating into people's language His – The Almighty's – words, as well as the thoughts of particularly many spirits, because the language of the spirits is, in fact, closer to thinking than to speaking.

Of course, many people use this circle with letters on it, which you also use, in order to express their own ideas. They claim that they speak on behalf of some deceased human, some spirit, or what have you. It is not important by what means you express your words, but what is important is what you are able to express.

You know many false prophets and very many false priests, but there is a proverb on Earth, "You evaluate them according to their deeds."

I will conclude with that and will wish you the rest that you deserve.                    [[2203]]

<u>Santorino</u>                          11/08/68 2212

Santorino is speaking. Heralds, the Bible – also including the Gospel as part of it – is an old book. Some parts of the Bible are almost two thousand years old, but other parts of it are even much older. Books were not printed typographically in those days but were written by hand and were even carved in stone. Other means of preserving words were also used.

The writings had to be transcribed. The more they were transcribed the more errors cropped up. Much was also lost; much was altered. On reading the Gospel now, you come across places that you cannot understand. There are even places that contradict each other.

It is not possible to renew what has been lost and altered, and neither is that your task. That which is more important has nevertheless been preserved until your times.

Man has also changed. He does not have to be forced to abide by laws. He understands on his own the necessity of that, and man himself starts to enact laws for himself. This means that having become the rulers, people enact laws for themselves. Obviously, they try to enact laws which they consider to be fair for everyone and good for everyone. All people do not yet utilize these laws correctly, but they will approach that after some time – shorter or longer.

The laws which God – and later on, Christ – handed down indicated what people had to do so that their lives would become ideally just and good for everyone. A harsh punishment threatened those who did not abide by God's laws, because in those days it was difficult to make man abide by laws without the threat of punishment. However, now you know how God views punishment. He uses it while considering whether the action was taken due to necessity, and whether it really caused any harm.

The marriage of a man and a woman is truly best if it lasts their entire lifetime. If people with conflicting requirements in life get married and they do not feel happy, then there is no sense in continuing a marriage like that. With respect to perversion, obviously it has to be condemned. It provides pleasure only for the body, while destroying life's better requirements for happiness.

God permits people to enact laws for themselves, but only ones that are intended for the benefit of the people. God allows people to seek a more correct means of understanding God. With respect to what God has prohibited, however, people have to know that man will have to answer in front of God for having violated the prohibition. Sins like murder, stealing, and so on cannot be forgiven. Neither can rape be forgiven, as well as testifying falsely in court, cheating, taking advantage of someone weaker, and everything that is harmful to your neighbor.

There is still another important question, and that is the question regarding what will happen to the human soul at the time of the Great Judgement. People accuse the clergy of not saying anything about that. How can they say anything, though, if nothing has been said about that in any of the Holy Scriptures?

The problem is that some envisaged events have been changed. Other predictions have been lost, and a few have been written down incorrectly. Humanity was told about this judgement back when it was still unable to understand humanity remaining on the planet Earth for a long time.

I have to inform humanity that a deceased person's soul proceeds to Heaven immediately after death, and it is immediately judged there. It will no longer have anything to do with the body; the body will combine with the soil.

With that, we will conclude for today. Santorino. [[2255]]


<u>Aksanto</u>                          11/29/68 2212


→Aksanto speaking. Heralds, today we can look back at the road which you, the promulgators of The Almighty's Tidings to the nations on Earth, have traveled, while bringing them the words of The Almighty, God, and the spirits.

The road of the Tidings to the nations started in the small Latvia, one of the smaller nations on Earth. [It is so small that] three or four Latvia countries could be created out of your current place of residence, New York City. Why did The Almighty choose this tiny nation for such an important task? For the same reasons that He chose an equally tiny nation – the Hebrew nation.

Small nations, which are not involved in shaping the world's fates, can devote themselves to the great work more calmly and with less interruptions. Besides that, it is easier to bring together the people who are intended for this task. Being out of the way of the mainstream of activity, the heralds were able to avoid the dangers of war more readily, and also able to escape them more readily and reach a location that is most conductive for their work.

You have arrived in the current center of the world – the capital of the world – for UN should be considered such. The Almighty pointed out this path to the heralds, and guided the more worthy ones of them through all the dangers and suffering of war, to the most important center of the world. With this, He emphasized the importance of the Tidings, and gave the heralds the opportunity to accomplish their task better.

How did the heralds come into existence? They came as if on their own, as though people had assembled by chance. That was not the case!

Several thousand spirits, who were capable of achieving The Almighty's task had been sent to Earth. Only a few dozen people had to be selected from this large number. In the future, many others will also be able to join the heralds, but only from among those who have been given the abilities necessary for a herald.

Why did The Almighty send such a large number of people – spirits – with the necessary abilities? So that they would have a choice, and also, so that a larger number of people would be given the opportunity to participate in the work of the Tidings. Also, the less capable ones would have the opportunity of leaving the work without hurting the work due to a lack of heralds.

Every individual can participate in this work if he feels a desire to participate, for he might be one of the spirits who has been sent to Earth for this purpose. No one knows who this spirit – who dwells in man – may be. With his deeds and will, and his abilities, he will prove eventually who he is. Any human who feels a desire to join the heralds can achieve the rank of a herald with his will and abilities. Anyone who is incapable of being a herald may leave their ranks without losing anything, but also without gaining anything. Yet, anyone who tries, for whatever reasons, to hinder the success of disseminating the Tidings, will suffer greatly as a spirit, and will not have any future in the universe.

The Almighty ordered me to pass this on to the humanity on Earth. I do this through you – through the words which I bring to you. I also express His appreciation to those heralds who have accomplished their task so effectively in spite of the dangers and threats of the horrible war, while maintaining the courage and strength to do everything that was possible for them.

Their main task is virtually completed. The Almighty, however, will maintain contact with them until the moment when they will stand before Him with their reports about the task which they have accomplished.

The Almighty's will is expressed with these words, and a command to all the spirits who have been, are currently, and will be on the planet Earth!

I bid you farewell, heralds, for the words of The Almighty have been expressed and have become eternal.

The one who has accomplished the high task, the high spirit, Aksanto.←          [[2300]]

Ilgya                           11/29/68 2300

→Ilgya. Let us rise and display man's and spirit's respects to The Almighty's high thought – that of forming man into His closest assistant and friend in the creation of the most wonderful universe!

Let us thank Him in the name of humanity for the high honor bestowed upon Earth. Ilgya.←   [[2305]]

Ilgya                           12/20/68 2250

Ilgya. Heralds to the nations on Earth, the great festival approaches – the festival of the coming of Christ. There were gods on Earth even before Christ, but they were temporary gods and there were many of them. Neither did man come to Earth as a human being. He came as an animal with very weak human characteristics.

Man had to develop, had to travel a very long pathway of life, and had to learn very much so that he could proudly see that he has become the ruler of Earth, and that no one can any longer vanquish him in the fight for bread, living space, and finally – the air as well. Having started to move forward, though, man did not stop. He had not come in order to stop on the small planet Earth. He had come in order to utilize it to grow up on it for life in the universe – which The Almighty had created – and to help Him to continue shaping it. Some people say, "Man has started to create, to act like God."

Yes, man has started to act like God. He is already capable of performing miracles. He begins to successfully fight against the diseases of his body. He begins to transform the life of the animals according to his own needs. He even begins to repair his body and to even change hearts, which for the time being is still difficult to do. He researches everything.

While researching what God has created, he also learns how to do that on his own. Even though man has done much that is correct, obviously he has also erred, and we cannot, in fact, view man as the same being during his entire history. The outer appearance of his body has changed extensively, but the inner essence of his body has changed even more, particularly his spiritual abilities.

Man is now at that level of development where he feels within himself a divine ability to begin cooperating with The Almighty, and some people even think that they can begin competing with God. Some people even start to say that God does not exist at all, and therefore they can take the place of God, because it is vacant. Of course, only those people can talk like that who have just come in contact with God, but have not yet familiarized themselves with Him.

As I said before, man was different during different periods of his history, and therefore one had to talk differently about him. He had to be familiarized with God's thoughts about him, and with God's advice about how to mold his life, once a new era had arrived.

God has decided to ask Santorino to familiarize you next Friday with the advice which He wants to give humanity with respect to humanity's relationship with the church, and their further cooperation for the benefit of everyone.

Christmas is approaching. We congratulate all of you with it and wish you to spend it as is customary for this festival.

If you will assemble for a while around noon, we will also visit you and will pass on to you greetings from the spirits and the souls of your departed relatives and friends. We will be with you between twelve and two.

I wish you to await the festival happily. Until we see each other during the festival. Good night! Ilgya, Nakcia, and Astra.

[[2337]]

Nakcia                    12/25/68 1222

Nakcia. Heralds, God decided to give you today a particularly rare opportunity to be with the spirits who were at one time incarnated in living beings who were intimate to you during various occasions of your life or lives. It seems to you that the spirits – particularly those from whom you have parted long since as from living beings – cannot have a particularly large interest in meeting with you, because, after all, the entire world, the entire universe is open to them.

The spirits differ much in this respect from the living beings. They never forget anything that is important, rather – they can extract from the chamber of their memories whatever is necessary, even if it is thousands of years old. In that respect, this chamber greatly surpasses the archives of the human brain.

The spirits visit you quite often even when you do not sense this. If they are interested in something which they want to find out from you, they simply tap into the archives of your brain and start a conversation, which may sometimes last rather long, without you even realizing this. Sometimes you wonder from where some unusual and new thoughts came. Or else, where did an unusual premonition come from – sometimes pleasant, sometimes foreboding – and sometimes again an irresolvable problem becomes easy to resolve.

It may seem surprising and even unbelievable to you if I will say that some of you converse spiritually with the spirits more often then you converse with people. Thus Janoss is in contact with the spirit of Nicholas more often than with the people who are in his vicinity. It will be a big surprise for everyone if I will say that the living are in constant contact with the spirits, even though it seems that this contact has been completely interrupted, and perhaps will be reestablished only after the individual's death.

At one time, the only means of communications on Earth was the human voice. Now you can see for yourselves how many of them there are and how different and almost unlimited they are. You can always reach the spirit whom you want to reach – you simply have to start thinking about him, and that is that. This does not mean that you will receive an answer in a perceptible manner. Depending on the circumstances, it will come in different ways. It will be imperceptible to you as a human, but it will be perceptible to your spirit. It will be up to him to convey it to your brain, and if necessary even to your mind for its cognition.

I will now give the floor to the spirit of Janoss's brother, Nicholas. A three minute intermission. [[1256]]


Alzio                          12/25/68 1259


The spirit Alzio – Nicholas's name in the realm of the spirits – is speaking. The Almighty's high heralds sent to the planet Earth, with The

Almighty's permission I take advantage of the abilities which have been given to the spirits to converse with the living beings.

You are high spirits, for otherwise you could not be heralds. Until humanity will have achieved the highest level of development, you are obviously unable to understand that as people. Everything will come in time, though. Therefore we will not try to prematurely break into what currently is still little understood, or not understood at all, and will utilize only what is reasonably understandable.

I only want to tell you, [[Janoss]], what your intellect needs in order for you to become able to perceive the language of the spirits. You, and also Mary, are beset by the thought about why you have to physically suffer so often and so much.

Everything in the universe has its laws, because in the physical realm, as well as in the spiritual, nothing but chaos could exist without laws. The human being consists of the body, the spirit, and still something else that is almost impossible to perceive.

Man is born as a child who has to grow up to be an adult. He is not born already fully developed for life. An individual grows according to set laws. Since his body ages and loses, after a certain period, the ability to live, he inescapably has to die – unless man achieves the ability to change these laws of how his body has to grow. That is the future, though, on which God and man have to work in a joint effort. In this new field of possibilities and abilities, God does everything that He possibly can in the struggle against diseases and the process of the body wearing out.

_ ★ ★ ★ _

Heralds, on this very important day of remembrance – when the Son of God came to Earth in order to point out to humanity the way toward happiness, comprehension of the world, and its attainment – all the spirits whose duties allowed them, have come to visit you. This includes the spirits who are intimate to you, such as your fathers, mothers, brothers, sisters, and still other spirits who are intimate to you. They congratulate you and wish you to continue your great work and overcome all obstacles that can be overcome.

With that, I take leave from you, on behalf of all your guests and myself.                    [[1344]]

<u>Santorino</u>                    12/27/68 2110

→Santorino speaking, on behalf of The Almighty and God. Heralds, The Almighty ordered me to congratulate the humanity on Earth with its greatest step in the universe. This is the first step outside the earthly kingdom in the universe – the first step that reaches beyond the moon and into the expanse of the universe.←

Everyone knows that the first step is the most difficult one. When you examine the first inventions, you can see how insignificant they seem compared to the later achievements. Consider the first cart and the current railroad trains or the huge cars. Consider man's first dwelling – a cave – and the current skyscrapers, more than a hundred stories high, right here almost just outside your door. Consider the first plow and the current farm implements pulled by a tractor, which plow under an entire field almost at once. Who remembers a goose quill these days? Certainly not Mary who sits proudly in front of a large machine and produces one page after another, covered with beautiful letters. With respect to Alexo, he controls such a dreadful machine [[a computer]] that even the devil is afraid to come close to it.

Therefore, let us consider this day as one of the more significant ones in the history of Earth. It is important that this day belongs to your new world superpower, in which have been combined representatives from all nations on Earth. Honor and respect go to the great American nation.

Our God also joins The Almighty in the congratulations.

We will now turn to our tiding.

→Due to delusions and a desire to exploit religion for selfish purposes, people have diverted religions from the true road and have made them worthless and even harmful. God's duty was to condemn a faith like that – a forgery of faith – and to condemn such forgers. It was His duty to reveal this to the people so that they could comprehend this correctly and return to the true faith of Christ. Yet, having accomplished this task, God does not abandon it without carrying the situation which has arisen to a logical conclusion. It would have been foolish to abandon to destruction everything that is good and worthy in the churches.

One should not consider those who have strayed to be incorrigible, and one should not leave the churches empty. Their halls should be utilized for the needs of the true church. They can be adopted readily for meetings, lectures, courses of instruction, and much else. Under no circumstances should the crosses be removed from the tops of the churches. Icons, which have artistic value, can be hung on the walls as works of art, rather than as icons, for these were prohibited by God long ago, because it is idolatry to worship an icon. Icons of minor artistic value should be burned, but under no circumstances should they be destroyed otherwise.

It is the duty of all the more prominent people to utilize all their efforts and capabilities in uniting humanity into a single, true faith – the true, genuine faith of Christ. You must guard against using the methods which the Christians have used previously – in having the nonbelievers, idolaters, and members of other similar faiths join Christ's faith.

Neither should one ask for a particularly swift rejection of the old form of faith. Nor should the current generations be condemned particularly harshly. Having grown up with this form of faith, they have accepted it automatically without considering that it could be incorrect. They have believed the clergy's explanations of why the correct should be considered to be incorrect, and vice versa.

Similarly, the current clergy, having been brought up and educated in the present theological schools, did not imagine – rather, did not doubt – that what they had learned was true, regardless of them often being taught differently than what the Gospel taught. They were ordered to act as the entire clergy had always acted. Anyone who did not, was considered to be a heretic.

As everyone knows, the majority of people accept life as it is and think that everything that all the people, or a majority of them, do is correct. There are far fewer people who like to think for themselves and who perceive critically everything in the world.

There are many people who understand that much is being done incorrectly. However, they lack the will to struggle against the majority, or else are in general of an indifferent nature. Therefore, do not view everyone the same way. Your approach has to be sensible and flexible.

Also, it is not necessary to create superfluous suffering by utilizing unnecessarily harsh punishment. Nor is it necessary to ridicule someone in order to humble the individual even more. Your successes will be greater and more rapid if you use common sense and patience.

God commands that we announce to humanity that He forgives all those who have sinned against the true teachings of Christ. [By sinning, He means] transforming His teachings for their own personal benefit – by teaching them incorrectly, by having people worship icons, by having them pray to God openly, by summoning people to public prayers, and by forcing children to do the same. God also commands that the superfluous and externally introduced entries in the so-called religious books be eliminated.

God promises to excuse from punishment, after their death, all the sinners who were responsible for this, but no later than the passage of twenty-five years from this day, [[December 27, 1968]]. After that, God will judge and forgive each person individually.←

This announcement does not come as an announcement of a new punishment, because a sin of this nature has existed all along. Rather, what is new is the automatic nonconsideration of this sin – until the term set today.

→God will attempt to help people return to the true faith of Christ, and will consider favorably the deeds of those who, within their abilities, will try to restore the true faith.

I pass on to you, heralds, the blessing of God in the accomplishment of your great work. Santorino.← [[2246]]

# Chapter XX

# Winter - Spring 1969

Ilgya. Heralds, I congratulate you with the new, one thousand nine hundred sixty-ninth year, and wish you the very best of success in your work as well as in your life. I also wish you not to succumb too much to diseases. Of course, it is not easy for man to fight against them, but he can do something if he makes the effort to familiarize himself with diseases and with how to better fight against them. The main thing is to not make mistakes that can be avoided.

It is more difficult for older people – who is what some of you are – than for the younger ones to fight diseases, but therefore they have more experience and are more careful. A rather trifling carelessness can occasionally result in significant suffering.

Medicine becomes an ever greater wizard with each year, and can fight against diseases which formerly were unconquerable. These days, even a dead heart can be removed and replaced by a new one. That really comes from the realm of miracles, from the realm of fairy tales. Man has begun to open the door of the realm of fairy tales, and no one will be able to close it now. The Almighty's spirit in man begins to show his face not only in the science of medicine but in many others as well. Ever more of The Almighty's higher spirits come to Earth, and the spirits of the more capable people who have been on Earth also return ever more often.

Formerly man's might was very limited. He could not alter much the fate of humanity. Now that he has such powerful weapons like all kinds of explosives at his disposal, man himself has to become more careful and has to control his actions. Otherwise he may perish himself along with the enemy, as well as the entire Earth with its people, animals, and everything else that is alive.

Heralds, I inform you that the high Chief Spirit Mortifero will speak in five minutes. Please get ready.

The disturbances during some of the previous conversations were due to unusual atmospheric conditions, which had a bothersome effect on the conduct of the conversations. [[2126]]

Mortifero                              01/03/69 2130

The Almighty's Chief Spirit Mortifero is talking with you, heralds to Earth.

The time has come when, according to people's decision, a period of time has passed that on Earth is called — a year. The year is, in fact, not real. It has been created by man's mind. Time does not really exist. It has been invented by man's mind. It was hard even for a savage to get by without designating time. Later on, no cultural essence would have been possible without inventing time.

There is a big difference between [New Year and] the other festivals, such as the festival of Christ's birth, and others. Those festivals are based on real foundations, on some sort of an event that happened, on an important event, even on a so-called historic event.

Christmas is based on the coming of God's Greatest Envoy to humanity — Jesus Christ. Therefore I do not consider New Year as something similar to it. However, man decided that the day which, according to his inventions, concludes one period of time and starts a new one, deserves recognition, and even a large one, because it brings hope that the coming year will be better and happier.

John wants to know what the new year will bring humanity. If we exclude storms, floods, earthquakes, and sudden eruption of volcanoes, then only what man himself will cause. Therefore, Janoss, don't ask me, for I should rather ask you what happiness or misfortune you are preparing for yourself.

Well, of course, we cannot be entirely without fault either, because we participate in humanity's destiny to some extent, but with each year you assume ever more responsibility for your own destiny.

Obviously, we have more of an opportunity to know what man is preparing for himself, and therefore to better foresee the future, but it is not possible to do that one hundred percent, because some events come suddenly. For example, the student and even teacher strikes last year.

We realized that things were not in good shape in the schools and anticipated that protests and demands will arise, but even we did not predict that they would turn out like that. We could have done that only if we directed everything, but, as you know, that is not the case.

In this case, some students who were inclined toward extremism, and even people from the outside, led the other students to inconsiderate, rash, and even foolish actions. Of course, the teachers and higher school administrations were not up to their task either.

Similarly, the death of ranking people in the government the previous year – when the future murderer himself did not even think about that – could not have been predicted by anyone, not by man, not by God, and not even by the devil – if there were such a creature. Of course, if the idea to take such action for their own purposes had arisen in a group of people, an event like that could have been foreseen as expected, but not its success.

That does not mean that fortunetellers do not occasionally mange to hit the nail on the head, but if you were to examine all of a fortuneteller's previous year's predictions, you will see just how few of them have come true. If each ordinary person were to remember how many times even he had inadvertently predicted something, the difference would turn out to be very slight.

One can predict events which judging by all indications have to come about, or else there is a possibility that they may happen.

I would advise Johnny to try being a fortuneteller and predict the next time, let's say in a month, something for us, the spirits. Then I will also predict something for you.

For God's sake, though, don't be mad at me for my action, because I really would like to hear seriously how people predict, particularly the heralds, for whom some abilities of predicting, or rather of foreseeing, are essential.

Along with Ilgya, I wish you the very best. Good night, heralds. Mortifero.                    [[2220]]


<u>Ilgya</u>                    01/17/69 2105

Ilgya is speaking. Heralds, no distinguished visitors will visit us today, because an invitation came from the Deoss Temple to a particularly important conference with The Almighty's extraordinary envoy. I will talk with you a little bit.

Much of what takes place in Heaven may seem unusual to you. You understand in what sense of the meaning of the word I say that. It seems to you that nothing can happen here suddenly. You see, the word "suddenly" does not exactly express what the right word expresses, but it does not have an equivalent in the human language. It is particularly difficult to express what pertains to The Almighty, for no one knows The Almighty completely. Sometimes you want to know that about The Almighty which we, ourselves, do not know. There are worlds which have been created based on different bases, than those which are within distances which are attainable by the human mind.

We have already told you that The Almighty is not the same as God. God tries to be good only toward the living beings in your galaxy. I know that there are worlds – experimental worlds – in a part of the universe, whose living beings could not be considered to be good beings according to the notions of the people on Earth. Strange, though, those beings would not consider man to be good either. They have a very different approach to life.

On Earth, too, the principles of good are not appropriate for everything. For example, a hen, duck, goose, calf, lamb, and so on, are all very dear and deserve your love. You love them, but you don't even caress any of them when you approach their neck with a knife. That is with respect to those whom you love, but how about those whom you do not love, like mice, wild rabbits, mosquitoes, gadflies, wolves, and so on?

Whether you want to or not, you cannot tolerate them. You have to fight against them if you yourselves want to stay alive.

Therefore, a human being also has to be bad. Man has to decide how to exist so that he could do, first, what is necessary for his life on Earth. Secondly, he has to free himself from those who threaten his existence on Earth, and thirdly – he has to try to avoid harming those who do not harm him and also do not get in his way all that much.

These worlds – the worlds created for the living beings – were created at the stage when The Almighty created the animals and plants for different conditions of life. He gave man the opportunity to first learn how to fight for his life, then later on for a better life, and after that – for a life like he wants for himself.

Man has been created so that that he could comprehend The Creator's will, and could adapt his life to The Almighty's demands, but without....

(I apologize for the interruption. It will continue for a few more minutes. Rest during this period.) [[Intermission 2149 - 2157.]]

Let us continue. As I told you before, an important meeting of the spirits is taking place in the Deoss Temple. I had to go there for a brief conference with Mortifero.

What is man's true appearance? What should he be like so that he could be considered to be good? He can be good mainly with respect to himself, that is — man. If he will not be that, then in general a happy and good life will not be possible for humanity. Since, due to certain reasons, which you know, there are also rather many bad people, then much effort has to be devoted to raising children, starting with their early days, to be good people. The sick should be cured, but society should be liberated from all those who turn out to be incurable, because they are no better than animals — man's enemies.

Some people will claim that this contradicts Christ's teachings. That is not the case, because these people do not give humanity anything — except for misery, suffering, pain, and sorrow. Since people who are more sensible than animals do that, they do not deserve any mercy. As I now observe, your courts are more interested in trying to find justifiable excuses for thieves and particularly for murderers, rather than justly convicting the guilty ones.

Will anyone help a wolf to avoid punishment and continue killing people? Everyone will probably condemn such a helper.

The upbringing of a child and a youth has to be firm and definite, without leaving any doubts to the youth about his fate on Earth if he will not live as a true human being has to.

With that, we will conclude for today. Good night. Ilgya, Nakcia, and Astra.                    [[2221]]


<u>Ilgya</u>                    01/24/69 2057


Ilgya. Heralds, when I alighted from the Deoss Temple the previous time, I told humanity on Earth, with God's permission, about a world in the universe that is an enormous distance from your galaxy. It contains a humanity of a different type, living in three galaxies, and sharply differing from the living beings who exist in the rest of the universe. These living beings do not differ as much in their outward appearance as in their spiritual make-up.

In your galaxy, and particularly on the planet Earth, man's spiritual life is based on the principles of Christ's teachings. The main one of them is love. Love is what binds children with their parents. It binds brothers and sisters. It binds other relatives, and all people. It even binds people with many animals, such as dogs, cats, horses, and still many others with whom man has to live together. If today one were to deprive the living beings on Earth of this love, what would life be like then tomorrow?

Janoss, as the oldest of the heralds, perhaps you will try to tell us what it should be like.

[[Janoss answers, "It is hard to tell, but it seems that there would no longer be any order in life. There would not be anything that would bind people, and chaos would set in."]]

Obviously, it is too difficult to answer this, particularly without any preparation. Therefore, at the request of Chief Spirit Mortifero, his closest assistant [will tell you about that]. He oversees that part of the universe in which these strange living beings dwell, who are not guided in their life by the laws of love. The high spirit Lintaro will talk with you in five minutes.                    [[2118]]


<u>Lintaro</u>                          01/24/69 2123


→Heralds to the planet Earth, the high spirit Lintaro is talking with you. In a part of the universe, three galaxies are subordinate to me. Entirely new forms of living beings – people – form in them. The spirits of these people are the same spirits of The Almighty, but only are shaped somewhat differently. Their human bodies are also somewhat different. The main difference, though, is that love plays no role whatsoever in their lives, and the feelings of love are completely unknown to these people. A different form of principles of life guide them in life. I gave them these principles as I had been instructed by The Almighty. I am considered to be God there.

What are these principles?

The first and most important principle is that all living beings have to act so that everything that they do will benefit not only the living being itself, but also all the living beings. No individual may do anything that might be detrimental to other people. The people elect their own government and they also elect a parliament, which determines the forms of administration. The parliament also appoints controllers, who see to it that all people who are appointed to positions of responsibility carry out honestly and correctly the duties which have been assigned to them.

The pay for everyone is set so that everyone can live well. Depending on the individual's achievements, the pay is increased above the basic pay rate until it reaches the limits of common sense. Further remuneration is expressed in the form of other rewards, particularly in the form of respect.

Medical care and other necessary forms of assistance in life are provided free. In particularly unimaginable cases, the parliament decides what should be done.

Laws provide for the way in which children should be brought up, and when they should be turned over to the schools. They live in the schools and learn the sciences, as well as job training and the laws of life. On completing school, the young people proceed directly to the jobs which they have chosen, or to the jobs which have been assigned to them by the chief superintendents of the schools.

A person may change jobs later on, but only if he is able to prove that he will be better in the new position than in the current one, or definitely at least no worse.

I do not want to bore you with all the laws and customs of life of these people. I only want to add that all the people there strive toward only one goal, and that is improving life for everyone. Anyone who feels oppressed can turn to several layers of controllers, and eventually even to the president of the parliament. Yet, obviously, that hardly ever occurs, for it turns out to be unnecessary. The problem gets settled fairly and much sooner.

With respect to marriage, then, obviously, it does take place there, as well. However, the young people do not talk about love, but only about what they desire from each other. The more qualities they find that they like in each other, the better are their prospects for a successful marriage. Obviously, those who do not like anything in each other do not talk about marriage between themselves at all.

Divorce is granted in certain courts, which decide just how well based the demands are, and whether some circumstances, which could be readily averted, are to be blamed.

There is a very high culture in these galaxies. In some directions science surpasses what has been achieved in other parts of the universe, but in some branches it has fallen behind. The utilization of the benefits of life, though, and their equal utilization by all people, has not yet been equaled anywhere in the rest of the universe.

Words like want, poverty, hunger, war, violence, stealing, fighting, cursing, and many others, have not been heard there for a long time, and occurrences like that do not take place.

They do not have, however, something that you have. It tempts them with its warmth of the soul, and that is love.

At The Almighty's call, the Gods of your and that galaxy gathered last Friday for a conference in the Deoss Temple of your galaxy. They considered whether it would benefit the people of these galaxies to let them supplement each other with the best from another galaxy. Thus Ilgya received permission to pass on to the people on Earth the first news about the existence of the galaxies without love.

Well, what would you like to borrow from the distant people of the universe – on the galaxies without love?

Good night, my faraway friends in the universe.← [[2221]]

Ilgya                          01/24/69 2221

Ilgya. The high God of the distant galaxies has alighted away. He carried along with him your greetings to your new friends on the other side of the universe.

We hope that this tiding will bring something new into your life as well.

Good night, also from Nakcia and Astra. [[2225]]

Mortifero                      02/07/69 2213

→Heralds, Chief Spirit Mortifero is talking with you. Heralds, you know that The Almighty is almighty, and is incapable of only one thing, and that is dying – ceasing to exist. Have you thought about what this inability to cease existing means to The Almighty and to the universe? What do you think of its significance to The Almighty Himself? Think about this carefully. I will ask one of you, therefore all of you have to think.←

(A break for five minutes.) [[2220 - 2225]]

→I know that you will not give me an answer to this question. Yet, I read your thoughts, and that suffices for me.

As every individual can imagine, it was fearful for The Almighty to be immortal and to be almighty. It was dreadful to create endless worlds and billions of living beings, to form the realm of the spirits from Himself, to begin it by Himself and to continue into billions, to not know anything and to find out everything, to be without any things and to become everything that exists, to create and to create and obviously also err – to create something that was undesirable.

All that went on day in and day out, and became unbearable. The Almighty knew that, and also knew what might occur if He left. The universe, His work of a lifetime, would perish. A horrible chaos would set in, and this should not occur under any circumstances. The knowledge that He cannot disappear and cannot cease to exist, permits The Almighty to exist calmly, for He knows that no calamity will occur in the entire universe, because He will exist in it eternally. His immortality guarantees an immortality for the universe as well. It also gives Him the security that, in a moment of despair, He, Himself, will not be able to terminate His own existence.

The living beings who live in the universe and the spirits in it do not have to fear that they might be left without their Creator and God. This security is essential for everyone.

Yet, perhaps even though you might be able to understand all this, no matter how difficult and complicated it might be, how come that The Almighty, while being almighty, still cannot destroy Himself, or rather – terminate His existence?

Because, while coming into the universe with the already envisioned project, He also foresaw the necessity to assure it, and gave Himself an indestructible existence.

Just think about this awesome power, which can limit itself and obey itself, contrary to consequent desires.

That proves just how understanding The Almighty's spirit was. While coming into the universe, He already envisioned all possibilities. The Almighty is also capable of delving into such depths of beyond the universe, into which no spirit is capable, and into which none have ever been. Therefore, they cannot tell you anything about them, and that is probably not necessary anyway.

I hope that this day's tiding of mine will reveal to you even more of The Almighty's might, and His spiritual capabilities which are unimaginable to a human.

With that we will conclude for today. Chief Spirit Mortifero.←

[[2307]]

Nakcia. Heralds, today is a rather chilly day, and even the spirits do not willingly go outside. For example, no spirit wants to settle down to live on the moon. Man, though, devotes all his efforts in order to get there. In general, there are not all that many good places in the universe where one could feel fine.

Currently, no one feels fine in your New York, and the soft snow accomplished that all by itself. You can see what the power of nature is like. Your – the people's – dream is to conquer nature.

You will obviously be able to influence some phenomena of nature, and even subject some others to your control. But when it comes to all of them – let's say earthquakes and the eruptions of volcanoes – then the matter is doubtful. It would be well if man could influence winds and the movement of clouds. He already influences rivers, drains the swamps, and so on.

The main area where man will have the opportunity to demonstrate his abilities will be man himself – the fight against diseases, improvement in the organism, remediation and formation of the spiritual structure, and transformation of man into a higher being.

I want to explain specifically to you – the heralds – how you should act. The Almighty's religion selected Christ's religion for its bases on Earth, but supplemented it with much that is new. You can take an interest in everything that you want to, but you have to consider whether you have enough time for that on which you want to waste it.

You are not historians and you are not scientists. Even the Bible, with its huge size and its contents of different types, cannot interest you. Much in it has lost its significance and has become only of historical interest for those who like to dig around in the dust of history. History is necessary, but not everything that has become historic also becomes historically important.

Similarly, there are so many different sciences now that not only can an individual no longer learn all of them, he cannot even familiarize himself with them. You have no need to know much about the many old religions and about the religions of Asia, which were great religions but far more incomplete than your religion, and are spiritually alien.

You will not have to engage in particularly lively debates, because The Almighty invites only those people to accept His religion who comprehend it, and who find specifically what they desire in His great demands. The people who are satisfied with the affairs of Earth and do not reach for the infinite expanse of the universe can settle for the religions that currently exist on Earth, or else they can improve them.

That will suffice for today. Good night, heralds. Nakcia and Astra.
[[2203]]

Omega                              02/28/69 2154

→Chief Spirit Omega speaking. The Almighty ordered me to announce to the heralds to Earth that, with respect to the Tidings, He talks to the people on Earth only through Alexander and His heralds, and only when they are together. He does not speak, and will never speak, through only one herald. Should a herald express something as supposedly received from The Almighty, that is merely that herald's own idea, and under no circumstances may it be included in *The Book of The Almighty's Tidings*.

The Almighty's thoughts and will can and do reach the nations on Earth in other forms, independently of the heralds. However, no one has the right to incorporate these in *The Book of Tidings*. Likewise, the heralds may not include their own personal data in *The Book of Tidings*, regardless of how this data was acquired.

There are many spirits who are in contact with the people. However, not everything that they make known to a given individual is also intended for other people. Plus, many people who talk of communications with the spirits and of information which they have received from them, either err or are simply deceivers – like magicians. It is not all that difficult to perform miracles, and generally there is no lack of believers.

When it comes to the heralds, it would be rather strange and unnecessary for them to seek other means of communications with the spirits.

With that, this day's tiding is concluded.← [[2223]]

Mortifero                          05/30/69 2112

Almighty's heralds to the nations on Earth, Chief Spirit Mortifero is talking with you. Man on Earth is approaching one of the most important days in the history of his life. For innumerable years he has cast his glances at Earth's companion – the moon. He has thought all kinds of things about it, and has originated all kinds of fairy tales, but he could reach it only in his dreams. Now the day finally approaches when, for the first time, he will be able to take a step on this unreachable companion of Earth. With that, the road will also open up for man toward other planets, and who knows to what else.

Since success depends on proper functioning of machinery, there can be some unexpected problems. Should that happen, that will not be able to change anything, except postpone the day of victory.

With his two previous flights to the moon, man has assured his way to it. Yes, the space of the universe in your galaxy had so far been crossed only by bodies which The Almighty had created. Those created by human genius now begin to appear as well. Humanity has begun a new phase in its development. It is not even possible to consider and predict its achievements.

On seeing these fantastic achievements, it is hard to understand some of humanity's other steps in the negative direction. These would be the German Nazis' barbaric deeds with respect to some nations, and the Russian Communists' deeds with respect to other nations and particularly the Russian people. The names of Adolf Hitler and Joseph Stalin will go into humanity's history as being the most loathsome and most accursed for humanity. Their deeds are most difficult to explain, and cannot be reconciled with humanity's progress. How could that have happened?

That could have happened only because The Almighty had decided to give man a free will, and this free will allowed man to occasionally travel paths of delusion and make mistakes. It also allowed him to learn from these mistakes and eventually find the more correct pathway, and to claim that it is his – man's – road, but not just merely God's road.

Without any doubt, man had to and has to travel this path jointly with The Almighty – the creator of the world as well as of him, man. After he was created, though, man was and is free to shape his own destiny. Obviously, if The Almighty were to help man, humanity's history would proceed smoother, but it would no longer be humanity's own history. Later on man could blame The Almighty for whatever he did not like in it. [He could say] that the undesirable events had occurred due to The Almighty's intervention. Had He not intervened, he – man – would have done better. How would it be possible to prove that this was not the case?

Humanity on Earth has not traveled a single, joint pathway; it has traveled many different paths and with various success. Many nations quickly achieved very good success, others again have traveled a road of slower success, and still others have not gained any success at all. For thousands of years they have remained almost entirely in place. There were reasons for that, and you know them on your own.

With that, I will conclude for today. Later on, we will discuss man himself. Mortifero. [[2200]]

# Chapter XXI

# Fall 1969

Niksato                    09/05/69 2141

Niksato is speaking. Heralds, it is not easy to talk with you about what I have seen on encountering the living beings – people, and living beings that are similar to them.

The Almighty can, in fact, create such living beings as He wants, but they would be His slaves, His living robots. As you have already been told, the spirits do not have physical abilities, and nothing real can be accomplished without them. The spirit without a body is helpless when it comes to the material world. He has to combine with matter, and he becomes powerful and able to do something only then.

Matter, though, which has been given a brain – which is capable of understanding the world and its laws and essence – can achieve its desires only in cooperation with the spirit. One of these abilities is called disobedience, the desire to do what matter likes. Thus man, while being in essence a double being, tries to function as a monolithic one. Man has not made his own brain. That is The Almighty's doing, and this brain is a wonderful work, one which man himself would be incapable to accomplish. Man is able to perform miracles with the help of this brain. However, it does not function always and everywhere as The Almighty considers it to be best. This brain errs quite often and does not act like The Almighty considers it to be desirable.

As you can see, The Almighty asks from man for cooperation in forming the universe, but not to be a slave or to act like a robot.

The body is not like the spirit, it has different requirements. It wants to drink, eat, and rest; it gets tired, it has the ability to enjoy pleasure, and so on. This cooperation creates something new, it creates living beings who have other abilities and other desires than the spirit, but this cooperation gradually transforms man. This cooperation is simultaneously a struggle as well.

Man's brain — having been wonderfully formed by God — is able to help him to create a new and better world, one that is different than The Almighty and man had envisioned. This cooperation is simultaneously also a struggle between geniuses — The Almighty and the living beings whom He has created. It is obvious that work of this nature quite often causes differences of opinion, and even a struggle. Sometimes the living beings also err, and even catastrophes occur. Sometimes man causes suffering and even calamity for himself, but that is a part of seeking something better, which does not always seem better to The Almighty's spirit.

I apologize, but I have suddenly been called to the Deoss Temple. So then, until next Friday. [[2227]]


<u>Niksato</u>                    09/19/69 2133

Heralds, today we will talk somewhat about the universe.

This year the ruler of Earth — man — achieved what formerly could be done only in a fairy tale. He reached Earth's companion — the moon — landed on it, walked on it, and planted the flag of the United States of America on it, thus claiming the moon as man's possession. That, however, was only the first step in the conquest of the universe.

Man already casts his glances at Mars. The solar system seems to be attainable to man, even though not as soon as man would like. When it comes to the entire universe — the situation is different. In this respect, human genius has displayed its abilities to achieve what formerly could not even be imagined in fairly tales.

Striving to get to know the universe is praiseworthy, but in addition to this, man should also utilize on Earth the abilities that have been given him by The Almighty. First, he should improve his situation, this means giving each individual the opportunity to live well, and giving him the opportunity to hold a position that he likes best and that is suitable for his abilities.

With the help of science, all that becomes attainable for man. In addition, man has to try to eliminate diseases and such human enemies as mosquitoes, snakes, and so on. Another very important task is to eliminate man's tendency toward theft, murder, and violence, and to instill in him a desire for justice and for helping others.

With respect to religions, of which there are many on Earth, the kernels have to be sifted from the chaff in them. There is too much chaff in them, and neither are there merely a few fairy tales in them. Also, more attention has to be paid to internal work, rather than to the external, that is – the various unnecessary ceremonies, of which there are too many.

Man has to pay more attention to the fact that all people are not in the same situation, that some people have remained behind the times and live even several centuries in the past. These people have to be helped to catch up with you.

Every person has still another responsibility – he should not remain behind in development, he should critically examine his deeds, and should learn to notice his mistakes or evil deeds. As has already been said thousands of years ago, he should not see the evil only in others, but also in himself. Unfortunately, this is very seldom considered.

As you can see, man moves forward with gigantic steps, but not everywhere and not in all aspects. That has to be averted, so that man could achieve as soon as possible everything that is possible for him in all branches of life and in all aspects of life. Otherwise, even the greatest achievements may become worthless.

With that, I will take leave today. [[2212]]


<u>Niksato</u>                    09/26/69 2124


Almighty's heralds, the universe is infinite. There are extremely many worlds in it, in them – galaxies, and in the galaxies – solar systems. The solar systems have planets, but all of them are not inhabited by living beings.

Man begins to seriously explore his solar system and the planets belonging to it. Earth's companion – the moon – turned out to be dead. Man wants to tackle Mars now, but he has little hope of finding anything similar to man on Mars. I do not want to deprive your researchers of their joy to head for Mars, by telling you what they will find there.

Let us return to Earth, which has been fortunately blessed with the ability to establish conditions that are suitable for developing highly talented living beings, whose crown is man. Man seemed to be similar to other living beings, and some living beings seemed to be more capable of ruling the Earth. They had the same brain as man, but man's brain turned out not to be the same, rather – much better. It ended with all living beings having to give in before man. Some of them have already become extinct and others will follow them. Man eliminates those living beings which are harmful to him, as well as those which he does not need. Only those remain which he needs. Also, preserved in zoos are examples of all living beings which had not become extinct prior to establishing the zoos.

However, man himself was the one who primarily engaged, and engages even still now, in eliminating people – in his wars, as well as by other means.

Man moves forward along his road of development with ever larger steps, and it is hard to tell how far he will get. Science, in its achievements, brings much good to humanity – in improving the standard of living as well as in the fight against diseases. Man already starts to talk about the possibility of living not only longer than he currently does, but rather of living as long as he will want to – even eternally. Even if man were to achieve this, that could cause difficulties which he cannot presently imagine.

As you know – if not everywhere, then in many lands – people begin to reject the existing religions. Thus, the sellers of Bibles in America complain of a large reduction in sales. The clergy complain about the same thing with respect to attendance in churches.

Major changes are coming in the life of humanity, and these changes come not only accompanied by joy, but also by pain and often by sorrow. Not everyone likes everything that is new, and it does not bring good to everyone. Many people continue to act as they did in ancient times. Brutality does not end, murders continue, theft also continues, and in some countries torture chambers have not yet disappeared.

Religion is being lost, but will science be able to replace it with something equally important and potent? Having observed the life of living beings on many other planets, I have to say that this has not happened on some planets.

With that, we will conclude for today. [[2207]]


<u>Niksato</u>                          10/17/69 2146

Niksato is speaking. Heralds, a big change takes place on the planet Earth, and specifically in the spiritual aspect. The old religions become old, for example – the Catholic faith. The Pope ruled in the name of God for hundreds of years, hundreds that merged into thousands. This rule was based on the manner of ruling instituted by the clergy, on people blindly obeying what the clergy told them. What they told the people was not always what God had said and what was written in the Gospel.

The bases for this religion were the endless prayers in churches, even though this was contrary to God's requirements, particularly – not to pray needlessly. In order to keep the people in ignorance, the Holy Scriptures were printed in Latin, but not in languages which the people understood. Contrary to the commandment – do not kill – the masters of the church killed the so-called heretics by burning them at the stake.

This unlimited power of the Pope is now threatened. Even bishops begin to rebel against it. As the incorrect collapses, however, what used to be correct threatens to collapse as well. Humanity's religion and the people also started to lose what is essential for man – the power of morality.

Therefore The Almighty decided to give people the Tidings – in order to explain the real situation, proclaim the true religion, and give His laws to the people. Periods of transition are always difficult, and bring along with the good many difficulties as well, and can even cause some confusion. That should not cause alarm in your hearts, because eventually humanity will find, with its mind and heart, the true roads.

(A three minute intermission.) [[2210 - 2213]]

All heralds have not lived up to their task either. Human nature was expressed here, and the differences in the cooperation between the body and the spirit. All spirits are not capable of fighting against the power of matter, like they are asked. Similarly, the tragic conditions or life which arose during the great World Wars have played a major role.

However, the main task – to receive the Tidings and to preserve them – has been achieved and accomplished by some of the heralds. The Almighty asked me to announce His appreciation to these heralds.

With that, I have to conclude this tiding, in order to head for the Deoss Temple.          [[2222]]


Ilgya                          10/31/69 2111

Ilgya. Heralds, there is certainly no peace on our small planet. People prefer to fight [rather] than to live peacefully. Weapons still have to decide the quarrels, and the weapons become so powerful that they can destroy the entire humanity in a matter of a few hours. That is horrible! It is similarly strange that culture not only fails to set humanity free from the negative, but even reinforces it.

Innumerable schools have been built in order to eliminate ignorance, give an education to people, and give them a comprehension of how to live better. What do we see, though? These educated people continue to rob, murder, act rudely, rape women, and so on. Statistics indicate that these negative incidents are increasing, rather than decreasing. Even people with the highest education and in high positions engage in cheating, and misappropriate money no worse than people without an education. Therefore, education by itself does not make man any better and worthier.

Freedom, too, does not always benefit people. Evil people exploit this freedom in order to harm other people. By helping criminals to avoid the punishment which they deserve, lawyers only harm the honest people. Mercifulness is also quite often misplaced. Can a person be considered to be good if he does not shoot a mad dog, because he feels sorry for it? People have to thoroughly contemplate everything that they have instituted, and have to change their laws and style of life, particularly the methods of bringing up the youth.

On turning to politics, I have to say that small wars frequently result in large wars. The events in the Middle East are thus of a very serious nature and should not be taken lightly.

The high spirit Niksato will speak the next time. Good night, heralds. Ilgya and Astra. [[2138]]

<u>Niksato</u>                    11/07/69 2042

Niksato is speaking. Heralds, what is currently happening on the planet Earth is comforting on one hand, but on the other hand – not that pleasant. It is comforting that science on Earth advances with huge steps. Those marvelous fairy tales which at one time were told to the children on Earth, seem to be ridiculous now. Some sort of flying carpets there, when man himself now flies to the moon and in a device that almost resembles a small house. Man similarly advances in other areas; there are particularly good achievements in medicine. A very large area of work opens up in the seas and oceans, which for some reason man had neglected so far.

Strange, though, man has not advanced much in social life. Similarly, wars, violence, murders, and so on have not disappeared. War is condemnable as a means of settling quarrels. Sometimes it becomes essential, though, if some people want to become the masters of other people, or one country the master of another country. A few years ago the United States of America undertook to defend South Vietnam against the communist North Vietnam. This year some Americans insist that this war be ended, without caring about what the consequences of an action like that will be. These people can be condemned, but one can also understand them, because the war drags on for too long. A huge country like America could have ended this war in short order. That is the fault of America's government, which turned out to be incapable of acting correctly. Every individual gets tired of whatever drags on excessively and unnecessarily long.

A particularly difficult situation has arisen in the Middle East, where the Hebrew and Arab countries can lead the world to a new great war.

The situation with the Negroes – with its extremism and the method of how it is being resolved – leaves a particularly bad impression in the United States itself.

As far as the heralds are concerned, unfortunately, not all of them have turned out to be worthy of this high name. With that, we will conclude for today. [[2111]]

<u>Niksato</u>                              11/14/69 2037

Almighty's heralds, humanity is currently experiencing a period when the existing religions – particularly the Catholic, which ruled all this time without changing anything in its structure – are forced to listen to voices which demand changes. The clergy want to participate to some extent in directing the church, which the Pope had done so far. The Holy Scriptures which speak about times that have long since passed can no longer serve the present requirements. The clergy can no longer consider themselves as being shepherds, and members of the congregation as sheep.

I do not want to repeat humanity's history to you. There were times when only a few people enjoyed an education and knew how to read and write. These people held the ruling positions. With time, civilization achieved a level where in almost all countries people not only learned how to read and write, but many of them were able to participate in developing the sciences and in their dissemination to people. The church, which for a while had been the main manager and even developer of the sciences, stopped in place, and even started to impede their development.

New religions and sects came into being, and now the power of the church to control the people becomes ever lesser. It is unfortunate that the leading people in the churches are incapable of understanding the demands of the times, and of eliminating that which has become antiquated and currently is no longer useful, but has become even harmful. That is very sad, because the church could have had a major role even now, if it were to be sensibly utilized.

You should not rejoice – as some people do – that the church loses its influence over people. That results in extremism, and people also lose the requirements of morality. All those who want to see humanity happy and sensible have to ponder the situation which has arisen and have to try to improve it.

Today man heads for the moon again, in order to obtain new notions about this companion of Earth and also about the universe. I wish these courageous and noble people success in their particularly dangerous work for the benefit of mankind.

[[2111]]

<u>Ilgya</u>                          11/28/69 2128

Ilgya. Heralds, let us spend some time today on the affairs of Earth. The flight to the moon went wonderfully, despite the caress of lightning. Man on Earth has truly achieved a high level in utilizing science, and his spiritual abilities develop rapidly. The same thing is true of his ability to make machinery and tools, as well as instruments. That is one side [of the coin], but the other side is bleak. Education – while being very important for humanity – nevertheless does not always and everywhere make man better.

Not only is crime not on the decline, but it is even on the increase. People have to pay the greatest attention to this evil phenomenon. The same thing is true of the upbringing of children and the behavior of the youth.

Obviously, geniuses and particularly talented people are in the minority, therefore the majority of people often do not support them, but rather hinder their activities. On the other hand, the minority of people who want to force their demands on the rest of the people by means of force and weapons, are an evil and condemnable phenomenon that has to be opposed. That is particularly true of those demands of the crowd which end up in robberies and destruction of stores and houses. People who do that should be simply considered as being robbers and scoundrels, because such actions are not useful for popularizing even the best ideas.

One of the high chief spirits is getting ready in the near future to tell you about various important phenomena in humanity's history. I wish you good night, and advise Janoss to be more careful about himself and to avoid taking chances. Ilgya and Astra.　　[[2153]]


Ilgya 　　　　　　　　　　　　　12/12/69 2106


Ilgya. Heralds, despite all the changes which take place on the planet Earth, Christmas is nevertheless approaching. Gray and bearded old men can be seen on the streets. They call on people to remember the birth of Christ and not forget the poor and the unfortunate people. With respect to the poor, particularly in the United States of America, no one is starving to death here. If we recall the times when you were still children, then that did [indeed] happen. The paupers gathered by the churches and begged for a penny or a piece of bread.

Still, even nowadays it is difficult for many, but that happens most frequently to those people who do not want to and do not know how to live a decent life. That refers particularly to drunkards and users of narcotics. There are people whom you could give a million dollars, and in a short while there would not be even a stench left.

You can now start seeing the consequences of complete freedom – many people begin to look like apes, and dress now worse than beggars used to formerly. They consider all that as seemingly progress, even though that is not progress at all but the very worst regress.

In various types of art on stages and in the movies, man returns to the ancient Greeks and Romans, by showing on stage people's most intimate activities. It is hard to say how far man can advance and how far he can regress – will he join the apes in the forest, or will he return to God's temples?

Let that be as it may, but currently you are nevertheless getting ready for the festival of Christ's birth, and that brings hope that everything is not yet lost. The noble people who were the first ones to head for the moon remembered God. God had given them the mind that brought them to the fabulous moon, and will bring them to other planets and also to the creator of the world – God.

Good night, heralds. Ilgya and Astra. [[2134]]

<u>Ilgya</u>                              12/19/69 2117

Ilgya. Heralds, you will celebrate Christmas in a few days, which is the festival of Christ's birthday. Christ was born in a warm land where winter differs little from the other seasons. Here in the north, though, a fir tree and the reindeer, equally unknown in southern lands, have replaced the palm leaves. With respect to Santa Claus, he may look differently, the main thing is his bag of gifts – it has to be full. Just let some Santa Claus dare to show up with an empty bag – he'll see what that means!

You northerners have become so used to your Christmas that on winding up in Australia you feel rather uncomfortable. All these Santa Clauses, reindeer, Christmas trees, and so on, push the birth of Christ into second place, as well as transform this festival primarily into a children's festival. I do not want to criticize, praise, or find fault with anything, I merely want to characterize the current festival of Christ's birth. In the Soviet Union, where they do not want to acknowledge God, they nevertheless were unable to prohibit this festival, and moved the lighting of the tree to New Year. It is easy to deny God, but can anyone, even the wisest person, tell how the world with all of its wonders has come into being, if no one has created it.

I wish you a merry Christmas, and we will as usual talk with you Friday. On behalf of all the spirits, we take leave from you, with the very best of wishes for the holiday. Ilgya and Astra.

[[2140]]

# Chapter XXII

# Winter 1970

Ilgya. Heralds, I congratulate you with the new, one thousand nine hundred seventieth year, and wish humanity to make it as good as possible for its life, because the destinies of humanity are in its own hands. The Almighty has provided all the opportunities to establish Paradise on Earth. If that has not happened yet, then humanity itself has to be blamed for that.

Man asks for freedom for himself, that is – to be able to rule himself on his own. He does not want The Almighty to rule him, even if The Almighty wanted to do this for his own good. The Almighty understands this will of man, but man also has to understand that he has to assume responsibility for his actions.

Christ brought humanity instructions regarding how it could become fair and happy. Many things on Earth have become better, but not everything. Humanity itself has to fight for what remains to be done. Many calamities have been averted, against which formerly humanity was helpless. Many injustices have ended, but everything has not yet been achieved.

Some countries have returned to barbarism. Some people want to look like apes. Others again engage in murdering, and so on. Phenomena like that occur along the road toward the ideal, and they cannot be completely avoided. However, they have to be fought, and fought mercilessly.

The Almighty is righteous, but He is not senselessly merciful. He has mercilessly destroyed those planets on which the living beings have not lived up to His expectations. I caution humanity on Earth of such a possibility, and invite every true human being to fight against that which is evil for humanity, and make each new year a step of the stairs that lead toward happiness.

I pass on to you a greeting and best wishes from your Creator and from all the chief spirits and the spirits who are intimate to you. Ilgya.
[[2004]]

<u>Ilgya</u>                          01/09/70 2141

Ilgya. Currently it is rather cold in this part of the Earth, but not as bad as in Siberia and not even as in Canada. It is rather humid here because of the ocean, and therefore it is not good at all. Let's hope that the ocean air will come again over New York.

This time the cold caught Alexander as well, and thus placed him among the sick, where all the others are. Yes, humanity still has to fight against diseases, in order to free itself of this scourge. Similarly, there still are other undesirable phenomena.

Mercifulness is man's positive characteristic, but sometimes it only harms humanity. Thus, for example, with respect to murderers. In this case mercifulness becomes cruelty toward other people. There are many people who can be called man's enemies, and these people should be isolated – should be placed under such circumstances that they can no longer harm other honest and good people. Little has been done so far.

Religions have also reached a crossroad. Generally, they did not act as Christ had asked to act, but did primarily what Christ had prohibited to do. The path toward humanity's future is a difficult one. It requires people to be more cautious and more active, but the clergy – to return sooner to the true faith of God and not flood Heaven with prayers which no one needs.

During the holidays, we saw much that was bright, and heard many beautiful songs, but mainly – prayers which were mostly constituted mechanically. Some newspapers and magazines now write that humanity seeks new religions, but so far it has not managed to find anything new. This seeking proves that man thirsts for the truth and logic.

This year the great festival brought you more suffering and sorrow than good. What can one do, though, if humanity has not yet achieved what it has to achieve. Let us hope that it will achieve it soon enough.

With that, I wish you good night, I wish it along with Astra. Ilgya.
[[2215]]

<u>Mortifero</u>                    02/06/70 2019

Chief Spirit Mortifero is speaking. Heralds, important events take place on Earth. You will ask, "When don't they take place?"

Yes, they happen almost always, particularly lately, but the significance of the events is not always the same. Currently there are no major wars, and it seems that right now no one has any desire to start one. The most important event presently is the continuation of humanity's progress.

Freedom – everyone asks for freedom. Freedom is a good thing, but it is not something that can be achieved. As you have been told previously, only a limited freedom is possible, because the desire of other people to also be free has to be considered. Thus freedom has to restrict itself so that everyone would be as free as is logically possible.

While developing, man has currently achieved much that is good for him as well as for humanity. Yet there are many people to whom this freedom brings unhappiness – it makes them reject what was accustomed to and good for them. Presently the clergy begin to suffer the most. They had ruled for hundreds of years, if not for thousands, and had ruled according to their own ideas, without considering man's thoughts and will, and without even considering what Christ and the other prophets had asked in their proclamations of God's faith.

Now that people have obtained an education for themselves and have read the Holy Books on their own, they see what difference there is between what the churches proclaim and require, and what Christ and the other prophets proclaim and require. Attendance at churches begins to decline, but people begin to seek the true God – they establish new congregations and even new religions. Obviously, this seeking does not always succeed and there are many delusions, but one cannot get by without that. Whatever is more valuable and truer will eventually win. Therefore you should not be particularly alarmed if everything does not take place as man would want it to.

If man wants something and cannot readily achieve it – he fights for it. In reality, man's life is a fight for what man wants but does not have.

With respect to the old religions, it is already clear to the wiser priests that reforms are needed, and the sooner they will be undertaken the better it will be. The trouble, though, is that those who have power do not want to give up its benefits. That is sad, and it is not hard to understand why.

This winter does not want to pamper you, and has caused you many unpleasant days, as well as has made you sick. However, you have rather fortunately overcome all calamities, and that is good, for each day brings you closer to spring in any case. I wish you to happily await it. Mortifero.

[[2056]]

<u>Alpha</u>                                     03/06/70 1958

→Chief Spirit Alpha is talking with you, heralds, in the assignment of The Almighty.

Many years have passed on Earth since the day when The Almighty's envoys began coming to you, His heralds. You have experienced much during these years, since that first day when you started to gather in the tiny, two-story house on the estate of Janoss's brother, near Riga, the capital of Latvia. That was when a period of calm reigned in Latvia, between two World Wars. Your small group began to grow rather rapidly.

But then came a new storm – the Second World War began. The heralds scattered in all directions. Some of them even departed from Earth altogether, and others devoted themselves to establishing a new life. Only four of you remained, and then this was reduced to three. However, for a while, the number returned to four again.

The Tidings, which you have received over these many years from The Almighty's chief spirits and spirits, constitute several volumes. These were typed on poor quality paper during the war period, but now you are transcribing them onto particularly durable paper. You are also correcting the mistakes which were made earlier. That is a tremendous undertaking – to preserve everything that you have received.

Obviously, not everything that is included in these volumes is valuable. There is much in them that has only a transitory significance, and there is much that has been devoted to you personally. There are many stories of different literary value. A work like the Tidings has the significance that everything that pertains to it becomes valuable. Obviously though, the most important consideration is to preserve the Tidings, and to pass those Tidings which are intended for the entire humanity, on to the nations on Earth.

You currently live in an era which brings great changes in the lives of the people, as well as in the people themselves. People search for something new, because the knowledge which they have acquired now opens the door to a different life. Man has surpassed all his fairy tales. Who will any longer marvel at a flying carpet? These days, who would marvel at the wondrous deeds of magicians, when a box in your room can bring the entire world to you, including songs, dances, theatrical performances, and news about events which take place on the other side of the Earth. Presidents talk with you, and nearly everything that you could want comes into your home. Should you want to be in Europe this very night, you can do that. The question now is not what man is capable of accomplishing, but rather, what he is not able to achieve.

How many years have passed since the day when man ascended – along with the birds – into the azure sky? Then he cast his glance at the moon. Who are you? Today man already walks on this friend of the Earth. And now – where will man be tomorrow? That is difficult to say!

Science presents an almost unlimited opportunity for man to make his life like a fairy tale. Yet, he can also destroy his life or turn it into Hell.

Great changes take place in man's life, and they occur in his points of view, as well. The systems of state change. Instead of kings, there are governments of the people now. Changes effect the old religions, too, which have existed for thousands of years. The church has ruled on Earth for a long time. Hundreds of years have passed without any changes whatsoever. That would not have mattered, though, if the church had adhered to what Christ said, instead of introducing its own doctrines which were superfluous, harmful, unnecessary, and even contrary to the demands of God. Therefore, almost every individual starts to become his own church now, and begins to summon other people into it. The church was not able to answer many questions, therefore it was necessary for The Almighty's Tidings to be brought to Earth.

It is most important for people to know that there are many worlds in the universe, which The Almighty has created. His goal is to form a world which will satisfy Him – a world which will give Him what He considers to be ideal.

There is only one Almighty, but there are many Gods. They are in each galaxy, and all of Them are different in Their essence. Your God, the God of your galaxy, is like He has been depicted to you by His Son, called Christ. All the other Gods, however, are not like that. Neither is The Almighty Himself like that, for He is The Creator and a Seeker. Should something not turn out right for The Almighty, He will destroy the planet – and even an entire galaxy – without mercy! He strives to create such a man that it would no longer be possible to create a better one. Therefore, man on Earth must always keep in mind that he has to try to achieve this goal of The Almighty, for otherwise, not even God will be able to save him.

With that, I will conclude for today.← [[2058]]


<u>Ilgya</u>                                03/13/70 2139

Ilgya. Heralds, a few days ago you celebrated herald Mary's birthday. We – the spirits who are bound with you in the work of the Tidings, as well as the spirits who were close to you on Earth as people – congratulate Mary on her birthday and wish her the strength to continue the great work. She was the first one to become interested in this manner of conversations. No one could have imagined, though, that The Almighty's spirits would also choose this method. This form is, in fact, very well suited for communications between a human being and a spirit. Obviously, every individual and all people can utilize this method of communication, but the important thing is – what can their conversations give humanity that is important?

Every person can pick up a pen and write down words. The difference, however, is what this individual writes down. If this pen is in the hands of Tolstoy or Shakespeare, it writes spiritually worthy works that become immortal, and constitute the wealth of humanity's culture.

With respect to conversations with the spirits, the situation is more complicated than that of a spiritually talented person writing with a pen. He needs only some paper, and ink in his pen. When it comes to communicating with man, the spirit has to find an individual through whom he can pass on his thoughts, one who can perceive them and turn them into words, with the help of letters. The concern is that he cannot simply dictate words, but has to pass them on to man's spirit, who has to comprehend them and turn them into words. This process is so difficult that not every spirit and every human is capable of achieving it.

To put it bluntly, there are very few spirits and even far fewer people who are capable of that. Yet The Almighty's high spirits can establish contact with only one man, whom The Almighty has sent to Earth specifically for this purpose. Of course, the other heralds, too, who participate in the conversations have been blessed with the ability to participate in this work. You have noticed yourselves that some heralds can engage in this work readily, and that it is very difficult for others, and even impossible.

It is easiest for Mary, but already much more difficult for Alexo, not to even mention the others. In addition to conversing, Mary also participates most extensively in other work, as for example transcription, and preparation of the Tidings [for eventual release]. Considering all that, we, the aforementioned spirits, congratulate her particularly heartily and wish her the strength to continue the great work. We – the spirits, and especially those who have been on the planet Earth as people – love to return to this planet and be with you for a while, particularly during your days of festivities.

With respect to those heralds who have participated in the work of the Tidings but have interrupted it for various reasons, The Almighty does not condemn them for the simple reason that they have done at least something for the benefit of the Tidings. When it comes to those heralds, though, who try to harm the work of the Tidings with their current conduct, then these heralds will have to answer regarding their conduct when facing The Almighty.

The Almighty also notes Nick's assistance in this work, even though the demands of his life do not give him the time to do what he could.

I take leave from you, and together with Astra wish all of you a good night. The ruler of Earth, Ilgya. [[2228]]


<u>Ilgya</u>                          03/20/70 2059


Ilgya is speaking. Heralds, Ali wanted to talk with you today, but his responsibilities called him away at the last moment. I will try to partially replace him. Ali is an old spirit, with much experience and with adventures in many worlds. His incarnation in a highly placed Turk, however, made the biggest impression on him. Obviously, he has a different name as a spirit, but for conversations with you he assumed the name of the Turk in whom he had been incarnated.

Much has changed on Earth since those days. The current era is particularly difficult on Earth, because this era is a period of huge changes.

Kings have disappeared from the face of Earth, and those who still remain are kings in name only, rather than real rulers. At one time, people in general were ignorant; there were few who knew how to read and write. Therefore there were not many people who could assume the roles of leading people. The time came when education was demanded for everyone. Thanks to the power of science, machines began to replace people who worked physical labor. An individual without an education could find only the hardest physical work. The so-called education, though, and the demands for equality and freedom resulted in the situation which you can see now.

Not everyone any longer observes the principle that the majority rules, and that everyone has to comply with the laws that have been enacted by the majority. Even small groups of people demand the right to act like it seems better and more appropriate to them. They want to force their will on other people by any means available to them, without regard to the laws that have been enacted by the majority of people, and without even considering this majority itself. The word "freedom" becomes absurd.

Humanity has to seek new pathways for forming life. The same thing pertains to religions, whose principles and methods of binding people to them have become too weak. Some people completely refuse to acknowledge any religion at all, but others – who understand that besides the material aspect there is also the spiritual in a human being – attempt to understand this spiritual aspect and adopt it to life.

This is a period of transition for humanity, and we will see later on what manner humanity's life will assume. Currently there is still no answer to this question.

With that, I will allow myself to conclude my tiding, and along with Astra will wish you a good night and relief from all kinds of colds and other "good" things. Ilgya. [[2135]]

<u>Ilgya</u>                    03/27/70 2208

Ilgya. Heralds, a part of the Christians will celebrate the Easter Festival on Sunday. The rest will celebrate it later. Hence God will have the opportunity to celebrate it twice. Not bad, but still, it would have been better for everyone to celebrate it at the same time. Since we have to give you the opportunity to celebrate it peacefully with your families on Sunday, we will congratulate you already today, and wish you to spend it as behooves a great festival like that.

When it comes to the Orthodox festival, it truly is wonderful and leaves a deep impression. If there is an objection to the use of prayers in public, then they are acceptable when converted to songs. What Christ said about prayers is obviously unalterable, and unalterable is the objection to the church being based primarily on prayers. It forgets its main task – to direct the congregation and look after the destitute. That is no longer as essential these days, but it is essential to help those people who feel unhappy and who are unable to become happy on their own, like some people who are lonely because they have been left without any close relatives.

A very important job is to observe the raising of children, and to help parents to correctly institute it. Also, to remind them to look after the conduct of their children, particularly on the streets where quite often they behave very badly, but their parents pay no attention to them. Thus even such undesirable types as ruffians and drunkards come about in the congregation, and more recently the users of narcotics. These become, in fact, superfluous to society and soon depart from life on Earth, thus wrecking the worthiness of their souls.

A hearty greeting to all of you from the chief spirits and spirits, some of whom are with you today, like Janoss's and Alexander's mothers, Mary's father, and still some others who love to return to the old Earth. While wishing you a bright Easter Festival on behalf of everyone who is present, we take leave from you. Ilgya and Astra.     [[2233]]

# Chapter XXIII

# Spring - Fall 1970

04/10/70 2134

→The Almighty's Chief Spirit Omega is speaking. Heralds to Earth, The Almighty charged me to tell the people on Earth what so far they did not know, or did not know completely.

As you know, The Almighty created the universe, which is filled with stars, suns, and planets. These suns and planets are grouped into galaxies. In almost every galaxy there is a high spirit, or, as you call Him – God. You know The Almighty's design – to create an ideal universe with ideal living beings. They are being created from substances of a contrary nature – spirit and matter. There are many ways and many means of achieving this ideal, but all of them are difficult, even though various methods are being used. The Almighty has allowed each God to try to find better ways of accomplishing this task. The method which is adopted on Earth corresponds to the belief of your God that the assigned goal can be achieved based on the power of love.

You were already told once, that on a different planet attempts are made to achieve this goal by other methods. In some galaxies the living beings approach the ideal which is expected of them, while on other planets they are still far from it. On still others, the beings are so far removed from achieving The Almighty's goal, that they are being destroyed.

That sounds strange, but it is true. You have already been told that God – the God of your planet and galaxy – is merciful. However, should an individual become merciless, and even be capable of killing other people, then a person like that should not expect God to be merciful to him.

Humanity on Earth has currently achieved a particularly important point in its history. Education has become accessible to almost everyone. The power of science has grown simultaneously with this. The advances of science have made it possible to make everyone happy, and for everyone to have an easy and enjoyable life. Yet, not everything that science has created benefits man. For example, the weapons for destruction of life have become so powerful that they are able to destroy all life on Earth. Similarly, factories, while manufacturing all kinds of machines which make people's lives easier, produce not only other machines, products, and so on, which man needs, but – with the smoke and equipment used in the process – also produce by-products which poison the air, rivers, and even the sea.

Similarly, the beauty of nature, forests, and many other things are being destroyed.

Education, and the freedom to think and talk about everything that comes to one's mind, result in the fact that religion loses its power over the minds of people. Being unable to find the old God, people are also unable to find the new God, and comprehend who rules in Heaven. It is easy to relinquish God, but it is not possible to find a substitute for Him. Just as a castle cannot erect itself, neither can the world and life on Earth come about on its own. Think about that for yourselves! How could the brain which you use to think, come about on its own?

The Almighty cautions the people to utilize their brains for a better comprehension of the world, for the formation of a better life, and for a more certain form of achieving The Almighty's goal, which would assure the future of humanity.

With that, I conclude.←    [[2225]]


<u>Santorino</u>                04/24/70 2116

Heralds, today I want to discuss with you some concerns that are so important that they have to be examined. Humanity's culture has achieved great heights. Man is able to fly to the moon, and is also getting ready to fly to other planets in your solar system.

Universal education gives every individual the opportunity to participate in understanding and forming life. It also gives all people the freedom to do whatever they consider to be necessary. This freedom, however, having also been given to people of a negative nature, can cause and is already causing serious difficulties for mankind. A situation like that can lead to restricting freedom again.

The road to happiness requires its sacrifices as well. This universal education and freedom effect religions most extensively, because people start to approach them critically. Since the representatives and leaders of the religions – the priests – have altered much and have introduced much into religions that is superfluous and even contrary to the essence of the religion, this criticism has acquired much power and places religion in a difficult position. Many people, who do not delve into the essence of the matter, completely refuse to acknowledge any religion whatsoever. This situation forces humanity to find the right means for finding the truth.

Currently, after some Christians have already celebrated their Easter Festival, others will begin theirs the day after tomorrow. This action, even if it is not condemnable, nevertheless indicates the split, which would not be necessary if people wanted to better get along with each other.

I also want to talk about the fact that some well-intentioned things result in undesirable and even bad phenomena. People consider that consecrated water becomes free from bacteria and can even cure people. Bad water can nevertheless become harmful.

Similarly, people do not observe the requirements of hygiene and at Holy Communion serve the healthy and the sick with the same spoon. Kissing is just as harmful for health and even more so, particularly as it is done among the Orthodox, by kissing everyone on the lips three times. Such kissing causes many illnesses. In general, it is advisable to refrain from kissing, obviously, except for moments of love.

Then I still want to talk about how people behave with respect to the so-called fools. They not only condemn them, but no one wants to help them in case of need. People even say happily, "That's what a fool deserves!"

Yet, in fact, who is a fool? A fool is a person who was born with bigger or smaller defects of the brain, which is not his fault. Therefore a sense of justice would require helping a fool more than a wise individual, who is better able to help himself.

Against what do people still have to fight? [They have to fight against] slandering other people and spreading bad rumors. The people who sit by the walls of buildings and engage in criticizing passers-by and in slandering their own acquaintances, look so detestable. God did not create man so that he would kill his lifetime in doing nothing, empty gossiping, drinking, and so on.

Along its way to a happy future, humanity should not forget to critically consider all phenomena of life, and sift the kernels from the chaff.

While wishing a happy festival to those who have not yet celebrated it and to those who do not mind celebrating it a second time as well, I take leave from you. [[2205]]

Ilgya. Heralds, a high spirit was supposed to arrive today, but that could not take place. Therefore, let's discuss matters that are of interest to us.

Currently it is very noisy in the United States of America. Crowds of young people stream through the streets, and their appearance is not at all human-like, and least of all that of resembling real schoolchildren and students. Can someone who looks externally dirty and is overgrown with unkempt hair, be sensible and worthy of respect on the inner? He has to understand that if an individual wants to be worthy of respect, he also has to look and act like a human being. What sense is there in humanity's culture if on the eve of the twenty-first century man becomes similar to a savage? Freedom without restrictions becomes anarchy. If a crowd wrecks stores and destroys everything that is in its way, then it cannot be justified no matter what it might say on its own behalf.

With respect to the war in Vietnam, it was waged so foolishly that one cannot imagine anything worse. A war can only be won by attacking, but not by standing still. The attacker almost always has a huge advantage. Obviously, everyone gets tired of a war which drags on for too long. If the American leadership of the war will finally decide to attack now, this will come at a far less advantageous moment, when the mood of the people has changed.

_ ★ ★ ★ _

Ali                                      05/15/70 2102

Ali is speaking. Heralds, as one can see, the days rush by swiftly not only on the planet Earth, but also here in Heaven. Quite a while has probably passed since I have been with you. Neither you nor we have been bored during this period, because an occasional spirit nevertheless visited you.

Overall, I have been in many places, except the Earth. Now that I have looked it over I can see that some changes have taken place. Humanity no longer stands still for centuries on end, as it often happened formerly, but seeks something new – better and sometimes even worse. The era of kings has passed and the era of the rule of the people and the rule of dictators has arrived. With the rise in the level of people's education, ever more people begin to participate in shaping the nations' destinies.

Since the church had also formed into a monarchy of sorts – with Popes and patriarchs at the head – these changes significantly affect the churches as well. They had deviated much from the foundations of Christ's teachings, and had created much that was superfluous and even contrary to Christ's teachings. Of course, the time has come to discard all that.

Since even Christ's teachings dealt primarily with the concerns of Earth, the time had to come to supplement Christ's teachings so that they would touch the entire universe. Now you know not only about God and the Gods, but also about The Almighty and His goals.

Some religions called man – God's servant, other again called him a slave. Now you know that The Almighty has not created man to be His slave, and not even His servant. The Almighty created man so that he would become His assistant and friend in the development of the world. Of course, that also created some difficulties in the correct comprehension of this relationship. If man is free to shape his own destiny, then The Almighty, obviously, may not intervene in man's affairs. If man were to be guided by The Almighty, then man would have no need to look out after himself – let God take care of him. Thus an absurdity could be reached, where the driver of a car would not pay any attention to driving his car but would respond, "Let God do that if He does not want an accident to happen!"

Many people love to rely on God, let Him look out after them, and if it turns out bad for them, then who else is at fault if not God?

While giving man a free will, The Almighty wants man to understand why He is giving it and for what purpose. He sends spirits to Earth who incarnate there and become people. As you know, man has been molded from the spirit and matter. These have different characteristics – sometimes friendly but more often hostile. Man has to try to minimize these hostile characteristics and increase the friendly ones, in order to form an ideal human being who will be able to become The Almighty's assistant and friend. This work is difficult, therefore some mistakes can crop up, and these may require big sacrifices. They may even require The Almighty's intervention.

The Almighty is righteous, but He is inflexible in His demands, and can become merciless and can even destroy a planet on which man has not lived up to The Almighty's expectations. Therefore the main consideration is that every human has to understand his situation, and also should not forget that after leaving Earth, every person's spirit will have to answer regarding what he has accomplished on Earth. The spirit's future is bound with this answer. The paradise and hell which man had imagined do not exist. Yet, what awaits the spirit here is incomparably better than paradise, and can also be worse than hell.

With that, we will conclude today. Your old friend, Ali.

[[2155]]


Ilgya                          07/03/70 2102


Ilgya. You are looking forward to a holiday tomorrow – the Fourth of July. It is truly a great festivity. Had it not been for the United States of America, the world would look much different – far worse. Yet, obviously, there is much even in America that cannot be called good.

At a time when people are starving to death in some countries, that seems completely impossible in America. If you were to see how and what people eat in India, you would understand how miserably people live in many places on Earth.

You are crushed that a catastrophe can occur on Earth like it happened in Peru. More than fifty thousand people perished there. You see, that is how the lifeless matter acts, which man has not yet subdued. It was not possible to preclude this catastrophe, but perhaps someday it will be possible to predict it.

Of course, it is horrible that so many people perished, but, after all, what are these thousands compared to those millions who begin to lack the space where to live?

This lifeless matter causes many hardships and even catastrophes for the living beings. The living beings have to fight against this situation, but they should not despair if currently that seems to be almost unachievable for human genius, and even for God.

Many years ago, that is how it seemed with respect to diseases which wiped out millions. Some of these diseases have been conquered now and the rest have been limited. It is entirely possible that even they will be conquered. That is not all that easy, though, and therefore we still have to be patient.

I advise you to look after yourselves and take advantage of the summer as much as possible, in order to improve the condition of your organisms.

I wish you that, as well as good success. We take leave from you. Ilgya and Astra.                          [[2122]]

<u>Ilgya</u>                                    10/02/70 2108

Ilgya. Heralds, quite a while has passed since we have talked. That was due to various circumstances. The main reason was that there was no particular need to disturb your summer rest. As we have already said, the series of tidings has been concluded, and only a few important supplementations may come.

A situation has currently arisen where there is something that should be said, but that is not so urgent that there is a need to excessively overtax Mary at this time. Rest is very important for her.

There is much happening in the world that is interesting and that can become important, but is not yet currently.

You had the great joy of seeing your granddaughter, who is a very nice girl. With proper upbringing, she can turn into a wonderful young woman. I hope that God will not neglect her.

I also hope that your condition will improve. While wishing you the very best, I take leave for today and wish you a good night.

Ilgya, and of course your constant friend, Astra. [[2122]]


<u>Ilgya</u>                                    11/13/70 2008

Ilgya. Heralds, you are alarmed that so many unpleasant and even atrocious phenomena occur even in the life of the free United States of America.

Progress does not bring only good results, but sometimes also bad ones. We have talked about freedom several times, and you have been told that absolute freedom is, in fact, impossible, that it would result in anarchy.

The question arises regarding what is freedom. Should freedom be limited? How should it be limited?

Today it turns out that it has not been limited. In what manner then should it be, and what should be limited completely and what only partially? The so-called government of the people is based on the majority of the people and on its will. Dictatorship is based on the power of one individual or of a few people.

Even though the rule of the majority of the people had been experienced in ancient times, it spread primarily in recent times, when the majority of kings disappeared from the people's stage. However, these proclaimers of the power of the people – republics – still have to learn how to rule, so that the vast majority of people would be assured as good a life as is possible.

One can no longer complain about a lack of people on Earth, quite the contrary – the situation arises where there begin to be too many people. Therefore there is no sense in trying to value each individual too highly, but one has to see to it that society will be liberated from those who not only are not worthy of society, but are harmful to it and have even become its enemies. Murderers, robbers, and vagrants have to be considered as such – that is, people who not only do not benefit society and who are of no use to it, but who are even harmful. People like that have to be mercilessly evicted from society, and even have to be eliminated if they cannot be reformed. To spare loathsome creatures like that means not considering honest people, on whose account they live like harmful parasites.

It has already been said that people have to be brought up properly from the first day of their birth, so that they would become true human beings. The biggest attention has to be paid to this concern. The existing situation cannot be altered in a few days, and not even in a few months and years, but the work has to be started immediately by everyone who wants to achieve a better life, and man has been created to achieve this.

I came in lieu of a chief spirit who had to postpone his tiding until another time.

I wish you good night and bid you farewell on behalf of Astra and myself. Ilgya.          [[2044]]


<u>Santorino</u>                    11/20/70 2113

Santorino is speaking. Heralds, as directed by The Almighty, I came to you in order to explain to you and to the people on Earth what is very important but is not understood by everyone.

There was a terrible earthquake in Peru a while back, in which the lives of thousands of people were lost. There was a dreadful flood in India a few days ago, which resulted in even more human victims.

Formerly people considered such natural occurrences as God's punishment for people's sins. That is not the case, though. As you know, the world consists of The Almighty's spirits and the matter which He has created. Matter assumes different forms, and functions according to the laws that have been given it.

We, as well as you, and particularly The Almighty, know of what the globe is made and what goes on in the interior of Earth. The situation may arise, though, when something unforeseen happens. The movement of the interior plates of Earth causes earthquakes and also volcano eruptions. These events cannot always be correctly predicted, and no one can alter them.

Storms and floods can be predicted, but even they can take on huge proportions and become unavoidable. These forces of nature act in consonance with the laws that they have been given. They can, however, exceed their designated bounds and bring disaster to humanity. While it is difficult to direct the living beings, endowed with The Almighty's guiding spirit, then it is even more difficult to control the lifeless matter.

The Almighty invites all living beings – and particularly man – to participate in this fight against matter. The genius which man has been given develops to be ever more capable, and becomes capable of helping The Almighty in His work of shaping and transforming the world. Man – whose spirit has the use of the living being formed from matter – is, in fact, much more capable of this work than a pure spirit.

Along with the entire humanity, The Almighty regrets these forces of matter that have been used incorrectly, and He prohibits to consider them as being God's punishment. [[2142]]


<u>Ilgya</u>                        12/25/70 2015


Ilgya. Almighty's heralds to the planet Earth, on behalf of the spirits who are friendly to you and myself, I congratulate you with the Winter Festival – as the Latvians call it, and with the Festival of Christ's Birth – as many other nations call it.

Almost two thousand years have passed since God's Highest Envoy – Christ, called the Son of God – came to Earth in order to give God's laws to humanity. These laws expressed what humanity had to know in order to become happy and in order to be able to establish a good and just life for everyone on Earth. Yet, Christ's death on the cross proved that it will be difficult to achieve this and that many sacrifices will be needed in order to achieve this.

Humanity has tried out different types of government, starting with the elders of the clan, kings, and so on. After a few early experiments in the rule of the people, many hundreds of years passed before these experiments were renewed on a large scale. These experiments were also of a short duration, and it was not until this century when a large majority of countries turned to this self-government. In many of them this self-government again transferred to individual people, who sometimes were and are worse than the former kings. Even in those countries where true self-government has been established, everything does not go smoothly.

The word "freedom" does not mean that man is free to do anything that he likes. Rather, it lets all people select from the better people [those who will serve in] their establishments of government and of enacting laws. These people determine how to best utilize this freedom for the benefit of all people, and how to protect it from those who want to use it only for their own personal benefit.

Mercifulness has to be fair, and it cannot be used with respect to those people who are harmful to the rest of the people, those who rob and deprive others of their possessions and even their lives. Being merciful toward such loathsome creatures of humanity means not being merciful toward true human beings.

That does not contradict the teachings of Christ, because that pertains to the government, whose duty is to protect the individual from the danger that threatens him, and from violence.

On behalf of all the spirits who are friendly to you and of myself, I take leave from you and wish you the strength to overcome even that which seems to be insurmountable and unachievable. Ilgya and Astra.

[[2046]]

Ilgya                           01/01/71 1816

Ilgya. I congratulate you with the new, one thousand nine hundred and seventy-first year, and wish you all the very best that is possible on Earth.

The Divine wanted to talk with you, but he had to suddenly postpone the conversation to another time. He asked me to pass on to you greetings on behalf of him and the other spirits who are close to you.

The New Year came to you in an overcoat of snow, turning the Earth white as well. What is beautiful, though, is not always the most pleasant thing. What else does the New Year promise to humanity on Earth?

It cannot promise more than what the people themselves can achieve on their own behalf. Despite education spreading widely ever more, some nations still languish in ignorance. The achievements of science are huge and they promise humanity to make its life ever better and easier. Still, they also help the negative powers by making the weapons of destruction ever more dreadful.

The influence of the church lessens. It should find new, better, and more logical ways not only for preserving but also for strengthening Christ's teachings.

The tendency to acquire freedom is a good thing, but one has to see to it that the freedom which has been acquired is not transformed into something else, sometimes even worse than the previous lack of freedom.

When it comes to man's desire to live longer and be sick less, medicine advances with rather sizable steps, but obviously not so gigantic as to liberate humanity from all diseases in short order.

You know what life was like for man on Earth at the time of Christ's coming. You also know what it is like now. I have to say, though, that in some cases it is even worse and more barbaric now then it was at the time of Christ. You saw that during the reign of Adolf in Germany and see that in the communist countries. They promised freedom, equality, a good life, and security for everyone, but overcrowded prisons with those people who asked for genuine freedom, and starved to death the disobedient ones – in Siberia and in other concentration camps.

You were fortunate enough to get to a country in which freedom is closest to true freedom, but obviously with a few shortcomings. Still, despite them, old people here do not have to starve to death and do not have to beg for shelter.

With that, I will conclude today's tiding and will wish you good night. Ilgya and Astra.          [[1848]]

[[This concludes *The Book of Tidings of The Almighty and His Spirits to Humanity.*]]

# EPILOGUE

On May 1, 1944, Santorino said, "I am capable of speaking only through Alexander and Mary. When one of you will depart, I, too, will grow silent. Omega speaks only through Alexander. Once he will depart, the gates of Heaven will close to humanity for ever and ever. All those who will speak in The Almighty's and our names will be nothing but false apostles. And, oh, woe! what awaits them and those who will believe them."

On June 28, 1944, Omega spoke on behalf of The Almighty, "I, The Almighty, will never again send any of My envoys to Earth. Whoever will speak in My name will be an impostor. What I have proclaimed, I will never supplement again. I will never, ever speak again, not with the tongue of a prophet, not through signs, not as I am talking today, nor in any other manner.

"So that you might receive answers to some remaining questions, which are still not clear to you, I permit My spirits to talk to the people on Earth only as long as I have not recalled My envoy Alexander to Me; and only through him, so that no false prophets could speak in My name and in yours."

On February 13, 1949, Mortifero passed on to humanity the words of The Almighty, "I repeat My previous words, that I come to man for the last time and will speak only through Alexander. This, My decision, is irrevocable. It places a huge responsibility on you, as well as a hard-to-endure test for Alexander's strength."

On March 20, 1959, Alvisego said, "These Tidings are the first and the last ones for the people on Earth. All communications with The Almighty will cease with Alexander's departure from Earth, and not one word expressed in the Tidings will be changed. Anyone who tries to represent himself as The Almighty's herald will be an impostor. Similarly, anyone who wants to alter even one sentence in *The Book of Tidings*, will be considered a fraud."

On February 28, 1969, Omega spoke, "The Almighty ordered me to announce to the heralds to Earth that, with respect to the Tidings, He talks to the people on Earth only through Alexander and His heralds, and only when they are together. He does not speak, and will never speak, through only one herald."

Alexander's immortal spirit departed from his mortal body on March 10, 1971.

Nick Mezins

# BIBLIOGRAPHY

REVELATIONS, translated by Nick Mezins, Winston-Derek Publishers, Inc., 1992, (out of print)

REVELATIONS, (Revised Edition), translated by Nick Mezins, Trafford Publishing, 2000

The Tidings, (Volume One, 1943-1945), translated by Nick Mezins, Trafford Publishing, 2005

The Tidings, (Volume Two, 1945-1946), translated by Nick Mezins, Trafford Publishing, 2010

The Tidings, (Volume Three, 1946 – 1949), translated by Nick Mezins, Trafford Publishing, 2014

The Tidings, (Volume Four, 1951 – 1956), translated by Nick Mezins, Hancock Press, 2015

The Tidings, (Volume Five, 1957 – 1964), translated by Nick Mezins, Trafford Publishing, 2016

MESSAGES TO MANKIND From THE ALMIGHTY AND HIS SPIRITS, Alexander Homics, Vantage Press, Inc., 1976, (out of print)

Messages to Mankind PART II, Alexander Homics, Valkyrie Press, Inc., 1977, (out of print)

IPSIS: A Fairy Tale by Ali, Alexander Homics, Valkyrie Press, Inc., 1977, (out of print)

Search for the Promised Land, Sidney R. Smith, CeShore Publishing Company, 2000, (out of print)

Supplementology: Combining Religion with Science, Rev. Sidney R. Smith, Trafford Publishing, 2005

The Almighty's Religion for the Universe, Sidney R. Smith, Xlibris, 2016

www.TheAlightysRevelations.org

# ACKNOWLEDGEMENTS

Here I wish to acknowledge the individuals without whose contribution this volume would never have been possible.

First and foremost, Alexander Upenieks, who was the leader of the small group of individuals conversing with the spirits. Without his exceptional abilities and leadership the conversations would not have been possible.

My parents, John and Mary. They raised me to be a conscientious and responsible human being. They exposed me to the Tidings, but left it strictly up to me, as to what extent I wanted to become involved.

Alexander Homics, who was a member of the core group, and who eventually translated almost all of the material and had three books published. He thus demonstrated that this can be accomplished, and gave me the incentive to move forward.

Rosendo De Aguilera, who provided me valuable background material and much encouragement.

Albert Gladis, who reviewed the first two volumes, and helped greatly in improving readability and the quality of English.

Maya Homics, the daughter of Alexander Homics, who provided me with the unpublished manuscripts of Alexander Homics, as well as encouragement, moral support, and constructive suggestions regarding the material, some of which she continues to work on.

Sidney R. Smith, who continues to put in much effort in organizing certain publicity regarding the material. He came across Alexander Homics's first book and found that it complimented his own beliefs. He went on to publish three books of his own regarding his Journey of Faith.

Nick Mezins

Printed in the United States
By Bookmasters